OUTSIDE LOOKING IN

EARLY METHODISM AS
VIEWED BY ITS CRITICS

DONALD HENRY KIRKHAM

NEW ROOM™
BOOKS

Outside Looking In: Early Methodism as Viewed by Its Critics

The General Board of Higher Education and Ministry leads and serves The United Methodist Church in the recruitment, preparation, nurture, education, and support of Christian leaders—lay and clergy—for the work of making disciples of Jesus Christ for the transformation of the world. The General Board of Higher Education and Ministry of The United Methodist Church serves as an advocate for the intellectual life of the church. The board's mission embodies the Wesleyan tradition of commitment to the education of laypersons and ordained persons by providing access to higher education for all persons.

The name *New Room Books* comes from the New Room, a historic building in Bristol, England, and place of John Wesley's study. Built in 1739, it is the oldest Methodist chapel in the world.

Outside Looking In: Early Methodism as Viewed by Its Critics

Copyright 2019 by New Room Books

New Room Books is an imprint of the General Board of Higher Education and Ministry, The United Methodist Church. All rights reserved.

All web addresses were correct and operational at the time of publication.

ISBN 978-1-945935-43-5

GBHEM Publishing is an affiliate of the Association of University Presses.

Scripture quotations are taken from The Authorized (King James) Version (public domain).

Cover image: "The Idle Prentice Executed at Tyburn," Plate X1 of Industry and Idleness, Illustration from *Hogarth Restored: The Whole Works of the celebrated William Hogarth*, re-engraved by Thomas Cook, pub. 1812 (hand-coloured engraving). Image number STC451140, Private Collection/The Stapleton Collection/Bridgman Images. License to use granted. Depicted is the procession of convicted felon Tom Idle to the gallows at Tyburn near modern-day Marble Arch, London. In the cart with Idle is Methodist Silas Told. The Methodists were mocked for their ministry to condemned felons, the practice of which grew out of their prison ministry at Oxford with the Holy Club.

For Phebe, sine qua non

Many years ago, my wife, Phebe, typed the first draft of my Duke PhD dissertation, which forms the basis of this book. On this occasion she has carefully read and reread drafts numerous times, correcting errors and making stylistic suggestions to improve the book's clarity and readability. This book, published the year we celebrate our fiftieth wedding anniversary, is dedicated to her.

Contents

Acknowledgments

The scholars, librarians, and institutions who helped with my original research are acknowledged in my dissertation.

Over the years several people have encouraged me to publish. I am grateful especially to Kenneth Rowe, Clive D. Field, and Stephen Gunter for their support.

A section of chapter 7, "Methodism and Politics," was published with the title "John Wesley's Calm Address: The Response of the Critics," in *Methodist History* 14, no. 1 (October 1975): 13–23. It is used by permission of Alfred T. Day, editor of *Methodist History*.

John Mossman, editor of the *Bulletin of the John Rylands University Library of Manchester*, and Clive D. Field have kindly granted permission for the use of Field's "A Revised Bibliography" in the revision in this book of the Short Title listing of Anti-Methodist pamphlets by year.[1] Diana L. Pesek, journals manager at Penn State University Press, and Clive D. Field have granted permission for the use of Field's "Supplemental Bibliography."[2]

I am indebted to Clive D. Field, whose extensive, thorough, and scholarly work on the bibliography of eighteenth-century anti-Methodist publications is an invaluable resource for the study of early British Methodism. He has been an enormous help in answering many questions and offering suggestions.

John Lenton, who has extensive knowledge of early Methodist preachers, has kindly provided birth and death dates for a number of preachers.

My publisher, M. Kathryn Armistead, has answered many questions, has given helpful advice, and has been very patient with me, as has my editor, Jennifer Manley Rogers. Reneé Chavez provided skillful copyediting. I thank them for their encouragement.

---

1 Clive Douglas Field, "Anti-Methodist Publications of the Eighteenth Century: A Revised Bibliography," *Bulletin of the John Rylands University Library of Manchester* 73 (Summer 1991): 159–280. Hereafter, "A Revised Bibliography."

2 Clive Douglas Field, "Anti-Methodist Publications of the Eighteenth Century: A Supplemental Bibliography," in *Wesley and Methodist Studies* (University Park, PA: Penn State University Press, 2014), 6:154–86. Hereafter, "A Supplemental Bibliography."

Abbreviations

AMP   Richard Green, *Anti-Methodist Publications Issued during the Eighteenth Century. A Chronologically Arranged and Annotated Bibliography* (London: for the author by C. H. Kelly, 1902).

BEWJW   Frank Baker and Richard P. Heitzenrater, eds., *The Bicentennial Edition of the Works of John Wesley,* 35 vols. planned (Nashville: Abingdon Press, 1976–).

ECCO   *Eighteenth Century Collections Online.*

ESTC   *English Short Title Catalogue,* formerly *Eighteenth Century Short Title Catalogue.*

JWCE   Frank Baker, *John Wesley and the Church of England* (Nashville and New York: Abingdon Press, 1970).

Letters (Telford)   John Telford, ed., *The Letters of John Wesley,* 8 vols. (London: Epworth Press, 1931).

MH   *Methodist History.* The Official publication of the Commission on Archives and History of The United Methodist Church, Madison, NJ.

ODNB   Online version of *The Oxford Dictionary of National Biography.*

ProcWHS   *Proceedings of the Wesley Historical Society* (London: 1899–).

WGW   *The Works of George Whitefield,* 6 vols. (London: for Edward and Charles Dilly, 1771–72).

Works (Jackson)   Thomas Jackson, ed., *The Works of John Wesley,* 3rd ed., 14 vols. (London: John Mason, 1829–31).

Introduction

With few exceptions, new religious movements in the history of Christianity have met with sharp opposition from established institutions. German Anabaptist groups in the sixteenth century and Quaker societies in seventeenth-century England are outstanding instances of sects that at the time of their origin encountered harsh persecution. The rise of Methodism in eighteenth-century England offers a further example. From the early years of the evangelical revival until the close of the eighteenth century, the movement provided fodder for controversy from both without and within. While much of the resulting material was scurrilous satire, there was also much serious theological debate and valid criticism of Methodism's deviation from normative Anglican doctrine, organization, and practice.[1]

From the outset, the term *Methodism* was used very loosely during the eighteenth century. Originally a derogatory epithet applied to the zealous band of young Oxford University students under John Wesley's leadership, from the 1740s until the end of the eighteenth century it was applied to all participants in the revival. Brothers Charles and John Wesley, George Whitefield, evangelical Anglicans, and Moravians were all designated "Methodist" at one time or another. Opponents made little attempt to note the distinctions among them but lumped them together under one large evangelical umbrella. Any who proclaimed an evangelical faith or who failed to follow accepted Anglican worship and practices were declared to be Methodist.

The opposition to the revival was many faceted—mob violence, attacks in periodicals, satires of Methodist characters in novels, ridicule in the theater, denial of the use of pulpits, and pamphlet opposition.

---

1 Among Methodism's serious critics were Edmund Gibson (bap. 1669–1748), bishop of London (1723–48); Thomas Church (1707–56), vicar of Battersea, prebendary of St. Paul's Cathedral, London, and lecturer at St. Anne's Church, Soho, whom Wesley described as "a gentleman, scholar, and a Christian"; George Horne (1730–92), an academic writer, fellow of Magdalen College, later president of the college, and vice-chancellor of Oxford University; and Thomas Secker, archbishop of Canterbury (1756–68).

An additional note: Although it was not in common use in the eighteenth century, the term "Anglican" has been employed throughout the book as a synonym for "pertaining to the Church of England."

Mob Outbursts

Hostility toward Methodism erupted in spasmodic outbursts of mob violence.[2] Riots, which were common in England in the eighteenth century, were caused in the main by unusually high corn prices or agitation for higher wages. Large-scale riots over religious matters, such as the 1780 Gordon Riots against Roman Catholicism, were rare.[3] Compared to the Gordon Riots, anti-Methodist riots were smaller and more localized, and occurred mainly in the early years of the evangelical revival.[4] Encouraged by their social superiors or incited by inflammatory sermons, on occasion mob leaders were bribed by handouts of cash or alcohol. Methodist property was sometimes damaged or destroyed, and Methodist preachers and people, including John Wesley himself, were physically assaulted, often bearing the scars for the rest of their lives.

Protest in Periodicals

From the journals and magazines of the period came a chorus of protest against most aspects of the Methodist revival. The earliest newspaper attack appeared in the London-based *Fogg's Weekly Journal*, no. 214, on December 9, 1732. In an anonymous letter dated November 5, the practices of the Oxford society called Methodist were compared to those of the Pietists of Saxony and the Jewish Essenes. The Methodists were charged with enthusiasm, self-righteousness, and hypocrisy—charges that later critics of Methodism would expand. When the Methodist leaders, Whitefield and the Wesley brothers, took to preaching out of doors in 1739, the columns of the periodical press carried renewed protests. Probably the most vicious and constant attacks came from the *Weekly Miscellany*, but the *Gentleman's*

---

2 Josiah H. Barr, *Early Methodists under Persecution* (New York: The Methodist Book Concern, 1916); John Dixon Walsh, "Methodism and the Mob in the Eighteenth Century," *Studies in Church History*, ed. G. J. Cuming and Derek Baker (Cambridge: Cambridge University Press, 1972), 111:213–27. Cf. David Neil Hempton, "Methodism and the Law, 1740–1820," *Bulletin of the John Rylands University Library* 70 (1988): 93–107. See also Field, "A Revised Bibliography."

3 Occasioned by Lord George Gordon's call for the repeal of the Catholic Relief Act of 1778 that was passed to reduce official discrimination against Roman Catholics, Protestant extremists marched on Parliament in support of the repeal. The march quickly degenerated into a week of rioting. *ODNB*.

4 For a fuller discussion of Methodism and the Gordon Riots, see chapter 7, "Methodism and Politics."

Magazine, the *Craftsman, Common Sense: or, the Englishman's Journal*, and *Scots Magazine* also carried anti-Methodist material. Supplementing articles and news items, anti-Methodist in tone, were letters and unfriendly reviews. *The Monthly Review*, betraying at first an anti-Methodist slant, by 1760 had become more disposed to fairness in reviewing plays. On the whole, *Lloyd's Evening Post* and the *London Magazine* were more favorable to Wesley and his followers, publishing their replies in their own defense.[5]

Attacks in Novels

Methodism was noticed unfavorably in eighteenth-century novels quite early. Samuel Richardson's *Pamela, or Virtue rewarded* (1740) and Henry Fielding's *Shamela* (1741) gave Methodism passing, though critical, notice.[6] Henry Fielding's short story, *The female husband; or, The surprising history of Mrs. Mary, Alias Mr. George Hamilton* (1746), based on a true story, relates the fictionalized tale of Mary Hamilton, a Methodist transvestite who, disguised as a man, marries another woman, Mary Price.[7] The tale is replete with anti-Methodist and highly sexualized content. Tobias Smollett's *Humphrey Clinker* (1771) contained the first appearance of a Methodist leading character in a novel. Rather than ridicule the Methodists, Smollett smiled at their foibles. Richard Graves's three-volume *The spiritual quixote, or, The summer's ramble of Mr. Geoffrey Wildgoose*, which appeared in 1772–73, parodied Wesley, Whitefield, and the Methodist movement.[8] The anonymous *The adventures of an actor in the characters of a Merry-Andrew, a Methodist-preacher and a fortune-teller, founded on the facts* was a 334-page novel with a number of incidents set in Ireland. There are strong anti-Methodist sentiments throughout the novel. The central character, Jack Merryman, an actor turned Methodist preacher, later forsook Methodism for a career as a fortune-teller.

---

5 Thomas Boswell Shepherd, *Methodism and the Literature of the Eighteenth Century* (London: Epworth, 1947), 211–12.

6 Ibid., 212–16, 219–26; cf. Frederick C. Gill, *The Romantic Movement and Methodism* (London: Epworth, 1954), 106–20.

7 205D-Fi. [Henry Fielding], *The female husband; or, The surprising history of Mrs. Mary, alias Mr. George Hamilton* (London: for M. Cooper, 1746). Mary Hamilton was arrested, tried, convicted, and punished for marrying another woman. See Field's introduction to the item in "A Supplemental Bibliography."

8 454-Gr. Richard Graves, *The spiritual quixote, or, The summer's ramble of Mr. Geoffrey Wildgoose* (London: for J. Dodsley, 1773).

Another character, Mandrake, also a Methodist preacher, remained faithful to his vocation.[9]

Ridiculed in the Theater

The theater presented unique possibilities as a popular vehicle for anti-Methodist attack. At its disposal was the most devastating weapon in the anti-Methodist arsenal: ridicule. At first groups of strolling players lampooned the revival from makeshift stages. The earliest anti-Methodist play Green named in his *Anti-Methodist Publications Issued during the Eighteenth Century, a Chronologically Arranged and Annotated Bibliography* (hereinafter, *Anti-Methodist Bibliography*) was *The mock-preacher*, which was anonymously published in 1739.[10] In 1743 Thomas Este, an early playwright, produced a one-act farce entitled *Methodism display'd* at the Moot Hall in Newcastle.[11] Then the gauntlet was picked up by legitimate theaters, condemned by Whitefield in preaching as "nurseries of debaucheries . . . the pest of our nation . . . the bane of true Christianity,"[12] responding with all-out attacks. Chief among the playwright opponents was Samuel Foote.[13] *The minor*, his hugely successful three-act satire on Whitefield and the Methodist emphasis on conversion and personal religious experience, was produced at the Haymarket Theater. Foote continued his assault on the movement and its leaders for twenty years, adding to his repertoire of plays with anti-Methodist

---

9 527C-Fi. *The adventures of an actor in the characters of a Merry-Andrew, a Methodist-preacher and a fortune-teller, founded on facts* (London: for the author, [1782?]).

10 025-Gr. *The mock-preacher* (London: C. Corbett, 1739). The subtitle claimed that the play had been produced both in the open-air at Kennington Common and at "many theatres."

11 154-Gr. Thomas Este, *Methodism display'd: a farce* (Newcastle upon Tyne: for the publisher, [1743?]). It was "alter'd and publish'd by Mr. Este from a farce call'd '*Trick upon Trick; or, The Vintner in the suds.*'"

12 Letters of George Whitefield, Letter CVIII, November 10, 1739, to Mr. N., Philadelphia, *WGW*, vol. 1 (London: for Edward and Charles Dilly, 1771).

13 298-Gr. Samuel Foote (1729–1777), British actor, theater manager, and dramatist, began his attack on Methodism in 1760 with *The minor, a comedy* (London: J. Coote, G. Kearsly, T. Davies, 1760). Ten editions were published between 1760 and 1830. See Shepherd, "Methodists and the Theatre of the Eighteenth Century," *ProcWHS*, vol. 20 (1935–36): 166–68, 181–85; vol. 21 (1937–38): 36–38; see also Shepherd, *Methodism and the Literature of the Eighteenth Century*, 189–204. For an excellent account of Foote's *The minor* and the controversy it aroused, see Mary M. Belden, "The Dramatic Work of Samuel Foote," *Yale Studies in English*, no. 80 (New Haven: Yale University Press, 1929), 81–106. See also Brett C. McInelly, "Laudere Cum Sacris: Methodism, Mimicry and Samuel Foote's The Minor," in *Restoration and 18th Century Theatre Research*, December 1, 2009.

allusions: *The orators* (1762),[14] and *The devil upon two sticks* (1778).[15] Other playwrights were not slow to follow Foote's example. Israel Pottinger's *The Methodist*, advertised as a continuation of *The minor*, was in print soon after.[16] So harsh was its attack, however, that it was considered too libelous to perform in public. Although it appeared in 1760, Joseph Reed's *The register office* was not performed until April 23, 1761, at Drury Lane.[17] *The hypocrite; a comedy*, taken from Moliere and Cibber, appeared in 1769.[18] Numerous adverse references to Methodism occur throughout the play.

Use of the Pulpit as a Weapon

During the eighteenth century Anglican discipline was lax.[19] As a result, there was no formal ecclesiastical machinery by which the episcopacy could censure the Methodist preachers. Despite this, there was powerful opposition to Methodism from a number of London clergy who took to their pulpits to condemn Methodism's doctrinal emphases and practices. Moreover, angered by Methodist teaching and innovative practices, the clergy gradually closed more and more Church of England pulpits to Whitefield and the Wesley brothers. So effective was this move during the early part of 1739 that John Wesley could find no more than six parishes where he was welcome to preach. On his return from Georgia, Whitefield, formerly the idol of London congregations, likewise found himself debarred from the city's pulpits.

---

14 341D-Ki. Samuel Foote, *The orators, as it is now performing at the new theatre in the Hay Market* (London: for J. Coote, G. Kearsley, and T. Davies, 1762). Another early edition was printed in Dublin. See Samuel Foote, *The orators; in which is introduced the trial of the cock–lane ghost. And a view of the Robin-Hood-Society, as it is performed at the theatres of London and Dublin* (Dublin: for Thomas Richey, 1762).

15 520A-Ki. Samuel Foote, *The devil upon two sticks, a comedy in three acts* (London: printed by T. Sherlock for T. Cadell, [1778]). Both Lyles, *Methodism Mocked*, 16, and McInelly, *Textual Warfare . . . and Methodism*, 116, designate Foote's *The lyar* (1764), as anti-Methodist. The text of the play, however, reveals no Methodist allusions or attacks.

16 Israel Pottinger (1735–1782) was a British author, dramatist, and satirist who followed Foote's pattern for attacking Methodism. *ODNB*. See 305-Gr. *The Methodist: A Comedy* (London: for I. Pottinger [1760?]).

17 314-Gr. Joseph Reed (1723–1787), playwright and poet, *The register-office: A farce in two acts* (London: for T. Davies, 1761). *ODNB*.

18 432B-Fi. The author of the *Alterations of the plain dealer* [Isaac Bickerstaffe], *The hypocrite: a comedy: as it is performed at the Theatre Royal in Drury-Lane*. Taken from Moliere and Cibber (London: W. Griffin, 1769). There were numerous editions and reprints. Isaac Bickerstaffe (1733–1812?) was an Irish playwright and librettist for comic operas. *ODNB*.

19 See "The Bishops and Higher Clergy" in chapter 1.

Pamphlet Opposition

The most consistent and characteristic form of opposition to Methodism came in unbound polemical tracts. If the twentieth century was the age of the paperback, the eighteenth century, along with the seventeenth, was the age of pamphleteering. The pamphlets of Swift, Defoe, and others were a recognized part of the political life of the age and served as a model for anti-Methodist publications as did anti-Puritan pamphlets of the previous century. Those who sought to check Methodism's progress had no need to fashion a new weapon—the pamphlet lay at their disposal. Anti-Methodist pamphlets poured forth in a variety of literary forms: sermons, open letters, episcopal and archidiaconal charges, theological treatises, dialogues, satires (poems, plays, prose, novels), biographies, histories, and extracts of earlier publications.

Pamphlet attacks against Methodism were prolific and multifarious. Those published in the British Isles between 1738 and 1800 number 651. If those publications that merely contained unfavorable allusions to Methodism, were in newspapers or periodicals, or were published in America were also included, the number would be in the thousands.

Countless historians and church historians have discussed the rise and expansion of the Methodist movement in England in the eighteenth century. The opposition to Methodism has been duly noted. The first chronicler of anti-Methodist writings was Curtis H. Cavender, who in 1846, under the pseudonym H. C. Decanver, compiled a *Catalogue of Works in Refutation of Methodism from its Origins in 1729, to the Present Time.*[20] A second edition followed in 1868. The preface of the second edition boasted titles to 362 anti-Methodist works. A close examination of Cavender's *Catalogue*, however, reveals that many of this number are outside the limits of this study since they were issued in the nineteenth century, deal with Methodism in America, are not hostile to Methodism but were actually written in defense of the revival, or are by Methodist authors. Cavender's bibliographical detail

---

20 H. C. Decanver [Curtis H. Cavender], *Catalogue of Works in Refutation of Methodism from its Origins in 1729, to the Present Time; of Those by Methodist Authors or Lay-Representation, Methodist Episcopacy etc., etc., and of the Political Pamphlets Relating to Wesley's "Calm Address to our American Colonies"* (Philadelphia: John Pennington, 1846). For an excellent and detailed discussion of the development of bibliographies of anti-Methodist pamphlets, see the introduction to Field's "A Revised Bibliography," 159–67, and "A Supplemental Bibliography," 54–57.

lacks precision—this may not have been all his fault. Perhaps all he had for some were advertisements in eighteenth-century periodicals in which titles were invariably shortened. He may also have been working from references in the works of other authors that did not give titles fully or correctly.

Luke Tyerman, the preeminent early biographer and historian of the evangelical revival, broke new ground. He was the first to note in detail anti-Methodist writings and sometimes to provide quite lengthy extracts or characterizations of them.[21] Though I am grateful for Tyerman's list of pamphlets, some of his characterizations betray his Victorian upbringing and adulation of Wesley.

Major research on anti-Methodist publications was carried out by Richard Green, a British Wesleyan Methodist preacher and scholar.[22] In compiling his *Anti-Methodist Bibliography*, Green relied heavily on Cavender and Tyerman. In a number of cases, unable to examine publications listed by Cavender, Green simply listed the entry and affixed the letter *D* to show the authority for the pamphlet's existence. Nor did Green have access to all the tracts Tyerman had seen and was forced to rely on Tyerman's characterization of them. By necessity, then, a good deal of Green's information was secondhand, and this led him unavoidably to repeat mistakes of earlier researchers. There are errors in titles and dates of publication. In a number of cases where a pamphlet is listed in Green anonymously or pseudonymously, it is now possible to provide the author's name. Such names are designated by the use of brackets. Earlier editions of some pamphlets have been discovered, and this has entailed redating and renumbering those items. It is possible also to eliminate other items listed by Green because they are duplicates. In a few cases, when he had not had the chance to examine the contents of certain pamphlets, he incorrectly categorized them as anti-Methodist because of their titles. For example: 009A-Ba., "The Kennington song," a broadside, was not an attack on the revival but a defense of George Whitefield's theology and practices. In consultation with Clive Field, it has been removed.

---

21 Luke Tyerman, *The Life and Times of Rev. John Wesley, M.A.*, 3 vols. (New York: Harper and Brothers, 1872). See also Luke Tyerman, *The Life and Times of Rev. George Whitefield*, 2 vols. (New York: Anson D. F. Randolph, 1877).

22 Richard Green, *Anti-Methodist Publications Issued during the Eighteenth Century, a Chronologically Arranged and Annotated Bibliography* (London: for the author by C. H. Kelly, 1902), hereinafter *Anti-Methodist Bibliography*; it became and remained the standard work on the topic for many years.

In 1973 I compiled a revised Green's bibliography, 1738–1791, as part of my PhD dissertation at Duke University.[23] Working under the supervision of Frank Baker, I was given access to Baker's short survey of British anti-Methodist works before its publication in the *Encyclopedia of Methodism*.[24] More important, Baker also gave me access to his richly annotated copy of Green, which contained numerous works not listed by Green. My visits to a dozen British and American libraries brought to light further new titles. I eliminated 246 of Green's 606 entries because they were duplicates, were printed after 1791, were published in the United States, were not stand-alone pamphlets, or were pro-Methodist in tone. I then added 132 new titles for a revised total of 492. As the dissertation was researched and written before the availability of the *Eighteenth Century Short Title Catalogue (ESTC)*, now named the *English Short Title Catalogue (ESTC)*, I relied in a number of cases on second or third editions of anti-Methodist pamphlets or, in a few instances, on secondary sources, such as Tyerman, that gave detailed mention of works critical of Methodism.[25]

Field meticulously researched and reordered the anti-Methodist corpus. His *Anti-Methodist Publications of the Eighteenth Century: A Revised Bibliography*, published in 1991, replaced Green and my own bibliography as the standard anti-Methodist bibliography. The revised bibliography, based on Baker's handwritten annotations on his copy of Green, my doctoral dissertation, the extensive examination by Field of the Methodist Archives and Research Centre at the University of Manchester, and online searches of the *ESTC*, removed 160 titles from Green's original 606 that were duplicates, reprints, or works published in America. A new cut-off date of 1800 was established to coincide with the parameters of the *ESTC*. Field added back a number of titles I had removed from Green. Green had included them to "show by implication the nature and virulence of the anti-Methodist spirit that prevailed at the time."[26] I removed them because they were apologetic for, rather than antagonistic toward, Methodism. Field has retained some of Green's "pro-Methodist" items that were not consistently favorable but were evidence of the nature and scope

---

23 Donald Henry Kirkham, "Pamphlet Opposition to the Rise of Methodism: The Eighteenth-Century English Evangelical Revival under Attack" (PhD diss., Duke University, 1973).

24 Frank Baker, "Anti-Methodist Publications (British)," *The Encyclopedia of World Methodism*, Nolan Bailey Harmon, general editor, 2 vols. (Nashville: United Methodist Publishing House, 1974), 1:119–22.

25 Field, "A Revised Bibliography," 159–280. An open-access version is available online.

26 Green, *AMP*, v.

of opposition to Methodism.[27] To the reduced number of 446, Field added 154 new entries to bring the revised total to 600.

Field's revised bibliography retains Green's chronological order and uses a revised version of Green's numbering. Entries have been assigned a letter succeeding the item number to designate the authority for the action—Gr. for Green, Ba. for Baker, Fi. for Field, and Ki. for Kirkham. To assist further research Field attached five helpful appendices—author, title, imprint, provincial imprint, and a chronology of anti-Methodist tracts in tabular form.

Since the publication of Field's revised anti-Methodist bibliography in 1991, more anti-Methodist publications have come to light. Field has produced a supplement, which contains 42 new titles published between 1739 and 1800. In many cases fuller or variant titles have been discovered, as well as reprints and new editions. The chronology, however, was not significantly modified, nor were there any new anti-Methodist literary or rhetorical devices discovered.[28] In preparation for this book, I have identified eight additional pamphlets with anti-Methodist sections. They have been assigned Green numbers: 386A-Ki. James Ibbetson, *A charge to the clergy of the archdeaconry of St. Albans*; 491-Ki. John Cox Greenwood, *Remarks on a wild oration, or funeral sermon, in memory of William Austin, late Methodist preacher at Bledlow . . . Also some remarks . . . delivered at Thame, by the Irreverend Mr. Well* [*sic*]; 538A*-Ki. Samuel Horsley, *The analogy between the light of inspiration and the light of learning*; 556-Ki. George [Horne], *A charge intended to have been delivered to the clergy of Norwich at the primary visitation*; 561-Ki. Samuel [Horsley], *The charge of Samuel, Lord Bishop of St. David's to the clergy of his diocese*; 607-Ki. *Preaching for bacon*; 608-Ki. *Methodism indeed; or, A satirical poem, in reply to one composed by a partialist*; 609-Ki. *The Methodist turned poet*. The first four are available online on ECCO. Because they contain anti-Methodist allusions, two additional plays by Foote have been assigned numbers: 341D-Ki. *The orators* (1763); and 520A-Ki. *The devil upon two sticks* [1778?].

A number of authors have examined opposition to the emerging Methodist movement in England. Josiah Henry Barr, in *Early Methodists under Persecution*, concentrates on mob violence, but has a chapter entitled, "The

---

27 Field, "A Revised Bibliography," 165. Field cites pamphlets 169-Gr., 173-Gr., 187-Gr., 188-Gr., 242-Gr., and 243A-Ba., which provide details of anti-Methodist riots as examples.

28 Field, "A Supplemental Bibliography," 154–86.

Methodists Vilified" that discusses literary attacks on Methodism.[29] Thomas Boswell Shepherd, in *Methodism and the Literature of the Eighteenth Century*, devotes two chapters to literary assaults on Methodism: chapter 9, "Methodists and the Theatre in the Eighteenth Century," and chapter 10, "Methodism as Seen in the Literature of the Age."[30] Shepherd's treatment of pamphlets is slight, but the strength of the book is that he places pamphleteering in the context of all literary opposition—the novel, poetry, and the theater. D. Dunn Wilson's *Many Waters Cannot Quench* places pamphlet attacks in the context of other forms of opposition.[31] Arthur Whitney, in *The Basis of Opposition to Methodism in England in the Eighteenth Century*, studied only a fraction of the attacks and relied heavily on early nineteenth-century pamphlets, particularly those printed in America.[32] Albert M. Lyles, *Methodism Mocked: The Satiric Reaction to Methodism in the Eighteenth Century*, in the main limits the pamphlets studied to those that are satire.[33]

Three important recent works are Brett C. McInelly, *Textual Warfare and the Making of Methodism*, which examines both pro- and anti-Methodist publications to show how the debate between the two shaped Methodism, strengthened the movement's identity, and gave impetus to its growth;[34] Misty G. Anderson's study, *Imagining Methodism in Eighteenth-Century Britain: Enthusiasm, Belief, and the Borders of the Self*, which analyzes Methodism's role in the eighteenth century in the formation of the modern British self;[35] and Simon Lewis, "Early Anti-Methodism as an Aspect of Theological Controversy in England, c.1738–c.1770."[36] Lewis integrates anti-Methodist publications into the wider English theological controversies of the eighteenth century.

---

29 Barr, *Early Methodists Under Persecution*, 200–222.

30 Shepherd, *Methodism and the Literature of the 18th Century*. See chapter 12.

31 D. Dunn Wilson, *Many Waters Cannot Quench: A Study of the Sufferings of Eighteenth-Century Methodism and Their Significance for John Wesley and the First Methodists* (London: Epworth, 1969).

32 Arthur Whitney, *The Basis of Opposition to Methodism in England in the Eighteenth Century* (New York: New York University Press, 1951).

33 Albert M. Lyles, *Methodism Mocked: The Satiric Reaction to Methodism in the Eighteenth Century* (London: Epworth, 1960).

34 Brett C. McInelly, *Textual Warfare and the Making of Methodism* (Oxford: Oxford University Press, 2014).

35 Misty G. Anderson, *Imagining Methodism in Eighteenth-Century Britain: Enthusiasm, Belief, and the Borders of the Self* (Baltimore: Johns Hopkins University Press, 2012).

36 Simon Lewis, "Early Anti-Methodism as an Aspect of Theological Controversy in England, c.1738–c.1770" (DPhil thesis, Oxford University, 2017).

This book, a revision of my Duke PhD dissertation,[37] incorporates the corpus of 642 anti-Methodist pamphlets from Field's bibliographies, adds ten new titles I located in preparation for this book, and deletes one,[38] bringing the total to 651. Field's parameters of 1738-1800 are used to coincide with the *ESTC*.

This study is limited to an examination of separately published anti-Methodist pamphlets that appeared in the British Isles during the eighteenth century. However, should you wish to delve more deeply into reactions to a pamphlet, you may be richly rewarded by letters, poems, and reviews in periodicals such as the *Gentleman's Magazine* and the *Monthly Review*. For an example of what is available, see the controversy surrounding Wesley's *Primitive Physic*.[39]

The aim of the book is to survey the corpus of anti-Methodist pamphlets, note the arguments and tactics of the pamphleteers, and provide a critic's view of the movement from outside looking in. In approaching the material, I have attempted to be open and sympathetic to the anti-Methodist authors and their works. Tyerman's and Green's nineteenth-century assessments were so colored by their adulation of Wesley and loyalty to Methodism that their authors were shocked by the vigor of the attacks and the scurrility of the allegations, thus preventing them from recognizing elements of truth in anti-Methodist writings. If one is to understand eighteenth-century Methodism, it is important to see it not only as Wesley and those sympathetic to it did, but to view it also through the eyes of those who stood outside the revival. Opponents frequently distort, and this must be acknowledged, but they present another perspective, sometimes even a corrective. A balanced assessment of Wesley and early Methodists will take note of the views of their critics and the extent to which the movement was shaped by opponents.[40]

The launch of the *Eighteenth-Century Collections Online (ECCO)* has made many anti-Methodist works more readily accessible to researchers. With the improved accessibility of anti-Methodist material and Field's bibliography and supplement likewise easily accessible online, it is hoped that this

---

37 Kirkham, "Pamphlet Opposition to the Rise of Methodism."

38 See item 009A, "The Kennington song," *Anti-Methodist Pamphlets, 1738–1800: A Short Title Bibliography*. The item is pro-Methodist.

39 *BEWJW*, vol. 32, *Medical and Health Writings*, ed. James G. Donat and Randy L. Maddox, "The Primitive Physic Controversy," appendix D, 675–729.

40 See McInelly, *Textual Warfare and the Making of Methodism*.

survey of the corpus will spur renewed interest in and further examination of anti-Methodist literature. The corpus remains, as Heitzenrater has noted, "the most overlooked primary sources for studying the Wesley brothers."[41]

Anti-Methodist authors are eminently quotable. Selections from their pamphlets are thus liberally interspersed throughout the book to allow opponents to be heard in their own words and to provide you with material otherwise inaccessible. Quotations from anti-Methodist pamphlets retain the original spelling and contractions, but capitalization, punctuation, and the use of italics has been modernized to aid reading. In the body of the book, the long, encyclopedic, eighteenth-century titles have been shortened to bring them into line with the short titles used in *ESTC*. For full titles you may consult Field's bibliography and supplement.

---

41 Richard P. Heitzenrater, "John and Charles Wesley: Life, Ministry and Legacy," in *T & T Clark Companion to Methodism,* ed. Charles Yrigoyen (London and New York: T & T Clark, 2010), 18.

CHAPTER 1

Source of Anti-Methodist Pamphlet Attacks

It is surprising how quickly Methodism attracted hostile attention. The movement had barely emerged in 1738 when anti-Methodist pamphleteers began their hostile onslaught—four pamphlets were published in 1738, and sixty-seven rolled off the presses in 1739.[1] Also surprising is the breadth of the source of attacks on Methodism and its principals. Pamphlet criticism of Methodism came from every quarter of English society: the bishops and higher clergy of the Church of England, the lower clergy of the Church of England, the universities, other Christian denominations (the Society of Friends, Baptists, Independents, and Roman Catholics), the Calvinist wing of Methodism, Wesley's ex-preachers, ex-Methodist laity, the secular community, and women.

The Bishops and Higher Clergy

For most of the eighteenth century, Anglican discipline was lax. From 1717 to the mid-nineteenth century, convocation—synodical assemblies of bishops and clergy from the two provinces of the Church of England, Canterbury and York—did not meet with any regularity. Emasculated the previous century, convocation had degenerated into a "do nothing" gathering of clergy.[2] When it did meet, it was purely ceremonial and showed great reluctance to enforce the canons of the Church of England or engage in serious reform.[3] Archbishop Thomas Secker (1693–1768) argued in 1761 that convocation's inactivity had been beneficial to the church. It showed that by having the clergy meet and do nothing, the English people "have nothing to fear from [the clergy], but rather expect all manner of good things."[4] Without formal ecclesiastical

---

1 Field, *A Revised Bibliography*, appendix 5.
2 See Norman Sykes, *From Sheldon to Secker: Aspects of Church History, 1660–1768* (Cambridge: Cambridge University Press, 1959), 36–67; Robert G. Ingraham, *Religion, Reform, and Modernity in the Eighteenth Century: Thomas Secker and the Church of England* (Suffolk, UK: Boydell, 2007), 157.
3 Ingraham, *Religion, Reform, and Modernity in the Eighteenth Century*, 158.
4 Ibid.

machinery by which bishops could censure the Methodist leaders and rein them in, the printing press became their weapon of choice.

In the formative years of the revival, it was the Wesleys' good fortune that John Potter (1673?–1747) was archbishop of Canterbury from 1737 to 1747, and, to a lesser extent, that Edmund Gibson (1699–1748) was bishop of London (1723–48).[5] The Wesley brothers were no strangers to either man. Potter, while bishop of Oxford (1715–1737), was John's confidant on matters concerning the Holy Club, and it was he who had ordained them—John as deacon on September 25, 1725, and as priest on September 22, 1728; Charles as deacon on September 21, 1735. Both John and Charles met with Potter several times and believed they had his confidence and support. Overall, the Wesleys' dealings with him were warm and respectful. On one occasion Potter expressed the hope that the Wesleys might "leaven the whole lump" of the Church of England.[6] On another, referring to the Methodist leaders, Potter reputedly said, "These gentlemen are irregular; but they have done good, and I pray God to bless them."[7]

The Wesley brothers also kept in fairly close contact with Gibson.[8] Gibson had ordained Charles priest on September 29, 1735, and it was with Gibson that the brothers met on a number of occasions to defend themselves against charges concerning their theology and practices.

On October 20, 1738, John and Charles spent most of the morning with Gibson, discussing their views of justification and assurance of salvation.[9] The following February, the brothers met with Potter, and later with Gibson.[10] Both

---

5 See chapter 4, "Methodism and the Bishops," in Baker, *JWCE*. Baker maintains that the Wesley brothers were eager to have good relationships with, if not support from, members of the Episcopacy, especially Gibson. The Wesleys' concern was to avoid, if possible, any ecclesiastical hindrance to the spread of the revival.

6 Charles Wesley, "Letter to Benjamin La Trobe," July 20, 1786 [not James Hutton, as Telford states in Wesley's *Letters* VIII, 267]. See Baker, *JWCE*, 359n7.

7 John Potter, Archbishop of Canterbury, *Works* 19:265n.

8 *ODNB*. Norman Sykes, *Edmund Gibson* (London: Oxford University Press, 1926), is an excellent biography of Gibson. Gibson was educated at Queen's College, Oxford. Before becoming bishop of London, Gibson had served as bishop of Lincoln (1716–1723). For John and Charles Wesley's interaction with the Anglican bishops, see Baker, *JWCE*, 58–73 and 88–105. See also Julia Wedgwood, *John Wesley and the Evangelical Reaction of the Eighteenth Century* (London: Macmillan, 1870), chap. 13, "The Church against the Methodists," 292–333.

9 John Wesley, October 20, 1738, in *Journals and Diaries II (1738–1743)*, ed. W. Reginald Ward and Richard P. Heitzenrater, vol. 19 of *BEWJW* (Nashville: Abingdon, 1976), 359. The Wesleys met with Bishop Gibson from 9:15 to 11:00 a.m.

10 Wesley, February 21, 1739, in *Journals and Diaries II*, 377. The Wesley brothers met with the archbishop from 9:15 until 10:00 a.m., when they met with Bishop Gibson.

Potter's and Gibson's meetings with the Wesleys were civil and reassuring. But Gibson's favorable attitude to Methodism did not last long. Despite the Wesleys' close contact with Gibson, the earliest, most critical, and most significant attack from the episcopacy came from Gibson's pen. As the author of the *Codex Juris Ecclesiastici Anglicani* (1713), he was recognized as the preeminent authority of his day on ecclesiastical law. He was thus uniquely positioned to critique the Methodist movement, particularly where he believed ecclesiastical law had been contravened.[11]

It was only natural that Gibson as bishop of London was the first to publish his concerns about the revival. An analysis of the anti-Methodist pamphlets issued from 1739 to 1741 provides evidence of Methodism's early impact on London. Of the 114 pamphlets issued in that three-year period, 67 were published in London in 1739.[12] The Methodist movement had clearly gained a foothold in the city. Further confirmation of the importance of London came in 1739 when Wesley established one of his headquarters there, known as the Foundery, in a converted cannon factory.

Such rapid growth in the Methodist movement could not be ignored by the Anglican hierarchy. Since the diocese of London ranked third in significance after the Archbishoprics of Canterbury and York it was incumbent upon Gibson to enter the fray. His *Pastoral Letter* of 1739, gently rebuking the Methodists for their enthusiasm, was the earliest anti-Methodist pamphlet published by a bishop. It became the first of a series of attacks by Gibson on Methodism.[13] He urged his readers to avoid the extremes of enthusiasm on the one hand, and lukewarmness on the other. "Both these mistakes," Gibson informed his flock, "being greatly prejudicial to religion and dangerous to the souls of men, I may well be justified, and specially at this time, in setting before you the great evil of each, and letting you see that Christianity lies in the middle way

---

11　Edmund Gibson, *Codex juris ecclesiastici anglicani, or The statutes, constitutions, canons, rubricks, and articles of the Church of England* (London: J. Baskett, 1731). Gerald Cragg maintains that Gibson was the "undisputed authority" for interpreting canon law. See introduction to "A Letter to the Right Reverend the Lord Bishop of London," in *BEWJW*, vol. 11, *The Appeals to Men of Reason and Religion and Certain Related Open Letters*, ed., Gerald R. Cragg (Nashville: Abingdon, 1976–), 327–31.

12　Statistics derived from Field, *A Revised Bibliography*, esp. appendix 5, and his *Supplemental Bibliography*.

13　029-Gr. [Edmund Gibson], *The Bishop of London's pastoral letter to the people of his diocese* (London: S. Buckley, 1739). Second, third, and fourth editions were published in 1739, a fifth in 1741, and a tenth in 1768.

between them."[14] Furthermore he chastised the Methodists for undermining the authority of parish clergy by "casting unworthy reflections" on them.[15] Gibson also criticized early Methodist practices such as field preaching, itineration, and extempore prayer. Despite his critique of Methodism, nothing in the *Pastoral Letter* precluded civil relationships with the Methodist leadership. Nevertheless, Gibson kept an eye on them. Over the next five years, he continued to be critical of the revival in print. His visitation *Charge* of 1741–42,[16] less moderate than his *Pastoral Letter,* contained many unfavorable allusions to Methodism, linking the movement to the excesses of Puritanism in the previous century.[17] An even sterner denunciation of the movement's practices came from his pen in the anonymously published *Observations upon the conduct and behaviour of . . . Methodists* (1744).[18] Gibson opened his assault by chiding the Methodists for not qualifying themselves or their meeting places under the Act of Toleration. The Methodists were no longer well-meaning but misguided Christians, Gibson claimed; they had become a sect and had no right to remain in the Church England. Accordingly, he issued an ultimatum to the Methodists to "either renounce communion with the established church or oblige themselves and their followers to have a greater regard to the rules and doctrine" of the church.[19] Summed up in a single sentence, the message of *Observations* was: Methodists are no longer Anglicans!

The attack continued in the anonymously published *The case of the Methodists briefly stated; more particularly in the point of field-preaching* (1744). In all probability Gibson was the author.[20] It set out the provisions

---

14 Ibid., 3.

15 Ibid., 24.

16 Officially titled *The charge of Edmund, Lord Bishop of London, to the clergy of his diocese, in his visitation begun in the year 1741, and finished in the year 1742.*

17 176A-Ba. [Edmund Gibson], *Directions given to the clergy of the diocese of London* (London: Edward Owen, 1744). His 1741–42 charge to the clergy was appended to a reissue of his *Directions to the clergy,* 1724, which called for greater diligence in the performance of ecclesiastical duties. The *Directions* were printed on pages 1–76; the *Charge* is to be found on pages 77–110.

18 164-Gr. [Edmund Gibson], *Observations upon the conduct and behaviour of . . . Methodists* (London: E. Owen, 1744). Gibson neither denied nor admitted authorship. For almost certain proof of Gibson's authorship, see Baker, *JWCE,* 364fn. This work was circulated among the religious societies before its publication. Following its release, copies were circulated by a number of bishops in their dioceses.

19 164-Gr. [Edmund Gibson], *Observations upon the conduct and behaviour of . . . Methodists,* 6.

20 170-Gr. [Edmund Gibson], *The case of the Methodists briefly stated* (London: for Edward Owen, 1744).

of the Act of Tolerance for establishing congregations: (1) members of such congregations should take loyalty oaths; (2) meetings should be held in houses and not in the open air; (3) the doors of places of worship should be left open during services.[21] Gibson pointed out that to prevent sedition, preaching in the fields was forbidden. Gibson became increasingly hostile to Methodism. Only two years before his death, the aged bishop aggressively criticized the movement in his 1746–47 diocesan visitation charge.[22] Gibson noted that the Methodists had not cooled their zeal in spreading their dangerous discipline and pernicious doctrines.[23] In addressing the diocesan clergy directly, Gibson did not mince words, but issued a battle cry: "Reverend brethren, I charge you all, lift up your voice like a trumpet, and warn, and arm, and fortify all mankind—against a people called Methodists."[24] Wesley could not let the *Charge* go by without rebuttal. His "Letter to the Right Reverend the Lord Bishop of London" is regarded as Wesley at his best as a controversialist—candid, but courteous.[25] A posthumously issued work by Gibson, *A caution against enthusiasm,* appeared in 1751 and went through several editions, the last being in 1818.[26] It reiterates much of what Gibson had written in earlier tracts. Wesley, a prolific and serious author, was a reluctant controversialist but could not let Gibson's attacks pass without rebuttal to correct facts and explain the movement to an ever-widening audience. His apologia for Methodism took the form of two appeals: *An Earnest Appeal to Men of Reason and Religion* (1743) and *A Farther Appeal to Men of Reason and Religion* (1745).[27]

Gibson's attacks on Methodism found support in Thomas Herring (1693–1757). Educated at Jesus College, Cambridge, Herring became archbishop of York, 1743–47, and later archbishop of Canterbury and primate of

---

21 Acts of Parliament, Act of Toleration, 1689, granted freedom of worship to dissenting Protestants, such as Baptists and Congregationalists.

22 206-Gr. [Edmund Gibson], *The charge of the Right Reverend Father in God, Edmund, Lord Bishop of London . . . 1746 and 1747* (London: no printer, 1747).

23 Ibid., 8, 10–11.

24 Ibid., 8.

25 John Wesley, introduction to "A letter to the Right Reverend the Lord Bishop of London [Edmund Gibson]" (1747), in *BEWJW*, 11:327–31.

26 232-Gr. [Edmund Gibson], *A caution against enthusiasm* (London: E. Owen and sold by W. Johnston, 1751).

27 Wesley, *BEWJW*, 11:37–94; *A Farther Appeal to Men of Reason and Religion*, pts. 1–3, 11:95–325. Although *A Farther Appeal* was in three parts, it was published in two stages and viewed as a single document.

England, 1747–57.[28] Herring entered the fray against the evangelical revival by issuing a circular in 1744 as a covering letter for distribution of Gibson's *Observations* to the clergy of his archiepiscopal province.[29] Herring reproved the Methodists for their "great indiscretion" of regarding their "enthusiastic ardour" as "the true and only Christianity." Herring further criticized Wesley for allegedly teaching that very few people could attain or understand the kind of Christianity the Methodists espoused. Moreover, it could not be practiced, Herring asserted, "without breaking in upon the common duties of life."[30]

Wesley felt compelled to deny Herring's charges and requested that the archbishop review both Wesley's former and present writings. If, after having read them thoroughly, Herring could still maintain his accusations against the Methodist leader, Wesley promised "before God and the world" to cease preaching.[31]

The next episcopal attack on Methodism came from Richard Smalbroke (1672–1749). Educated at Trinity College and Magdalen College, Oxford, Smalbroke became bishop of St. David's, Wales (1724–31), and then Lichfield and Coventry (1731–49).[32] A keen controversialist, he expressed strong opposition to the evangelical movement within his diocese. His 1741 visitation charge did not mention Wesley or Whitefield by name but referred to "men of an enthusiastical temper"—clearly an inference to the Methodist leaders. The charge was not published immediately but issued in 1744 after

---

28 *ODNB.*

29 Wesley makes note of Herring's circular letter in *A Farther Appeal to Men of Reason and Religion*, pt. 1 (1745) *Works*, 11:118. "I was shown a kind of circular letter, which one of those whom 'the Holy Ghost hath made overseers' of his church* I was informed, had sent it to all the clergy of his diocese!" [*The (then) archbishop of York]. No copy of Herring's circular appears to have been preserved. It is possible, however, based on Wesley's critique of the document, to partially reconstruct it. See Wesley, *A Farther Appeal to Men of Reason and Religion, in BEWJW,* 11:117–19.

30 Ibid.

31 Ibid. There is speculation that Herring, using the alias "John Smith," was the eminent anonymous correspondent who carried on a long, serious, and respectful theological debate with Wesley in a series of six letters dating from September 1745 to March 1748. See Albert C. Outler, ed., *John Wesley* (Oxford: Oxford University Press, 1964), 3. Others, principally Tyerman, based on Henry Moore, *Life of the Rev. John Wesley* (London: for John Kershaw, 1825), identify Smith as Bishop (later Archbishop) Thomas Secker. See Tyerman, *The Life and Times of the Rev. John Wesley,* 1:500. Neither Outler nor Baker believes there is enough evidence to identify Smith. See Outler, *John Wesley,* fn.1, 1; and Baker in *Letters* 11, (1740–1755), *BEWJW,* ed. Frank Baker (Nashville: Abingdon, 1976–), 26:138n18.

32 *ODNB.*

Methodism had made successful inroads into Staffordshire. At the center of Smalbroke's critique of Wesley was the charge that he was an enthusiast who confounded the "extraordinary with the ordinary operations of the Spirit," a common charge made against the Methodists.[33] Smalbroke was convinced that a united force of Methodism and Deism would destroy the established Church.[34] Unable to ignore Smalbroke's charges, Wesley penned a lengthy rebuttal for inclusion in *A Farther Appeal*.[35]

The most vociferous, elaborate, and notoriously scurrilous attacks from the church hierarchy came from George Lavington (1684–1762). Educated at New College, Oxford, he was bishop of Exeter from 1746 to 1762.[36] As "neither an author nor preacher of note," Lavington was far from the most distinguished man on the episcopal bench.[37] Lavington was moved to join the barrage of anti-Methodist pamphleteers after an anonymous tract appeared in 1748, purporting to be an extract from his visitation charge to his diocese, endorsing Methodist practices.[38] It was a hoax, of course, but it so infuriated Lavington that he issued a hostile disclaimer pointing an accusing finger at the Methodists. He nursed his wounds until he could release the first part of his rambling *Enthusiasm of Methodists and papists compar'd*. The largest of all pamphlet assaults on Methodism, it was published anonymously in three parts, in 1749, 1751, and 1752, each part approximately doubling the size of the preceding one.[39] Methodists, Lavington asserted, were nothing more than "a set of pretended reformers—a dangerous and presumptuous sect, animated

---

33 202-Gr. [Richard Smalbroke], *A charge deliver'd to the clergy of the diocese of Lichfield . . . 1744 and 1745* (London: John and Paul Knapton, 1746), 64.

34 Ibid. See also 167-Gr. Richard Smalbroke, *A charge deliver'd to the . . . clergy in . . . the diocese of Lichfield . . . 1741* (London: J. and P. Knapton, 1741).

35 John Wesley, *A Farther Appeal to Men of Reason and Religion*, pt. 1 (1745), in *BEWJW*, 11:141–66.

36 *ODNB*.

37 For Gerald R. Cragg's assessment of Lavington, see his introduction to "Open Letters to Dr. George Lavington," in *BEWJW*, 11:353–58.

38 *A letter to the Right Reverend Father in God George, Lord Bishop of Exeter, occasioned by his Lordship's late charge to the clergy of the diocese*, 1748. For a more complete account of Lavington's motivation to issue an anti-Methodist attack, see Baker, *JWCE*, 104.

39 213-Ga. [George Lavington], *The enthusiasm of Methodists and papists compar'd* (London: for J. and P. Knapton, 1749). Wesley responded in "A letter to the author of *The enthusiasm of Methodists and papists compar'd*," in *BEWJW*, 11:359–76. Wesley followed this up with a much longer and detailed response, "A second letter to the author of *The enthusiasm of Methodists and papists compar'd*," in *BEWJW*, 11: 380–429.

with an enthusiastical and fanatical spirit."[40] Unable to find any merit in the revival, Lavington set out to demonstrate that the worst features of Roman Catholicism were duplicated in Methodism. His final thrust at the Methodists came in 1752 in a letter to Wesley.[41] Wesley felt compelled to ignore much of what Lavington had written in the letter, and responded only briefly to charges such as enthusiasm, itinerancy, lay and field preaching by boys and women, and maligning the clergy. Lavington's assault on Methodism was unbecoming of the episcopal office. It "deserved," Julia Wedgwood wrote in the late nineteenth century, "to be coupled with the men who flung dead cats and rotten eggs at the Methodists, not with those who assailed their tenets with arguments, or even serious rebuke."[42]

Thomas Secker (1693–1768), archbishop of Canterbury from 1758 to 1768,[43] though pleading against harsh treatment of the Methodists, chided them in his 1762 visitation charge for advancing "unjustifiable" notions and prejudicing parishioners against their "proper ministers."[44] Secker's temperate attitude toward the Methodists may have been formed by his numerous (mostly friendly) personal contacts with Wesley.[45]

One of the most formidable episcopal attacks came from William Warburton (1698–1779), bishop of Gloucester from 1760 to 1769, a longtime critic of Wesley and Methodism. It ranks as one of the most "perverse and abusive" anti-Methodist publications.[46] Warburton's attack on Wesley placed him in good company as the bishop assaulted in print some of the leading figures

---

40 Lavington, *The enthusiasm of the Methodists and the papists compar'd,* pt. 1, preface. In 1754 Lavington released the work in a two-volume edition including all three parts. Of note is the republication of the work in 1820 and a new edition by the Reverend Richard Polwhele in 1833.

41 239-Gr. [Lavington], *The Bishop of Exeter's answer to Mr. J. Wesley's late letter* (London: John and Paul Knapton, 1752). Wesley responded in "A Second Letter to the Lord Bishop of Exeter in Answer to His Lordship's Late Letter" in *The Appeals to Men of Reason and Religion and Certain Other Open Letters, Works,* 11:435–36.

42 Julia Wedgwood, *John Wesley and the Evangelical Reaction of the Eighteenth Century* (London: Macmillan, 1870), 131.

43 *ODNB.*

44 341A-Ki. Thomas Secker, *The charge designed to have been delivered by the archbishop of Canterbury to the clergy of his diocese* . . . (London: no printer, 1762). Secker studied medicine and graduated with an MD from Leiden University before returning to England and entering Exeter College, Oxford.

45 Baker, *JWCE,* 30.

46 *ODNB.* Warburton served articles and practiced as a solicitor before studying Latin and Greek in preparation for ordination. He was one of the most "perverse and abusive" of all Wesley's opponents. Introduction, "A Letter to the Right Reverend the Lord Bishop of Gloucester" (1763) in *BEWJW,* 11:459–63, esp. 459–60.

of the age: David Hume, man of letters; Edward Gibbon, respected historian and scholar; and Robert Lowth, professor of poetry, Oxford University, and later bishop of London. Gerald Cragg summed up Warburton's career as "a long sequence of discreditable brawls."[47] Warburton's two-volume *Doctrine of grace* (1763), reiterating the old charge of enthusiasm, was directed in the main at Wesley, accusing him of falsely claiming apostolic gifts and grace.[48] It was the last major work to come from the Anglican hierarchy in opposition to Methodism.[49]

Four additional bishops, however, warned their dioceses in print of the dangers of the movement. The first, Richard Richmond (d. 1780), bishop of Sodor and Man from 1773 to 1780, issued a broadside circular to the clergy of his diocese in 1776 that attacked the "profane and blasphemous, extempore effusions of these pretenders to the true religion," and charged them with having "private meetings, assemblies, and congregations contrary to the doctrine, government, rites and ceremonies of the Established Church, and the civil and ecclesiastical laws" of the Isle of Man.[50] Although Methodism is not mentioned, it is clearly implied. Hoping to stem the tide of Methodism's growth on the island, Richmond called upon the clergy of his diocese to be "diligent and to use [their] utmost endeavours to dissuade [their]respective flocks from following, or being led or misguided by, such incompetent teachers, and to exhort, incite, and invite them to devoutly read the holy Scripture, to attend reverently the blessed sacraments of their parish church, and the ghostly advice of their own ministers."[51]

The second, Shute Barrington (1734–1826), bishop of Salisbury from 1782 to 1791, in his inaugural visitation charge in 1783, issued a warning to the clergy of his diocese that the "present shameless profligacy, avowed libertinism, infidelity, and superstition in every shape are making a most alarming

---

47 "A letter to the Right Reverend the Lord Bishop of Gloucester," in *BEWJW*, vol. 11.

48 342-Gr. [William Warburton], *Doctrine of grace* (London: for A. Millar and J. and R. Tonson, 1763).

49 A voracious reader, Warburton earned standing in the literary realm. As one of the most eminent of all of Wesley's opponents, Warburton could not be ignored. Wesley responded in "A Letter to the Right Reverend the Lord Bishop of Gloucester" in *BEWJW*, 11: 467–538.

50 *ODNB*. Richard Richmond, "Circular letter to the several rectors, vicars, chaplains, and curates within the Isle and diocese of Man," transcript printed in Tyerman, *The Life and Times of the Rev. John Wesley*, 3:229.

51 Ibid.

progress."[52] Like Richmond, Barrington did not name his foe, but it is clear that he had the Methodists in mind. He railed against those persons "who profess rigid piety, who propagate their wild conceits with much eagerness . . . who themselves vent the most extravagant notions."[53]

The third was Samuel Horsley (1733–1806), archdeacon of St. Alban's, bishop of St. David's from 1788 to 1793, bishop of Rochester from 1793 to 1802, and bishop of Asaph from 1802 to 1806. In his 1790 charge to the clergy of the Rochester diocese, he raised concern about the prevalence of the Methodists in the diocese and their tendency to antinomianism. But more critical, he thought, was their tendency toward enthusiasm: "The great crime and folly of the Methodists consists, not so much in heterodoxy, as in fanaticism; not in perverse doctrine, but rather in a disorderly zeal for the propagation of the truth."[54] The immediate remedy, and the best security, Horsley claimed, was a laity forewarned against the seduction of false teachers.[55] Earlier, as archdeacon of St. Albans, Samuel Horsley, in an ordination sermon at Gloucester Cathedral on September 9, 1787, attacked the lack of education among Methodist preachers. The prerequisite for preaching, Horsley said, was an education that included the study of ancient languages, Jewish history, and all parts of the Scriptures. Any who claimed to be qualified for preaching but who lacked sufficient education were, he considered, enthusiasts.[56]

The fourth, George Pretyman Tomline (1750–1827), tutor and secretary to the younger Pitt, became bishop of Lincoln from 1787 to 1820. Tomline was known for his strong anti-Catholic and anti-Calvinist tendencies. To these he added contempt for the Methodists. Tomline launched an attack on them in his visitation charge in 1800.[57] Although he did not mention them by name, it is clear that the Methodists were his target. He warned against those

---

52 528E-Fi. Shute Barrington, *A charge delivered to the clergy of the diocese of Sarum* (Oxford: no printer, 1783), 11–15. A second edition appeared in 1791. Barrington was educated at Merton College, Oxford. *ODNB.*

53 Barrington, *A charge delivered to the clergy of the diocese of Sarum*, 11–15.

54 561-Ki. [Horsley], *The charge of Samuel, Lord Bishop of St. David's, to the clergy of his diocese*, 33.

55 Ibid.

56 538A*-Ki. Samuel Horsley, *The analogy between the light of inspiration and the light of learning.*

57 589-Gr. [Sir George Pretyman Tomline], *A charge delivered to the clergy of the diocese of Lincoln 1800* (London: for Cadell and Davies, Rivingtons, White, Hatchard, Lunn, 1800). Tomline was educated at Pembroke College, Cambridge. *ODNB.*

whose "especial gift or grace . . . supersedes the necessity of education and of regular ordination."[58] Such leaders seduced the people from their appointed ministers and separated them from communion with the church.[59] Tomline called for action. "We must," he wrote, "oppose energy to violence, zeal to enthusiasm, vigilance to cunning, piety to infidelity, and Christian firmness, forbearance and charity to the shafts of envy and malice, ridicule, and ignorance."[60] Ten years earlier Wesley had twice written to Tomline. The first letter, in March 1790, was a plea from the aged Methodist leader for toleration of the movement.[61] The second letter, dated June 26, 1790, reminded Tomline of the loyalty of the Methodists to both church and state, and asked why the bishop would want to drive the Methodists out of the church.[62] At issue was the Act of Toleration. On legal advice the majority of the Methodist preachers and chapels were licensed according to the act. But Methodists had in some instances been refused the license unless they declared themselves Dissenters. Wesley refused to make such a declaration. Although the Methodists were loyal members of the Church of England, the bishop was treating them cruelly and disingenuously: "They desire a licence . . .Your Lordship refuses it, and then punishes them for not having a licence! So, your Lordship leaves them only this alternative, 'Leave the church or starve.'" For all intents and purposes Tomline's action, Wesley complained, was "persecution," and he urged an end to it: "For pity's sake suffer the poor people [the Methodists] to enjoy their religious as well as civil liberty!"[63]

A surprising omission from the list of episcopal critics of Methodism who ventured into print is Joseph Butler (1692–1752), bishop of Bristol from 1738 to 1750, and later bishop of Durham (1750–1752). Educated at Oriel College, Oxford, Butler was a theologian and philosopher of note. He is best known for his *Analogy of Religion, Natural and Revealed* (1736), and his refutation of Deism. Just as he had done with Gibson in London, Wesley sought to be on good terms with Butler in Bristol, the location of the New Room, another of his regional headquarters. Wesley met

---

58 [Tomline], *A charge delivered to the clergy of the diocese of Lincoln*, 18–19.

59 Ibid.

60 Ibid., 20.

61 Wesley, Letter to Dr. Pretyman Tomline, bishop of Lincoln (March 1790), *Letters*, 8:209.

62 John Wesley, Letter to Dr. Pretyman Tomline, bishop of Lincoln (June 26, 1790), *Letters*, 8:224–25.

63 Ibid., 225.

with Butler on three separate occasions, the first in early summer 1739, and then on two more occasions, August 16 and 18. The first interview lasted about fifteen minutes, the second about an hour, and the final one approximately one hour.[64] During the second meeting Butler told Wesley that his view of the Methodist leaders had changed from a positive to a negative one: "I once thought you and Mr. Whitefield well-meaning men. But I can't think so now for I have heard more of you—matters of fact, Sir. And Mr. Whitefield says in his *Journal*, 'There are promises still to be fulfilled in me.' Sir, 'pretending to the extraordinary revelations and gifts of the Holy Ghost is a horrid thing, a very horrid thing.'" Butler asked then about reports he had heard of people falling into fits at society meetings. Wesley admitted that they did and that he prayed over them. To which Butler commented, "Very extraordinary indeed!" Asked for his advice, Butler replied, "I will give it you very freely. You have no business here. You are not commissioned to preach in this diocese. Therefore, I advise you to go hence."[65] Wesley's hope for a supportive episcopal presence in Bristol was dashed. Butler's antipathy to Methodism and his disdain for Wesley and Whitefield became well-known and oft quoted. Given the intensity of his anti-Methodist feelings, it is curious that Butler remained aloof from joining in the pamphlet attacks on the Methodists. Perhaps Butler had other means.

Butler took Josiah Tucker (1713–99), a promising young Anglican priest serving at All Saints' Church, Bristol, under his wing and mentored him. Tucker shared Butler's dislike of the Methodists. No doubt Butler encouraged Tucker to be one of the earliest Bristol anti-Methodists to engage in pamphleteering. The first three of Tucker's assaults, published in 1739, singled out Whitefield for attack.[66] The fourth, published in 1742, entitled

---

64 Appendix B, Wesley's interview with Bishop Butler, August 16 and 18, 1739, *BEWJW*, vol. 19, *Journals and Diaries II (1738–1743)*, ed. W. Reginald Ward and Richard P. Heitzenrater (Nashville: Abingdon, 1990), 471–74. See also Frank Baker, "John Wesley and Bishop Joseph Butler," *ProcWHS* 42 (May 1980): 93–99.

65 150-Gr. Josiah Tucker, *A brief history of the principles of Methodism* (Oxford: for James Fletcher, 1742).

66 005A-Ba. Josiah Tucker, *Bristol 30 March 1739* (Bristol: no printer, 1739). See John Wesley's earliest defense of the emerging revival in Bristol, introduced, transcribed, and annotated by Randy L. Maddox, in *Wesley and Methodist Studies*, 6:124–53. 036-Gr. [Josiah Tucker], *A complete account of the conduct of . . . Mr. Whitefield* (London: by C. Corbett, 1739). 040-Gr. An impartial hand [Josiah Tucker], *The life and particular proceedings of the Rev. Mr. George Whitefield* (London: for J. Roberts, 1739).

A brief history of the principles of Methodism, was written by Tucker at the request of Hugh Boulter, archbishop of Armagh and primate of Ireland, previously bishop of Bristol, to provide an "authentic account of the divisions and quarrels of the Methodists."[67] The bulk of the pamphlet, thirty-one out of fifty-two pages, deals with Wesley. Tucker believed Methodism was strongly influenced by William Law, whose eclectic theology borrowed from both Calvinism and Arminianism. Methodism, Tucker alleged, was also strongly influenced by the Moravians. From them Wesley selected "a medley of principles;" a very "extraordinary and odd composition, full of contradictions," such as the ideas that conversion was instantaneous, that faith alone justified, that assurance of salvation was possible, and that the saved ceased to sin.[68] Wesley found Tucker a formidable and dispassionate opponent, and worthy of a reply. His rejoinder to Tucker, "The principles of a Methodist," appeared in 1742.[69]

Five of Methodism's clerical opponents were eventually elevated to the episcopal bench. Once they had assumed higher responsibilities, the great majority no longer railed against the revival. This may be explained by the fact that they served in the episcopacy at a time when anti-Methodist zeal had cooled. Richard Hurd (1720–1808), fellow of Emanuel College, Cambridge, and one of the Whitehall preachers, later became bishop of Lichfield and Coventry from 1774 to 1781, then bishop of Worcester from 1781 to 1808, declining the primacy in 1783 for health reasons.[70] John Douglas (1721–1807), vicar of High Ercall, Shropshire, a young man when he attacked the Methodists in print in 1755, was elevated to the See of Salisbury in 1791.[71] Four important pamphlets came from John Green (1705–79), dean of Lincoln and vice-chancellor of Cambridge (formerly Regius Professor of Divinity and

---

67 150-Gr. Tucker, *A brief history of the principles of Methodism*, preface, 5. It is sometimes claimed that it was Joseph Butler who requested Tucker to produce this pamphlet, but such claims are erroneous. It is more than likely that Butler, although he did not initiate the endeavor, encouraged it.

68 Ibid., 32.

69 John Wesley, "The principles of a Methodist," vol. 9, *The Methodist Societies History, Nature, and Design*, ed. Rupert Davies, *BEWJW*, 47–66.

70 237-Gr. Richard Hurd, *The mischiefs of enthusiasm and bigotry* (London: for J. Gleed, 1752). *ODNB*.

71 *ODNB*. 237-Gr. [John Douglas], *An apology for the clergy, with a view to expose the groundless assertions of a late commentator . . .* (London: S. Bladon, 1755). A second edition was published in 1755.

royal chaplain). Green was consecrated bishop of Lincoln in 1761 and died in office in 1779.[72] Samuel Hallifax (1733–90), a twenty-seven-year-old fellow of Trinity Hall when he criticized the evangelical doctrine of justification by faith alone, was elevated to the episcopal see of Gloucester from 1781 to 89, and later was translated to St. Asaph, in 1789. He died in 1790.[73] George Horne (1730–92), fellow of Magdalen College, academic writer, university administrator, and chaplain to George III from 1771 to 81, became bishop of Norwich in 1790.[74] He was the only one of these five bishops to publish anti-Methodist criticisms while serving in the episcopacy. Too ill to deliver his 1791 *Charge* to the Norwich diocese in person, Horne had the charge printed and distributed throughout the diocese.[75] Horne died in 1792. In the *Charge* Horne chided the Methodists for having "more zeal than discretion" by opening an "asylum for penitents" in London that "took in people of all persuasions, without exception to any." The inference, Horne claimed, was that "souls might be saved as well without, as within a church; perhaps better." The Methodists' neglect of Anglican rules led to their despising them. The logical end, said Horne in a veiled reference to the consecrations of Thomas Coke and Francis Asbury as superintendents for America, was the establishment of a "spurious episcopacy."[76]

The bishops, despite their hostility to the Methodist movement in print, took no decisive action against its leaders. Apart from the small number of bishops already mentioned, the episcopal bench was by and large silent. The

---

72 *ODNB*. Green wrote four pamphlets critical of Methodism before his episcopal appointment. 205B-Ba. John Green, *An appeal to the oracles of God* (London: for J. Hart, 1746). 271A-Ki. John Green, *Eight sermons preached in the parish church of St. Saviour's, Southwark* (London: printed for J. Fuller and J. Scott, 1758). 294-Gr. Academicus [John Green], *The principles and practices of the Methodists considered* (London: printed for W. Bristow, 1760). A second edition, corrected, was published in 1761. 315-Gr. Academicus [John Green], *The principles and practices of the Methodists farther considered* (Cambridge: for J. Bentham, 1761). A second edition was published in 1761.

73 290-Gr. Samuel Hallifax, *Saint Paul's doctrine of justification by faith* (Cambridge: J. Bentham, 1760).

74 Horne had attacked Methodism in 1755 and 1761. *ODNB*. See 250-Gr. George Horne, *Christ and the Holy Ghost the supporters of the spiritual life* (Oxford: printed at the theatre for S. Parker, [1755]), and 330-Gr. George Horne, *Works wrought through faith a condition of our justification* (Oxford: Clarendon, [1761]). Wesley thought highly of Horne and responded to him in "A Letter to the Rev. Mr. Horne (1762)," *BEWJW*, 11:437–58. Horne is best known for his *Commentary on the Psalms* (Oxford, 1771), which went through many editions.

75 556-Ki. George Horne, *A charge intended to have been delivered to the clergy of the diocese of Norwich at the primary visitation* (Norwich: Yarington and Bacon, 1791).

76 Ibid., 22–24.

majority preferred to follow the policy of quieta non movere (do not move settled things) and left the Methodists alone. However, the printed opposition that issued from those few who engaged in debate with the leaders of the revival was some of the strongest critique that Methodism had to face. The publications of Gibson, Lavington, and Warburton were particularly effective in stirring up strong anti-Methodist sentiments in their dioceses and beyond.

Archdeacons joined bishops in deploring the spread of Methodism. Perhaps the best-known archdeacon to attack Methodism was Henry Stebbing (bap. 1687–1763), preacher at Gray's Inn and chaplain to George II, archdeacon of Wiltshire (1735–63), and chancellor of the diocese of Sarum. One of the earliest anti-Methodist pamphleteers, Stebbing published his first anti-Methodist tract, *A caution against religious delusion*, in 1739. It was followed by two other anti-Methodist pamphlets: *An earnest and affectionate address to the . . . Methodists* (1745), and *The doctrine of justification by faith* (1757).[77]

In 1763 Thomas Rutherforth (1712–71), Regius Professor of Divinity, Cambridge, and archdeacon of Essex, delivered a series of four charges to his clergy, the main burden of which was enthusiasm, particularly anti-intellectualism and illiteracy. The Methodist doctrine of assurance, Rutherforth complained, was so full of contradiction and evasion that "it is scarce possible to collect from thence any consistent opinion which they will abide by."[78] James Ibbetson, archdeacon of St. Albans (1754–1781), in his 1765 *Charge*, deplored the increase of Methodism and popery in his archdeaconry and the neglect of the Book of Common Prayer in some churches.[79] John Tottie ([1711]–74), rector

---

77 *ODNB*. 017-Gr. Henry Stebbing, *A caution against religious delusion* (London: for Fletcher Gyles, 1739). 200-Gr. A. B. [Henry Stebbing], *An earnest and affectionate address to the people called Methodists* (London: J. Oliver, 1745). By 1815 this pamphlet had been issued in seventeen editions. 267-Gr. A Clergyman [Henry Stebbing], *The Doctrine of Justification by Faith in Jesus Christ* (London: L. Davis and C. Reymers, 1757).

78 343-Gr. Thomas Rutherforth, *Four charges to the clergy of the archdeaconry of Essex* (Cambridge: J. Bentham, 1763), 2–3, 8, 39. Rutherforth was educated at St. John's College, Cambridge, graduating at age sixteen. In 1743 he was elected a fellow of the Royal Society, and in 1745 he became Regius professor of divinity at Cambridge and was awarded the DD degree. In 1752 he became archdeacon of Essex. *ODNB*. Wesley responded in "A letter to the Rev. Dr. Rutherforth (1768)," *BEWJW*, 9:373–88.

79 386A-Ki. James Ibbetson, *A charge to the clergy of the archdeaconry of St. Albans* ([London]: for Benjamin White, 1776), 33–34. Ibbetson was educated at Exeter College, Oxford, served as rector of Bushey, Hertfordshire, prebendary of Lincoln, and archdeacon of St. Albans. James Ibbetson papers, 1746–1775, at Pitts Theology Library, Candler School of Theology, accessed December 5, 2018, https://findingaids.library.emory.edu /documents/P-MSS030/

of St. Martin's, Worcester, and archdeacon of Worcester, in 1766 warned the clergy of the archdeaconry to beware of the Methodists.[80] The archdeacon of Winchester, Thomas Balguy (1716–95), accused the Methodists in 1769 of making an outright assault on the established order.[81]

The Lower Clergy

If the bishops and higher clergy did not use the power of the printed word against Methodism as extensively as they might have, the lower ranks of the clergy certainly more than made up for the reluctance of their superiors to go to press. Compared to the virtual trickle of pamphlets from the bishops, the lower clergy released a devastating flood of printer's ink in an attempt to disparage the movement. Not all Anglican clergy were opposed—there were notable exceptions—but the London clergy, in the main, were unreservedly vocal in their opposition to the revival, particularly in 1739 and 1740, when London's pulpits were not only closed to Whitefield and Wesley but rang with sermons antagonistic toward Methodism.

Some who attacked the revival in print were highly influential clergy in positions where they had significant audiences for their anti-Methodist attacks. Most held important London lectureships.[82] Several went on to achieve fame and preferment. Among the more significant early critics were: Arthur Bedford (bap. 1668–1745), chaplain to H. R. H. Frederick, Prince of Wales, and to the Haberdashers Hospital at Hoxton;[83] Tristram Land, fellow of Clare Hall, Cambridge, curate of St. James' Garlickhithe, and lecturer of the united

---

80 384-Gr. John Tottie, *Two charges delivered to the clergy of the diocese of Worcester . . . 1763 and 1766* (n.p.: no printer, [1766]). Tottie was archdeacon of Worcester 1742–1774. "Archdeacons: Worcester," in *Fasti Ecclesiae Anglicanae 1541–1857*, vol. 7, *Ely, Norwich, Westminster and Worcester dioceses*, ed. Joyce M. Horn (London, 1992), 113–14, on British History Online, accessed December 5, 2018, http://www.british-history.ac.uk/fasti-ecclesiae/1541-1847/vol7/pp113-114.

81 423A-Ki. Thomas Balguy, *Sermon preached at Lambeth Chapel on the consecration of the bishop of . . . Llandaff* (London: L. Davis and C. Reymers, 1769). Balguy was educated at Cambridge and was a disciple and admirer of Bishop Warburton. Upon Warburton's death Balguy was invited to succeed his mentor but declined due to ill health. *ODNB*.

82 Employed by the parish vestry, lecturers were expected to assist with the incumbents' preaching duties. They often had responsibility for the Sunday afternoon worship services and for performing most of the midweek preaching. See Jennifer Farooq, *Preaching in Eighteenth-Century London* (Suffolk, UK: Boydell, 2013), 22.

83 003-Gr. Arthur Bedford, *The doctrine of assurance* (London: Charles Ackers, 1738). 130-Gr. Arthur Bedford, *The doctrine of justification by faith stated* (London: C. Rivington, 1741). *ODNB*.

parishes of St. Anthony and St. John the Baptist;[84] Joseph Trapp (1679–1747), priest, poet, and pamphleteer, rector of Harlington, Sussex, and lecturer at St. Martin-in-the-Fields, formerly the first professor of poetry at Oxford, from 1708 to 1718, and manager for Henry Sacheverell at his trial in 1709;[85] Thomas Church (1707–56), educated at Brasenose College, Oxford, became vicar of Battersea, prebend of St. Paul's Cathedral, and lecturer at St. Anne's, Soho.[86]

In the late 1750s and 1760s, three well-known London preachers issued scurrilous assaults on the Methodists: William Dodd (1729–77), lecturer at St. Olave, Hart Street, chaplain of Magdalene Hospital, formerly lecturer at West Ham and St. James' Garlickhithe, and chaplain to the king in 1763, who was hanged for forgery in 1777;[87] John Free (1711–91), vicar of Runcorn, Cheshire

---

84 009-Gr. Tristram Land, *A letter to the Rev. Mr. Whitefield* (London: J. Roberts, 1739). 133-Gr. Tristram Land, *A second letter to the Rev. Mr. Whitefield* (London: J. Roberts, [1741]).

85 A popular preacher at Oxford, Sacheverell, in a very contentious speech in 1709 that attacked Dissenters and Catholics, was charged with incensing violence. He was tried by parliament and found guilty. *ODNB*.

For Trapp's anti-Methodist pamphlets see 010-Gr. Joseph Trapp, *The nature, folly, sin and danger of being righteous over-much* (London: L. Gilliver, 1739). There were five editions by 1758. 040-Gr. Joseph Trapp, *The nature, usefulness and regulation of religious zeal* (London: Lawton Gilliver, [1739]). 093-Gr. [Joseph Trapp], *The true spirits of the Methodists and their allies* (London: Lawton Gilliver, 1740). 123-Gr. Joseph Trapp, *A reply to Mr. Law's "Earnest and Serious Answer"* (London: L. Gilliver, 1741).

86 049-Gr. Thomas Church, *An explanation and defence of the doctrine of the Church of England* (London: J. Roberts, 1739); 165-Gr. Thomas Church, *A serious and expostulatory letter to the Reverend George Whitefield* (London: M. Cooper, 1744); 185-Gr. Thomas Church, *Remarks on the Reverend Mr. John Wesley's last journal* (London: M. Cooper, 1745); 205-Gr. Thomas Church, *Some farther remarks on the Rev. Mr. John Wesley's last journal* (London: M. Cooper, 1746). Thomas Church, *Dictionary of National Biography* (London: Smith, Elder, 1887), 4:305–6. Wesley regarded Church as a respectful and scholarly opponent.

87 William Dodd was educated at Clare Hall, Cambridge, and was ordained a priest in the Church of England. *ODNB*. In London he was known for his extravagant lifestyle, which left him deeply in debt. In an effort to clear his debt he forged a bond in the amount of £4,200 in the name of his former pupil the Earl of Chesterfield. Caught, he was tried, convicted, and imprisoned. An attempt to obtain a royal pardon for him failed, and he was sentenced to be hanged at Tyburn. In a twist of irony Dodd, who had railed against the Methodists, now sought their solace in his final days. John and Charles Wesley ministered to him in the jail on several visits. Two days before his execution, John spent time with Dodd and found him repentant and resigned to his fate: "Such a prisoner I scarce ever saw before, much less such a condemned malefactor. I should think, none could converse with him without acknowledging that God is with him." See John Wesley, February 15 and 18, 1777, and June 25, 1777, *BEWJW*, vol. 23, *Journals and Diaries VI (1776–1786)*. For his anti-Methodist publications, see 280-Gr. William Dodd, *Cautions against Methodism* (London: L. Davis and C. Reymers, [1759]). 332A-Ba. [William Dodd], *A conference between a mystic, an Hutchinsonian, a Calvinist, a Methodist, a member of the Church of England, and others* (London: L. Davis and C. Reymers, 1761).

and East Coker, Somerset, lecturer of Newington, Surrey, and Sir John Leman lecturer of St. Mary at Hill;[88] and John Downes (c. 1691–1759), rector of St. Michael, Wood Street, and lecturer of St. Mary-Le-Bow.[89]

Strong opposition from London's clergy was supplemented by printed attacks from clergy in other cities and the rural areas. Chief among them were Josiah Tucker (1713–99), vicar of All Saints', Bristol, and minor canon of the College of Bristol;[90] William Bowman (ca. 1703–44), vicar of Dewsbury, Yorkshire;[91] Thomas Dockwray (1689–1760), fellow of St. John's College, Cambridge University, vicar of Wallsend, and lecturer of St. Nicholas Church (later Cathedral), Newcastle;[92] John Kirkby (1705–54), rector of Blackmanstone, Kent; [93] Theophilus Evans (1693–1767), sometime chaplain to the Gwynnes of Garth (Sarah Gwynne married Charles Wesley in 1749);[94] Thomas Green, vicar of Wymeswould, Leicestershire;[95] and Robert Potter

---

88 The Reverend John Free was educated at Oxford and was headmaster of St. Olave's Grammar School before becoming vicar of East Crocker, Somerset. He received the income from both parishes but never took up residence in either place, employing instead curates to do the work. *ODNB*. 273-Gr. John Free, *A display of the bad principles of the Methodists* (London: by the author, 1758). 274-Gr. John Free, *Rules for the discovery of false prophets* (London: E. Owen, 1758). 275-Gr. John Free, *Dr. Free's edition of the Rev. Mr. Wesley's first penny letter* (London: E. Owen, 1758). 276-Gr. John Free, *Dr. Free's edition of the Rev. Mr. John Wesley's second letter* (London: by the author, 1759). 277-Gr. John Free, *Dr. Free's remarks upon Mr. Jones's letter* (London: E. Owen, 1759). 278-Gr. John Free, *The whole speech, which was delivered to the reverend clergy* (London: by the author, 1759). These were reprinted in 286A-Ki. John Free, *A controversy with the people called Methodists* (London: W. Sandby, 1760). In 1758, in an attempt to gain preferment, he published 273-Gr. *A display of the bad principles of the Methodists*. To appoint a Methodist to a parish, Free warned, would damage both church and state. At issue was the role of good works in salvation. Wesley replied in *A letter to the Rev. Dr. Free* (May 2, 1758), and a *Second letter to the Rev. Dr. Free* (August 24, 1758). Free responded in a sermon at the University Church, Oxford, and published it in a pamphlet, 274-Gr. *Rules for the discovery of false prophets*. For Wesley's letters see *BEWJW*, 9:316–30.

89 282-Gr. John Downes, *Methodism examined and exposed* (London: for John Rivington, 1759). See Wesley's reply: Wesley, Letter to the Rev. John Downes (1759), in *BEWJW*, vol. 9, *The Methodist Societies: History, Nature, and Design*, ed. Rupert E. Davies (Nashville: Abingdon, 1989), 350–66.

90 See earlier discussion of Josiah Tucker in this chapter.

91 094-Gr. William Bowman, *The imposture of Methodism display'd* (London: printed for Joseph Lord, 1742).

92 156A-Ba. Thomas Dockwray, *The operations of the Holy Spirit imperceptible* (Newcastle, UK: John White, [1743]). *ODNB*.

93 217-Gr. John Kirkby, *The impostor detected* (London: for M. Cooper, 1750). *ODNB*.

94 235-Gr. [Theophilus Evans], *The history of modern enthusiasm* (London: printed and sold by W. Owen and W. Clarke, 1752). *ODNB*.

95 249A-Fi. Thomas Green, *A dissertation on enthusiasm* (London: J. Oliver, 1755). 269-Gr. Thomas Green, *Justification* (London: J. Oliver and T. Payne, 1758). *ODNB*.

(1721–1804), poet, translator, pamphleteer, and curate (later prebendary) of Norwich.[96]

Two of the of most biting satirical poems ridiculing Methodism came from priests of the Church of England. Evan Lloyd (1734–76), vicar of Llan-vair Dyffryn Clwyd, Denbighshire, authored *The Methodist, a poem*,[97] and Nathaniel Lancaster (1701–75), former chaplain to the prince of Wales, and from 1737 rector of Stanford Rivers, Essex, penned the scurrilous *Methodism triumphant*.[98]

The majority of pamphlets that came from the clergy of the established church listed the authors' names and livings. Others were published pseudon-ymously under such titles as "Presbyter of the Church of England," "Clericus," "Curate in the Country," and "A Country Curate." To these must be added tracts issued anonymously but that, judged by their contents, were clearly the work of men in Anglican orders.

The Universities

As members of the Holy Club at Oxford and as graduates later, the three leaders of Methodism, the Wesley brothers and Whitefield, were well known for their ties to Oxford University. That printed attacks emanated from the universities is not surprising--universities were, in effect, an arm of the Church of England, were staffed by clergy, and attendance was restricted to members of the established church. What is surprising is that it was not until the 1750s and 1760s, a decade or more after the Evangelical Revival's emergence in England, that pamphlet attacks on Methodism came from the universities.

A number of Oxford clergy took the opportunity, when invited to preach before the university from the pulpit of St. Mary's Church, to attack the revival. Preachers were appointed from the various colleges in turn by the vice-chancellor. All masters of arts of two or more years' standing who were also presbyters or deacons of the church were eligible to receive the invitation

---

96 272-Gr. [Robert] Potter, *On the pretended inspiration of the Methodists* (Norwich: W. Chase, 1758). *ODNB.*

97 379-Gr. The author of *The powers of the pew* and *The curate* [Evan Lloyd], *The Methodist: A poem* (London: Richardson and Urquhart, 1766). *ODNB.*

98 387-Gr. [Nathaniel Lancaster], *Methodism triumphant* (London: J. Wilkie, 1767). For attribution of authorship see John Nichols, *Literary Anecdotes of the Eighteenth Century*, 6 vols. (London: for the author, 1812), 2:30. *ODNB.*

to preach. The sermons of the following clergy were published after their delivery from St. Mary's pulpit: Tipping Sylvester, fellow of Pembroke College, Oxford, and lecturer of St. Bartholomew the Great, London;[99] Thomas Griffith, fellow of Pembroke College and rector of Bishopstoke, Hampshire;[100] John Free;[101] Thomas Hitchcock, fellow of St. John's College and Whitehall preacher;[102] George Horne, fellow of Magdalene College;[103] John Allen, vice-principal of Mary Magdalene Hall;[104] George Croft (1747–1809), an Anglican priest, who was chosen as Bampton lecturer at Oxford in 1786;[105] and William Hawkins (1721–1801), educated at Pembroke College, Oxford, a writer and preacher who held the posts of prebendary of Wells Cathedral and fellow of Pembroke College. He had formerly been professor of poetry at Oxford (1751–56). In 1787 he was chosen to provide the Bampton Lecture in 1787.[106] From the pulpit of St. Peter's-in-the East, Oxford, Methodism was denounced by Thomas Randolph (1701–83), president of Corpus Christi College,[107] and John Allen.[108]

In 1768 Methodists at Oxford came under heavy fire when six young protégés of the Countess of Huntingdon were expelled from St. Edmund Hall by the vice-chancellor, David Durell (1728–1775), because of their alleged enthusiasm and illegal meetings in private houses for prayer. The expulsion

---

99 002-Gr. Tipping Sylvester, *The scripture doctrine of regeneration stated* (London: for Charles Rivington, 1738).

100 002-Gr. Thomas Griffith, *The use and extent of reason in matters of religion* (Oxford: printed at the Theatre for S. Parker, 1756).

101 For a list of Free's anti-Methodist pamphlets, see footnote 88.

102 329-Gr. Thomas Hitchcock, *The mutual connexion between faith, virtue, and knowledge* (Oxford: printed at the Theatre for James Fletcher, [1761]).

103 For additional information on George Horne, see notes 74 and 75 of this chapter.

104 317-Gr. John Allen, *No acceptance with God by faith only* (London: for Messrs. Whiston, White, and Withers, [1761]).

105 The Bampton Lectures at Oxford were founded in 1780 by a bequest from John Bampton. The first lecture was held the same year. Croft published his Bampton lectures as 536A-Ki. George Croft, *Eight sermons preached before the University of Oxford* (Oxford: Clarendon Press, 1786). He later published 574-Gr. *Thoughts concerning the Methodists and the established clergy* (London: for F. and C. Rivington, 1795). *ODNB*.

106 *ODNB*. 411A-Ki. William Hawkins, *The pretenses of enthusiasts considered* (Oxford: Clarendon, 1769). 411B-Ki. William Hawkins, *The pretenses of enthusiasts, as grounded in the articles of the Church, considered confuted* (Oxford: Clarendon Press, 1769).

107 341-Gr. Thomas Randolph, *The use of reason in matters of religion* (Oxford: printed at the theatre, [1762]).

108 417A-Ki. John Allen, *The enthusiast's notion of election to eternal life disproved* (Oxford: for S. Parker and D. Prince, 1769). *ODNB*.

sparked a pamphlet war. In all, eight tracts were written against the students in support of the vice-chancellor's action.[109]

Little printed criticism came from Cambridge University. In 1769 Samuel Hallifax published the only known anti-Methodist sermon preached at Cambridge.[110] In all probability, however, there were further pulpit attacks on the revival emanating from Cambridge.

Other Denominations

Anglicans were not alone in their opposition to Methodism. Critical pamphlets came from members of the Society of Friends, Baptist, Independent, and Roman Catholic churches.

The Society of Friends

Friends who adhered strictly to the peculiar Quaker emphases looked upon Methodism as a threat. Their similarities with the evangelicals were considered too superficial, and their variance on matters of discipline and doctrine too deep, for close cooperation.[111] Joanna Hawkins, an obscure Quaker, attacked Wesley and his preachers in print in 1749.[112] John Rutty (1697–1775), a prominent Dublin Quaker, physician, and naturalist, believed that although the similarities between the two movements were great, the differences were greater and needed to be clearly enunciated and adhered to.[113]

Although Methodists proselytized among the Quakers, often successfully, the traffic was not all one-way. Methodists trickled into Friends' societies.

---

109 See S. L. Ollard, *The Six Students of St. Edmund's Hall Expelled* (London: A. R. Mowbray, 1911).

110 290-Gr. Hallifax, *Saint Paul's doctrine of justification by faith.*

111 For Wesley and the Society of Friends, see Frank Baker, *The Relations between the Society of Friends and Early Methodism* (London: Epworth, 1949), esp. 22. According to Baker it was the mystical aspect of Quaker spirituality (quietism) that most separated the two societies. See also John C. Bowmer, "The Relations between the Society of Friends and Early Methodism" in *London Quarterly and Holborn Review* 175 (1950): 148–53, 222–27.

112 214A-Ki. Joanna Hawkins, *Letter to John Wesley* ([London]: no printer, 1749). There is doubt that Hawkins was a Quaker. Her name does not appear in the online or card catalog of the Library of the Friends' House, London, or in the *Dictionary of Quaker Bibliography*. Melissa Atkinson, email to author, October 19, 2017. If she was not a Quaker, she was knowledgeable about and sympathetic toward them.

113 444-Gr. Johannes Catholicus [John Rutty], *An essay towards a contrast between Quakerism and Methodism* (Bristol: William Pine, 1771). *ODNB.*

Converts from Methodism—John Webb,[114] Thomas Burton,[115] and John Helton (1732–1817)[116]—attacked their former denomination in print. John Curtis (?1716–1753) claimed falsely to be a former Methodist.[117] Wesley's criticism of Robert Barclay's *Theses Theologicae* in *A Letter to a person lately join'd to the people call'd Quakers*, drew an able rejoinder from John Fry (1728–1787), the Quaker poet of Sutton Benger, Wiltshire.[118]

Baptists

The earliest printed criticism of the revival by a Baptist came from Anne Dutton (1695–1765), widow of Baptist pastor Benjamin Dutton, and a keen controversialist in her own right. Her letter to John Wesley on the perseverance of saints was published in 1742.[119] The apparent effectiveness of Methodist proselytizing among Baptists drew a number of attacks strongly asserting Baptist principles and practices. Among the tracts was the anonymously published *A plain and familiar dialogue between a steady and wavering Christian*.[120] More formidable was a pamphlet by Gilbert Boyce (1712–1800), Baptist minister at Coningsby for sixty years.[121] The statement of faith issued by the Baptist assembly that met at Kettering, Northampton, in June 1781,

---

114 248-Gr. John Webb, *An appeal unto the honest and sincere–hearted among the . . . Methodists* (London: for the author, 1753).

115 206A-Ki. T. B. [Thomas Burton], *A friendly letter to John and Charles Wesley* (London: for the author, 1747).

116 506-Gr. John Helton, *Reasons for quitting the Methodist society* (London: printed by J. Fry and Co., 1778).

117 John Curtis was a Bristol Quaker and traveling preacher. He falsely claimed to have been a Methodist who left the movement to join the Friends. See Wesley, May 1, 1749, *Journals and Diaries III, BEWJW*, 20:269–70. See also *ProcWHS* (1897): 59–62.

118 208A-Ba. [John Fry], *Some remarks on a pamphlet, Intituled, "A letter to a person lately joined with the . . . Quakers"* (London: S. Clarke, 1761). For anti-Methodist publications authored by Quakers, see 206A-Ki., 207A-Ba., 208A-Ba., 214A-Ki., 248-Gr., 444-Gr., 506-Gr., and 565B-Fi.

119 146-Gr. [Anne Dutton], *A letter to the Reverend Mr. John Wesley, in vindication of the doctrines of absolute, unconditional election* (London: John Hart, 1742). She followed this up with a further publication in 1747: 206B-Ki. [Anne Dutton], *A letter on perseverance* (n.p.: no printer, 1747). I have not seen this item, but it is cited in *Notes and Queries, Twelfth Series*, no. ii (July–December 1916), 338, *ProcWHS* 6 (1917–18): 47. See JoAn Ford Watson, "Anne Dutton: An Eighteenth Century British Evangelical Woman Writer," in *Ashland Theological Journal* 30 (1988): 51–55.

120 216B-Ki. *A plain and familiar dialogue between a steady and a wavering Christian* (London: for the author, 1749).

121 428-Gr. Gilbert Boyce, *A serious reply to the Rev. Mr. John Wesley* (Boston: C. Preston, 1770).

contained a slight attack on Methodism.[122] William Kingsford of Barton Mills, Suffolk, engaged in a heated controversy with the Methodists, denying Wesley's alleged accusation that the Baptists were sheep stealers, and defending vigorously the necessity of believers' baptism.[123] One of Wesley's strongest political critics in 1775 after publication of *A calm address* was Caleb Evans (1737–91), a Bristol Baptist minister.[124] In all, sixteen anti-Methodist tracts came from Baptist sources.[125]

Independents

Concern over Methodist proselytizing among Independents (also known as Dissenters and Congregationalists) sparked criticism from an anonymous Congregationalist who blamed "sheep stealing" by evangelical preachers for the decline of attendance at Independent churches.[126] In the 1770s a number of Dissenters took Wesley to task for his political views. Among them were Joseph Towers (1737–99), sometime pastor of a Presbyterian church at High Gate, and his brother, John (?1747–1804), who was pastor of an Independent church in the Barbican, London;[127] Rowland Hill (1744–1833), late eighteenth-century Calvinist Evangelical; [128] James Murray (1732–82), Dissenting minister of High Bridge Chapel, Newcastle, and advocate for enlightenment principles;[129] and

---

122 526A-Ki. *The nature of faith* (n.p.: no printer, 1781), esp. 11, 14.

123 539-Gr. William Kingsford, *A vindication of the Baptists* (Canterbury: printed by J. Grove, and sold by J. Marsom [in London], 1788). 543A-Ki. William Kingsford, *Three letters to the Rev. Mr. Wesley* (Canterbury: for the author by J. Grove, London, 1789).

124 For a discussion on Evans and his pamphlets, see chapter 7, "Methodism and Politics."

125 See 146-Gr., 153-Gr., 206B-Ki., 233-Gr., 234-Gr., 428-Gr., 482-Gr., 483-Gr., 492-Gr., 525-Gr., 526A-Ki., 527B-Fi., 539-Gr., 542C-Ki., 542C-Fi., 543A-Ki.

126 385-Gr. An Independent [Samuel Newton], *The causes and reasons of the present declension among the Congregational churches* (London: J. Johnson and B. Davenport, 1766).

127 446-Gr. [Joseph Towers], *A letter to the Rev. Mr. John Wesley in answer to his late pamphlet entitled "Free thoughts on the present state of public affairs"* (London: printed for J. Towers, 1771). 473-Gr. J. T. [John Towers], *Elihu's reply*.

128 451-Gr. [Rowland Hill], *Friendly remarks occasioned by the spirit and doctrines contained in the Rev. Mr. Fletcher's 'Vindication'* (London: for E. and C. Dilly, 1772). 497-Gr. Rowland Hill, *A full answer to the Rev. J. Wesley's remarks upon a late pamphlet* (Bristol: sold by T. Mills, also by T. Valance and J. Matthews, London, [1777]). *ODNB*.

129 407-Gr. [James Murray], *Sermons to asses* (London: printed for J. Johnson, T. Cadell, and W. Charnley at Newcastle, 1768). 480A-Ki. A Gentleman of Northumberland [James Murray], *A grave answer to Mr. Wesley's "Calm address"* [Newcastle upon Tyne: no printer, 1775]. 492A-Ba. A Gentleman of Northumberland [James Murray], *A compleat answer to Mr. Wesley's observations upon Dr. Price's essay* (Newcastle: T. Robson, 1776). 505-Gr. James Murray, *The finishing stroke to Mr. Wesley's "Calm address"* (Newcastle upon Tyne: T. Robson, 1778). See chapter 7, "Methodism and Politics," for a fuller discussion of the role of Dissenters in criticizing Wesley's political views.

Joseph Hart (1712–1768), minister of the Independent Chapel, Jewin Street, London, and hymn writer.[130]

Renowned eighteenth-century Dissenter, theologian, and natural philosopher Joseph Priestley (1733–1804) joined his brethren in assaulting the reputation of the deceased Wesley by publishing a number of letters, chiefly correspondence between John and his brother, Samuel, concerning the Epworth "rectory ghost." The supposed supernatural phenomenon was nothing more, he opined, than servants playing tricks on the family.[131]

Roman Catholics

An indication that the Roman Catholic Church feared the loss of communicants to Methodism is seen in the title of Bishop Richard Challenor's anonymously published *Caveat against the Methodists—shewing how unsafe it is for any Christian to join himself to their society, or to adhere to their teachers.* First published in 1760, this work went through three editions by 1787, indicating that Methodism continued to have an appeal among Roman Catholics.[132] Challenor (1691–1781), educated at the English College, Douai, a Catholic seminary in France, became the Roman Catholic bishop of England and served in that capacity for forty years, from 1741 to 1781.

A flurry of Roman Catholic attacks on Methodism came in the 1780s. These were not concerned with proselytizing but with Wesley's support for the militant Protestant Association.[133] Wesley's main antagonists were Arthur O'Leary (1729–1802), a Capuchin friar from Dublin,[134] and John Whittingham, a Coventry seedsman, who joined O'Leary in dispute with Wesley on this issue.[135]

---

130 127-Gr. Joseph Hart, *The unreasonableness of religion* ([London]: for the author, 1741). *ODNB.*

131 554-Gr. Joseph Priestley, *Original letters by the Reverend John Wesley and his friends.* See Richard P. Heitzenrater, *The Elusive Mr. Wesley: John Wesley as Seen by Contemporaries and Biographers* (Nashville: Abingdon, 1984), 2:169–70, 176. *ODNB.*

132 311D-Gr. [Richard Challenor], *A caveat against the Methodists* (London: printed for M. Cooper, 1760). The pamphlet went through seven editions in England. Editions in Dublin and America appeared in 1808 and 1817, respectively.

133 See chapter 7, "Methodism and Politics."

134 525C-Ki. Arthur O'Leary, *Mr. O'Leary's remarks on the Rev. Mr. Wesley's letters* (Dublin: printed in London, reprinted for J. Coghlan, 1780). 527-Gr. Arthur O'Leary, *Miscellaneous Tracts* (Dublin: Tho. McDonnel, 1781). *ODNB.*

135 525B-Ki. The Old Fashion Farmer [John Whittingham], *To the public* (Coventry: [no printer], 1780).

The Calvinist Wing of Methodism

One of the main sources of attack came from within the confines of Methodism itself. Originally the term *Methodism* was an inclusive one, gathering people of differing theological positions under one large evangelical umbrella. Tensions on matters of doctrine were evident early in the movement but broke into the open in 1741 with Whitefield's printed criticism of Wesley's sermon "Free Grace."[136] Although Whitefield and Wesley reconciled personally, from 1741 the revival was divided into two camps—Calvinist and Arminian. An undercurrent of strong disagreement continued, giving rise to outbursts of hostile pamphlets from time to time. The relationship between the two wings of Methodist became even more turbulent after 1770, when Wesley issued strongly Arminian Minutes of Conference.[137] Wesley and Whitefield had learned to live and work in an uneasy alliance, despite differences of doctrine, but the new generation of Calvinists—Richard Hill (1732–1808), his brother, Rowland (1744–1833), and Augustus Toplady (1740–1778)—prized their theological orthodoxy. In the 1770s Calvinist "elect" and Arminian "saint" battled each other with a ferocity unbecoming their Christian profession. Through the dispute John Fletcher stood beside Wesley, championing the Arminian position.[138]

Wesley's Ex-Preachers

A number of Wesley's early lay preachers left Wesley's branch of Methodism. Of the seven who were itinerating in the 1740s, only one—Thomas Westell (1719–1794)—remained in connection with Wesley. Of the sixty-two preachers who were itinerating in 1745, thirty-six either withdrew or were expelled from Methodism.[139] It is little wonder that several of Wesley's former preachers joined the ranks of his literary opponents. Some were motivated to enter into controversy with their former leader because of theological differences. Helton's pamphlet resulting from his conversion to Quakerism,

---

136 The long and often bitter controversy between the two wings of the revival is the subject of chapter 9, "Calvinist 'Elect' and Arminian 'Saint' at War."

137 Ibid.

138 Ibid.

139 See W. Stephen Gunter, *The Limits of "Love Divine": John Wesley's Response to Antinomianism and Enthusiasm* (Nashville: Kingswood Books, 1989), 181, 313n1–3. Statistics are based on William Myles, *A Chronological History of the People called Methodists*, 4th ed. (London: Cordeaux, 1813), 446–49.

already noted, is an example.[140] Also noted earlier are the printed attacks of former Methodists John Webb and Thomas Burton. John Curtis (1716?–53), a Bristol Quaker, had falsely claimed to be a member of the Methodist Society who had left it.[141]

The earliest preacher to leave Wesley and to dispute with him in print was Joseph Humphreys (1720–1785) who became a Calvinist. One of Charles's early converts and first lay preacher to assist Wesley in England, Humphreys later received both presbyterial and episcopal ordination.[142] Better known than Humphreys was Thomas Maxfield (d. 1784), one of Wesley's pioneer and trusted preachers for more than twenty years. He was ordained by William Barnard, bishop of Derry, Ireland, to assist Wesley but left him and established his own chapel in Moorfields. Although Maxfield separated from Wesley in 1763 over the doctrine of Christian perfection, it was not until 1767 that he put his complaints about Wesley into print, claiming that Wesley misrepresented him in the *Short History of Methodism*.[143] Maxfield's biography of his wife, Elizabeth, contained a second attack on Wesley.[144] Wesley's response to the embittered Maxfield, entitled *A letter to the Rev. Mr. Thomas Maxfield*, was dated February 14, 1778, and signed, "Your injured, yet still affectionate brother, John Wesley."[145] Michael Moorhouse, an itinerant for fourteen troubled years before leaving the connection at the Conference of 1786, circulated an appeal to all of Wesley's preachers in 1786, full of personal grievances against Wesley and his fellow preachers.[146] He later incorporated much of the appeal into his lengthy *Defence of Mr. Michael Moorhouse*, a rambling, repetitious, and petty diatribe.[147] Nicholas Manners, an itinerant (1759–1784),

---

140 506-Gr. Helton, *Reasons for quitting the Methodist society.*

141 207A-Ba. *Letter to the author of a pamphlet entitled, "A letter to a person lately join'd to the . . . Quakers."* 248-Gr. Webb, *Appeal unto the honest and sincere-hearted among the people called Methodists and Quakers.* 206A-Ki. [Burton], *A friendly letter to John and Charles Wesley.*

142 136A-Ba. Joseph Humphreys, *A letter to the members of the religious societies* (Bristol: printed by Benj. Hickey, 1741). See Baker, *JWCE*, 82–83.

143 390-Gr. [Thomas Maxfield], *A vindication of the Rev. Mr. Maxfield's conduct* (London: G. Keith, 1767).

144 512-Gr. Thomas Maxfield, *A short account of God's dealings with Mrs. Elizabeth Maxfield* (London: J. W. Pasham, 1778).

145 John Wesley, "A Letter to the Rev. Mr. Thomas Maxfield, Occasioned by a Late Publication," 1778, *BEWJW*, 9:418–24.

146 535A-Ki. Michael Moorhouse, *An appeal to all honest men* (n.p.: no printer, 1786).

147 545-Gr. Michael Moorhouse, *The defence of Mr. Michael Moorhouse* (Leicester: Ann Ireland, 1789).

severed his ties with Methodism over the doctrine of original sin and attacked his former colleagues in three pamphlets.[148] John Atlay (1736–1805), Wesley's book steward, left the connection in 1783 to become the minister of the rebellious congregation of Dewsbury Chapel after the trustees had refused to meet the demands of the Conference, and Wesley had withdrawn his preachers. The defense of the trustees' action that appeared in 1783 came, in all probability, from John Atlay.[149]

In the Calvinist-Arminian debate of the late eighteenth century, one of those who attacked Wesley most strenuously was John MacGowan (1726–80), a Scottish-born minister, who had at one time been a Methodist lay preacher before joining the Independents. In 1780 he attacked a number of Wesley's anti-Calvinist writings.[150]

The earliest full-length biography of Wesley—the three-volume *Memoirs of the late Rev. John Wesley*—came from the disappointed ex-preacher John Hampson (1753–1819). Hampson's disaffection with Wesley came to a head in 1784 with the exclusion of his name from the "Legal Hundred"—the membership of the Methodist Conference as defined in the Deed of Declaration (1784).[151]

Ex-Methodist Laity

Not all the laity who joined the Methodist societies remained loyal to Methodism. We have noted already that Thomas Burton, John Helton, and John Webb threw in their lots with the Quakers and took their former religious associates to task in print.[152] Thomas Moorhouse, an obscure Methodist

---

148 538A-Fi. Nicholas Manners, *A full confutation of the Rev. Mr. John Fletcher's appeal* (London: R. Hindmarsh, 1787). 540A-Ba. Nicholas Manners, *Remarks on the writings of the Rev. J. W.* (Hull: George Prince, 1788). 540B-Ba. Nicholas Manners, *Preachers described and the people advised* ([Hull]: no printer, [1788]).

149 542B-Ba. [John Atlay], *A reply to what the Rev. Dr. Coke is pleased to call the state of Dewsbury House* (n.p.: no printer, 1788). 550A-Ba. [John Atlay], *Letters that passed between the Rev. John Wesley and Mr. John Atlay* (London: J. Matthews, [1790]).

150 401-Gr. The Shaver [John MacGowan], *Priestcraft defended* (London: printed for G. Keith, 1768). This work went through twenty-six editions by 1818. 402-Gr. The Shaver [John MacGowan], *A further defence of priestcraft* (London: G. Keith, 1768). 525-Gr. John MacGowan, *The Foundry budget opened* (London: printed for G. Keith, J. Johnson and James MacGowan, 1780).

151 560B-Ba. John Hampson, *Memoirs of the late Rev John Wesley*. For a fuller discussion of Hampson, see chapter 6, "The Church in Danger."

152 See the section titled "Society of Friends" in this chapter.

layman, published two curious pamphlets attacking the revival.[153] Richard Tompson attacked the doctrine of assurance by publishing his correspondence with Wesley on the subject.[154]

The best-known attack by a former Methodist layman is James Lackington's *Memoirs* (1791).[155] Lackington (1746–1815), a prosperous London bookseller who had been given a start in business with a loan from Wesley's pioneering lending fund, vehemently assailed his benefactors, equating Methodism with enthusiasm. He lived to regret what he had written in his biography concerning the movement. Recanting in his *Confessions* (1804), he retracted much, but the damage had been done.[156]

The Secular Community

The religious community found itself embroiled in controversy with Methodism. If it could not ignore the evangelical revival, neither could the secular community. Because Methodism was not a direct threat, critique in the secular realm was less extensive and differed in focus. Matters of theology and church organization exercised priests and prelates, but secular people were not interested in the subtleties of doctrine or the novelty of structure that were a part of Methodism. Much of the criticism that emanated from the secular community was satirical. Secular critics found features in both leaders and movement to ridicule.

Professionals

Several physicians—Samuel Bowden (fl.1733–61), nonconformist poet and physician of Frome, Somerset;[157] James Makittrick Adair (1728–1802), phy-

---

153 391-Gr. Thomas Moorhouse, *A sermon preach'd . . . at Otley-Cross* (Leeds: no printer, 1767). 528D-Ki. Thomas Moorhouse, *A view of practical Methodism* ([London]: no printer, [1783]).

154 Richard Tompson was a founding member of the Fetter Lane Society. From 1755 to 1756 he and Wesley corresponded concerning the doctrines of assurance and Christian perfection. Tompson published the correspondence in 1760: 286-Gr. *Original letters between the Reverend Mr. John Wesley and Mr. Richard Tompson* (London: printed for L. Davis and C. Reymers, 1760). See Wesley, *Letters*, 26:566–71, 574–80, in *BEWJW*.

155 560-Gr. James Lackington, *Memoirs of the first forty–five years of the life of James Lackington* (London: by the author, [1791]).

156 James Lackington, *The confessions of J. J. Lackington in a series of letters to a friend* (London: R. Edwards for the author, 1804).

157 249-Gr. Samuel Bowden, *Poems on various subjects* (Bath: T. Boddely, 1754). 371A-Ba. [Samuel Bowden], *The Methodists welcome to Pewsey* ([London]: no printer, 1765).

sician and medical writer educated at Edinburgh;[158] William Hawes (1736–1808), philanthropist, founder of the Royal Humane Society, and physician to a London dispensary;[159] John Rutty (1697–1775), Quaker, naturalist, and Dublin physician;[160] and Samuel Norman, member of the Corporation of Surgeons in London, and a surgeon at Yatton, a village in North Somerset[161]—turned from their professional responsibilities to issue criticism of the revival. William Fleetwood, a London apothecary, assailed the Methodist doctrine of perfection.[162]

Capel Lofft (1751–1824) and John Hough were London lawyers (Lofft a member of Lincoln's Inn, Hough a member of the Inner Temple) who attacked Wesley in print.[163]

Tradesmen

Curious assaults on Whitefield came from John Harman, a London watchmaker and astrologer,[164] and Thomas Inglefield, a tanner, in King John's Court, Southwark.[165] A more serious author was Thomas Sheraton (1751–1806), Baptist minister and renowned cabinetmaker. He is best known, along with Thomas Chippendale and George Hepplewhite, as one of the "big three" eighteenth-century English furniture designers and makers. He was critical of Wesley, Whitefield, and the Methodists in general.[166]

---

158 378-Gr. Peter Paragraph *pseud.* [James Makittrick Adair], *The Methodist and mimick* (London: printed for C. Moran, 1766).

159 488-Gr. William Hawes, *An examination of the Rev. Mr. John Wesley's "Primitive physic"* (London: printed for the author and sold by J. Dodsley, 1776). *ODNB.*

160 444-Gr. Johannes Catholicus [John Rutty], *An essay towards a contrast between Quakerism and Methodism* (Bristol: William Pine, 1771).

161 See Field's annotations to 542C*-Fi. Samuel Norman, "The great apostle unmask'd." *A Supplemental Bibliography,* 176–77.

162 131-Gr. William Fleetwood, *The perfectionists examin'd* (London: printed for J. Roberts, 1741).

163 504-Gr. Capel Lofft, *Observations on Mr. Wesley's second "Calm address"* (London: printed for E. and C. Dilley, 1777). 341B-Fi. John Hough, *The pastor* (London: published by Mr. Williams, [1762]).

164 319-Gr. John Harman, *The crooked disciple's remarks upon the blind guide's method of preaching* (London: for the author, [1761]). 360A-Fi. John Harman, *Remarks upon the life, character and behaviour of the Rev. George Whitefield* (London: by the author, 1764).

165 125-Gr. Thomas Inglefield, *An answer to a sermon preach'd at Rotherhith* (Sarum: printed for the author, 1741).

166 527B-Fi. Thomas Sheraton, *A scriptural illustration of the doctrine of regeneration* (Stockton: for the author by R. Christopher, 1782), 46–47, 54–55. *ODNB.*

Women

Very few women attacked Methodism in print. Not surprisingly, of the six who have been identified, two were members of the Society of Friends—Joanna Hawkins and Catherine Phillips. In elevating the Scriptures, Wesley and his preachers, Hawkins claimed, denigrated the Holy Spirit's guidance, thus refusing to obey the Spirit's dictates.[167]

Catherine Phillips (1627–1794) was an itinerant Quaker minister and publisher of numerous tracts. One, entitled *Reasons why the people called Quakers cannot so fully unite with the Methodists*, was a defense of the Quakers' refusal to participate financially with the Methodists' overseas mission to blacks in the West Indies and Africa.[168] Phillips reiterated some of the traditional Quaker critiques of Methodism, such as their use of sacraments, the Church of England's rites and ceremonies, and their reliance on "human appointments," and not those of the Holy Spirit.

Anne Dutton (c.1692–1765) an eighteenth-century hymnist, Calvinist controversialist, and wife of Benjamin Dutton, a clothier turned minister of the Baptist Church, Great Grandsen, Huntingdonshire, was a theologian in her own right. She carried on published correspondence with some of the major religious and evangelical leaders of the age, among them John Wesley. Her pamphlets challenging Wesley's Arminian theology were printed in 1742, 1743, and 1747.[169]

Ann Downes, widow of John Downes, who had been rector of St. Michael, Wood Street, London, published a letter in reply to Wesley's letter addressed to her late husband.[170] Wesley's comment on reading Mrs. Downes's letter to him was dismissive: "There is nothing extraordinary in it but an extraordinary degree of virulence and scurrility."[171]

---

167 214A-Ki. Hawkins, *A letter to John Wesley*, 1, 7.
168 565B-Fi. Catherine Phillips, *Reasons why the people called Quakers cannot so fully unite with the Methodists* (London: James Phillips, 1792).
169 146-Gr. [Dutton], *A letter to the Reverend Mr. John Wesley* (London: John Hart, 1742). 153-Gr. [Anne Dutton], *Letters to the Reverend Mr. John Westley*. 206B-Ki. [Dutton], *A letter on perseverance*. No copy of this has been located.
170 286B-Ki. [Ann Downes], *The widow Downes's answer to the Reverend Mr. John Wesley's letter* (London: for the author, [1760]). For the letter to which she is replying, see John Wesley, *A letter to the Rev. Mr. Downes* (London, 1759), *BEWJW*, 9: 350–66.
171 *BEWJW*, 9:351.

An essay on schism, with several discourses contrary to the Methodist-doctrine, written by Mary Hill, appeared in 1745.[172] Nothing is known of her other than the title and contents of her pamphlet. No explicitly Methodist reference occurs in the pamphlet, but the destructive nature of Antinomianism, a popular anti-Methodist target, is singled out for attack. To this she added the charge of schism, also a common focus for opponents of the revival, blaming the divisiveness in the church on "proud and self-conceited persons" who "are brain sick in the fond estimation of their own opinions, and heart-sick by a feverish zeal for the propagation of them."[173]

Mary O'Brien (d. 1790), an Irish novelist, playwright, and poet, published *The pious incendiaries* in 1785, using the pseudonym "A Lady." The work was a dramatic poem in seven cantos which dealt with the anti-Catholic feeling prevalent in the Gordon Riots.[174]

Katharine Pimm was the wife of Joseph Pimm, a band and Methodist society member at the Foundery. Influenced by a dream, Joseph sent Wesley a donation of £100 in 1742 toward the construction of the Orphan House at Newcastle-on-Tyne.[175] Initially Katharine agreed to Joseph's substantial gift, but later changed her mind and denounced Wesley in a four-page pamphlet, *A true and faithful account of some of the transactions and horrid impositions of Doctor Westley [sic] set forth in the case of Mrs. Catherine Pimm*.[176] Much to Wesley's relief, Joseph subsequently repudiated his wife's account in a published *Letter from Mr. Joseph Pimm to the Rev. Mr. Broughton*, 1745.[177]

Charlotte MacCarthy (fl.1745–68) was an English author who published under the pseudonym "Prudentia Christiania."[178] Her *Letter . . . to the bishop*

---

172 200B-Fi. Mary Hill, *An essay on schism* (Salisbury, UK: Benjamin Collins, 1745).

173 Ibid.

174 532B-Ba. A Lady [Mary O'Brien], *The pious incendiaries* (London: printed for the author, 1785). *See The Cambridge Guide to Women's Writing in English*, ed. Lorna Sage (Cambridge: Cambridge University Press, 1999), 476.

175 Charles Wesley to John Wesley (December 16, 1742), in Frank Baker, ed., *BEWJW*, vol. 26, *Letters II, 1740–55* (Nashville: Abingdon, 1976–), 96.

176 200C-Fi. Katharine Pimm, *A true and faithful account of some of the transactions . . . of Doctor Westley* (Southwark: printed for T. Hinton, [1745]).

177 See John Wesley to Elizabeth Hutton (January 18, 1745/6), *Letters II*, in *BEWJW*, 26:184. This letter contains details of the event.

178 For identification, see "Irish Women's Writings and Traditions" in *The Field Day of Irish Writing* (New York: New York University Press, n.d.), 5:795. Her work is strongly tinged with a concern for women and social justice.

of London (1769) does not mention Whitefield or Wesley by name but clearly infers them in several places of the text. MacCarthy leveled harsh criticism at Wesley, whom she contended operated from base motives of financial gain. Her main attack was on the alleged antinomianism of Wesley in teaching "righteousness without works." [179]

---

179 423-Gr. Prudentia Christiania [Charlotte MacCarthy], *A letter from a lady to the bishop of London* (London: printed for J. Brown, [1769]), 7–8.

CHAPTER 2

The Methodist Caricature

Opponents in disputes often resort to the use of caricature to depict each other. Truth is distorted, issues are oversimplified, and labels are attached. By means of caricature eighteenth-century critics of Methodism implanted in the popular mind an image of the "typical" Methodist. In 1765 Wesley wrote of this caricature:

> It is not easy to reckon up the various accounts which have been given of the people called Methodists; very many of them far remote from the truth as that given by the good gentlemen in Ireland: "Methodists! Ay, they are the people who place all religion in wearing long beards."[1]

The caricature was spread most effectively by word of mouth as people circulated rumors or elaborated on stories they had heard about Methodists. It was further shaped and nurtured by anti-Methodist publications, particularly pamphlets.

The anti-Methodist image was in sharp contrast to the image the Methodists projected of themselves in their own literature as pious and righteous people intent on reforming the Church of England from within. What Methodists spoke of as virtues, anti-Methodists portrayed as vices—piety became hypocrisy; reliance on divine inspiration, enthusiasm; yearning for intimacy with the divine, sentimentalism; striving for righteousness, a new puritanism; reviving the Church of England's former doctrinal emphases, heresy; believing themselves to be God's instruments of renewal, satanic delusions. As in any caricature, the typical Methodist described above bore some resemblance to the truth, but it was far from a complete and accurate portrayal of the movement's members. The caricature did great harm to the cause of the evangelical revival. Many who may have been sympathetic to the movement were prejudiced against it from the outset.

---

1 Wesley, "A Short History of Methodism" (1765), in *BEWJW*, vol. 9, *The Methodist Societies: History, Nature, and Design*, ed. Rupert E. Davies, 367–72, specifically 357.

Epithets

Epithets, singling out some feature to ridicule, were hurled in print at the Methodists. The comparative "youthfulness" of the Wesley brothers and Whitefield was often mocked. Tristram Land called them "young quacks in divinity;"[2] John Downes referred to them as "novices in divinity."[3] Others, capitalizing on the Methodists' emphasis on inspiration, referred to them as "newly-illuminated, self-experienced zealots,"[4] or "deceivers," "babblers," "men of capricious humors, spiritual slight, and canting craftiness."[5] The unconventional behavior of Methodist preachers prompted epithets such as "buffoons in religion," "mountebanks in theology,"[6] and "grievous wolves."[7] If the preachers were "deceivers," Methodist society members were "the deceived." The author of *The progress of Methodism in Bristol* derided Wesley's devotees as "priest-ridden," "hood-wink'd people," and "giddy-sheep."[8] Believing Methodists to be Satan's emissaries rather than God's ambassadors, Evan Lloyd derogatorily referred to them as "soldiers for hell's church militant."[9] Usually those who used nicknames for the evangelicals did not make any attempt to distinguish between the various groups within the revival. However, using a play on the names of four of the principals, Mrs. Downes dubbed their followers "Whislers, Wiflers, Madmen, and Romancers." An explanatory footnote added that the four were Wesley, Whitefield, Madan, and Romaine.[10]

Methodist

The derogatory labels were many and varied—among them "Bible moths" "Sacramentarians," "Supererogation Men," and "Methodist"—but the label

---

2 009-Gr. Land, *A letter to the Rev. Mr. Whitefield*, 5.

3 282-Gr. Downes, *Methodism examined and exposed*, 6.

4 104-Gr. *A Presbyter of the Church of England, A modest and serious defence of the author of 'The whole duty of man'* (London: for J. Roberts, 1740), 5.

5 018-Gr. John Wilder, *The trial of the spirits* (Oxford: printed at the Theatre for the author, 1739), 3–5.

6 040-Gr. [Tucker], *The life and particular proceedings of the Rev. Mr. George Whitefield*, 79.

7 282-Gr. Downes, *Methodism examined and exposed*, 4.

8 156-Gr. An Impartial Hand, *The progress of Methodism in Bristol* (Bristol: J. Watts, 1743), 14, 17, 19.

9 379-Gr. The author of "*The powers of the pew* and *The curate* [Evan Lloyd]," *The Methodist: A poem*, 49.

10 286B-Ki. [Ann] Downes, *The widow Downes' answer to the Rev. Mr. John Wesley's letter*, 9.

that stuck was "Methodist."[11] The epithet "Methodist" was originally applied as early as 1732 to the group of young Oxford students. As the evangelical revival spread through the efforts of Whitefield and the Wesley brothers, the term "Methodist" was applied to all who involved themselves in the work of the revival. Even those unconnected with the major figures found themselves being dubbed "Methodist." In the 1750s and '60s, evangelicals who remained within the Anglican fold—Martin Madan, William Romaine, John Berridge, and Henry Venn, for example—could not escape the opprobrious title.[12] The term "Methodist" was a great umbrella under which to assemble all who espoused an evangelical faith and were diligent in the performance of their ecclesiastical responsibilities. Calvinist and Arminian (Whitefield and Wesley), loyal Anglican and Dissenter (Romaine and Cudworth), were all lumped together; their distinctions barely noticed, or deliberately blurred.[13]

In a number of his writings, John Wesley gave his explanation of how the title Methodist came into currency. He believed that it was the "exact regularity" of the lives of the Oxford Holy Club members that reminded a young Christ Church College scholar of an ancient sect of physicians, called Methodists, who placed their patients under stringent regimens.[14] If this is how Methodists understood the origins of the nickname, it was not how critics

11 For a detailed discussion of the origin of the name Methodist, see Richard P. Heitzenrater, *Mirror and Memory, Reflections on Early Methodism* (Nashville: Kingswood Books, 1989), 13–32. See also Baker, *JWCE*, 25–26.

12 Martin Madan (1726–1790), educated at Christ Church, Oxford, was a barrister, hymnist, and ordained Evangelical clergyman closely connected to Lady Huntingdon. For several years he was chaplain of Lock Hospital, London. William Romaine (1714–95), son of a French protestant who had fled to England after the revocation of the Edict of Nantes, was educated at Christ Church, Oxford. Initially attracted to Wesley's theology, Romaine later became an ardent follower of Whitefield and an able exponent of evangelical theology imbued with Calvinism. John Berridge (1716–1793), educated at Clare College, Cambridge, was an Evangelical Anglican priest, vicar of St. Mary's, Everton, itinerant revivalist, and hymnist. Henry Venn (1725–97), an Anglican priest educated at Cambridge, was curate in Surrey, curate at Clapham, London, and later vicar at Huddersfield, Yorkshire. He ended his career as vicar of Yelling, Huntingdonshire. A close friend of John Wesley, Venn asked if Wesley would allow him oversight of Methodist societies in his parish. His request, however, was refused. *ODNB*. Also see Danker, *Wesley and the Anglicans*, 147–51.

13 William Cudworth (1717–1763) a staunch Calvinist, was minister of the Independent Church, Margaret Street, London. Previously he had been in charge of Whitefield's school at the Tabernacle. By 1747 he was superintendent of five London congregations known as the Hearers and Followers of the Apostles. *ODNB*.

14 John Wesley, "Second Letter to the Reverend Dr. Free" (1758), in *Works* 9:321–30; Wesley, "Short History of Methodism," in *Works* 9:367–72.

did. Several opponents believed that the leaders of the revival had chosen the name for themselves. As early as 1740 Samuel Weller put forward the suggestion:

> [I]nstead of contenting themselves with being called by the general name of Christians, [the Methodists] have taken an appellation perhaps thro' a judicial inadvertence or infatuation, which the Spirit of God has peculiarly appropriated to the adversary of mankind, and to those who are leagued with him in enmity to the interest of righteousness and true holiness.[15]

Another anti-Methodist author, also implying that the Oxford group had christened themselves "Methodists," contended that they rejoiced in their new title: "If I am not misinformed, by one who was a member of your club, ye were in no ways displeased at being called (if ye did not give yourselves the title of) Methodists; at your first setting up."[16] John Free rejected Wesley's explanation of the similarities between the Holy Club's strict regulation of their members' lives and the school of physicians. Free hinted that Wesley was attempting to make a derogatory title respectable.

> Having . . . dipped into Dr. Friend's History of Physick and met with such a sect of physicians, you thought it would look better if you affected to be their relations, choosing . . . to draw upon you the denomination of quacks.[17]

Opponents of the Methodists offered fanciful interpretations of the name Methodist. Samuel Weller claimed that the word *Methodism* was used in Scripture. There, it had evil connotations. It was, he thought, therefore, a most appropriate designation for the eighteenth-century evangelicals:

> The word is only twice used throughout the New Testament. [A footnote adds: Ephesians IV: 14, and VI: II.] In the first of those texts the word μεθοδεία or Methodism is translated lying in wait or watching to take an advantage of any one: And in the other it is rendered by the word wiles or stratagems: And in both places

---

15 098-Gr. [Samuel Weller], *The trial of Mr. Whitefield's spirit* (London: T. Gardner, 1740), 3.

16 188A-Ki. A layman of the Church of England, *Remarks on a late pamphlet intitled 'A brief account of the late persecution,'* 35.

17 276-Gr. Free, *Dr. Free's edition of the Rev. Mr. John Wesley's second letter*, 39.

> denotes that cunning craftiness, whereby evil men, or evil spirits
> lye in wait to deceive.[18]

Weller's etymological explanation surfaced again in the 1750s. Nathaniel Fletcher claimed, "The students at Oxford . . . derived their name from μεθοδεία, i.e. occulta et fraudulenta circumventio."[19] Theophilus Evans gave it wide circulation, praising his source as a "learned and judicious writer."[20]

Some anti-Methodist writers found the name "Methodist" inappropriate, claiming that the new movement displayed anything but strict regulation and order: "Order or method is wholly disregarded amongst them: Their teachers are not orderly set apart for that sacred function; neither is there anything like church-discipline amongst them: Their prayers and preaching are also without any method, and all things belonging to their way of worship is in utter confusion."[21] More typical were opponents, like Bishop Warburton, who thought that the title Methodist was descriptive of evangelicals' fetish for order and methodicalness:

> They tell us what to expect, in the very appellation they assume.
> For Methodism implies a set of manners, squared out by the rule
> and compass; and when made a name of distinction, it declares
> those manners are to be strictly and invariably observed, as the
> sacred badge of brotherhood.[22]

John Free alleged it was the methodical way the Methodists recorded insignificant and trivial actions in their diaries that gave them their name.[23]

Influence of William Law

A number of the important early critics of Methodism associated the beginnings of the movement with William Law (1686–1761), the great eighteenth-century English mystic and ascetic. Joseph Trapp declared Law to be the spiritual

---

18 098-Gr. [Weller], *The trial of Mr. Whitefield's spirit*, 2–3.

19 217A-Ki. Nathaniel Fletcher, *A vindication of the 'Methodist dissected'* (Halifax: no printer, 1750), 9.

20 235-Gr. [Evans], *The history of modern enthusiasm*, 108.

21 210-Gr. Fletcher, *A Methodist dissected*, 2.

22 342-Gr. [Warburton], *The doctrine of grace*, 192.

23 274-Gr. Free, *Rules for the discovery of false prophets*, iv. Reprinted in 286A-Ki. *Controversy with the people called Methodists*.

father of Methodism. Law's *A practical treatise upon Christian perfection* (1726), Trapp believed, was "one of the most pernicious books that has been published in this age . . . When the sect of Methodists first started up, I imputed it very much to that book; and so did others, as well as I."[24] Josiah Tucker agreed—Law's writings were the formative influence on the Methodists while at Oxford.

> Before the Methodists came abroad into the world, and whilst they were forming their systems and opinions in the University they chose to put up themselves chiefly under the direction of the writings of Mr. William Law . . . For they looked upon the gentleman as their tutor, tho' not resident upon the spot . . . as their schoolmaster to bring them unto Christ.[25]

William Warburton expressed the intimate connection between Law and the Methodist revival picturesquely: "Mr. W. Law begat Methodism and Zinzendorf rocked the cradle."[26] In *Methodism Triumphant,* Law is depicted as an archetype of John the Baptist, who "marked the path" for Wesley.[27] Law was blamed for a number of aspects of Methodist theology. Tucker believed Law's doctrines were a hodgepodge of borrowings from antithetical systems—he took what he liked from Calvinism and Arminianism and rejected what he disapproved of in each. This eclecticism, Tucker believed, was the source of the division between the two wings of Methodism in 1741—Whitefield lifted out the Calvinist emphases in Law's system; Wesley, the Arminian. Critics found other instances of Law's influence on Wesley, such as the doctrine of the total depravity of humanity and the insistence on self-denial as a necessary Christian duty.[28] John Brownsword believed that the Methodists had learned their doctrine of renunciation from Law. Like their mentor, the Methodists espoused what amounted to a "leveling principle" by teaching that

---

24 123-Gr. Trapp, *A reply to Mr. Law's "Earnest and serious answer,"* 6–7.

25 150-Gr. Tucker, *A brief history of the principles of Methodism,* 7.

26 342-Gr. [Warburton], *The doctrine of grace,* 152. Count Nicholas Zinzendorf (1700–1760) from 1722 on was the leader of a branch of the *Unitas Fratrum* with two centers, one at Herrnhut and the other at Marienborn. He later became the first bishop of the Moravian Church.

27 387-Gr. [Lancaster], *Methodism triumphant,* 77.

28 95-Gr. Thomas Whiston, *The important doctrines of original sin* ([London]: for John Whiston, 1740), 6.

the renunciation of all the world's goods was commanded by Jesus.[29] One pamphleteer believed Law was one of the principals of Methodism because there was no difference between them in the articulation of the doctrine of self-denial. Law, he said, was "the best writer of the party."[30] Law's ascetic austerity and mystical doctrines were the subject of much criticism. Obviously, the intent of linking the names of Law and Methodism was to transfer the distaste of the former to the latter. Anti-Methodists had only to mention that Methodism was the spiritual offspring of Law, and the opprobrium surrounding Law attached itself to the revival.

Definitions of Methodism

Methodism was variously defined by opponents. Some definitions centered on a particular leader of the revival. A Methodist, suggested the author of *The question whether it be right to turn Methodist considered* (1745), is "one that hears and follows the doctrines of Mr. Wesley, and those preachers who teach a much stricter rule and method of life."[31] For some, similarity in doctrine did not seem to be a point of definition: "the people that go under this denomination are of so many sorts, it is almost impossible to mention them all: some are called Inghamites,[32] some Moravians, and some Wesleyans; some hold one sort of principles, and some another."[33]

Others thought there was enough unity in theological emphases for this to be a part of the definition. William Dodd defined Methodists as those who "hear their preachers . . . attend their meetings and approve their distinguishing doctrines and practices."[34] The defining point for some critics of Methodism was its alleged anti-Anglican stance: Methodism was an organization of

---

29 043-Gr. Note the full title of John Brownsword, *The case of the rich young man in the gospel endeavoured to be set in a clear light, and the levelling principle of selling all, and giving it to the poor, as drawn from that passage, and lately advanced and taught by some, proved to be ill grounded* (London: for George Strahan, 1739), 11, 14.

30 297-Gr. Alexander Jephson, *A friendly and compassionate address to all serious . . . Methodist* (London: printed and sold by C. Jephson, 1760), i.

31 190-Gr. *The question whether it be right to turn Methodist considered*, 2.

32 For a brief biographical note on Benjamin Ingham and the societies he formed, known as Inghamites, see footnote 173 in this chapter.

33 210-Gr. Fletcher, *A Methodist dissected*, 1.

34 280-Gr. Dodd, *Cautions against Methodism*, 27. A second edition was published in 1759 and a third in 1769.

religious groups that all agreed in opposing the Church of England. Free, in *Rules for the discovery of false prophets* (1758), distinguished Methodists as

> a set of enthusiasts, who under the pretense of being true members of the Church of England, either pervert its doctrines relating to faith and works, and the terms of salvation, so as to make them repugnant to the Holy Scripture; or else offend against the order and discipline of natural religion, and still under the pretense of being members of the Church of England, or at least Christians.[35]

Later in the same pamphlet, Free distinguished between two types of Methodists: first, the "Dissenter type," led by Whitefield and Wesley, who established their own societies and their own ecclesiastical machinery; second, the "Church of England type," those who sought and assumed Church of England preferments, like William Romaine, Henry Venn, and Richard Elliot. This second type he considered "rather more dangerous as they raise no suspicions of that sort among the deluded common people, while they assume legal titles, and pass with them for *Rector* of _____ *Vicar* _____ of . . . and then add that they . . . are the *true ministers* of the Church of England."[36]

Just how broad the definitions had become can be seen in Downes's *Methodism examined and disposed* (1759). Anyone who departed from eighteenth-century pulpit conventions was suspect of being Methodist:

> I am not ignorant upon what weak and slender grounds a suspicion of that sort is apt to be found. Sometimes a preacher unhappily incurs it in his voice, manner, gestures, pronunciation, nay, even his very countenance—sometimes by the pathos of his stile. And the vehemence of his address. Sometimes by his being misunderstood by his less attentive, or distinguishing hearers . . . But then sometimes again, he brings it upon himself; as by heaping scripture upon scripture, either foreign to his subject, or unconnected with his matter; by a studied and more frequent repetition or hackneyed use of the adorable name of Jesus, than is either prudent, or decent; by being fond of rapturous expressions, and high flights of piety, soaring quite beyond the regions of reason and common sense. [37]

---

35 274-Gr. Free, *Rules for the discovery of false prophets*, 1758, vi.
36 Ibid.
37 282-Gr. Downes, *Methodism examined and exposed*, 94–95.

Not all critics of Methodism were happy with such indiscriminately loose definitions. They recognized it was sometimes a convenient weapon for unjustified attack and feared that "the worldly and lukewarm may stigmatize the more serious and regular Christians with the name of Methodists as a name of the utmost reproach and infamy."[38] Thus, they attempted to be more responsible in their use of the term. Regular and constant attendance upon the Church and living a sober and exemplary life did not automatically mean that one was a Methodist.

Enthusiasm

The caricature of the Methodist was sketched in bold and sweeping strokes. The most prominent feature was "enthusiasm." No charge was more consistently leveled at Methodism than this. Although it was more commonly used in the early attacks, there remained pamphleteers who assailed Methodists with it even late in the century.[39] Joseph Priestley expressed the sentiment of many later critics. He praised the Methodists for putting aside earlier marks of enthusiasm: "[Y]ou who are now called Methodists, are a very different set of people, and much more rational, than those who were first distinguished by that name."[40]

The word "enthusiasm" is of Greek origin and meant "inspired by a god," implying a direct communication between the deity and human beings. In the seventeenth and eighteenth centuries, it meant the spurious claim of immediate divine inspiration and the gift of extraordinary powers from the Holy Spirit. Several critics tried their hands at defining the term. One of the earliest was Joseph Trapp: "By enthusiasm is meant a person's having a strong but false persuasion, that he is divinely inspired; or, at least, that he has the Spirit of God some way or other; and this made known in a particular and extraordinary manner."[41] Central to the anti-Methodist definition of enthusiasm was the conviction that such claims of inspiration were ill grounded and

---

38 280-Gr. Dodd, *Cautions against Methodism*, 28.

39 543-Gr. *Methodism unmasked* (London: G. Riebau, [1789]); 555-Gr. *A review of the policy, doctrines and morals of the Methodists* (London: printed for J. Johnson, 1791); 536A-Ki. Croft, *Eight sermons preached before the University of Oxford*.

40 554-Gr. Priestley, *Original letters by the Rev. John Wesley and his friends*, 19.

41 010-Gr. Trapp, *The nature, folly, sin and danger of being righteous over-much*, 39.

> nothing more but the more natural effect of a heated imagination, violent passion, and the like . . . And imagined revelations and visions may as effectually enter into a troubled brain, as well as many strange things fix themselves in the head of a person in a high fever; which he so firmly believes to be true (though there is no reality in them) that it is impossible at that time to persuade him to the contrary.[42]

Some critics went further in their definitions and distinguished between an enthusiast and an impostor. An enthusiast, they believed, was genuinely convinced that inspiration came immediately from the Holy Spirit, even if such a conviction was false. Such people allowed "heated imagination" and emotions to rule their actions. On the other hand, an impostor "acts against the dictates of his own conscience, pretends to raptures and visions, knowing they are counterfeit and false, and his sole purpose is to deceive, knowing himself to be a deceiver."[43]

One opponent suggested that although inspiration might indeed be from a supernatural source, the source was not God, but Satan. Methodism, asserted John Kirkby, "advances the same wicked Spirit [Satan] into the place of God himself, making his diabolical illusions and suggestions pass for the operations of the Holy Ghost."[44]

The distinguishing traits of an enthusiast were itemized by various anti-Methodist writers. The following list outlines Edmund Gibson's eight ways that enthusiasts see the Holy Spirit's special workings in their lives and ministry:

- They claim to have extraordinary communications with God and a greater-than-ordinary assurance of the presence of God is with them.

- They use language that implies a special and immediate mission from God.

- They claim thoughts and actions that are under the guidance of divine inspiration.

- They claim their preaching and its effect are the work of a divine power.

---

42 249A-Fi. Thomas Green, *A dissertation on enthusiasm*, 58.

43 235-Gr. [Theophilus Evans], *The history of modern enthusiasm* (London: W. Owen and W. Clarke, 1752).

44 217-Gr. Kirkby, *The impostor detected*, 40.

- They boast of sudden and surprising effects wrought by the Holy Spirit as a result of their preaching.

- They boast of their ability to prophesy.

- They use scriptural phases, particularly apostolic ones, and even of Christ, to describe themselves and their work.

- They profess to preach a new gospel, unknown to the majority of the clergy and people in a Christian country.[45]

John Green pointed out the dangers of enthusiasm:

> Our own persuasion how strong and steadfast so ever, cannot be that kind and degree of conviction, on which we can securely depend. Zealots, the most blind and intractable zealots, have acted and suffered under the settled influence of this persuasion. Opposite opinions have been maintained and persisted in by different parties, under the same confident assurance of the divine illumination.[46]

Enthusiasm, opponents believed, would undermine the whole fabric of Christian faith. The enthusiasts' faith had no rational foundation; it was blatant subjectivism—faith without external verification. This made it impossible to argue with an enthusiast, William Dodd complained, because the enthusiast used different rules:

> [N]ever attempt to reason or dispute with an enthusiast; no good can ever come from it; for such persons have no intention to come over to your opinions: they only talk to convert and save you, as they are pleased to phrase it; they have a short method of baffling every argument which may be urged either from reason or Scripture rightly understood, by telling you, that "they have eyes, and you have not; that they see, and you do not," and if this be the case, how vain is it to reason with those who are endowed with another sense, with a faculty of knowledge and discernment denied to you?[47]

---

45 029-Gr. [Gibson], *The bishop of London's pastoral letter*, 16–22. W. Stephen Gunter, *The Limits of "Love Divine,"* 18. Gunter reduces the eight types to four: extraordinary communications, special vocations and spiritual accomplishments, unusual piety, and a new gospel message, 19–24.

46 315-Gr. Academicus [John Green], *The principles and practices of the Methodists farther considered*, 21.

47 280-Gr. Dodd, *Cautions against Methodism*, 34.

Enthusiasm thrived, anti-Methodists contended, among the ignorant and those deprived of good religious training. The uneducated and the un-churched were easily converted to enthusiasm, because they were "apt to admire everything that seems strange and uncommon."[48] Lavington lamented that mentally and emotionally unstable people were easily proselytized by enthusiasts:

> [A] cunning man, having under his management persons of ten-
> der nerves and weak brains, of a tractable disposition, or rather
> indisposition of mind or body, may infuse such doses of wild
> doctrine, as easily to work them up into whatever *strange sights*
> the arch-enthusiast pleaseth.[49]

Critics pointed to the dire consequences of enthusiasm. It fostered fa-naticism, and fanaticism "[begat] an aversion, then hatred, and at last ends in some degree of persecution and cruelty."[50] Lavington expressed many opponents' fears when he drew a connection between enthusiasm and im-morality: "'Tis observable in fact, that a multiplicity of wives, and promiscuous use of women has been the favorite tenet of most fanatical sects."[51] When enthusiasts' imagination run wild, their emotions are raised to fever pitch, and their passions are inflamed. Without reason to guide them, virtue no longer informed their actions, and impure desires went unchecked. Immorality was an inevitable consequence of enthusiasm, argued Thomas Green.[52] Enthusi-asts were "libertines," Theophilus Evans contended: "[T]he grossest sins, as incest, adultery. and murder, &c. are no sins in them because they are the elect; but are abominable sins in others, because they are the reprobates."[53] Enthusiasm was identified, further, with insanity. Lavington claimed it had driven numbers "into direct madness and distraction, either of the moaping, or the raving kind; or both of them, by successive fits; or into the manifold symptoms of a delirium and phrenzy."[54] Incidents were reported where the

---

48 249A-Fi. Thomas Green, *A dissertation on enthusiasm*, 59.

49 225-Gr. [Lavington], *The enthusiasm of Methodists and papists compar'd*, pt. 3, 115.

50 126-Gr. *A comparison between the doctrines taught by the clergy . . . and . . . Whitefield* (London: printed for A. Smith, 1741), 2.

51 225-Gr. [Lavington], *The enthusiasm of Methodists and papist compar'd*, pt. 3, 61.

52 249A-Fi. Thomas Green, *A dissertation on enthusiasm*, 88.

53 235-Gr. [Theophilus Evans], *A history of modern enthusiasm*, 2nd ed., xii.

54 225-Gr. [Lavington], *The enthusiasm of Methodists and papists compar'd*, pt. 3, 12.

madness brought about by enthusiasm led to suicide.[55] One critic feared that enthusiasm would encourage the spread of atheism.[56] Another predicted an easy transition from enthusiasm to Roman Catholicism.[57]

Enthusiasm not only endangered individuals; it threatened society. In the enthusiasm of the early Methodist movement critics saw the revival of Puritan enthusiasm, which led to social disorder and the overthrow of the Stuart monarchy in the mid-seventeenth century. The anonymous author of *A compleat account of the conduct of that eminent enthusiast Mr. Whitefield* (1739) urged his readers to learn the lessons of history.[58] These sentiments were echoed by critics, including Bishop Edmund Gibson in his 1739 *Pastoral letter*: "This nation, in the time of our forefathers, had sufficient experience of the mischief and contempt that may be brought upon religion by inspired tongues and itching ears."[59]The foregoing paragraphs illustrate the nature of the charge of enthusiasm that was leveled at the early Methodists. While responsible critics, such as Gibson, documented specific charges of enthusiasm in the writings and activities of the Methodists, other, less responsible critics made generalized attacks on alleged enthusiasm. All too frequently anti-Methodist authors used the charges as a term of personal abuse. It became a convenient label: "enthusiast" and "Methodist" were synonymous.

Anti-Intellectualism

One of the aspects of Methodism that infuriated its eighteenth-century opponents was the Methodists' alleged deprecation of learning. The Methodist leaders were portrayed as anti-intellectual. John Green, in noting that John Berridge advocated that "everyone is qualified to preach the gospel, who has the gift of utterance," accused him of making "unwearied endeavors . . . to depreciate the value, and decry the use of, human learning."[60] Samuel Weller

---

55 315-Gr. Academicus [John Green], *The principles and practices of the Methodists farther considered*, vi.

56 167-Gr. [Smalbroke], *A charge deliver'd to . . . clergy in . . . the diocese of Lichfield . . . 1741*, 1–2.

57 315-Gr. Academicus [John Green], *The principles and practices of the Methodists farther considered*, 88.

58 036-Gr. [Josiah Tucker], *A compleat account of the conduct of Mr. . . . Whitefield*, 11.

59 029-Gr. [Gibson], *The Bishop of London's pastoral letter*, 29.

60 294-Gr. Academicus [John Green], *The principles and practices of the Methodists considered*, 7–8.

complained of Whitefield, "[T]his gentleman's quarrel is . . . with learning in general."[61] A number of critics agreed with Weller, observing that Whitefield advised the Methodists to lay aside formal education. The strongest statements came from one who signed his pamphlet "W. C." He believed that the Methodists had been taught that

> all human learning must be superfluous lumber, with which the more the head is stuffed there is less room for spiritual furniture; all philosophy, whether natural or moral, all the liberal arts and sciences, history, mathematics, poetry, painting and musick, together with the learned professions of law and physick are vain.[62]

Methodism depreciated learning so strongly, it was suggested they placed it on a level with sin. Nathaniel Lancaster remarked:

> Spirit of new birth!
> Extend thy pity to this man of sin,
> Unhappily o'erwhelmed in the gulph
> Of human erudition, and defil'd
> With all the turpitude of carnal sense.[63]

The writings of some Methodist leaders, Whitefield, Berridge, and Seward, provided ample evidence for opponents that Methodists disdained secular learning. John Green culled quotations from the above Methodists to show they played down the role of learning and emphasized the Christian's inner receptivity to spiritual truths. The epithets the Methodists attached to the Anglican clergy confirmed, said Green, that Methodists were anti-intellectual. Whitefield's antipathy to learning was evidenced in his reference to well-educated clergy as "letter-learned divines, polite reasoners, modern rabbis, men of head-knowledge, &c."[64]

Not only were Methodists branded as anti-intellectual; they were portrayed as irrational. For the eighteenth century, known as the "Age of Reason,"

---

61 098-Gr. [Weller], *The trial of Mr. Whitefield's spirit*, 42.

62 398-Gr. W. C., *Remarks upon the Reverend Mr. Whitefield's letter to the vice–chancellor* (Oxford: printed at the Theatre for J. Fletcher, 1768), 28; cf., 124-Gr. *Mr. Whitefield's doctrines considered and confuted* (Ipswich: by the author, 1741), 27–28.

63 387-Gr. [Lancaster], *Methodism triumphant*, 16.

64 315-Gr. Academicus [John Green], *The principles and practices of the Methodists farther considered*, 9.

this was a cardinal sin. There was nothing unreasonable about the Christian religion—faith had a rational base. Anti-Methodists believed Methodists did not appreciate that faith was built on reason. In his *Essay on faith* (1768), John Rotheram contended, "Reason leads to faith. Reason pleads for it . . . Reason flies to faith as its only protector."[65] Another critic, James Penn, advised the Methodists that reason and Christianity were inseparable: "If Christianity cannot stand the test of reason, it is a religion of no authority. Everyone concerned for the glory and honour of the Supreme Being ought to declare against and expose it, and mankind should be taught some other way to happiness. When arguments from reason fail, or are defective, it is time to abolish Christianity, and to seek for or invent some new religion."[66] Methodism's Anglican critics did not deny the necessity of revelation but insisted that revelation was always of a reasonable character. John Green articulated the eighteenth-century Church of England belief in the preeminence of reason:

> The clear deductions of that reason, which God has given us, cannot I think be overturned by any subsequent revelation of his will, which he may be pleased to give. For we cannot suppose the Deity to contradict himself in the discoveries which he may vouchsafe to communicate to us, or that what he makes known in one way should be repugnant to what he makes known in another way. . . Even that part of it, relating to God's nature or providential administration, which may greatly exceed the utmost reach of our capacity, yet must not be contradictory to the clear notices or dedications of our reason. It must appear credible, before anyone can receive it as true.[67]

Religion and reason, for some critics, were almost synonymous.

Anti-Methodists contended that Methodists made religion irrational—they denigrated reason and in its place extolled fancy. They made pretended inspiration superior to all rational examination and thus destroyed the authority of the Christian religion. Individual intuitions, they affirmed, were superior to reason. Methodists were contemptuous of reason, explained the author of

---

65 380-Gr. John Rotheram, *An essay on faith and its connection with good works* (London: W. Sandby, 1766), 230.

66 338-Gr. James Penn, *Various tracts* (London: Charles Say, [1762]), 108.

67 315-Gr. Academicus [John Green], *The principles and practices of the Methodists farther considered*, 13–15.

A fine picture of enthusiasm (1744): "This power in man, by which alone he can resemble his Maker, they degrade as carnal and devilish. They tell you, that they have another, a more spiritual medium thro' which they discern the truth."[68] The Methodists' denigration of reason was deliberate—critics believed Methodists denied the validity of reason because reason was the weapon consistently used to defeat their theological propositions. It was feared that because the Methodists replaced reason with individual whim in matters of religion, they might do the same in other matters. With reason no longer controlling emotions, Methodists might give vent to their religious feelings in wild and extravagant behavior:

> Fix'd principles wou'd zeal's bright flame restrain,
> And cool too fast the fever of their brain:
> From reason free, they give their frenzies wing,
> Groan, weep, rave, rant, confess, exhort, and sing.[69]

Thomas Hitchcock warned his readers that if the Methodists were successful, society might revert to the dark ages: "[S]hall we therefore run back again into the times of ignorance and barbarism, and dishonour God by rejecting the gifts and endowments and advantages that he has given us?"[70]

Insanity

The logical outcome of the Methodists' irrationality, critics opined, was insanity. For many opponents, Methodism and insanity became synonymous. Wesley records people expressing it simply: "[T]hey were mad; they were Methodists."[71] As early as 1739, Joseph Trapp leveled the charge of madness:

---

68 174-Gr. Eusebius [Caleb Fleming], *A fine picture of enthusiasm* (London: J. Noon, 1744), 16.

69 516-Gr. [William Combe], *The saints* (London: for J. Bew, 1778), 3–4. Combe (1742–1823), was an English author of miscellaneous prose and satirical verse. A series of seven anti-Methodist works published from 1778 to 1779 were attributed to him: 516-Gr. *The saints* was the first in a series of poetic satires. It was followed by 517-Gr. [William Combe] *Perfection* (London: for J. Bew, 1778); 518-Gr. Author of *The saints* [William Combe], *The temple of imposture* (London: for J. Bew, 1778); 519-Gr. Author of *The saints* [William Combe], *The love-feast* (London: for J. Bew, 1778); 520-Gr. Author of *The saints* [William Combe], *Sketches for tabernacle frames* (London: for J. Bew, 1778); 521-Gr. [William Combe], *Fanatical conversion* (London: for J. Bew, 1779); 523-Gr. [William Combe], *Voltaire's ghost* (London: for J. Bew, 1779).

70 329-Gr. Hitchcock, *The mutual connexion between faith, virtue and knowledge*, 25.

71 Wesley, August 30, 1766, *Journal and Diaries V* (1765–1775), in *Works* 22:58.

"They have been made stark mad and received into Bedlam as such."[72] Lavington did much to confirm this aspect of the caricature in the public mind.[73] Warburton believed Wesley's conversions were not to be confused with what the Church of England called regeneration but were "turning fools into mad-men."[74] Methodist preachers were accused of having such a great impact as to fill "Bedlam and the several mad-houses in England with shoals of patients."[75] William Woolley, author of *A cure for canting*, claimed that the proprietors of every mad-house within twenty miles of London hailed Rowland Hill as their benefactor.[76]

James Lackington, as late as 1791, confirmed the caricature that Methodists drove people to insanity. He estimated that thousands who "occasionally" heard Methodist sermons went mad.[77] The satirists had a heyday with this charge. Combe gleefully noted how convenient it was that the Foundery, Wesley's headquarters in London, was located near Bedlam, the lunatic asylum.[78] The author of the *Memoirs of the life of a modern saint* suggested that Methodist preaching houses were, for all intents and purposes, "mad houses." He suggested further that Whitefield be allowed to assume control of Bedlam and use it as a center for preaching since he had "already several disciples in this sanctuary."[79] Another author carried this idea further and recommended that the Methodists, instead of building chapels, should construct insane asylums.[80] Anti-Methodists hinted satirically that the leaders of the revival deliberately chose the way of madness. Nathaniel Lancaster, in his mock epic, *Methodism triumphant* (1767), has the hero (John Wesley) at the end of a sermon invoke divine mania:

---

72 010-Gr. Trapp, *The nature, folly, sin and danger of being righteous over-much*, 37. Bedlam, formerly known as St. Mary Bethlehem Hospital, was England's first mental institution. Londoners abbreviated the name to Bethlem and often pronounced it "Bedlam."

73 225-Gr. [Lavington], *The enthusiasm of Methodists and papists compar'd*, xxvii–xxxi.

74 342-Gr. [Warburton], *The doctrine of grace*, 211.

75 348-Gr. Samuel Charndler, *An answer to the Reverend John Wesley's Letter to William, Lord Bishop of Gloucester* (London: printed for the author, 1763), 4.

76 569-Gr. William Woolley, *A cure for canting* (London: sold by Jordan and Ridgeway, 1794), 3.

77 560-Gr. Lackington, *Memoirs of the . . . life of James Lackington*, 87.

78 516-Gr. [Combe], *The saints*, 7.

79 320A-Ba. *Memoirs of the life of a modern saint* (London: printed for H. Ranger, 1761), 87.

80 232B-Ba. A Country Gentleman [William Evans], *A letter to the Reverend Mr. M—re B—k—r* (Dublin: printed for Peter Wilson, 1752), 18–19.

Oh! how unequal to the arduous height
Of this great theme, without thy mighty aid,
O thou celestial source of ecstasies
Of visions, raptures, and converting dreams
Awful ebriety of new-birth grace!
Thee Mania, I invoke my pen to guide,
To fire my soul and urge my bold career.
"O mania! O phantasia, pow'rs divine."[81]

Hypocrites

Methodists were also branded as hypocrites. Their outward show of piety, it was claimed, hid the ugliness of their inner lives. William Russel described them as "a set of sly, canting and deceitful persons, who have God in their mouths but the Devil in their hearts."[82] Critics called them "counterfeit saints," "diabolical seducers," "wolves in sheeps' clothing."[83] The author of *A wolf in sheep's cloathing* dubbed Methodists thus:

A lawless sect who spurn all honest worth,
Call nonsense faith, old puritanic cant new birth,
Who like fell ruffians act the Christian part
And learn all rules of piety by art.[84]

A number of opponents drew parallels between the Methodists and the Pharisees condemned by Jesus. "Meek lambs without, proud Pharisees within," remarked Combe.[85] Some listed examples of pharisaic hypocrisy found in the journals published by the leaders of the revival: protestations of humility; well-publicized scrupulosity with respect to pastimes; deliberate neglect of their physical appearance; strict observance of the Sabbath; long prayers and frequent devotions in public places; statements that they

---

81 387-Gr. [Nathaniel Lancaster], *Methodism triumphant*, 78.
82 566A*-Fi. [William Russel], *A short address to the public* (n.p.: no printer, 1793). Russel was curate of Pershore in the diocese of Worcester.
83 217-Gr. Kirkby, *The impostor detected*; 378-Gr. Peter Paragraph *pseud.* [Adair], *The Methodist and mimick*, 15.
84 575C-Fi. *The wolf in sheep's cloathing: a fragment addressed to the Methodistical clergy* (London: no printer, 1795), 4.
85 516A-Ki. [William Combe], *The fanatic saints: or, Bedlamites inspired* (London: for J. Bew, 1778), 12. This item is a new edition of 516-Gr. *The saints*.

were superior to the Church of England clergy—such were the marks of feigned piety.[86] Anti-Methodists believed that the Methodists practiced their pseudo-religion for their own ends. The motive, John Kirkby suggested, was adulation:

> To insinuate themselves into the good opinion of the multitude is the grand end of all the outside piety . . . The aim of their devotion is to draw the minds of men rather to the worship of themselves, than to the worship of God.[87]

So strong was their desire for popularity that, under the mask of being saints, Methodists often stooped to unscrupulous means to entice disciples to join them: "Some do it with a present of money in hand, or with a yearly allowance; others promise them constant employment in their trade or business; and some again grant their followers a greater liberty to gratify their lusts than the gospel of Christ doth allow."[88] The author of A letter from a deist suggested an easier way—the Methodists should make converts among innkeepers. "If once you can gain the land lord and his family . . . he will raise your recruits."[89]

Samuel Bowden satirized the lack of principles shown by these "counterfeit" saints:

> Ye pious enthusiasts! who riot and rob,
> With holy grimace, and sanctify'd sob:
> Ye saints in rebellion—far worse than the sword,
> who cheat—pray—and lie in the name of the Lord.
> How modest these innocent Methodist elves,
> Who curse half mankind, but are righteous themselves:
> Those who plunder the poor, are surely accurst,
> And of all rogues—the sanctify'd rogue is the worst.[90]

---

86 118-Gr. J. Trevor, *A short history of the Donatists* (London: printed for T. Cooper, 1741), 30–33. 354-Gr. An Enemy to Pious Fraud, *A sovereign remedy for the cure of hypocrisy and blind zeal* (London: T. Becket and P. Hondt, 1764), 23.

87 217-Gr. Kirkby, *The impostor detected*, 3.

88 366-Gr. A Presbyter of the Church of England, *The doctrines of Methodism examined and confuted* (London: no printer, 1765), 9.

89 222E-Fi. *A letter from the deists to the chief rulers amongst the Methodists* (Dublin: printed and sold by the booksellers and hawkers, 1750), 12.

90 249-Gr. Samuel Bowden, "The mechanic inspired," in *Poems on various subjects* (Bath: printed for T. Boddley, 1754), 213, 216.

Some opponents claimed the Methodists were taught the art of hypocrisy by Satan. Evan Lloyd portrayed the devil tutoring young Whitefield:

> To hide your blemishes use paint
> To screen the villain play the saint
> Affect religion, church frequent,
> Kneel, seem to pray, and keep up Lent—
> Charity too must be display'd,
> But charity in masquerade.[91]

William Combe insinuated that the Foundery had been established by Wesley expressly for the purpose of training Methodists to be hypocrites.

> Adults for training to the F—d'ry go.
> In holy go-carts there, by due degrees,
> They're taught to snivel, groan, cant, whine, and wheeze
> Heart-melting tones of wheedling intercession,
> Boanergy, on mobs to make impression;
> Stage-tricks, to fill the gloomy soul with fear,
> And wring from guilt a shilling, and a tear.[92]

One of the tricks Wesley's disciples were trained in was that of false humility: "They reduce the virtue of humility to mere form—to turn up the white of their eyes—sometimes to shut their eyes—to speak in a deep, slow, and hollow tone—to mouth well their words—wring their hands—sigh and groan in time—always to look down."[93]

One satirist produced a devastating broadside (1785) that purported to be a recipe for making a Methodist:

A Receipt How to Make a True Methodist

Take the herbs of hypocrisy, and the roots of spiritual pride, of each two handfuls, two ounces of ambition, vainglory and impudence, of each a sufficient quantity; boil them over the fire of sedition, until you perceive the ingredient to swim on the top, then add to them six ounces of the sugar of deceit, and one quart of dissembling tears, put them into the bottle of envy, and stop

---

91 379-Gr. [Lloyd], *The Methodist, a poem*, 44.

92 516A-Ki. [Combe], *The fanatic saints*, 18. This is a new edition of 516-Gr.

93 516-Gr. [Combe], *The saints*, 12–13.

it with the cork of malice. When these ingredients are subsided, then make them into pills, warm at five in the morning and seven in the evening, take them with the tongue of slander, and go into the society-house to hear nonsense and stupidity, and by way of exercise, fall into pretended fits, then go home, cant, sing hymns, say prayers, till you are heard all round the neighbourhood, this will produce such an effect that your chief study will be to cheat all you have dealings with, play the whore under the cloak of sanctity, revile the church, rail against the ministers of government, and when opportunity suits, cut the throat of all your opposers. These ingredients if they are well prepared are an infallible receipt, and without which you cannot be a True Methodist.[94]

A note at the bottom of the broadside announced that the ingredients could be purchased in London at a warehouse near Tottenham Court and Moorfields (close to Whitefield's and Wesley's preaching houses). For the convenience of those in the country, the Methodists planned new warehouses in almost every market town.[95]

Sentimentalism

Methodists were caricatured as sentimental religionists. Adversaries noted the extensive use of "Jesus" and "Christ" and such phrases as "precious Lord," "Lamb of God," and "Christ's blood" in the Methodist sermons and publications. The vocabulary with which they described their relationship to members of the Trinity was considered extravagant, intimate, and even amorous. Satirists delighted in ridiculing the practice. Lancaster's saint exclaims:

> Dost thou not see, we're darlings of the skies
> How fond we lean, and roll ourselves on Christ?
> Kisses, caresses, and endearing smiles

---

94 534A-Ba. "A receipt how to make a true Methodist" ([London]: no printer, 1785). This broadside went through a number of editions. One had a woodcut of a Methodist preacher (possibly either Wesley or Whitefield) preaching to a throng of people in the open air. In one hand the preacher holds a Bible; in the other, some money bags.

95 Ibid.

> Confirm the passion—whilst we this imbibe
> The sweet effusions of a breath divine.[96]

So intimate with Christ were the Methodists that they were urged to "wade to the knees in Christ's blood with exquisite raptures of joy and pleasure."[97] It was further suggested that the Methodists spoke and wrote in this manner to hide deficiencies in their doctrine and method of reasoning.[98] The Methodists were severely criticized also for using their sentimental and amorous vocabulary in conversing with, and writing to, members of their own societies. Edmund Gibson charged the Methodists with using "tender and melting terms and phrases" such as "a sweet society of ministers and exhorters," "poor, dear precious lambs," and "I send you a thousand kisses."[99] John Free took the cue from Gibson and attacked Whitefield and the Methodists for resorting to "religious-amorous or melting and rapturous expressions."[100] Their utterances made the Methodists appear foolishly sentimental and irrational. Observed one critic, "No allegory, illusion, or evasive interpretation can reconcile [their use of such expressions] with true religion, sound reason, or . . . common sense."[101] Critics might take offense at the language the evangelicals used because it showed no reverence toward the Almighty, but for the Methodists its use developed "an emphasis of spiritual intimacy as a mode of piety."[102]

Spiritual Arrogance

Another of the aspects of the Methodists' preaching and publications that infuriated opponents was the application of scriptural phrases to themselves. Thomas Church accused the Methodists of talking in the style of apostles, thus

---

96 387-Gr. [Lancaster], *Methodism triumphant*, 70. For a similar satire, see 341C-Fi. J. Helme, *A specimen of preaching* (London: printed for John Bird, 1762). A second edition, with additions by a friend of the author, was printed in London by N. Young in 1766. John Wesley's abhorrence of terms of endearment in the Moravians' hymns, and even to those in Charles's hymns, should be noted.

97 341C-Fi. Helme, *A specimen of preaching*, 14.

98 174-Gr. Eusebius [Fleming], *A fine picture of enthusiasm*, 24.

99 164-Gr. [Gibson], *Observations upon the conduct and behaviour of . . . Methodists* (London: E. Owen, 1744), 17.

100 274-Gr. Free, *Rules for the discovery of false prophets*, 35–36.

101 248A-Ba. A Lay-man, *A few queries concerning the growth of Methodism* (Dublin: no printer, 1753).

102 William Gibson and Joanne Begiato, *Sex and the Church in the Long Eighteenth Century* (I. B. Tauris, 2017), chap. 5, "Evangelicals, Sex and Respectability."

implying that they too possessed extraordinary powers and had received an extraordinary commission.[103] Not only did they draw parallels between themselves and the apostles, but George Lavington charged them with comparing themselves to the patriarchs, prophets, and even Christ himself:

> They cannot open the Bible, and thereby turn the holy scriptures into a lottery, but they are sure of a prize; some panegyric upon themselves and proselytes; or some special direction and instruction. They cannot read, or hear, lessons, psalms, epistles and gospels; but they have sagacity enough to find something peculiarly concerning themselves . . . As if the whole Bible were a sort of prophecy (designed at least by way of accommodation) of their mission; and entirely interested in the honour and advancement of their valuable persons, and important whims.[104]

Anti-Methodists found Whitefield's injudicious metaphors comparing himself with Christ in his autobiography, *A short account of God's dealings with the Reverend Mr. George Whitefield* (1740), nothing short of blasphemy.[105] One author admonished Whitefield for taking upon himself "the office of a thirteenth Apostle."[106] Even Wesley was criticized on this point. One author commented that the individual reading Wesley's journals and other writings "will be often at a loss to know whether it is St. Paul or John Wesley that is speaking to him."[107] Methodist preachers were accused of following the example of their leaders, by comparing their sufferings and indefatigable labors to those of Christ.[108] This aspect is satirized in *A journal of the travels of Nathaniel Snip.* Echoing Matthew 10:14, the entry for April 3 reads, "Early

---

103 049-Gr. Church, *An explanation and defence of the doctrine of the Church of England*, 12.

104 213-Gr. [Lavington], *The enthusiasm of Methodists and papists compar'd*, pt. 2, 27. See also 469-Gr. A saint from the Tabernacle, *A sermon upon the turf*, 2nd ed. ([London]: for the author, 1776), 10–11.

105 005-Gr. [T. Gib], *Remarks on the Reverend Mr. Whitefield's journal* (London: for the author, [1738], v. See also 006A-Ba. A Gentleman of Oxford [Ralph Jephson], *The Methodists dissected* (Oxford: by the author, [1739]). It was reprinted in 1740 with the title *The expounder expounded.* A second edition appeared in 1743 under the title *Methodism and enthusiasm fully displayed.* See second edition, 18.

106 148-Gr. A True Lover of the Church and Country, *Some observations upon the conduct of the famous Mr. W—field* (Edinburgh: no printer, 1742), 8.

107 161-Gr. [Thomas Sharp], *Remarks on a book intitled 'An earnest appeal to men of reason'* (Newcastle: no printer, 1743), 6.

108 268-Gr. [Thomas Mortimer], *Die and be damned* (London: S. Hooper and A. Morley, 1758), 25–26. A second edition, revised and enlarged, was printed in 1758, and a third in 1761.

in the morning I left Hull—at my departure I shook the dust off my shoes at them (dirt I should have said, for in truth it was wet weather) in token of my giving them over to their vanity, and the lust of the flesh."[109] Several critics labored to show how greatly the Methodists differed from the apostles. Trapp believed the difference lay in the fact that while the apostles were falsely reviled and persecuted, the Methodists were rightfully so. No charges could be proved against the character and behavior of the apostles, but charges against the Methodists had been documented.[110]

Spiritual arrogance was a distinguishing trait of the Methodists. Tristram Land, in his *Letter to the Rev. Mr. Whitefield* (1739), claimed that Methodists "look upon themselves as exquisite pictures of holiness . . . whilst they represent us as dumb dogs, profane and carnally minded."[111] John Roche, in 1751, agreed with him: the Methodists "are in the general as immodest and unlimited in the praise of themselves, as in the defamation of others."[112] The journals of Whitefield and Wesley, it was claimed, were full of arrogant statements; indeed, some parts were nothing more than essays in self-congratulation. Whitefield's manner of publishing the successes of his ministry offended many anti-Methodists:

> I must further tell you, that your common way of publishing what success you have had in other places;—of the many solicitations to return to them, in order to preach the gospel, as if it's being preached depended on you;—That your appellations, my dear hearers, my soul loves you, &c. and now and then relating your private experiences in public are very disgusting, have a flattering appearance, and look as if you would make them subservient to ends I hope you do not intend.[113]

Critics believed that the spiritual arrogance of the leaders of Methodism was contagious, and cited instances where it had spread to the rank-and-file

---

109 324-Gr. Nathaniel Snip *pseud.*, *A journal of the travels of Nathaniel Snip*, 16.
110 093-Gr. [Trapp], *The true spirit of the Methodists and their allies*, 16. See also 166-Gr. J. B. /A Gentleman of Pembroke College, Oxon., *A letter to the Reverend Mr. Whitefield occasioned by his pretended answer to the first part of the 'Observations on the conduct and behaviour of the Methodists'* (London: M. Cooper, [1744]), 46.
111 009-Gr. Land, *A letter to the Rev. Mr. Whitefield*, 4.
112 226A-Ki. John Roche, *Moravian heresy* (Dublin: for the author, 1751), 292.
113 266A-Ba. Probator, *A letter to the Revd. Mr. George Whitefield* (n.p.: no printer, 1757), 2.

members.[114] The height of arrogance, opponents believed, was the alleged claim that they were the sole dispensers of the gospel. Nathaniel Lancaster's Saint warned all who would know salvation that they must turn to Methodism:

> High as you are, to us you must descend:
> Th' obstetric med'cines in our hands are lodg'd;
> And we, alone, dispense the heav'nly boon—
> The cure infallible for souls diseas'd.[115]

Opponents implied that the Methodists made Christianity and Methodism synonymous and believed themselves to be the sole custodians of the keys to heaven: "[N]o man can be a good Christian . . . who does not enter into Christianity by the door of Methodism."[116] One satirist explained "Almost Christians" (Wesley's phrase to mean nominal Christians) as "a contemptuous name among the saints for all but their own sect."[117]

Censoriousness

Closely allied to the trait of arrogance was that of censoriousness. Opponents believed Methodists were so bigoted in their opinions that they stood in judgment upon all who differed. Methodists were likened to papists who condemned in a lump, as heretics, all but themselves.[118] John Witherspoon complained:

> [T]hey are so free with their anathemas and curses, as if God had entrusted them with the keys of the bottomless pit, and with all given them a commission to consign over those to everlasting fire, who, in the judgement of the whole impartial world, must be look'd upon as intelligent and honest, as good men, and as good Christians, as themselves.[119]

Anti-Methodists were offended by the way the Methodist leaders cited

---

114 235-Gr. [Theophilus Evans], *A history of modern enthusiasm*, 2nd ed., 111.

115 387-Gr. Lancaster, *Methodism triumphant*, 39.

116 354-Gr. An Enemy to Pious Fraud, *A sovereign remedy for the cure of hypocrisy and blind zeal*, 19.

117 520-Gr. Author of *The saints* [Combe], *Sketches for tabernacle-frames*, 28.

118 210-Gr. Nathaniel Fletcher, *A Methodist dissected*, 7–8.

119 356-Gr. A. T. Blacksmith *pseud.* [John Witherspoon], *Enthusiasm delineated* (Bristol: printed for the author, 1764), 23.

their opponents to the bar of judgment. Lavington referred to it as an "audacious custom . . . an uncharitable presumption."[120] Methodists, the bishop suggested, seemed to believe that everything would be determined in their favor, and judgment passed against all those whom they prosecuted. Warburton found in Wesley's comments on disasters that befell some of his critics an illustration of the Methodist leader's belief that what happened to his opponents was the immediate execution of heavenly judgment. A rector who had preached against the Methodists suddenly became unable to preach again and died as he was carried from the pulpit. Another opponent later hanged himself. Warburton remarked that Wesley's judgments were "fulminated with the air of one who had the divine vengeance at his disposal."[121] The author of *Mumbo chumbo* (1765) scorned the Methodists for this practice:

> But say, Ye bold presumptuous men! how dare
> You brandish high the everlasting rod
> 'Gainst righteous souls who do their Maker fear?
> Will you thus impudently lie for God?[122]

Critics found in the alleged censoriousness of the Methodists a distinct lack of Christian charity. They wondered how followers of Jesus could exercise such a judgmental attitude toward others:

> Art thou commission'd, by that suff 'ring Lamb
> Whom you pretend to follow, thus to damn?
> Hath punishment to thy department fell?
> Hath heav'n to thee consign'd the keys of hell?[123]

Fearmongers

Not only were the Methodists accused of calling down judgment on others and striking fear into the hearts of their hearers, but it was suggested that they actually enjoyed doing it. Early Methodists were caricatured as disciples of fear. As fear is ever predominant in weak minds, Thomas Mortimer

---

120 213-Gr. [Lavington], *The enthusiasm of Methodists and papists compar'd*, 123.
121 342-Gr. [Warburton], *The doctrine of grace*, 147.
122 364-Gr. *Mumbo chumbo*, 17.
123 517-Gr. [Combe], *Perfection*, 34.

contended, fear was at the center of the Methodists' lives.[124] Whereas love was the motivation for Christians, only fear, suggested Evan Lloyd, could direct Methodists.

> [They] from a coward dread of law
> Owe all their virtue to their awe
> . . . tho' they seem so true, and just,
> So strictly faithful to their trust,
> Will, if you take the gallows down
> Out-pilfer half the rogues in town.[125]

The task for Methodist preachers was to terrify people into being good. This they accomplished by means of hell-fire sermons. Not content with the New Testament depiction of hell, the Methodists, said their critics, allowed their imaginations to run riot.[126] Details of a literal hell and the agony of doomed sinners were vividly described. "This," claimed James Lackington, "the Methodists called 'shaking the people over the mouth of hell.'"[127] Whitefield, Wesley, Romaine, and Berridge, as well as illiterate lay preachers, all reveled, it was alleged, in portraying sinners terrified before an "angry God."[128] John Harman printed what he alleged was a transcript of one of Whitefield's sermons. In the discourse Whitefield was obsessed by the idea of hell:

> Hark! Hark! (Holds both his hands up above his head and roars.)
> I hear the noise of the damn'd souls in hell, shaking their chains
> which they want to get loose from, to come to torment us here!—
> See! See! the devil dragging off the damned souls to hell.[129]

---

124 268-Gr. [Mortimer], *Die and be damned*, 22.

125 379-Gr. Author of *The powers of the pew* and *The curate* [Evan Lloyd], *The Methodist: A poem*, 51.

126 For the Methodists' attitude to hell see David Dunn Wilson, "The Importance of Hell for John Wesley," *ProcWHS* 34 (March 1963): 12–16.

127 560-Gr. Lackington, *Memoirs of the . . . life of James Lackington*, 87–88.

128 320A-Ba. *Memoirs of the life of a modern saint*, 58; 387-Gr. Lancaster, *Methodism triumphant*, 35, 76–77; 519-Gr. Author of *The saints* [Combe], *The love-feast*, 31–32; 294-Gr. Academicus [John Green], *The principles and practices of the Methodists considered*, 28–29; 560-Gr. Lackington, *Memoirs of the . . . life of James Lackington*, 84; 324-Gr. Nathaniel Snip *pseud.*, *A journal of the travels of Nathaniel Snip*, 10.

129 319-Gr. Harman, *The crooked disciple's remarks upon the blind guide's method of preaching*, 18.

So terrifying were some of Whitefield's hell-fire sermons, it was claimed, that while trying to convert a six-year-old boy, he frightened him to death.[130]

Theophilus Evans described a Methodist sermon on hell. The preacher depicted "hell's flames flashing" in the faces of the damned as they drop into the bottom of hell.[131] J. Helme printed in 1762, what he claimed was a *"Specimen of [Methodist] Preaching."* Fear of hell was an important ingredient: "Some here present will go part of the way up the ladder toward heaven— Some one step,—some two,—some three,—and some will get to the vertex of the ladder and then tumble down to hell."[132]

Libertines

The Methodists of popular imagination were antinomians. By espousing justification by faith alone, it was commonly believed they rejected the necessity of good works. Timothy Scrub warned that antinomianism "annuls all religious obligations whatever; and sets at once at naught the commandments of God; . . . If they are to be justified, at all events, merely by an act of faith, then there is an end of all morality, and religion, and virtue."[133] In a similar vein, another wrote: "Methodists (at least their lay preachers) teach, that Christians are under no obligation to observe the Ten Commandments; that Christ has done all for us, and that we need, therefore, do nothing for ourselves."[134] Methodists had made Christianity too easy! John Downes noted that they had found "a safer and smoother passage, by divesting themselves of the incumbrances of moral duties."[135] One satirist entitled his work *A plain and easy road to the land of bliss.*[136] John Green hinted that the Methodist motive for making Christianity easier was to gain greater popularity. "A Methodist when he preaches up salvation by faith alone, will draw numbers about him; if he does it in the

---

130 138C-Fi. *Remarks on Mr. Whitefield* ([Edinburgh]: no printer, 1741). This item was a broadside and was sold for a penny. A vindication of Whitefield with the title *Observations upon the 'Remarks on Mr. Whitefield'* (Edinburgh: no printer 1741), appeared in October 1741.

131 235-Gr. [Theophilus Evans], *A history of modern enthusiasm*, 2nd ed., 119.

132 341C-Fi. Helme, *A specimen of preaching*, 12.

133 012-Gr. Timothy Scrub, *A letter to Robert Seagrave, M.A.* (London: J. Roberts, 1739), 19.

134 349-Gr. Richard Hardy, *A letter from a clergyman to one of his parishioners who was inclined to turn Methodist* (London: for the author, 1763), 22–23.

135 282-Gr. Downes, *Methodism examined and exposed*, 40.

136 337-Gr. *A plain and easy road to the land of bliss* (London: for W. Nicoll and W. Tesseyman in York, 1762).

utmost latitude of the antinomian principles and to the absolute exclusion of all works, he must be expected to draw much greater."[137] The anonymous author of *A review of the policy, doctrines, and morals of the Methodists* (1791) confirmed Green's assessment made thirty years before.[138] It was the "new and easy passage to heaven" which had gained Methodism such numerous disciples: "One need not be surprised to see so many of dishonest principles and profligate morals enlist under this standard [Methodism]. Many . . . dishonest, lustful, treacherous, the tyrants of their families, have in the decline of life taken shelter under this zealous profession."[139]

While Methodists claimed to be God's agents for reforming the nation, anti-Methodists believed the opposite. The antinomianism of the Methodist movement was creating widespread irreligion: "Most certain it is," wrote a country curate, "that a down-hill reformation will roll on very fast."[140] It was not only that Methodist doctrines failed to encourage good works, but Lavington contended that some of its tenets fostered immorality and vice. The doctrines of assurance and perfection, he believed, turned Methodists into libertines.[141] Theophilus Evans supported Lavington's contention. He believed that "the most zealous of the party now in a great measure wallow in lust and sensuality."[142] Westley Hall, Wesley's brother-in-law, became the prime illustration of the immorality of the Methodists.[143] Those who mentioned Hall implied that he was typical, rather than the exception. Hall's reputation rubbed off on Whitefield and John Wesley as they, too, were charged with indiscretions with women. Trapp accused the Methodists in

---

137 294-Gr. Academicus [John Green], *The principles and practices of the Methodists considered*, 22.

138 555-Gr. *A review of the policy, doctrines, and morals of the Methodists.*

139 Ibid., 10–12, 20.

140 371-Gr. Country Curate, *The self–commissioned apostle an impostor*, 29. See also 010-Gr. Trapp, *The nature, folly, sin and danger of being righteous over-much*; 249A-Fi. Thomas Green, *A dissertation on enthusiasm*, 145, 149; 205-Gr. Church, *Some farther remarks on the Rev. Mr. John Wesley's last journal*, 118.

141 213-Gr. [Lavington], *The enthusiasm of Methodists and papists compar'd*, pt. 2, 146.

142 235-Gr. [Theophilus Evans], *The history of modern enthusiasm*, 2nd ed., i.

143 Westley Hall was an eighteenth-century Anglican priest. A former student of John Wesley at Oxford and a member of the Holy Club, Hall married Wesley's sister, Martha. He later became a polygamist and his reputation was an embarrassment to the Wesleys and the Methodist movement. See Stephen Gunter, *Limits of Love Divine*, 186–87; 193–201. See also, Henry Abelove, *The Evangelist of Desire: John Wesley and the Methodists* (Stanford: Stanford University Press, 1990).

1739 of welcoming into their midst "women of a most infamous and prostitute character."[144] By such malicious accusations and innuendo Methodism's name was besmirched.

Satirists inferred that the Methodist doctrine of justification meant that sinners did not have to cease their sinful actions. A footnote in *A journal of the travels of Nathaniel Snip* explained:

> A gentleman being in company with a common prostitute, observed to her that he heard she was become a Methodist: She told him, she thanked God she was.—How then, replyed he, can you reconcile this way of living with the doctrine you profess?—Oh, cried she, I am very easy in that respect; for as I am convinced my precious soul is wedged above, I am quite careless what becomes of my body here below.[145]

Former Methodist James Lackington helped further the impression that Methodists were immoral. He noted that the parish of Wellington was deeply troubled. "For, if (said they) the Methodist society continues, we shall have the parish full of bastards." Lackington claimed the problem was with some Methodist women whose desires were insatiable: "[O]wing to their having husbands too spiritual. . . [they] receive assistance from the husbands of others."[146]

Heretics

Many anti-Methodists pictured the Methodists as heretics. Wesley contended that the Methodists preached the doctrines of the Church of England, but few of his critics would grant him that point.[147] They believed that in Methodist theology and practices, old heresies were being revived. In 1739 the author of the satiric *The Methodists: An humorous burlesque poem*, inveighed against the movement as the epitome of heresy:

> O Britain! miserable land!
> Fools of all sorts still crowd thy strand!
> Projectors, chymists, priests of Rome!

---

144 010-Gr. Trapp, *The nature, folly, sin and danger of being righteous over-much*, 55.
145 324-Gr. Snip *pseud.*, *A journal of the travels of Nathaniel Snip*, 29.
146 560-Gr. Lackington, *Memoirs of the . . . life of James Lackington*, 244, 236–37.
147 See chapter 3, "Doctrinal Deviation."

French prophets, pietists, all come,
And now to crown 'em all in one,
The Methodists the work have done.[148]

Twenty years later, London clergyman John Downes found himself in agreement with the poet's assessment. Methodists might be new in name, but their principles were old: "[T]heir doctrines or notions square or coincide with many of the oldest and rankest heresies that ever defiled the purity and disturbed the peace of the Christian Church." Downes linked Methodists with a number of ancient heresies, alleging similarities between Methodism and Gnostics, Montanists, Donatists, Simonians, and Valentinians.[149]

In 1745 Zachary Grey, in his *Serious address to lay-Methodists,* explained in detail Methodism's resemblance to Gnosticism on the basis of a common pretense to divine inspiration, "proudly arrogating to themselves a more than common share of it, and on this pretense, by their own authority to the revealed will of Christ, they blasphemously father'd, their monstrous heretical notions, upon the dictates of the Divine Spirit."[150]

Methodism's alleged parallels with Montanism were noted by many opponents. In this case, however, it was not doctrines but practices that were compared. Montanists, one critic believed, "were the original pattern of our present Methodists."[151] A lengthy pamphlet, *Montanus redivivus; or, Montanism revived in the principles and discipline of the Methodists,* written by James Clark, an Irish Anglican priest, catalogued the similarities between the two movements: both used laity from the lower classes as evangelists; showered contempt upon the clergy of their day; encouraged devotees to neglect their social and family responsibilities in order to immerse themselves in spiritual concerns; misused monies raised by contributions; rejected those who differed from them as not being Christians; and gave such adulation to their leaders as amounted to idolatry.[152]

---

148 026-Gr. *The Methodists: An humorous burlesque poem* (London: John Brett, 1739), 27.

149 282-Gr. Downes, *Methodism examined and exposed,* 26.

150 186-Gr. A Sincere Protestant [Zachary Grey], *A serious address to lay Methodists* (London: printed for William Russell, 1745), 19.

151 253B-Ki. Christophilus, *A serious inquiry whether a late epistle from . . . Charles Wesley to John Wesley be not an evident mark of their being fallen into one of the. . . wiles of the devil* ([London]: by the author, 1755), 15.

152 287-Gr. James Clark, *Montanus redivivus* (Dublin: H. Saunders, 1760), passim. Cf. 217-Gr. Kirkby, *The impostor detected,* 4–5; 282-Gr. Downes, *Methodism examined and exposed,* 20–25; 213-Gr. [Lavington], *The enthusiasm of Methodism and papists compar'd,* 1–9.

Methodists were also identified with Donatists. Joseph Trapp made the allegation in 1739.[153] Within two years there appeared *A short history of the Donatists,* the appendix of which (actually half the pamphlet) compared the Donatists and Methodists. Both heretical groups believed they were the only true Christians, railed at the clergy of the established church of the day, attempted to usurp pulpits belonging to the established church, met for communion in private houses, caused feuds in families, claimed to preach purer doctrine, and engaged in immoral practices.[154] Ancient heresies were not the only ones Methodists allegedly embraced. Doctrines from Anabaptism had been borrowed by Whitefield and his fellow preachers: "The spawn of Muncer, scattered here, produced a fruitful progeny of heretical and schismatical opinions, from most of which Mr. W. has borrowed something."[155] Theophilus Evans added the French Prophets to the list.[156] The accounts of frenzied conversions of the prophets during the reign of Queen Anne were paralleled by those of the Methodists.[157] William Fleetwood, a London apothecary, agreed. The Methodists were "more like French enthusiasts" than true Christians.[158] Samuel Bowden suggested that Methodists were the offspring of an unholy alliance of Rome and the French Prophets: "The spawn of French prophets and mendicant friars."[159]

Some of the most bitter charges of heresy were laid at Wesley's door by the Calvinist wing of Methodism, particularly after the printing of the *1770 Minutes of Conference.* Richard Hill fired off a volley of pamphlets attacking Wesley's doctrinal orthodoxy. Wesley's tenets were, he wrote in his *Review of all the doctrines taught by the Rev. Mr. John Wesley* (1772), a

---

153 010-Gr. Trapp, *The nature, folly, sin and danger of being righteous over-much,* 55.

154 118-Gr. Trevor, *A short history of the Donatists.*

155 032-Gr. A Curate in the Country, *Observations on the Reverend Mr. Whitefield's answer,* 36.

156 The French Prophets were a section of the French Huguenots who believed prophecies that the French Church would collapse in 1690. In preparation they trained hundreds of child-prophets to keep the apocalyptic spirit alive. Defeated in a civil war in France, they joined other Huguenots in diaspora in England and Europe, where they gained a following. In England they operated within and at the fringe of the Methodist revival. See Hillel Schwartz, *The French Prophets: The History of a Millenarian Group in Eighteenth-Century England* (Berkeley: University of California Press, 1980).

157 235-Gr. Theophilus Evans, *The history of modern enthusiasm,* 2nd ed., 130.

158 131-Gr. Fleetwood, *The perfectionists examin'd,* 3.

159 249-Gr. Bowden, "The mechanic inspired," in *Poems on various subjects,* 213.

"mixture of Pelagianism, Semi-Pelagianism, Arminianism, Popery, Mysticism, and Quakerism."[160]

Critics gave Methodism a bad name by connecting the movement with other discredited denominations. Similarities with the Quakers were exploited. In calling the Friends "one of the most pestilential sects that ever infested the Christian Church," and showing how alike the Methodists were, Joseph Trapp then transferred the opprobrium from one to the other.[161] Numerous critics tarred Methodism with the same brush they used for Quakerism. An example is James Bate's booklet *Quakero-Methodism; or a Confutation of the first principles of the Quakers and the Methodists* ([1739]).[162] Zachary Grey, in comparing the journals of Quaker founder, George Fox, with those of George Whitefield, found striking resemblances: "Both [are] fond of the same phrase and diction and their pretences to inspiration, to a very intimate familiarity with the Deity, and the power of working miracles, are of the same stamp and authority." Only on the question of tithes and attitude toward the sacrament was there any difference.[163] The author of the broadside *The parallel reformers* (1740), found the Methodists actually on the side of the Friends on all matters. Whitefield was portrayed as attacking tithes, the liturgy, and baptism—he was a schismatic establishing a new and flourishing sect.[164] As late as 1766, Methodist tenets were still being likened to Quaker doctrines.[165]

Moravianism Duplicated

Contemporary opinion, official and popular, held that Methodism and Moravianism were of the same stock. Critics of Methodism took delight in showing how much they had in common. Josiah Tucker published in 1742 what he claimed was a brief history of the revival, in which he attempted to show that one of the formative influences on Wesley's theology was Moravianism. They "infused strange particularities into him about the assurances of grace and

---

160 449-Gr. The author of *P. O.* [Sir Richard Hill], *A review of all the doctrines taught by the Rev. Mr. John Wesley* (London: for E. and C. Dilly, 1772), 92.

161 010-Gr. Trapp, *The nature, folly, sin and danger of being righteous over-much*, 61.

162 042-Gr. James Bate, *Quakero-Methodism* (London; John Carter, [1739]).

163 110-Gr. [Zachary Grey], *The Quaker and Methodist compared* (London: for J. Milan, 1740), iii.

164 109-Gr. *The parallel reformers* (London: J. Lewis, 1740).

165 385-Gr. An Independent [Samuel Newton], *The causes and reasons of the present declension among the Congregationalist churches*, 5–6.

justification." Wesley's visit in 1738 to the Moravian settlement at Herrnhut, founded by Count Zinzendorf, made him a firm disciple of the Brethren.[166] From them he learnt that conversion was instantaneous, faith alone justified, the converted had full assurance of their salvation, and the born-again Christians no longer sinned.[167] The belief that the Methodists were spiritual offspring of the Brethren persisted. An Irish author in 1752 stated that John and Charles Wesley "were the followers of Count Zinzendorf and falling off from him were excommunicated by him."[168] Thomas Church, an important critic of the revival, believed that Wesley's interest in, and commendation of, the Moravians had encouraged their growth in England. Their expansion, he thought, was due in part to Wesley's introduction of bands, modeled on the German Moravian pattern, into Methodism. This, he commented, "in all probability induced . . . them to settle here."[169] Church had no time for the Moravians, since their teaching resulted, he believed, in "scandalous contempt of all piety and goodness."[170] As Methodism espoused almost identical tenets, Church feared the consequences would be the encouragement of irreligion. Both the Brethren and the Methodists were attacked by John Roche, a Dublin clergyman, in his *Moravian Heresy* (1751). He denounced the Moravians as antinomians and more dangerous than the Methodists. Although sympathetic to the Methodists, Roche believed that "their practice and discipline savored too much of Moravianism to be tolerable."[171] Some opponents of the revival failed to distinguish between Moravians and Methodists. Both were enthusiasts; both adopted unusual practices; both preached unacceptable doctrines; both were leading their followers into separation from the Church of England; both were suspected of being puppets of foreign powers intent on rebellion. In 1740 William Bowman, vicar of Dewsbury and Aldbrough, Yorkshire, claimed in an open letter to his parishioners, entitled *The imposture of Methodism display'd*, that he was prompted to write because of "the rise of a certain modern sect of

---

166 Wesley visited Herrnhut, Saxony, in August 1738, to see the place where the Moravians lived and to witness firsthand their ethos and religious practices. Wesley, August 1, 1738–August 14, 1738, *Journals and Diaries I (1735–1738)*, in *Works* 18:266–73, 291–93.

167 150-Gr. Tucker, *A brief history of the principles of Methodism*, 21, 32.

168 235A-Ba. *A general view of the principles and spirit of the predestinarians* (Dublin: printed for G. Faulkner, 1752), 59.

169 185-Gr. Church, *Remarks on the Reverend Mr. John Wesley's journal*, 12.

170 Ibid., 24.

171 226A-Ki. John Roche, *Moravian heresy*, 286.

enthusiasts call'd Methodists."[172] He singled out Benjamin Ingham and Charles Delamotte as leaders of the new sect.[173] At the time of the publication of this tract (1740), Delamotte was closely in touch with the Moravians. Ingham handed his societies over to the Brethren within a year or two. Since some pamphleteers confused Methodists and Moravians, James McConnell's solution was to lump them together and christen them "Moravian Methodists."[174]

Papists

Opponents reveled in making the connection between Methodism and Roman Catholicism. Methodists were labeled "papists," their teachings and practices called "popish," and their leaders indicted as "Jesuits." Such similarities as could be found to exist between the two were exploited to the full by anti-Methodist authors.

The earliest critics of Methodism did not charge the movement with popery directly but implied that as an ally of Rome, it was actually aiding and abetting the Roman Catholic Church.[175] The satiric poem *The Methodist: A poem* (1766) took a further step—Methodism was an instrument of Rome. The new religious movement sprang from a pact between Satan and the Roman

---

172 094-Gr. The full title of Bowman's attack is *The imposture of Methodism display'd; in a letter to the inhabitants of the parish of Dewsbury, occasion'd by the rise of a certain modern sect of enthusiasts (among them) call'd Methodists* (London: printed for Joseph Lord, 1740). William Bowman was a graduate of Emmanuel College, Cambridge University, BA 1727–28; MA 1731. He was vicar of Aldborough, Yorkshire from 1730 to 1744. He succeeded his father, Thomas, as vicar of Dewsbury, and held the appointment of chaplain to Charles, Earl of Hopetoun. See J. A. Venn, *Alumni Cantabrigiensis* (London: Cambridge University Press, 1922–1954).

173 *ODNB*. Benjamin Ingham (1712–1772) was educated at Queen's College, Oxford. There he met John and Charles Wesley and joined the Holy Club. Shortly after ordination he accompanied the Wesleys to Georgia. On the journey there he was deeply impressed by the behavior and beliefs of the Moravians, who were also traveling to Georgia. On his return to England, he began to preach in pulpits of the churches in the Yorkshire diocese and form religious societies. Banned from the diocesan pulpits, he took to preaching in barns and private houses. In 1741 he placed his societies under Moravian control. Charles Delamotte, a young Anglican layman, also accompanied the Wesleys to Georgia. John used Delamotte in the colony as a kind of assistant in his parish work, to teach, catechize, and on rare occasions when Wesley was absent from Savannah, perform pastoral care, and perhaps even preach. See Baker, *JWCE*, 51, 79. Deeply influenced while in Georgia by the Moravians, Delamotte was finally received into the Moravian Church in 1761. See P. J. Lineham, "Charles Delamotte," in *Dictionary of Evangelical Biography 1730–1860*, vol. 1., ed. D. M. Lewis (Oxford: Blackwell, 1995).

174 204-Gr. James McConnell, *Mr. Cennicks laid open* (Dublin: for J. Gowan, 1746).

175 010-Gr. Trapp, *The nature, folly, sin and danger of being righteous over-much*, 66; 093-Gr. [Trapp], *The true spirit of the Methodists and their allies*, 33–34.

Catholic Church to win England back to papal allegiance.[176] A part of the title of a 1745 pamphlet proclaimed that "their [the Methodists'] religion is an artful introduction to popery, and directly in support of it."[177] It was Bishop Lavington's three-part attack that firmly linked the revival with popery. Lavington scoured Catholic history for examples of fanaticism, and then attempted to demonstrate that they were duplicated in Methodism: "Our modern itinerant enthusiasts are treading in their [Roman Catholic] steps and copying their example; their whole conduct being but a counter-part of the most wild fanaticisms of the most abominable communion, in its most corrupt ages."[178]

The leaders of the revival were branded as Jesuits. At first there were only vague hints to this effect. The author of *A fine picture of enthusiasm* (1744) suspected that "the Jesuit is masked, at least, in one character."[179] The net was cast wider by Zachary Grey: "[M]ay not some of those gentlemen, who inveigh so bitterly against the church establish'd, be papists in disguise?"[180] The Methodists denied the charge, but the denial fell on deaf ears and the charge persisted. Lavington reminded his readers that the history of the Jesuit mission to England in the sixteenth century showed that "a Jesuit's or enthusiast's declaiming against popery [was] no test of their sincerity."[181]

Charges of popish practices were multifarious: Like Roman Catholics, Methodists claimed salvation was available only to those of their own flock; Methodists encouraged the use of images (examples of band and class tickets with crucifixes imprinted on them had allegedly been found); what went on in band and classes by way of intimate spiritual examination resembled closely popish private, auricular confession; prayers for the dead were used by Methodists—this countenanced the Catholic doctrine of purgatory; Methodists sold absolutions of sin comparable to Roman indulgences; while Roman Catholics placed infallibility in popes or councils, Methodists invested it in their leaders or those of their followers who had reached perfection; Methodists inculcated

---

176 379-Gr. The author of *The powers of the pew* and *The Curate* [Evan Lloyd], *The Methodist: a poem*, 11, 12.

177 See the title of 194-Gr. An Impartial Hand, *An essay containing evident proofs against the Methodists, from certain of their secret articles and practices that their religion is an artful introduction to popery, and directly in support of it* (London: by the author, [1745]).

178 213-Gr. [Lavington], *The enthusiasm of Methodists and papists compar'd*, pt. 1, iii.

179 174-Gr. Eusebius [Caleb Evans], *A fine picture of enthusiasm*, iv.

180 186-Gr. A sincere protestant [Zachary Grey], *A serious address to lay Methodists*, 3.

181 213-Gr. [Lavington], *The enthusiasm of Methodists and papists compar'd*, pt. 2, 184.

the popish practice of celibacy; Methodism preferred the monastic life and set up the Foundery as a kind of Jesuit college to achieve this.[182]

Critics delighted in drawing analogies between the revival's leaders and the great Catholic saints. Lavington, in 1749, listed the excesses of the Catholic saints Ignatius, Francis founder of the Friars Minor, Dominic, Catherine of Sienna, and Anthony of Padua and quoted what he believed were parallels from the journals and other writings of Whitefield and Wesley.[183] A decade earlier, Samuel Weller had drawn similar parallels between Methodists and the thirteenth-century mendicant orders of Catholicism.[184]

The tenets of Methodism, furthermore, were linked with those of Catholicism. An Irish writer noted: "Nor is there a single article peculiar to Methodism, or any other sect of fanaticks, or enthusiasts, that was not spawned out of the dirt, and dregs of popery."[185] Anti-Methodists conjectured that Wesley's distinction between "opinion" and "essential truth" opened the door for countenancing Catholic theological errors.[186]

Suspicions about Methodism's similarities to Catholics were confirmed when Wesley issued his Letter to a Roman Catholic (1749).[187] Critics noted that Wesley did not ask Roman Catholics to leave or change their religion, nor did he criticize Roman opinions or liturgy, but emphasized areas of agreement. The conclusion to be drawn, thought an anonymous author, was that "Mr. Wesley's sentiments are nearly allied to those of the Church of Rome."[188] This belief was fostered, too, by those who were appalled at

---

182 094-Gr. Bowman, The imposture of Methodism display'd, 46; 174-Gr. Eusebius [Caleb Fleming], A fine picture of enthusiasm, 24–25; 194-Gr. Impartial Hand, An essay containing evident proofs against the Methodists, 10, 15–16; 213-Gr. [Lavington], The enthusiasm of Methodists and papists compar'd, pt. 2, 166; 516-Gr. [Combe], The saints (London; for J. Bew, 1778); 531-Gr. John Muirhead, A review of the principles of such Methodists as are under the direction of . . . Wesley (Kelso: J. Palmer, 1784), 29; 517-Gr. [Combe], Perfection, 33.

183 213-Gr. [Lavington], The enthusiasm of Methodists and papists compar'd pt. 1, 9–12.

184 098-Gr. [Weller), The trial of Mr. Whitefield's spirit, 3.

185 248A-Ba. A Lay-man, A few queries concerning the growth of Methodism, 13.

186 John Wesley, "Orthodoxy, or right opinion, is at best a slender part of religion, if it can be allowed to be any at all," A Plain Account of the People called Methodists in a letter to the Revd. Mr. Perronet, Vicar of Shoreham, Kent, in Works, vol. 9, The Methodist Societies: History, Nature, and Design, ed., Rupert E. Davies, 253–280.

187 John Wesley, "A Letter to a Roman Catholic," Works (Jackson), 10:80–86.

188 467-Gr. A faithful warning to the followers of the Reverend John Wesley (London: Keith, Buckland & Lewis & Mathews, 1744), iv.

Wesley's recommendation of writings by Catholics, and by his publishing extracts of Catholic works such as *The Life of M. de Renty* (1741).[189]

Most accusations about the similarities of Methodism and Roman Catholicism were vague. Opponents did not bother to indicate precisely the alleged correlations between Methodist and Roman Catholic theology. The Calvinists who attacked Wesley's doctrinal stance, however, were different. To a person, they believed that Wesley and those who followed him in assuming an Arminian position on salvation had apostatized. Wesley's Methodism taught justification by works—a popish doctrine. The Hill brothers and Augustus Toplady combed Wesley's writings for statements that, when quoted out of context, made him seem more than sympathetic to Rome. John McGowan, formerly one of Wesley's local preachers who became a Calvinist, reported that in the early 1780s, with the relaxation of the government's attitude to Roman Catholic worship, large numbers of Methodists had begun to frequent Catholic chapels in Manchester and Lancashire. His explanation was: "This attachment of the Wesleyans to the popish worship can arise from nothing but the oneness of the doctrine published in Mr. Wesley's and the popish chapels."[190]

Anti-Methodist authors exploited the political undertones of the epithet "papist." The Jacobite supporters of the Stuart dynasty were identified in the popular imagination with the papists. The two terms "papist" and "Jacobite" were used interchangeably as forms of insult. By linking "Methodist" and "papist" opponents made use of the tactic of guilt by verbal association and stigmatized Methodists as "Jacobites," and thus part of the political underground.[191] Even when they were not stereotyped as papists and Jacobites, Methodists were depicted as schismatics, subverting the ecclesiastical establishment. Since church and state were so closely aligned in the eighteenth century, an attack on the church was also an attack on the state.[192]

Ascetics

Methodism's antagonists believed that the Methodists' zeal for righteousness amounted to a new kind of Puritanism. They portrayed Methodists as going to

---

189 213-Gr. [Lavington], *The enthusiasm of Methodists and papists compar'd*, pt. 2, 172–78.
190 525-Gr. MacGowan, *The Foundry budget opened*, 47.
191 For a fuller discussion of this aspect see chapter 7, "Methodism and Politics."
192 See chapter 6, "The Church in Danger," for a fuller account.

extremes in religious life. Joseph Trapp's seminal pamphlet *The nature, folly, sin and danger of being righteous over-much* (1739), established the pattern for attacks on the excessive righteousness of the revival's participants. Trapp warned:

> To be constant and frequent in prayer, and other religious exercises, is the duty of every Christian; but . . . to spend so much time in those exercises as to neglect all other necessary duties, or even any one other necessary duty, is contrary to his duty.[193]

One adversary contended that the Methodists had turned the virtue of righteous living into a vice: "Being over-righteous is a sin, a very great sin indeed."[194] Bishop Gibson admonished the Methodists for self-righteous fanaticism by raising "religion to greater heights and greater abstractions from common life, than Christ and his Apostles made and designed it."[195] The Methodists had made the practice of religion so difficult, he thought, that it would discourage people from spiritual endeavors. The end result would be that religion would be restricted to a few. Satan's plan, Tristram Land suggested, was to give the Methodists an overdose of religion to destroy their faith.[196]

Methodists, Trapp alleged, looked down on those who did not meet their unrealistic standards. Excessive righteousness engendered spiritual pride. Opponents delighted in showing that despite the Methodists' ascetic religiosity, they were sinners like everyone else.[197] Activities such as rigorous fasting and regular hours for prayer were criticized as making the Christian life too austere.[198] James Lackington illustrated the dangers of fasting. In one London family, he claimed "the mistress was deprived of her senses, and the maid literally fasted herself to death."[199] There were other instances, reported John Maud, rector of Steeple Giddings and vicar of St. Neots, where their striving for virtuous living had made some Methodists virtual recluses.[200]

---

193 010-Gr. Trapp, *The nature, folly, sin and danger of being righteous over-much*, 7.
194 025-Gr. *The mock–preacher*, 27–28.
195 029-Gr. [Gibson], *The bishop of London's pastoral letter*, 30.
196 009-Gr. Land, *A letter to the Rev. Mr. Whitefield*, 9.
197 174-Gr. Eusebius [Caleb Fleming], *A fine picture of enthusiasm*, 25.
198 018-Gr. John Wilder, *The trial of the spirits*, 17.
199 560-Gr. Lackington, *Memoirs of the . . . life of James Lackington*, 319.
200 191-Gr. John Maud, *An apology for the clergy, in a letter to a gentleman of fortune* (Cambridge: R. Walker and T. James, 1745), 11.

The indifference of the Methodists to material things was criticized—they were careless in dress; they never washed or mended their clothes.[201] One satirist ridiculed the extent to which Whitefield carried his abstinence and mortification:

> A lousy pate was deemed humility; foul linen heavenly contemplation; . . . a patched gown justification by faith; and dirty shoes, was walking with God . . . [Satan] taught him that religion consisted wholly in nastiness; that heaven was easiest attacked from a dunghill; and that the surest way for a man to obtain it was by his sloth and sordidness.[202]

Methodism had made religion a negative thing; the Christian life was reduced to misery; life was joyless. Eighteenth-century Anglicans looked upon Methodists as laughterless spoilsports who disapproved of all fun.[203] James Lackington recounted the dullness of his early life as a Methodist: "From a gay, volatile, dissipated young fellow [I] was at once metamorphosed into a dull, moping, praying, psalm-singing fanatic, continually reprehending all about me for their harmless mirth and gaiety."[204] Another author wondered if there had ever been a true Methodist "without that sad and dismal Devil's painting in his countenance."[205] Bishop Warburton, accepting the caricature of the joyless Methodist, believed that Wesley had resolved, after his conversion, never to laugh again.[206]

The caricature was complete. Enthusiasm, anti-intellectualism, irrationality, insanity, hypocrisy, censoriousness, spiritual vanity, antinomianism, immorality, heresy, popery, sentimentalism, fear mongering, asceticism—the features of the "typical" Methodist were drawn from such charges. It was a sketch so absurd as to cause Methodism to be ridiculed wherever it showed its face.

---

201 See the scurrilous introduction to 293-Gr. [John Beveridge], *A fragment of true religion* (London: for J. Williams, 1760), iii–iv.

202 006A-Ba. A Gentleman of Oxford [Ralph Jephson], *The Methodists dissected* (Oxford: for the author [1739]). Reprinted in 1740 under the title *The expounder expounded*. See second edition with changed title, 139–Ki., A Gentleman of Oxford [Ralph Jephson], *Methodism and enthusiasm fully displayed*, 58.

203 174A-Ba. William Howdell, *Religion productive of joy and consistent with politeness* (York: Caesar Ward, 1744), 6–8.

204 560-Gr. Lackington, *Memoirs of the . . . life of James Lackington*, 156.

205 476-Gr. *A letter to a friend on the subject of Methodism* (n.p.: no printer, 1775), 26–27.

206 342-Gr. [William Warburton], *The doctrine of grace*, 193.

CHAPTER 3

Doctrinal Deviation

The closing of Anglican parish pulpits to the leaders of the Methodist revival in 1739 was due in the main to the movement's distinctive doctrines, which critics believed were not in harmony with those of the Church of England. Wesley, however, continually disclaimed any doctrinal differences between the Church of England and Methodism. Asked in what points of theology the Methodists differed from the Church, Wesley replied, "To the best of my knowledge, in none. The doctrines we preach are the doctrines of the Church of England: indeed, the fundamental doctrines of the Church, clearly laid down, both in her Prayers, Articles, and Homilies."[1]

Throughout his career Wesley was "scrupulously loyal" to his theological heritage and insisted that Methodist doctrine was Church of England doctrine.[2] Recounting a sermon preached on October 15, 1739, he declared, "I simply declared the plain old religion of the Church of England, which is now almost everywhere spoken against, under the new name of Methodism."[3] In several of his apologiae, Wesley defended his claim that he stood fairly and squarely within the Anglican tradition.[4] Even as late as 1777, on the occasion of the laying of the foundation stone of his new chapel at City Road, London, he reminded his listeners that Methodism was "the old religion . . . the religion of the Church of England."[5] Throughout his life, to support his statement that he preached authentic Anglican theology, Wesley appealed to the principal documents of the sixteenth-century Anglican Reformation—the Thirty-nine Articles, the Book of Common Prayer, and the Book of Homilies—but always

---

1 John Wesley, September 13, 1739, *BEWJW*, vol. 19, *Journals and Diaries II (1738–1743)*, ed. W. Reginald Ward and Richard P. Heitzenrater (Nashville: Abingdon, 1976), 96.

2 Gerald Cragg, introduction to vol. II, *The Appeals to Men of Reason and Religion*, in *BEWJW*, 9.

3 John Wesley, October 19, 1739, *BEWJW*, 19:106.

4 John Wesley, *A Farther Appeal to Men of Reason and Religion*, pt. 1 (1745) in *BEWJW*, 11:105–202.

5 John Wesley, Sermon 112, "On Laying the Foundation of the New Chapel," in *BEWJW*, vol. 3, *Sermons III*, ed. Albert C. Outler (Nashville: Abingdon, 1976–), 585.

as they were interpreted in the works of the seventeenth-century theologians.[6] It is not surprising that his detractors, a generation nurtured on John Locke, John Tillotson, and Samuel Clarke, viewed his tenets as aberrations of the theological heritage they venerated. Wesley may have been in tune with historic Anglicanism, but he was out of tune with its eighteenth-century manifestation.

Methodist orthodoxy on such matters as the Trinity and the nature of Christ was never questioned. It was the Methodists' evangelical tenets that Anglicans found offensive. Salvation was the center of Methodist theology— the preachers of the revival were concerned chiefly with pointing their listeners to "the way to heaven."[7] Methodist preaching in 1739 and the 1740s focused on the saving work of Christ and human appropriation of that work in their lives.[8] Whitefield and the Wesleys called on their hearers to repent and become "new creatures" in Christ. Just as Jesus challenged Nicodemus to be born again, so the Methodists urged the crowds that followed them to experience the "new birth."

Regeneration and assurance were the earliest Methodist doctrines to receive criticism. Attacks on those doctrines, which came as early as 1738, continued throughout the 1740s and 1750s, but were less frequent in the 1760s and thereafter. Also assailed early was the Methodist emphasis on the doctrine of the Holy Spirit. Disparaged in a number of pamphlets before 1745, the main assault came after that date, culminating in 1763 in Warburton's *Doctrine of Grace*. The Methodist formulation of the doctrine of justification was criticized in the 1740s also, but the strongest opposition to it came in the 1750s and 1760s. Although Wesley's emphasis on Christian perfection was

---

6 See Gerald C. Cragg, introduction to *The Appeals to Men of Reason and Religion*, in *BEWJW*, 11:9. Only biblical quotations in Wesley's writings outnumber references to the Anglican Standards: the Thirty–nine Articles, the Book of Common Prayer, and the Book of Homilies.

7 John Wesley, *BEWJW*, vol. 1, *Sermons on Several Occasions (1–33)* (1746), ed. Albert C. Outler (Nashville: Abingdon, 1984), preface, 105. See Colin Williams, *John Wesley's Theology Today* (New York: Abingdon, 1960), 39–41; Rupert Davies, "The People Called Methodist, Our Doctrines," in Rupert Davies and Gordon Rupp, eds., *History of The Methodist Church in Great Britain* (London: Epworth, 1965), 147–48; Theodore Runyon, *The New Creation: John Wesley's Theology Today* (Nashville: Abingdon, 1998), chap. 1, "The Renewal of the Image of God," 13–25; and chap. 2, "Grace in the New Creation," 26–70.

8 Outler notes that "the burden of [Wesley's] evangelical message was always the same; the references were almost monotonous. He speaks of 'preaching Christ,' of 'offering Christ,' of 'proclaiming Christ,' and 'declaring Christ.'" Albert C. Outler, *Theology in the Wesleyan Spirit* (Nashville: Tidings, 1975), 46.

also noticed unfavorably in the early years of the revival, the most forceful attacks upon it appeared in the 1750s and 1760s, and mainly from the Calvinist wing. In spite of their importance, Methodist emphases on providence, persecution, and "catholicity" received a good deal less criticism.

Use of Scripture

Underlying much of the criticism of Methodist theology was opposition to the way the Methodists viewed and used or abused the scriptures.[9] Evangelicals claimed to stand with the Reformers on the principle of sola Scriptura. In matters of faith and practice, scripture, they said, was their final authority. It was the norm by which all their doctrines were to be judged.

Critics recognized that the Methodists knew their Bible but charged that they did not understand how to use it. The Methodists, critics maintained, were too fond of proof-texting, wrenching biblical quotations out of their contexts and stringing them together to buttress their tenets. Such use of scripture, opponents said, violated the integrity of the Bible. Leveled at Whitefield and Wesley from the outset of the revival, this criticism followed the evangelicals all their careers.[10] Minor figures in the Methodist movement also came under fire for this practice.[11] Summed up by John Downes in 1759, the charge was that Methodists

> pretend to build all their doctrines or notions upon Scripture authority; but then, it is by wresting and straining those sacred books, putting texts to the tortures, and racking them till they will speak to their purpose, dealing arbitrarily with them . . . and to say all at once, practising every means or method of perversion.[12]

While the Methodists were occasionally accused of interpreting the scriptures too literally, a more common charge was that they ignored the literal sense

---

9 For Wesley's use of Scripture, see Scott J. Jones, *John Wesley's Conception and Use of Scripture* (Nashville: Kingswood Books, 1995), and Mark L. Weeter, *John Wesley's View and Use of Scripture* (Eugene, OR: Wipf and Stock, 2007), 151–54.

10 205C-Ki. W— D— [William Dowars], *Errors in part discovered*, 5; 256-Gr. One of the Clergy/Clericus [Caleb Fleming], *A letter to the Revd. Mr. John Wesley, occasioned by his 'Address to the Clergy'* (London: M. Cooper, 1756), 4; 245-Gr. John Parkhurst, *A serious and friendly address to the Reverend Mr. John Wesley* (London: for J. Withers, 1753), 16–17; 034-Gr. Bate, *Methodism displayed; or, Remarks upon Mr. Whitefield's answer*, 3.

11 See 217A-Ki. Nathaniel Fletcher, *A vindication of the 'Methodist Dissected,'* 13–14.

12 282-Gr. Downes, *Methodism examined and exposed*, 34–35.

and delighted in allegorizing. In the hands of the Methodists, averred Thomas Davies, the Bible had been "miserably burlesqued and twisted into every fanciful meaning that a heated imagination might suggest."[13] As evidence of this, he noted an instance of a Methodist preacher who, in expounding the parable of the good Samaritan, alleged that the two pence given to the innkeeper for the care of the wounded man were to be understood as symbols of the Old and New Testaments.[14] Another author contended that the Methodists took delight in expounding the most obscure books of the Bible (particularly the Song of Solomon and the Revelation of John) because such writings afforded "the widest play for the imagination, and . . . fancy is laid under no restraint."[15]

The typological interpretation of the Old Testament employed by a number of Methodist authors (particularly the Calvinists) offended some critics. Evangelicals saw Christ foreshadowed in many obscure Old Testament details. Though some passages were capable of such an interpretation, the Methodists stretched the meaning of others to make their typological interpretations fit.[16]

Strong objection was taken to the alleged subjective approach of the Methodists to scripture. In claiming they received direct inspiration when reading scripture, Methodists emphasized private judgment. They rejected all aids (especially reason and learned expositions of the scripture) in interpreting what they read, setting themselves up as their own infallible interpreters.[17] The conspicuous subjectivism of Methodist biblical interpretation was contrasted with the method approved by the Church. Bishop Gibson explained that difficulty in understanding obscure passages was resolved, not by appeal to immediate inspiration, but by "comparing scripture with scripture, and by just and regular reasonings upon it, where need is, by having recourse to the expositions of writers of known learning and judgement."[18]

---

13 490A-Ki. Thomas Davies, *Rational religion recommended* (Lewes: William Lee, 1776), 32.

14 Ibid. 315-Gr. Academicus [John Green], *The principles of the Methodists farther considered*, 69.

15 555-Gr. *A review of the policy, doctrines and morals of the Methodists*, 24.

16 252-Gr. [Douglas], *An apology for the clergy with a view to expose the groundless assertions of a late commentator*, 26–28.

17 272A-Ki. [Robert] Potter, *An appendix to the sermon on the pretended inspiration of the Methodists* (Norwich: printed and sold by W. Chase, 1758), 21; 268-Gr. [Thomas Mortimer], *Die and be damned* (London: printed for S. Hooper and A. Morley, 1758), 17; 282-Gr. Downes, *Methodism examined and exposed*, 54.

18 029-Gr. [Gibson], *The bishop of London's pastoral letter*, 28.

Other authors suggested further rules of textual criticism that the Methodists might use: the text should be read in the original Greek or Hebrew; a passage should be understood in its proper context; the purpose of the author of a particular book should be ascertained.[19] Wesley's Roman Catholic opponent, Bishop Challenor, chided the Methodists for setting aside tradition as the means for checking their own interpretations of the scripture. "What," he asked, "more intolerant pride and self-conceit can there possibly be, or rather, what more extravagant madness than for any one private Christian to think himself wiser than the whole Church of Christ?"[20] Scriptural images were frequently used by Methodist leaders (chiefly Whitefield) in describing their work and the revival's progress. Such metaphoric applications of biblical phrases, critics charged, was an inappropriate, even blasphemous, use of scripture.[21]

Wesley's *Explanatory Notes upon the New Testament* was published in 1755.[22] As well as explanatory notes, this volume carried the full text of the New Testament, which included a number of changes by Wesley. Disclaiming altering for altering's sake, Wesley claimed to adhere closely to the King James Version. Some passages, however, he changed, claiming that either a better rendition of the original Greek was necessary, or that the Authorized Version's meaning was not clear. It might have been expected that such a major publication as this would have received much critical notice, but such was not the case. The only attack of any substance came in a 1756 pamphlet entitled *An expostulatory letter to the Rev. Mr. Wesley*. The bone of contention of the authors was that Wesley's amendment of the biblical text was arbitrary.

---

19 254-Gr. Griffith, *The use and extent of reason in matters of religion*, 20–21; 353A-Ba. A Professor of Christianity, *A scriptural account of the doctrine of perfection* (London: for T. Becker, 1763), 5.

20 311D-Gr. [Challenor], *A caveat against the Methodists*, 14.

21 For a fuller discussion of this aspect, see chapter 2, "The Methodist Caricature."

22 John Wesley, *Explanatory Notes upon the New Testament* (London: William Bowyer, 1755).

They chided him for not designating the changes he had made and of not noting the reasons for his changes.[23]

A further attack on Wesley's *Notes* appeared in Gilbert Boyce's defense of baptism by immersion. Boyce charged Wesley with deliberately tampering with scripture. Where the Authorized Version of Acts 8:33–39 read: "They went down both into the water, both Philip and the eunuch," Wesley printed, "They both went to the water." Wesley made a similar change in Mark 1:9, where he substituted "at" for "in"— the text reading "Jesus . . . was baptized at Jordan," rather than "in Jordan." Boyce advised Wesley to refrain from allowing his anti-Baptist prejudices to influence his translation of the Bible.[24]

Bibliomancy and Sortilege

Other customs for decision-making at which anti-Methodists scoffed were the casting of lots, a practice known as *sortilege*, and opening the Bible at random, a practice known as *bibliomancy*.[25] Both Whitefield and Wesley employed these methods on occasion and defended their use as a last resort. Scripture and reason were the Christian's guides, but when they failed to provide firm direction, Wesley believed that the use of lots or opening the Scriptures at random was warranted.[26] Moreover, since those methods were not expressly forbidden in scripture, they could be employed.

Antagonists, however, could find no justification for the practices. Opening the Bible at random, Thomas Church wrote, was a misuse of scripture

---

23 265-Gr. B., W., C., G., M., J., &c. [Fawcett], *An expostulatory letter to the Rev. Mr. Wesley*, 12–15. This tract was possibly written by the Reverend Richard Fawcett, lecturer at St. John the Evangelist, Leeds (1732–57), and lecturer at St. Peter's, Leeds (1757–70). See handwritten attribution of authorship to Richard Fawcett on the title page of the pamphlet held at General Theological Seminary, New York. It was purportedly written, however, by several of Wesley's lay preachers, whose initials are listed in the pamphlet; it may have been written by Richard Fawcett, a prominent Bradford merchant, Methodist class leader, and local preacher for almost fifty years. See James Norton Dickons, *Kirkgate Chapel, Bradford, and its associations with Methodism* (Bradford, UK: privately printed, 1903), 43. Those who signed the *Letter* claimed to be Wesley's preachers, who were offended by many of the requirements for the clergy set forth in Wesley's *Address*.

24 428-Gr. Boyce, *A serious reply to the Rev. Mr. John Wesley*, 127. Boyce claimed Wesley allowed his "opinion and practises" to influence his translation of New Testament verses from the Greek.

25 See Weeter, *John Wesley's View and Use of Scripture*, 151–54. See also E. H. Sugden, ed., *The Standard Sermons of John Wesley* (London: Epworth, 1964), 2:96–97n22.

26 John Wesley, "The Principles of a Methodist Farther Explained," (1746), §8, in *Works*, vol. 9, *The Methodist Societies: History, Nature, and Design*, 160–237, 201–2.

and led the Methodists into many idle and fanciful interpretations, while drawing lots to determine difficult issues was rash and extravagant. In sum, "prudence is set aside and affairs of moment [are] left to be determined by chance."[27] Bishop Lavington stigmatized the customs as "heathen superstition."[28] Even the Methodists' most distinctive doctrines had been chosen by lot, contended satirical poet William Combe.[29] Former Methodist James Lackington recorded how he was cured of bibliomancy and sortilege while still a young apprenticed shoemaker living with his master's family. Forbidden by his master's wife from attending a Methodist meeting, James was locked in the house. When he turned to the scriptures for guidance, the Bible fell open at the text "He has given his angels guard over thee, lest at any time thou shouldest dash thy foot against a stone."[30] Believing this to be a message of divine intervention, young Lackington ran up two flights of stairs to his room and jumped from a window, bruising his feet and ankles so severely it took him a month to recover. James's rash act also bruised his ego: "Some few admired my amazing strength of faith, but the majority part pitied me as a poor, ignorant, deluded and infatuated boy."[31]

Inspiration

The frequent charge of enthusiasm made against the Methodists was based on their teaching of the Holy Spirit. The Methodists asserted that the Holy Spirit could and did, in a direct manner, inspire eighteenth-century Christians. Anglican critics in opposing this position drew a clear distinction between the Holy Spirit's "extraordinary" and "ordinary" operations or gifts. The extraordinary gifts had been given by the Holy Spirit to the apostles and the early church, while the ordinary gifts were bestowed by the Spirit upon all people in all ages.

Extraordinary gifts were entrusted to men and women in the apostolic and early church to enable them to achieve rapidly the propagation of the

---

27 205-Gr. Church, *Some farther remarks on the Reverend Mr. John Wesley's last journal*, 121, 124.

28 213-Gr. [Lavington], *The enthusiasm of Methodists and papists compar'd*, 71–74.

29 521-Gr. [Combe], *Fanatical conversion*, 14.

30 Matthew 4:6, as cited in 560-Gr. Lackington, *Memoirs of . . . the life of James Lackington*, 53–54.

31 560-Gr. Lackington, 53–54.

faith. Robert Potter explained how the conditions of the world in the first three centuries necessitated special gifts:

> When the apostles first receiv'd their commission to spread the gospel to all nations, their minds were praepossess'd in favour of a carnal law and their understandings thereby peculiarly indispos'd to receive the spiritual doctrines of the gospel: hence that abundant effusion of the Holy Ghost to enlighten their minds, to remove their prejudices, and guide them into all truth. The world around them was also praeengag'd in religious institutions whose nature, genius, and spirit were directly opposite to the dictates of the everlasting gospel: They had to contend with the violence and obstinacy of the Jews, the pride and scorn of the philosophers, and the passions and interests of mankind at large: to overcome these it was requisite that Christ shou'd work with them "thro' mighty signs and wonders by the power of the spirit of God." They were also to stand before counsels and synagogues and rulers and kings; to suffer all that malice cou'd inflict and humanity endure, persecutions, and torments, and deaths: to support them under this fiery trial the assistance of the Comforter was necessary.[32]

The consensus among leading eighteenth-century clerics was that the extraordinary gifts of the Holy Spirit had been limited to the first three centuries. Once Christianity was established, they were withdrawn, no longer needed in a church that had advanced from infancy to maturity. Like pieces of "scaffolding of a palace now compleated," wrote Warburton, "they were removed once their usefulness had passed."[33]

Christianity, then, could be divided into two dispensations: the first was the apostolic period (from Christ to the third century), in which special gifts of the Holy Spirit were bestowed; the second was the post-Constantine period (from the third to the eighteenth centuries), when the Holy Spirit bestowed only ordinary gifts. Those who lived in the second dispensation had no claim to the extraordinary gifts of the first.[34]

---

32 272A-Ki. [Robert] Potter, *An appendix to the sermon on the pretended inspiration of the Methodists*, 25.

33 342-Gr. [Warburton], *The doctrine of grace*, 192, 112–13. See also 042-Gr. Bate, *Quakero-Methodism*, 22, and 029-Gr. [Gibson], *The bishop of London's pastoral letter*, 12.

34 338-Gr. Penn, *Various tracts*, 117–18. See also 167-Gr. Smalbroke, *A charge deliver'd to the reverend the clergy . . . in the diocese of Lichfield . . . 1741*, 8–9; 156A-Ba. Dockwray,

The miraculous gifts of the Holy Spirit given to the early church were: healing of diseases, power to suspend or control the laws of nature, speaking in tongues, interpreting tongues, exorcism, prophetic dreams and visions, and dramatic conversions.[35] In contrast, the ordinary gifts were: the illumination of the Christian's understanding of the gospel, the encouraging of devotion to Christ, and the sanctification of the Christian's life. Critics charged that Methodists made too many claims for the Holy Spirit's work in the present age. Warburton, in accusing Wesley of laying "claim to almost every apostolic gift and grace; and in as full and ample a measure as they were possessed of old," expressed the charge succinctly.[36] Claims that they received not only the Holy Spirit's ordinary, but the extraordinary gifts, sounded like blasphemy to people of the Age of Reason. Demands that the Methodists prove their claims were issued from a number of quarters. Since the disputants believed that the early Christian leaders had verified their claims to special inspiration by working miracles, Methodists were called upon to validate their alleged gifts in like manner. Thomas Church threw down the gauntlet: "Miracles were wrought to support their [the apostles'] pretences to inspiration. These were, and still are, the proper demonstrations of the Spirit, the only proofs that an extraordinary power of the Holy Ghost came upon them. Whoever, therefore, pretends to such a power must make good his claim by the same proofs."[37] Other critics issued similar challenges; they made it plain that unless the Methodists could support their claims by performing miracles, they would be considered enthusiasts.[38]

Disputants believed the Methodist doctrine of inspiration smacked of subjectivism. The teaching that the effects of the Holy Spirit were 'sensible'—that people could know they were inspired because of an inner sensation—offended rationality. How could such sensations be distinguished from those

---

The operations of the Holy Spirit imperceptible, 7–10; 342-Gr. [Warburton], The doctrine of grace, 3; 029-Gr. [Gibson], The bishop of London's pastoral letter, 12.

35 034-Gr. James Bate, Methodism displayed; or, Remarks upon Mr. Whitefield's answer, 13; 342-Gr. [Warburton], The doctrine of grace, 123–38.

36 342-Gr. [Warburton], The doctrine of grace, 116.

37 049-Gr. Church, An explanation and defense of the doctrine of the Church of England, 52.

38 167-Gr. Smalbroke, A charge deliver'd to the . . . clergy in the diocese of Lichfield . . . 1741, 46. See similar statements in 018-Gr. Wilder, The trial of the spirits, 15; 094-Gr. Bowman, The imposture of Methodism display'd, 4; 315-Gr. Academicus [John Green], The principles and practices of the Methodists farther considered, 31–32.

created by the imagination? Critics agreed that they could not—the Holy
Spirit's activity was not open to human perception.

> How to distinguish . . . heavenly motions and suggestions from the
> natural operations of our own minds, we have no light to discover;
> the Scriptures being herein entirely silent, or rather declaring that
> the operations of the Holy Spirit are not subject to any sensible
> feelings or perceptions. For what communications can there be
> between feelings or touches which are properties peculiar to body
> or matter, and the suggestions of the Spirit which are of a quite
> different nature? [39]

Thomas Green reminded Methodists of the saying of Jesus concerning the
Spirit:

> Our Saviour compares them [the Spirit's communications] to the
> wind, whose sound we hear, but cannot tell whence it cometh,
> John 3:8 . . . So that though the Spirit may produce great and good
> effects in us, and we are in no doubt about the Spirit's indwellings
> and operations; yet we cannot say that such a particular thought
> or opinion was owing to the Spirit's immediate direction.[40]

Critics of Methodism agreed. Foote's fictional Shadrack Bodkin parodied
the Methodists' experience that the Holy Spirit's influence was discernable:

> One day I was sitting cross legged on my shop board [and] I felt
> the spirit within me, moving upwards and downwards, and this
> way and that way, and tumbling and fumbling. At first I thought
> it was cholic.[41]

On another occasion Bodkin described "thumps, scratches, and bumps" on
his breastbone emanating from the Spirit within him.[42]

In the journals of the early Methodists (particularly Whitefield's), antagonists found numerous instances where the evangelicals had been too freely

---

39 156A-Ba. Dockwray, *The operations of the Holy Spirit imperceptible*, 11–12.

40 249A-Fi. Green, *A dissertation on enthusiasm*, 11–12. See 034-Gr. Bate, *Methodism displayed; or, Remarks upon Mr. Whitefield's answer*, 23; 272-Gr. [Robert Potter], *On the
pretended inspiration of the Methodists*, 21–22; 380-Gr. Rotheram, *An essay on faith and
its connection to good works*, 110.

41 341D-Ki. Foote, *The orators*, 44.

42 Ibid., 41–42.

attributing feelings, thoughts, and decisions to divine influence. Gibson declared himself suspicious of the Methodist leaders for "making inward, secret and sudden impulses the guides of their actions, resolutions and designs."[43] Methodists would be judged, their critics told them, not by their assertions that they were being guided by the Holy Spirit, but by the quality of their lives—lives "of piety and virtue and obeying to the utmost of our power all the laws and commandments of Jesus Christ. For the doing of his commandments is the only test he makes of being his disciples."[44] A prudent Christian would not say, "I have the Holy Spirit," but rather leave it to others to make the judgment from the person's behavior.

Although Anglican critics scorned the Methodists for placing too great a reliance on direct inspiration, Quakers maintained the opposite, that the Methodists slighted the Holy Spirit. Wesley, Joanna Hawkins said, by relying too heavily on Scripture for guidance, refused to follow the Spirit's dictates. Methodist preachers, like their leader, were "Bible adorers." All Methodists ought to put aside "the dead letter," and wait in silence for the Spirit's direction.[45]

Providence

Reflection on past events convinced the Methodists that the hand of God had guided their lives and protected them. On numerous occasions in their journals, Whitefield and Wesley attributed natural events to supernatural instigation, convinced that such instances of divine interference with the natural order of things were performed on their behalf. While the Methodists jubilantly announced providential intervention in their lives, their contemporaries indignantly denied the assertions. It was irrational, complained John Brownsword, "to suppose providence interfering in every minute circumstance of life, which consider'd in itself, might have no tendency either to good or evil, but [is] entirely indifferent as to either."[46] T. Gib found Whitefield's thanking God for diverting a waterspout the height of absurdity—it was not a miracle wrought

---

43 164-Gr. [Gibson], *Observations upon the conduct and behaviour of . . . Methodists*, 14; 039-Gr. J. B. [John Brownsword], *Remarks on the continuation of Mr. Whitefield's journal* (London: for T. Cooper, 1739), 2, 3, 11.

44 156A-Ba. Dockwray, *The operations of the Holy Spirit imperceptible*, 11–12.

45 214A-Ki. Hawkins, *A letter to John Wesley*, 1, 7.

46 039-Gr. J. B. [Brownsword], *Remarks on the continuation of Mr. Whitefield's journal*, 2.

for Whitefield's safety, but a natural phenomenon.[47] It was blasphemous to see the hand of God in every fortuitous event in life. Antagonists reminded the Methodists that God did not operate the world for the benefit of a favored few. Thomas Church, commenting on passages from Wesley's journal, wrote, "I know of no ground either from scripture, reason, or experience, for a good man to hope or pray for such immediate reliefs, as the ceasing of rain, the moon's breaking out, &c. to prevent his suffering through wet and cold."[48]

Bishop Lavington found in the Methodists' doctrine of providence evidence of their arrogance—Whitefield's hoarseness disappears just before preaching; Wesley is freed from the effects of a fever while speaking at a love feast; the rain and storms are controlled for their benefit: "You see the peculiar privileges of such conceited favourites of heaven. The common course of providence must be altered for their sake; and all nature be made subservient to their whimsical dispensations."[49]

Resentment was expressed at the evangelicals' insistence that Methodism had been providentially raised up to revive the nation. In denying that God was using the movement as an extraordinary instrument for his work, Bishop Gibson challenged the leaders: "Whether they have given, or can give, any proof, either that God is now bringing-about such extraordinary work; or, if they were, that they are the persons singled-out, and employed by [God], to carry it on."[50]

Persecution

Wesley maintained that Christians must suffer because they are righteous. Salvation and persecution appeared to him to be inseparable: "Though a man may be despised without being saved, yet he cannot be saved without

---

47 005-Gr. T. G. [T. Gib], *Remarks on the Reverend Mr. Whitefield's journal*, 26.

48 205-Gr. Church, *Some farther remarks on the Rev. Mr. John Wesley's journal*, 132. See similar comments in 294-Gr. Academicus [Green], *The principles and practices of the Methodists considered*, 17; and 536A-Ki. Croft, *Eight sermons preached before the University of Oxford*, 180–81.

49 213A-Ki. [Lavington], *The enthusiasm of Methodists and papists compar'd*, pt. 2, 50. See also 213-Gr. [Lavington], *The enthusiasm of Methodists and papists compar'd*, pt. 1. The second edition of 1749 and the third edition of 1752 included both part 1 and part 2 (the latter originally listed as 213A-Ki).

50 164-Gr. [Gibson], *Observations upon the conduct and behaviour of . . . Methodists*, 22; 185-Gr. Thomas Church, *Remarks on the Reverend Mr. John Wesley's last journal*, 61; and 205-Gr. Church, *Some farther remarks on the Rev. Mr. John Wesley's last journal*, 125.

being despised."[51] Moreover, he asserted, suffering was "the badge of [the Christian's] discipleship, the stamp of [his or her] profession; the constant seal of [one's] calling."[52] Whitefield agreed: "The people of God are to expect little else but trouble and trial while they are in this world . . . All who would seek and serve the Lord Jesus, must be despised, hated, scoffed, slandered, and evil intreated."[53] Although the Methodists expected persecution, and were constantly prepared for suffering, they did not seek it.

It is hardly surprising that the Methodists' attitude toward persecution received criticism. Opponents could not accept the belief that persecution was the test by which all Christians should verify their lives: "Our Lord . . . pronounced them blessed that are persecuted for the sake or on account of righteousness. but he does not say that they are blessed unless they are so persecuted; nor can it, I think, be fairly inferr'd . . . that all that will live godly in Christ shall suffer persecution."[54] The Methodists, some detractors inferred, embraced persecution because of a martyrdom complex. Whitefield, John Brownsword believed, actually rejoiced in his afflictions: "[He] makes no difference between thanking God immediately for sufferings sent by [God] . . . and thanking God in those sufferings."[55] An anonymous author in 1744 claimed that the Methodists, believing that they would remain an insignificant sect unless persecuted, were disappointed that they had been largely ignored.[56] Another writer claimed Whitefield "knew nothing could secure him the affection of his proselytes, and increase their number, so much as enduring persecution with resignation; nothing he knew could give him greater assurance of a more respectable establishment than receiving frequent indignities and the artful hinting 'such were the disgraces the primitive apostles endured.'"[57] Wesley, likewise, William Warburton maintained, believed

---

51 Wesley, Letter to Samuel Wesley, Sr. (October 10, 1735), 23, in *BEWJW*, vol. 25, *Letters I (1721–1739)*, ed. Frank Baker (Nashville: Abingdon, 1976–), 407.

52 John Wesley, Sermon 23, "Upon the Lord's Sermon on the Mount, III," in *BEWJW*, vol. 1, *Sermons I*, ed. Albert C. Outler, 510–30.

53 George Whitefield, Sermon LVI, "An Exhortation to the People of God," in *WGW*, 6:361. See also Sermon LV, "Persecution Every Christian's Lot," *WGW*, 6:345–60.

54 240-Gr. *Candid remarks on some particular passages . . . in Mr. Whitefield's . . . sermons* (Reading: C. Micklewright, 1752), 12.

55 039-Gr. J. B. [Brownsword], *Remarks on the continuation of Mr. Whitefield's journal*, 8.

56 174-Gr. Eusebius [Fleming], *A fine picture of enthusiasm*, iv.

57 522-Gr. *Methodism and popery dissected and compared* (London: Fielding and Walker, 1779), 41–42.

persecution was a prerequisite for his movement's numerical success. Denied real persecution from the church and state, Wesley sought it, Warburton claimed, in the "mock persecutions . . . of the mob," making more of them than they were in reality, "[Wesley] expatiates on every adventure with such circumstances, that there is hardly a turnip-top ever thrown at his sacred pate, which has not had the honor of being recorded."[58]

Catholicity

Fundamental to Wesley's thought is his distinction between doctrine and opinion. He stated it as early as 1742 in *The Character of a Methodist*: "[A]s to all opinions which do not strike at the root of Christianity, we think and let think."[59] He expressed it even more boldly seven years later in *A Plain Account of the People Called Methodists*: "[O]rthodoxy, or right opinions, is, at best, but a slender part of religion, if it can be allowed to be any part of it at all."[60] The same year Wesley developed and preached a sermon entitled "Catholic Spirit." Though he was adamant about what were essential doctrines (those vital to salvation), he insisted that differences in modes of worship, church polity, and theological opinion (speculative theology) ought not to preclude those who love Christ from uniting in witness to their faith: "Let all opinions alone on one side and the other: 'only give me thine hand.'"[61] Wesley's theological principle of catholicity was contested vehemently. His statement invited confusion—which beliefs were essential and which were opinions? Disputants alleged that Wesley dismissed the need for correct doctrine and tolerated heresy. Theophilus Evans's distorted commentary was: "Let them be as heterodox as a bewildered fancy can make them, provided they are Methodists, they are safe enough."[62]

John Kirkby satirized Wesley's willingness to embrace those who differed from him theologically: "If we will not allow his church to pass for holy; yet we are forced to grant it in his own way to be catholic. And that is by making

58 342-Gr. [Warburton], *The doctrine of grace*, 187–90; cf. 263–365.

59 John Wesley, "The Character of a Methodist" (1742) in *BEWJW*, 9:32–46, §1.

60 John Wesley, *A Plain Account of the People Called Methodists in a Letter to the Revd. Mr. Perronet* (1749), in *BEWJW* 9:253–80, 1.2.

61 John Wesley, Sermon 39, "The Catholic Spirit," in *Works*, 2:89.

62 235-Gr. [Evans], *The history of modern enthusiasm*, 117.

it perfectly reconcilable to persons of all opinions."[63] Warburton contended that Wesley no longer distinguished between orthodox and heretical doctrine and was attempting to deal the death blow to Christianity.[64] The Calvinists agreed with Wesley's Anglican critics. John Erskine warned: "If once men believe that right opinion is a slender part of religion, or no part at all, there is scarce anything so foolish; so wicked, which Satan may not prompt them to, by transforming himself into an angel of light."[65] Wesley was much misunderstood—even Joseph Priestley thought the Methodist leader was little concerned with doctrine.[66]

The consequences of Wesley's catholicity were feared. Lavington believed it would usher in popery.[67] The author of *The Methodists* concurred—satirically he linked Methodism's origin to satanic inspiration to strengthen Rome:

> For your [Rome's] good,
> I've form'd a new religious brood,
> Where all the various sects in one,
> In my alembick mixt are thrown . . .[68]

John Kirkby thought contempt for the Church and its sacraments would occur: "Thus we have the only sacraments of baptism and the tremendous body and blood of Christ depreciated as no other than superstitious modes of worship, circumstances of small concern, things which deserve not a thought."[69]

Not only were there evil consequences, but the positive outcome supposed by Wesley was never realized, Samuel Martin contended. The Methodist leader's preaching love for those who differed in opinion and practice had little effect on his followers. It was impossible to find a Methodist who was not a "bigot for Methodism."[70] Whitefield, like Wesley, espoused catholicity of spirit. His sole question was, "Are you a Christian?"[71] In a sermon on

---

63 217-Gr. Kirkby, *The impostor detected*, 20, 23.
64 342-Gr. [Warburton], *The doctrine of grace*, 156–58.
65 363-Gr. [John Erskine], *Mr. Wesley's principles detected* (Edinburgh: for William Gray, 1765), 6.
66 554-Gr. Priestley, *Original letters by the Rev. John Wesley and his friends*, xxii.
67 213-Gr. [Lavington], *The enthusiasm of Methodists and papists compar'd*, pt. 2, 171.
68 026-Gr. *The Methodists: An humorous burlesque poem*, 15.
69 217-Gr. Kirkby, *The impostor detected*, 20–23.
70 376-Gr. [Samuel Martin], *A few thoughts and matters of fact concerning Methodism* (Edinburgh: sold by W. Gray, 1766), 9.
71 George Whitefield, "Letter CXXV," in *WGW*, 1:126.

spiritual baptism, he wrote, "Don't tell me you are a Baptist, an Independent, a Presbyterian, a Dissenter, tell me you are a Christian, that is all I want."[72] By contrast to Wesley, Whitefield's catholicity drew little criticism. It did, however, raise the wrath of Adam Gib (1704–1778), minister of Bristow Street Church, Edinburgh, and a member of the Associate Presbytery, who flayed Whitefield:

> The panacea, the all-heal medicine that he applies to the divided church is not merely an antidote against Presbyterian, Episcopal, Popish, or Independent forms of communion, but it is such a catholick love as will make light of all forms of communions, from a notion that these things which are beneficial, and so worthwhile, may be found under any of these communions; and if all form of church communion be so trifling it must be neither scriptural, reasonable, nor needful.[73]

It was not merely his private opinion that Gib voiced. When the Associate Presbytery met in December, 1742, it, too, lashed out at Whitefield's "latitudinarian tenets," complaining that Whitefield was teaching that "any particular form of church-government is denied to be of divine institution, and under a pretence of catholick love, a scheme is laid for uniting parties of all denominations in church communion, in a way destructive of the Christian faith."[74]

Original Sin

Original sin was a fundamental doctrine of the Methodists. Wesley believed that human beings by nature were filled with evil. Before God, humans were devoid of all good—wholly fallen. Their souls were totally corrupt.[75] Whitefield painted the total depravity of humans in even bolder strokes and

---

72 George Whitefield, *Eighteen Sermons*, rev. by Andrew Gifford (Springfield, MA: Thomas Dickinson, 1808), 247.

73 142-Gr. Adam Gib, *A warning against countenancing the ministrations of Mr. George Whitefield* (Edinburgh: David Duncan, 1742), 30.

74 172-Gr. Secession Church-Associate Presbytery, *Acts of the Associate Presbytery* (Edinburgh: T. W. and T. Ruddimans, 1744), 109.

75 Wesley, Sermon 44, "Original Sin," *BEWJW*, 2:172–85. See also Sermon 141, "The Image of God," in *BEWJW*, 4:292–303.

darker colors.[76] Both Wesley and Whitefield believed the doctrine rested on three principal bases: it was a part of the divine revelation contained in the Scriptures, the Thirty-nine Articles articulated it, and human experience corroborated it.

The very things that the Methodists thought confirmed the doctrine, critics believed actually denied it.[77] First, neither the term nor the concept of original sin was biblical: "It is nowhere . . . declared in scripture that the soul is by nature sully'd and contaminated with all that horror and darkness, and all those gloomy passions, with which they [the Methodists] overwhelm it."[78] Second, opponents rejected the Methodists' literal interpretation of the Church's Article IX of Original Sin. The article, it was claimed, was ambiguous: "Whoever preaches or believes [it] . . . in the strictest and most rigorous sense makes man absolutely passive . . . as a mere machine in its different movements all contrived by the hand of the Artist."[79] Third, human experience denied total depravity. Anti-Methodist authors made much of this point. Eighteenth-century Anglicans were more optimistic about humanity than were their Methodist contemporaries. Humanity's benevolence was in evidence everywhere, they said. Humanity's goodness, not depravity, prevailed.[80] Since humans performed good deeds, they could not be completely evil. God's image in humans had not been obliterated by the fall. Anglican cleric Thomas Whiston maintained it "still retains some distant resemblance to his great original . . . Still his . . . features wear the indelible marks of power and distinction."[81] The fullest attack on the Methodists' argument that the doctrine of original sin was confirmed by personal experience and observation of humanity appeared in a rejoinder to Wesley's comments on John Taylor's

---

76 Whitefield, Sermon XIII, "The Potter and the Clay," in *WGW*, 5:202–6.

77 See Simon Lewis, A 'Diversity of Passions and Humours': Early anti-Methodist literature as a disguise for heterodoxy in *Literature & History* 26, no. 1 (2017): 3–23. Lewis argues for a more nuanced view of eighteenth-century anti-Methodist authors taking note of their theological diversity.

78 095-Gr. Whiston, *The important doctrines of original sin*, 6.

79 Ibid., 21.

80 035-Gr. A Curate of London, *A short preservative against the doctrines reviv'd by Mr. Whitefield* (London: printed for John Clarke, [1739]), 3.

81 095-Gr. Whiston, *The important doctrines of original sin*, 3. Little is known about Thomas Whiston. He graduated from Trinity College in 1735, was ordained deacon in 1736, and was ordained priest in 1738. This pamphlet marked Whiston's debut as an author. His occupation at the time he published the above pamphlet is unknown.

seminal *Scripture-Doctrine of Original Sin.*[82] That there was general wickedness in the world, Taylor did not deny. But that it was due to the effect of
original sin, he could not accept: "The general wickedness of mankind hath,
always and everywhere been the wickedness of single persons, and therefore
we may account for the wickedness of any number of single persons in the
same way that we account for the wickedness of any one man." Humans
have no sinful propensity. Individuals sin because they choose to sin. When
temptation confronts them, they yield.[83]

The imputation of Adam's sin to contemporary human beings, disputants
contended, was blasphemous. It was unreasonable to suppose that a just and
loving God would punish men and women for sins committed by Adam and
Eve thousands of years beforehand—sins for which contemporary Christians
were in no way responsible.[84]

One of the most consistent attacks on the Methodist formulation of the
doctrine of original sin came from one of Wesley's ex-preachers, Nicholas
Manners, who contended that, as a consequence of the work and death of
Christ, all human beings were born into the same state of original purity as
Adam before the fall. Scripture, he said (quoting Romans 5 and 1 Corinthians
15), taught that Christ wiped out the effect of sin. Infants were not corrupt at
birth. Human nature had been renewed at its roots. "Holy souls," he wrote,
"as naturally flow from it as unholy ones would have done, if it had not been
renewed.[85] If people sin, it is because they have chosen freely to do so. People
alone are responsible for their sin.[86]

---

82 392A-Ba. John Taylor, *A reply to the Reverend John Wesley's 'Remarks on . . . original
sin'* (London: printed and sold by M. Waugh, 1767). Taylor (1694–1761) was an ordained
Presbyterian cleric who served a church, Kirkstead Abbey Chapel, Lincolnshire, before
being called to be co-pastor with Peter Finch of the Presbyterian Church, Norwich. He
finished his career as divinity tutor at the newly opened Warrington Academy. Taylor
became a recognized and influential Hebrew scholar. *ODNB.*

83 392A-Ba. Taylor, *A reply to the Reverend John Wesley's 'Remarks on . . . original sin,'* 205.

84 See 495-Gr. Thomas Herring, *Letters from the late Most Reverend Dr. Thomas Herring*
(London: J. Johnson, 1777), 7. See also 217A-Ki. Fletcher, *A vindication of the 'Methodist
dissected,'* 7.

85 540B-Ba. Manners, *Preachers described and the people advised,* 11.

86 540A-Ba. Manners, *Remarks on the writings of the Rev. J. W.,* 30–31; 544-Gr. Nicholas
Manners, *A full confutation of the Rev. John Fletcher's appeal* (Hull: T. Briggs, 1789), 11–12,
19–21; 540B-Ba. Manners, *Preachers described and the people advised,* 11.

Justification by Faith

A battle of major proportions was waged over the doctrine of justification by faith.[87] In the 1740s Anglicans attacked the Methodists on the role they accorded works in justification. Early critics failed to note the distinctions between the two wings of the movement—Calvinist and Arminian—despite the fact that there were greater differences between them than those between Anglicans and Wesley's branch of Methodism. In the main the attacks in this period countered the Calvinist expression of the doctrine, although more often than not it was not designated as such.[88] A more concentrated assault did not occur until the 1750s and 60s. The sharp controversy between Anglican and Calvinistic Methodists over this doctrine led some mid-century authors to remark that it was the chief cause of division in the Church.[89]

All Methodists, it was said, drew a sharp line between faith and works. Works (called "filthy rags" by Whitefield and the Calvinists) played no role in justification. The implication of this made opponents apprehensive. The Methodists seemed intent on repudiating Christian responsibility by preparing the way for a resurgence of antinomianism. Justification by faith alone, said one critic, was "a pernicious doctrine and subversive of all the moral part of Christianity."[90] Both Gibson and Henry Stebbing, when they discussed the Methodists' doctrine of justification, rattled the skeleton of antinomianism by citing "historical evidence" that the elevation of faith over works depressed morals.[91]

---

87 First published in 1746 Wesley's sermon, "Justification by Faith," was, Outler claims, the "earliest full summary of Wesley's soteriology . . . It is a landmark sermon to which all subsequent ones may be compared." Outler, an introductory comment to sermon 5 "Justification by Faith," in *BEWJW*, 1:181–82.

88 236-Gr. *A plain account of justification* (Norwich: W. Chase, 1752); 267-Gr. A Clergyman [Henry Stebbing], *The doctrine of justification by faith in Jesus Christ*; 269-Gr. Thomas Green, *Justification by faith*; 289-Gr. Samuel Martin, *Two discourses* (London: P. Vaillant, 1760); 290-Gr. Samuel Hallifax, *Saint Paul's doctrine of justification by faith* (Cambridge: J. Bentham, 1760); 296-Gr. William Law, *Of justification by faith and works* (London: for J. Richardson, 1760); 317-Gr. Allen, *No acceptance with God by faith only*; 329-Gr. Hitchcock, *The mutual connexion between faith, virtue, and knowledge*; 330-Gr. Horne, *Works wrought through faith a condition of our justification*.

89 269-Gr. Green, *Justification*, 25–8, vi–vii. Cf. 267-Gr. A Clergyman [Stebbing], *The doctrine of justification by faith in Jesus Christ*, 25–28; 289-Gr. Martin, *Two discourses*, iii.

90 137-Gr. *A letter from a gentleman in the country to his friend in Edinburgh* (Edinburgh: no printer, 1741), 12. A second edition was printed in 1741.

91 200-Gr. A. B. [Stebbing], *An earnest and affectionate address to the people called Methodists*, 13. 206-Gr. [Gibson], *The charge of the Right Reverend Father in God, Edmund, Lord Bishop of London . . . 1746 and 1747*, 8–11.

The distinction, critics claimed, between good and evil, virtue and vice, had been blurred by the Methodist doctrine. If people were justified without regard to their works, it did not matter whether they performed good or bad deeds. "What kind of a God did this imply?" critics asked. Justification by faith demeaned the nature of God. It made God irrational. It represented "the unerring discoverer of all things and the rewarder of every man according to his works as apprehending things differently from what they really are, and as treating good and evil exactly alike."[92]

By denying works a place in justification and emphasizing faith, the Methodists had, antagonists contended, sunk once more into rampant subjectivism. Wesley's definition of faith as "a sure trust, which a man hath, that Christ loved him, and died for him," reduced faith to the level of impulse and feeling. The Methodists resolved "all religion into instantaneous faith, and faith itself into impulses and mere animal sensations," damaging "the nature of faith, by turning it into an act of sense, and natural perception."[93] Faith and works, Anglicans reminded the Methodists, were inseparable. They had been wedded by God, and what God had joined together, the Methodists ought not to put asunder.[94] There was no argument for justification by works, but opponents, with arguments invariably drawn from St. James's epistle, defended the necessity of people performing good works in order to be justified.[95] In emphasizing the necessity of good works, most anti-Methodists were careful to avoid giving the impression that they were considered meritorious—they did not earn God's approval. The accepted Anglican position, according to William Dodd, was that

> no works of imperfect, sinful, dependent creatures can possibly be
> meritorious and avail before God, to procure pardon or life; but this
> by no means renders those works unnecessary, which, considered
> in themselves, are so acceptable to God, so honourable to man,
> so beneficial to the community; and without the practice of which

---

92 035-Gr. A Curate of London, *A short preservative against the doctrines reviv'd by Mr. Whitefield*, 17–18.

93 190-Gr. *The question whether it be right to turn Methodist, considered*, 44–5.

94 125-Gr. Inglefield, *An answer to a sermon preached at Rotherhith*, 10; 130-Gr. Bedford, *The doctrine of justification by faith stated*, 4; 296-Gr. Law, *Of justification by faith and works*, 4; 330-Gr. Horne, *Works wrought through faith a condition of our justification*, 25.

95 032-Gr. A Curate in the Country, *Observations on the Reverend Mr. Whitefield's answer*, 18; 018-Gr. Wilder, *The trial of the spirits*, 6.

no Christian can ever have any rational ground of acceptance with
the great judge of heaven and earth.[96]

Methodism's fundamental error, critics suggested, was that it taught that
a human being's salvation was unconditional, whereas the Scriptures, they
believed, taught that one must fulfill certain requirements for salvation. The
distinction between what God did and what human beings did in justification
was clearly drawn in the Bible:

> The primary cause of our salvation is the boundless love of God;
> the meritorious cause the perfect sacrifice of Christ; but the formal
> cause or condition by which it is obtained, is obedience to the will
> of God, as far as it is revealed, or may be known by mankind.[97]

Human beings, then, receive God's pardon only after they have complied
with the conditions God has laid down—repentance, faith, and obedience.
This does not mean that we earn or deserve God's acceptance; salvation
remains God's gift.[98]

Thomas Church provided a definition of what Anglicans meant by
condition:

> Its full meaning is no more than it is a causa sine qua non; it is the
> very lowest of causes indeed; very improperly stiled a cause, but
> it is something necessary to be done, as we would attain that of
> which it is a condition. Thus the condition of a bond or will is that,
> without which we shall be subject in the forfeiture, or deprived
> of the advantage.[99]

Article IX in the Thirty-nine Articles, Church argued, did not totally exclude works
from justification. They were excluded only as meritorious, and in no other way.[100]

---

96 332A-Ba [Dodd], *A conference between a mystic, an Hutchinsonian, a Calvinist, a Methodist, a member of the Church of England, and others*, 87.

97 271A-Ki. Green, *Eight sermons preached in the parish church of St. Saviour's*, 115–16. See a similar statement in 405-Gr. Thomas Randolph, *The doctrine of justification by faith explained* (Oxford: printed at the theatre for J. Fletcher and Co., 1768), 17.

98 104-Gr. Presbyter of the Church of England, *A modest and serious defence of the author of 'The whole duty of man'* (London: J. Roberts, 1740), 29; 105A-Ki. Smyth, *A curious letter from a gentleman to Mr. Whitefield*, 13; 226A-Ki. John Roche, *Moravian heresy* (Dublin: for the author, 1751), 323–24; 289-Gr. Martin, *Two discourses*, 53–55; 330-Gr. Horne, *Works wrought through faith a condition of our justification*, 8.

99 185-Gr. Church, *Remarks on the Rev. John Wesley's last journal*, 25–26.

100 205-Gr. Church, *Some farther remarks on the Rev. Mr. John Wesley's last journal*, 26.

In opposing Methodist "solafidism," critics restated the Anglican concept of twofold justification, composed of initial and final justification. Initial justification they described as an individual's initial restoration to God's favor. Such acceptance by God, though based on the merits of Christ's righteousness and death, was conditional upon the person's repentance and faith. Initial justification, however, did not guarantee a place in heaven. The justified one was expected to grow in grace. Faith must issue in good works. Second justification, or final salvation, occurred at the last judgment. Here the basis of justification is faith and works together.[101] As previously noted, criticism of the doctrine of justification in the 1750s and '60s was primarily aimed at the Calvinist wing of Methodism. Much of what Anglican opponents had to say, Wesley would have agreed with. He, too, was concerned that the Calvinist doctrine might lead to antinomianism. Although he had, immediately after 1738, placed less importance on the concept of a second or final justification conditional upon obedience or good works, by 1740 he had embraced the concept and was articulating it in controversy with antinomian opponents.[102]

Regeneration

The doctrine of the "new birth" or regeneration was central to Wesley's teaching, but it was very unpopular among eighteenth-century Anglicans. Wesley sought to explain it in his sermon "On the New Birth," a formal statement that would rebut many of the criticisms of the doctrine.[103] The extent to which Anglicans were disturbed by the Methodist doctrine of regeneration can be seen in the fact that between 1738 and 1741 nine pamphlets appeared that were primarily directed at the tenet by title.[104] Numerous pamphlets in the

---

101 Numerous anti-Methodist tracts stated the doctrine of twofold justification. Among the most important were: 095-Gr. Whiston, *The important doctrines of original sin*, 39. 160B-Ba. [Smith], *The notions of the Methodists farther disprov'd* (Newcastle: no printer, 1743), 7–9; 271A-Ki. Green, *Eight sermons preached in the parish church of St. Saviour's*, 166; 236-Gr. *A plain account of justification*, 7–11; 296-Gr. Law, *Of justification by faith and works*, 16; 330-Gr. Horne, *Works wrought through faith a condition of our justification*, 19.

102 See Harald Lindstrom, *Wesley and Sanctification* (London: Epworth, 1950), 205.

103 John Wesley, Sermon 45, "On the New Birth," § 45, *BEWJW*, 2:187–201. In the introduction to the sermon, Outler describes it as "a distillation of more than 60 oral sermons on John 3:7," 186.

104 See 002-Gr. Silvester, *The scripture doctrine of regeneration stated*; 008-Gr. Skerret, *The nature and proper evidence of regeneration*; 009-Gr. Land, *A letter to the Rev. Mr. Whitefield*; 133-Gr. Land, *A second letter to the Rev. Mr. Whitefield*; 017-Gr. Stebbing, *A*

first years of the revival also attacked the doctrine either in passing or in some detail. To a person, disputants believed the Methodists had distorted the accepted Anglican doctrine. None would have disagreed with Ralph Skerret's assessment—the orthodox tenet had been "palpably misrepresented by subtle and designing men."[105] In place of the Church's doctrine, the Methodists, it said, espoused Quaker or Anabaptist tenets.[106]

Whitefield and Wesley taught the necessity of adult regeneration. Between baptism and adulthood, they believed, sin invalidated the effects of infant regeneration. All adults, even those who had been baptized as infants, needed to be born again in a spiritual rebirth called regeneration.[107] Methodists, then, acknowledged two regenerations—one occurring at the infant's baptism, the other in the adult's conversion. They were separate and successive. In no way were they incompatible. Moreover, the Methodists claimed that they had not made a radical departure from the traditional Anglican position. The Methodists' critics, however, disagreed: the two regenerations were irreconcilable; the teaching of the second regeneration was a fundamental break with Church of England theology.

Anglican doctrine, disputants argued, knew only one regeneration—baptismal regeneration. In baptism the Holy Spirit renewed the infant inwardly, water being the outward and visible sign. Regeneration and baptism were one and the same thing. "We should go to our baptism for the date of our regeneration," insisted Tipping Silvester.[108] Ralph Skerret stated the contemporary Anglican position: "The washing of baptism outwardly, and the inward

caution against religious delusion; 039-Gr. J. B. [Brownsword], *Remarks on the continuation of Mr. Whitefield's journal*; 049-Gr. Church, *An explanation and defence of the doctrine of the Church of England*; 107-Gr. Daniel Waterland, *Regeneration stated and explained* (London: for W. Innys and R. Manby, 1740), 106; 095-Gr. Whiston, *The important doctrines of original sin*.

105 008-Gr. Skerret, *The nature and proper evidence of regeneration*, vi.

106 039-Gr. J.B. [Brownsword], *Remarks on the continuation of Mr. Whitefield's journal, 32*; 049-Gr. Church, *An explanation and defence of the doctrine of the Church of England,* 25; 349-Gr. Hardy, *A letter from a clergyman to one of his parishioners who was inclined to turn Methodist*, 2–6.

107 For an examination of the Methodist teaching on baptism, see Bernard G. Holland, *Baptism in Early Methodism* (London: Epworth, 1970), 63. Holland notes that Wesley believed that usually by the age of nine or ten, conscious sin had vitiated infant regeneration. See also Ole E. Borgen, *John Wesley and the Sacraments: A Theological Study* (Nashville and New York: Abingdon, 1972).

108 002-Gr. Silvester, *The scripture doctrine of regeneration stated*; cf. 005-Gr. [Gib], *Remarks on the Reverend Mr. Whitefield's journal*, 32.

sanctification of the Holy Ghost are the chief and only [qualifications] for gaining admittance into the kingdom of heaven." [109] In baptism, John Brownsword explained, the infant became a new creature, wholly regenerated.

> For hereby [in baptism] is he regenerate, and become a new creature, converted from a child of wrath by nature, to one of the sons of God by adoption and grace. And then, as a testimony of his new birth, the Holy Ghost is there-upon sent into his heart . . . baptism is said to confirm and seal unto us the free pardon and forgiveness of our sins.[110]

Eighteenth-century Anglicans equated baptism with the scriptural doctrine of new birth. Nowhere, they claimed, could they find a biblical injunction for a second new birth. Regeneration, advised Tristram Land, was unrepeatable, a once-in-a-lifetime-affair: "Here [in baptism] the Church supposes they have been regenerate and born again, and so does not command them to be baptized or born again a second time for to be born more than once in a scriptural sense, is just as impossible, as to be born twice in a natural."[111]

Methodists were accused of misapplying the term *regeneration* to mean repentance. Neither the Church of England nor the early church, said Henry Stebbing, had given this connotation.[112] Disputants acknowledged that human beings, since they continued to sin after baptism, needed to repent. But sin committed after baptism never blots out the effects of regeneration. It was incorrect to teach, Brownsword insisted, that regeneration and repentance were the same thing:

> A person may be actually regenerated, or become a new man, by being born of water and the Holy Spirit, and after this new birth, follow a wicked course of life for a while, and then at last entirely forsake those wicked ways. But yet this forsaking his wicked ways can never be deemed a regeneration or new birth: For the Holy

---

109 008-Gr. Skerret, *The nature and proper evidence of regeneration*, 10.
110 039-Gr. J. B. [Brownsword], *Remarks on the continuation of Mr. Whitefield's journal*, 36.
111 009-Gr. Land, *A letter to the Rev. Mr. Whitefield*, 27–28. See similar statements in 107-Gr. Waterland, *Regeneration stated and explained*, 8; 049-Gr. Church, *An explanation and defence of the doctrine of regeneration*, 2; and 190-Gr. *The question whether it is right to turn Methodist, considered*, 27–8.
112 200-Gr. Stebbing, *An earnest and affectionate address to the people called Methodists*, 9.

> Spirit of God was [not] sent into hearts at baptism as a guest to tarry
> only for a night or two, but as an inhabitant, to dwell and remain
> with us, as an earnest of our inheritance until the redemption of
> the purchased possession.[113]

Critics were willing to admit that some, having fallen deeply into sin, required a radical change in their lives—conversion. Thomas Church spoke of it as "recovery from any dangerous distemper which would have otherwise destroy'd the child of God."[114] Conversion, however, was to be clearly distinguished from regeneration since they differed with respect to "the effective cause or agency." Daniel Waterland (1683–1740), an orthodox High Churchman, and master of Magdalene College, Cambridge, was adamant that in regeneration (baptism) the individual is passive. It "is the work of the Spirit . . . singly, since water really does nothing." Conversion, in contrast, is "the work of the Spirit and man together. Man renews himself, at the same time that the Spirit renews him: . . . [it] is the result of their joint-agency."[115] Conversion was not necessary for all. Some people, critics maintained, having led good Christian lives since childhood, had no need of it. Waterland asked, "Must they be called upon to recollect the day, week, month, or year of their conversion or regeneration, who from their Christian infancy have never been in an unconverted or unregenerate state at all? "[116] To justify their dramatic conversions, Methodists, some said, exaggerated their sins or lied concerning them.[117] The author of *The harlequin Methodist* purports to be a Methodist preacher who has undergone a dramatic conversion. The contrast between his old life and the new man he has become is stark:

> Thro' all the whole circle of vice,
> Dear brethren, I often have run,
> Whores, horses, and drinking and dice

---

113 039-Gr. J. B. [Brownsword], *Remarks on the continuation of Mr. Whitefield's journal*, 40. See also 190-Gr. *The question whether it is right to turn Methodist considered*, 27.

114 049-Gr. Church, *An explanation and defence of the doctrine of the Church of England*, 22.

115 107-Gr. Waterland, *Regeneration stated and explained*, 14. For a further example of a High Church view of original sin, see also J. Bate, *An essay towards a rationale of the literal doctrine of original sin* (London, 1752), 52; *A rationale of the literal doctrine of original sin; or A vindication of God's permitting the fall of Adam, and the subsequent corruption of our human nature* (London, 1766), 91–92.

116 107-Gr. Waterland, *Regeneration stated and explained*, 14.

117 476-Gr. *A letter to a friend on the subject of Methodism*, 8–9.

> And thought all religion but fun;
> But now, so my stars have decreed,
> My follies I see, tho' full late,
> I'm made a new man, ah! Indeed
> And faithfully regenerate.[118]

Claims to instantaneous conversion were also criticized. Though within God's power, instantaneous conversion of unbelievers or habitual sinners was not, opponents said, God's normal method. "The purification of the heart," wrote Archdeacon Tottie, "is a gradual work . . . The Christian life is progressive . . . We may daily gain strength and advance more in faith, knowledge, and virtue."[119]

Anti-Methodists objected strenuously to the evangelicals' insistence that conversion was a sensory experience—something an individual might feel happening to his or her life. Methodists supposed conversion to be, wrote Henry Stebbing, "the work of God's Spirit, and so far, they are right, but they will have it to be a sensible operation; an operation which may be felt and distinguished as the hand of God upon them; overpowering, as it were, the soul."[120] The evidence of conversion was not to be found in a person's experience but in practical righteousness—a virtuous life and quiet performance of the duties of one's station.[121]

The bizarre physical agitations that accompanied Methodist conversions, commonly called "pangs of the new birth" offended the religious proprieties of conservative and rational Anglicans. They found talk of such behavior bizarre and unscriptural. The Bible nowhere recorded that violent physical convulsions or screaming fits were the usual accompaniment of conversion.[122] Anglican critics feared that the Methodists' insistence on referring to conversion as regeneration might destroy the institution of baptism. Thomas Green

---

118 *The harlequin Methodist. To the tune of an old woman cloathed in grey* (n.p.: no printer, [1739]). Broadside.

119 384-Gr. [Tottie], *Two charges delivered to the clergy in the diocese of Worcester . . . 1776 and 1766*, 368. Sudden conversion was attacked also in: 029-Gr. [Gibson], *The bishop of London's pastoral letter*, 27; 049-Gr. Church, *An explanation and defence of the doctrine of the Church of England*, 23; 210-Gr. Fletcher, *A Methodist dissected*, 10; 380-Gr. Rotheram, *An essay on faith and its connection with good works*, 193.

120 017-Gr. Stebbing, *A caution against religious delusion*, 7–8.

121 008-Gr. Skerret, *The nature and proper evidence of regeneration*, 23, 26–27; 018-Gr. Wilder, *The trial of the spirits*, 15.

122 For a fuller discussion of this aspect see chapter 8, "Methodists at Worship."

sounded the warning: "To preach up regeneration, or direct baptised persons to wait for the new birth, may tend in some measure to perplex the minds of several and perhaps make them slight their baptism as an institution of little power and signficancy."[123]

If the clergy of the Church of England felt threatened by the Methodists' teaching on regeneration, so too did the Baptists. Several Baptists expressed fear that the evangelicals might undermine the doctrine of believers' baptism and the practice of total immersion. In 1749 an anonymous Baptist attacked the Methodists for continuing the "unscriptural" practice of infant baptism.[124] Much later in the century, two other Baptists, Gilbert Boyce and William Kingsford, issued stronger attacks on infant baptism.[125]

Assurance

The doctrine of assurance preached by the Methodists first came under fire in a sermon by Arthur Bedford in 1738 and continued to be strongly criticized into the 1760s.[126] As late as 1753, John Parkhurst, in remarking that it was one of the principal doctrines of Methodism, noted that they rarely preached "without mentioning it, yea insisting upon it."[127] The novelty of the doctrine attracted attention to it. One author contended that it had "never [been] heard of in Christendom for 1,500 years together."[128] Others traced the doctrine to the Moravians, claiming that the Methodists had adopted it uncritically from them.[129]

---

123 249A-Fi. Green, *A dissertation on enthusiasm*, 131.

124 216B-Ki. *A plain and familiar dialogue between a steady and a wavering Christian*, 19.

125 428-Gr. Boyce, *A serious reply to the Rev. Mr. John Wesley*; 539-Gr. William Kingsford, *A vindication of the Baptists*; 543A-Ki. Kingsford, *Three letters to the Rev. John Wesley* (Canterbury: for the author by J. Grove, 1789).

126 003-Gr. Bedford, *The doctrine of assurance*. Bedford (1668–1745) published numerous sermons on doctrinal subjects. Wesley found his sermon on assurance both deficient and disturbing. He visited him on October 6, 1738 to express his disappointment and belief that it had done great harm to God and his brother, Charles. Bedford's explanation of assurance, Wesley said, was "weak from beginning to end" and was totally different from what the Methodists taught. "We speak," Wesley told him, "of an assurance of our present pardon, not (as he does) of our final perseverance." John Wesley, October 6, 1738, *BEWJW*, vol. 19, *Journals and Diaries II (1738–1743)*, ed. W. Reginald Ward and Richard P. Heitzenrater, 15.

127 245-Gr. Parkhurst, *A serious and friendly address to the Reverend Mr. Wesley*, 28.

128 248A-Ba. A Lay-man, *A few queries concerning the growth of Methodism*, 11.

129 286-Gr. *Original letters between the Reverend Mr. John Wesley and Mr. Richard Tompson*, 24; 332A-Ba. [Dodd], *A conference between a mystic . . .* , 64–65.

Assurance meant to the Methodists an awareness that God had forgiven their sins. Wesley grounded his doctrine in Romans 8:16, "The Spirit itself beareth witness with our spirit, that we are the children of God" and defined assurance as "an inward impression on the soul, whereby the Spirit of God directly witnesses to my spirit, that I am a child of God; that Jesus hath loved me, and given himself for me; and that all my sins are blotted out, and I, even I, am reconciled to God."[130]

Wesley's doctrine, opponents believed, appeared to base divine forgiveness on people's emotional experience of having received it. To the anti-Methodists this was arrant subjectivism. Some Christians, they objected, never experienced a consciousness of their forgiveness. John Parkhurst contended that faulty biblical exegesis led Wesley into subjectivism. The context of Romans 8:16, he maintained, did not support Wesley's belief that the witness of the Holy Spirit was known by an "inward impression on the soul." The verse, taken in context, meant that God's love, through the Holy Spirit's influence, is manifest in the Christian's love.[131]

For a number of years following his conversion in 1738, Wesley was inclined to insist that assurance was necessary for justification and to assert that those who did not possess an inner sense of pardon were not justified.[132] The equation of assurance with justification drew a host of attacks on Wesley. Richard Tompson, one of a number who disputed the issue, wrote, "[It is] neither of the essence of faith; neither is it essentially connected with it."[133] Thomas Green could find no scripture to support the claim that assurance was necessary to salvation:

> It is a very rash declaration to pronounce those as damned already, who only say they hope to be saved, but do not pretend to [have] . . . assurance of it . . .The gospel nowhere teaches us that

---

130 John Wesley, Sermon 10, "The Witness of the Spirit I," *BEWJW*, 1:269–284; and Sermon 11, "The Witness of the Spirit II, *BEWJW*, 1:285–98, were written twenty years apart (1746, 1767), but they were meant to be read together and seen as an exposition of the crucial doctrine of assurance, which was pilloried by anti-Methodist critics.

131 245-Gr. Parkhurst, *A serious and friendly address to the Reverend Mr. John Wesley*, 12–13.

132 See Rupert Davies, "The people called Methodists 1. Our Doctrines" in Rupert Davies and Gordon Rupp, eds., *History of the Methodist Church*, 147–79, esp. 165.

133 286-Gr. *Original letters between the Reverend Mr. John Wesley and Mr. Richard Tompson*, 9. Cf. 003-Gr. Bedford, *The doctrine of assurance*, 5; 245-Gr. Parkhurst, *A serious and friendly address*, 6–7; 267-Gr. [Stebbing], *The doctrine of justification by faith in Jesus Christ*, 30.

... assurance is to be one of the conditions of our salvation, or a necessary motive or means of comfort for the due performance of our duty.[134]

The Church of England, many critics alleged, taught a doctrine of assurance, but what the Methodists taught was a distorted version of it. Whereas the Book of Homilies spoke of an "assurance of hope," the Methodists preached an "assurance of certainty." The assurance of hope occurs, Bedford said, when we fully believe that we are lost and undone by nature and must utterly perish in that condition; when we are fully assured that the death of Christ is sufficient satisfaction for all our sins, and his merits imputed to us will make us perfectly holy in the sight of God the Father. . . . [We hope that] we shall obtain the promises which are given in general terms to all that believe . . . though we never have an assurance of certainty as to our particular case.[135]

Thus, Christians hope for salvation rather than claim certainty of it. An individual's claim to be sure of his or her own salvation amounted to an "assurance of certainty." It was tantamount to a belief that the individual could not fall from grace. The possibility of having such certainty Anglican critics vigorously denied. The ordinary Christian, wrote John Roche, has "no power given him to discover a certainty of his state with respect to futurity."[136] Doubt as to the Christians' final outcome is never banished, argued Thomas Green:

When Christians . . . consider their own infirmity, and how easily they may fall short of what is required of them, they will proceed with fear in the work of their salvation, not a slavish fear indeed, but a filial one: a fear that includes firm trust and confidence in God, as a kind and merciful father . . . I would place a well-grounded hope of salvation as a due medium between assurance and distrust.[137]

---

134 249A-Fi. Green, *A dissertation on enthusiasm*, 140.
135 003-Gr. Bedford, *The doctrine of assurance*, 21–22.
136 226A-Ki. Roche, *Moravian heresy*, 310. See similar statements in 021-Gr. Charles Wheatly, *St. John's test of knowing Christ* (London: J. Nourse, 1739), 19; 343-Gr. Rutherforth, *Four charges to the clergy of the archdeaconry of Essex*, 59–60; 190-Gr. *The question whether it be right to turn Methodist considered*, 29; 160A-Ba. [Smith], *The notions of the Methodists fully disprov'd*; 160B-Ba. [George Smith], *The notions of the Methodists farther disprov'd* (Newcastle: J. White, 1743); 160A-Ba. and 160B-Ba. were reprinted in London for Jacob Robinson under the combined title of *The notions of the Methodists fully disprov'd*.
137 269-Gr. Green, *Justification*, 147.

Anti-Methodists conceded that assurance of certainty had been given to some—the Old Testament patriarchs, the apostles, and early Christian martyrs, those whom God had called to extraordinary service or great suffering. However, as the task of the eighteenth-century church was not comparable to the tasks of the apostolic and early church, there was no need for the gift of assurance of certainty.[138] Some were willing to allow that God still granted the assurance of certainty in their own age, but that only a select few (the Methodists not among them) received such a gift.[139]

Controversy over assurance was partly due to fear of its implications. Joseph Trapp's comment that it led either to despair or presumption initiated a criticism that was reiterated by many:

> We have despair on the one hand, presumption on the other. The former part of this doctrine tends to plunge into despair those who, whether with, or without reason, have not this strong persuasion of their being in a state of salvation; and the latter to confirm in the height of presumption those who, without reason have it.[140]

On the one hand, to boast of assurance was presumptuous. It smacked of spiritual pride and was thus contrary to the whole tenor of Scripture, which stressed humility. The satirist assailed the Methodists' pride in boasting about their assurance:

> Christian-assurance in the gospel-sense
> They [the Methodists] construed into matchless impudence.[141]

Assurance, if possessed, said Arthur Bedford, ought not to be paraded, but concealed, unless the individual is called to martyrdom.[142] On the other hand, because it seemed to base divine forgiveness on "feelings," it led many to despair about their salvation. Henry Stebbing explained:

> If a man is never to think well of himself, till he experiences

---

138 003-Gr. Bedford, *The doctrine of assurance*, 5.

139 286-Gr. *Original letters between the Reverend Mr. John Wesley and Richard Tompson*, 47. Cf. 021-Gr. Wheatly, *St. John's test of knowing Christ*, 24.

140 010-Gr. Trapp, *The nature, folly, sin and danger of being righteous over-much*, 45–46.

141 516-Gr. [Combe], *The saints*, 7.

142 003-Gr. Bedford, *The doctrine of assurance*, 13–4. See also 297-Gr. Jephson, *Friendly and compassionate address to all serious . . . Methodists*, 11; 210-Gr. Fletcher, *A Methodist dissected*, 11–2.

something within himself, which he has not yet experienced, and which he cannot be assured beforehand that he ever shall experience so long as he lives; this will lead him to cast off all hope in God, and to give himself up to despair.[143]

A number of other clergy echoed Stebbing's concern: making feelings the criteria for judging assurance induced despair.[144]

Antinomianism, it was suggested, was an outcome. Those who felt assured, believing themselves secure in their salvation, would neglect good works. Assurance, said Bishop Gibson, "leads the people into . . . a neglect of the gospel-means of attaining [salvation] . . . It supersedes the means of grace, and all endeavours to grow in grace, that man be much concern'd to labour, who is already secure of his reward?"[145] Henry Stebbing contended that antinomianism was also the outcome for those who despaired because they were unable to claim assurance: "It cuts up virtue to the very root; for he who has no hope in God can have no heart to serve him."[146]

Late in life Wesley acknowledged that he and Charles had modified one aspect of their early teaching on assurance, which had been strongly criticized by their opponents. They no longer insisted that assurance was necessary for salvation: "When, fifty years ago," he commented to Melville Horne, "my brother Charles and I, in the simplicity of our hearts, taught the people that, unless they knew their sins were forgiven, they were under the wrath and curse of God, I marvel they did not stone us. The Methodists, I hope, know better now: we preach assurance as we always did, as a common privilege of the children of God; but we do not enforce it under the pain of damnation, denounced on all who enjoy it not."[147]

---

143 017-Gr. Stebbing, *A caution against religious delusion*, 16–17.

144 003-Gr. Bedford, *The doctrine of assurance*, 15; 005-Gr. T. G. [Gib], *Remarks on the Rev. Mr. Whitefield's journal*, 6–7; 167-Gr. [Smalbroke], *A charge delivered to the . . . clergy in . . . the diocese of Lichfield. . . 1741*, 1; 349-Gr. Hardy, *A letter from a clergyman to one of his parishioners who was inclined to turn Methodist*, 41.

145 206-Gr. [Gibson] *A charge of the Right Reverend Father in God, Edmund, Lord Bishop of London . . . 1746 and 1747*, 12–13; 049-Gr. Church, *An explanation and defence of the doctrine of regeneration*, 41.

146 017-Gr. Stebbing, *A caution against religious delusion*, 17.

147 First published in Robert Southey, *The Life of Wesley and the Rise and Progress of Methodism* (New York: W. B. Gilley, 1820), 1:258, this comment has been duly noted by many. Melville Horne (1761–1841) served for a time as one of Wesley's itinerants. He was ordained priest and served as curate to John Fletcher at Madeley, Shropshire.

Perfection

The doctrine of perfection was of pivotal importance in Wesley's Methodism. Wesley regarded it as a peculiar heritage entrusted to the Methodists by God.[148] Use of the term "perfect," however, created confusion and misunderstanding. Controversy surrounded it throughout the century, Anglicans and Calvinists joining in a battery of charges that forced Wesley to clarify his statements concerning it in a series of publications.[149] When he published his *Plain Account of Christian Perfection* in 1766, an apologia for the doctrine, Wesley asserted that his views had not changed from 1725 to 1765. If he had not changed them, they had undergone considerable modification in those years. In his early sermons there are statements on the complete absence of sin in the justified believer.[150] Wesley's early underemphasis on the continuance of sin in justified believers, and his talk of perfection, infuriated his contemporaries, who accused him of teaching that regeneration made the individual sinless. They were alarmed, moreover, that as a consequence of his preaching this doctrine, numbers of his followers had begun to claim complete freedom from sin. In 1741 Joseph Humphreys expressed concern that many Bristol and Kingswood Methodists claimed they "are without sin in thought, word, or deed; that they neither commit sin nor have sin, that they are sanctified throughout in soul, body, and spirit; being wholly deliver'd both from the power and from the very inbeing of all sin."[151]

Much of the controversy over this doctrine was due to disputants attributing to Wesley more than he intended. He defined sin as a voluntary transgression of a known law. The justified Christian was sinless only insofar as he or she did commit voluntary sin.[152] Wesley never suggested that perfection

---

148 John Wesley, Letter to Robert Carr, at Brackenbury, September 15, 1790, *Letters* (Telford) (London: Epworth, 1931), 8: 237–38.

149 See also Wesley, "Thoughts on Christian Perfection" (1760) in *BEWJW*, vol. 13, *Doctrinal and Controversial Treatises II*, ed. Paul Wesley Chilcote and Kenneth J. Collins (Nashville: Abingdon, 2013), 54–80; Wesley, Sermon 40, "Christian Perfection," *BEWJW*, 2:97–124; Sermon 43, "The Scripture Way of Salvation," *BEWJW*, 2:153–69.

150 Wesley, Sermon 1, "Salvation by Faith," *BEWJW*, 1:109–130; Sermon 2, "The Almost Christian," *BEWJW*, 1:131–41; Sermon 17, "The Circumcision of the Heart," *BEWJW*, 1:398–414; Sermon 12, "The Witness of Our Own Spirit," *BEWJW*, 1:299–313, where Wesley teaches that the justified Christian is freed from sin. He later modified his views. See Wesley, Sermon 13, "On Sin in Believers," *BEWJW*, 1:314–34.

151 136A-Ba. Humphreys, *A letter to the members of the religious societies*, 16–17.

152 John Wesley, Sermon 19, "The Great Privilege of Those That Are Born of God," *BEWJW*, 1:436.

would remove a person's creaturely limitations—human beings were never free of error or ignorance.[153] Despite such disclaimers, opponents argued that Wesley was guilty of preaching "angelism." Josiah Tucker believed Wesley taught that one could be "free not only from willful sins, from sins of delibera- tion and choice, but also from moral frailties, weaknesses and imperfections, i.e., from such slips and failings in our duty, arising from surprize, hurry of temptation, or any other pitiable circumstances, that are really and properly sins of infirmity."[154] No human being could attain such perfection.

Calvinists charged Wesley with not appreciating the extent of human depravity. Conversion and sanctification never completely blot out the effects of original sin. Christians, though accepted by God, remain sinners through- out their lives. Sin continues to permeate everything they do or think. The Calvinist stance was summarized by Mrs. Anne Dutton:

> 'For tho' by the Holy Ghost's work in regeneration he has given us a new, and holy nature, and wrought a universal change in the soul: Yet is not the soul wholly new, entirely holy, and univer- sally changed . . . And so long as the soul is imperfect, so long sin doth, and will abide in all the powers and faculties thereof: even all sin, the seeds, or habits of all sin: a whole body of sin, not this or that member only, but a body, for the completeness of parts . . . man . . . having both the new, and old nature in him . . . sinneth daily, the holiest of his actions being mixt with sin. And he often falls into acts of sin either more inward, or outward, in heart, or life.[155]

Wesley's doctrine of perfection, Calvinists argued, was unscriptural. None of the Old Testament people of faith made claims to perfection, nor did any of the men and women of the New Testament. Indeed, Paul, the great apostle, many times remarked upon his own imperfection.[156] At fault, the Calvinists said, was Wesley's exegesis of Scripture. He had misinterpreted certain pas- sages from the First Epistle of John. In his sermon "On Christian Perfection,"

---

153 John Wesley, Sermon 62, "The End of Christ's Coming," *BEWJW*, 2:481–82.

154 150-Gr. Tucker, *A brief history of the principles of Methodism*, 38.

155 153-Gr. [Anne Dutton], *Letters to the Reverend Mr. John Wesley*, 16–17, 21; 131-Gr. Fleetwood, *The perfectionists examined*, 27, 30.

156 131-Gr. Fleetwood, *The perfectionists examined*, 46; 205C-Ki. W. D. [Dowars], *Errors in part discovered*, 44.

Wesley contended that 1 John 1:8, "If we say we have no sin" should be read as "If we say that we have not sinned"—thus making it refer to commission of sin in the past.[157] Critics, rejecting this interpretation, insisted that the author of the epistle wrote concerning sin in the present. John's phrase "whosoever abideth in him [Christ] sinneth not" (1 John 1:9) ought not to be taken to mean that the sanctified Christian no longer sins, but that he or she eschews sin; "[H]e doth not make a trade and business of sinning," because he has been born of God.[158]

Calvinists complained that Wesley set perfection too low. He taught that perfection was attainable on earth; they believed that it was not. The only perfection that a human being could claim on earth was not his or her own but an alien one—Christ's. Mrs. Dutton explained: "I see so much imperfection in my graces and duties, that I am glad to run by faith, out of my imperfect self, into my perfect Jesus, and to see my beauty in his fairness, and my blackness swallowed up in his comeliness."[159] Human partial sanctification on earth would be made whole in heaven. Augustus Toplady reminded the Arminian wing of Methodism in 1770 that those who wished to see "a perfect saint" must go to heaven, since "there only are the spirits of just men made perfect. This earth, on which we live, never bore but three sinless persons: our first parents, in the short state of innocence; and . . .Christ, in the days of his abode below."[160] Wesley's Anglican critics also believed that the doctrine of perfection on earth was unscriptural. They contended that although the Bible taught that humans could achieve a degree of perfection on earth, it was a limited perfection. As the Christian grows in grace, he or she imitates (with the Holy Spirit's assistance) the perfection of God as seen in Christ. It is gradual and progressive—humans always remain imperfect, but they move toward perfection.[161]

---

157 John Wesley, Sermon 40, "On Christian Perfection," *BEWJW*, 2:115–16.

158 353A–Ba. A Professor of Christianity, *A scriptural account of the doctrine of perfection*, 6. Cf. 336-GR. W. P., *An answer to Mr. C___ P___'s letter to Mr. P___e* (London: no printer, 1762), 6.

159 153-Gr. [Anne Dutton], *Letters to the Reverend Mr. John Wesley*, 50.

160 427-Gr. Augustus Montague Toplady, *A caveat against unsound doctrines* (London: for Joseph Gurney, 1770), 54–55.

161 185-Gr. Church, *Remarks on the Reverend Mr. John Wesley's late journal*, 60; 205-Gr. Church, *Some farther remarks on the Rev. Mr. John Wesley's late journal*, 115–16; 226A-Ki. Roche, *Moravian Heresy*, 315; 133-Gr. Land, *A second letter to the Rev. Mr. Whitefield*, 21.

The consequences of the doctrine alarmed opponents. Calvinists believed that it led to the doctrine of works righteousness. If humans were capable of perfect obedience, they could claim that they merited salvation. Perfect Christians had no need of a savior. Christ's death upon the cross was thus rendered unnecessary.[162] Anglicans suggested that teaching perfection encouraged people to indulge in self-delusion and self-righteousness. Those who claimed to be in a state of perfection allowed spiritual pride to dominate their lives and hold others in contempt. Those who professed perfection were satirized as Pharisees:

> None live such holy lives as they;
> However this appears notorious.
> These holy ones are the most censorious
> . . . .
> The pharisee (with proud disdain)
> His boasted virtues did proclaim:
> The publican went off the winner,
> Who did confess himself a sinner.[163]

Despair was another outcome. Those who could not live up to the expectations of a perfect life became despondent with their attempts.[164]

Richard Hill maintained that Wesley's distinction between infirmities and sins was too easily misapplied. Some who professed perfection excused a person's sinfulness as the result of human frailty.[165] William Combe expressed Hill's concern satirically by alleging that the doctrine of perfection

---

162 194-Gr. An Impartial Hand, *An essay containing evident proofs against the Methodists*, 49; 449-Gr. Author of *P.O.* [Hill], *A review of all the doctrines taught by the Reverend Mr. John Wesley* (London: for E. and C. Dilly, 1772), 49; 531-Gr. John Muirhead, *A review of the principles of such Methodists as are under the direction of . . . John Wesley* (Kelso: J. Palmer, 1784), 25; 094-Gr. Bowman, *The imposture of Methodism display'd*, 45; 206-Gr. [Gibson], *The charge of the Right Reverend Father in God, Edmund, Lord Bishop of London, at the visitation of his diocese in the years 1746 and 1747*, 16–17; 164-Gr. [Gibson], *Observations upon the conduct and behaviour of . . . Methodists*, 10.

163 156-Gr. An Impartial Hand, *The progress of Methodism in Bristol*, 25.

164 206-Gr. [Gibson], *The charge of the Right Reverend Father in God, Edmund Lord Bishop of London . . . 1746 and 1747*, 17; 351-Gr. *A word in season* (London: M. Lewis, 1763), 5–6.

165 449-Gr. The author of *P. O.* [Hill], *A review of all the doctrines taught by the Rev. Mr. John Wesley*, 55–56.

was a facade behind which the Methodists practiced loose living.[166] In his *Perfection. A Poetical Epistle* (1778) Combe vilified the imperfect behavior of a self-styled "perfect Methodist preacher":

> For sanctity, and rapes on babes, well-known;
> Perfection's child—a suckling of your [Wesley's] own.
> With him perfection's graft brought forth, good fruit,
> In faith an angel, and in works a brute . . .
> Thus thro' delusion's mist perfection leads
> God's chosen people to the worst of deeds.[167]

Satirists alleged that the tenet of perfection masked immorality, not only among the Methodists at large, but also in Wesley himself. Combe scurrilously wrote:

> 'Perfection only saves'—John gravely cries;
> Mark how his life his tenet justifies!
> 'The husband of one wife' this saint appears;
> Who wou'd suspect his sanctity and years?
> . . . Whilst on sin of wantonness he dwells,
> His own weak flesh at sev'nty-five rebels.[168]

Although he never claimed perfection himself, Wesley was willing to accept self-evidence from those who professed attainment. Reliance on others' estimates of their own spiritual condition was naiveté on Wesley's part, said John Muirhead, ridiculing the doctrine's subjectivism: "He appeals to the experience of some of his votaries: 'I knew such and such person in such and such a condition.' And he appears to give the same credit unto this kind of knowledge, that he does unto 'Thus saith the Lord,' or unto the experience of the saints recorded in scripture."[169]

Pervading much of the criticism of Methodist theology was the suspicion that subjectivism had replaced rationality as the grounds for theological judgment. The evangelicals appeared to appeal to the emotions rather than

---

166 516-Gr. [Combe], *The saints* (London: J. Bew, 1778), 40, 44. A new edition was published in 1778 under the title of *The fanatic saints; or Bedlamites inspired*. 517-Gr. [Combe], *Perfection: a poetical epistle* (London: J. Bew, 1778), 10–11.

167 517-Gr. [Combe], *Perfection*, 10–11.

168 516A-Ki. [Combe], *The fanatic saints*, 26–27.

169 531-Gr. Muirhead, *A review of the principles of such Methodists as are under the direction of . . . John Wesley*, 22.

the mind. Heart had replaced head—a Christian knew something was right if experience rather than reason confirmed it. Private judgment was emphasized. Individuals established themselves as their own infallible interpreters of truth.

Fear that the implications of Methodism's distinctive doctrines were dangerous prompted many attacks. Opponents of Methodism believed that the danger of antinomianism was raising its ugly head once more in many Methodist tenets.

CHAPTER 4

Innovative Practices

I t was not the novelty of their theological emphases alone that brought upon the Methodists such violent disapproval—the irregularity of their practices attracted even more vehement censure than did their "new" doctrines.[1] Critics of the revival were aghast at the extent of irregular practices adopted by Whitefield and Wesley. These attacks were not just reactions to the novelty of Methodist practices; they were, as Henry Rack states, expressions of "social alarm and outrage."[2] Observers were astonished as one by one the unwritten Anglican canons of good taste were rejected by the Methodists. It seemed that Methodists, as they adopted one unsanctioned behavior after another, were bent on abandoning all social and religious propriety.

Infiltration of Religious Societies

It became clear very early that the Methodists were intent on assuming control of the religious societies that had sprung up in England at the end of the seventeenth century under the influence of Anthony Horneck, minister at the Savoy Chapel, London.[3] Informally related to the Church of England, each society was under Anglican clergy leadership. The rules of the societies enjoined members to diligence in private devotion and regular attendance upon the worship services of the Church of England. At the onset of the evangelical revival, the societies were in decline, but numbers of them still survived in London, Westminster, and Bristol.[4] The Methodist leaders provided

---

1 Cragg, *BEWJW*, vol. 11, *The Appeals to Men of Reason and Religion, and Certain Related Open Letters*, 23–32. Cragg asserts that many of the attacks on the methods used by the Methodists grew out of their offending the religious proprieties of the age.

2 Henry D. Rack, *Reasonable Enthusiast: John Wesley and the Rise of Methodism* (Philadelphia: Trinity Press International, 1989), 280.

3 Anthony Horneck (1641–1697), a German Protestant who migrated to England and became an influential and popular evangelical preacher and one of eight chaplains to King William. *ODNB*.

4 John S. Simon, *John Wesley and the Religious Societies* (London: Epworth, 1921), 17–27; John Walsh, Origins of the Evangelical Revival, in C. V. Bennett and J. D. Walsh, eds., *Essays in Modern Church History* (London: A. C. Black, 1966), 144–5; Richard P. Heitzenrater, *Wesley and the People Called Methodists* (Nashville: Abingdon Press, 1995), 21–24; Henry Rack, *Reasonable Enthusiast*, 186–7.

the existing societies with an impetus for renewal, but their infiltration into the leadership threatened the Church of England's control. During 1738 and 1739 Anglican divines watched with mounting concern and expressed grave fears that the Methodists' control of the societies would result in schism from the Church of England.

In 1738 T. Gib addressed a thirty-two-page pamphlet to the religious societies, warning them against Whitefield's dangerous doctrines. The young Methodist preacher's enthusiasm, Gib claimed, was causing needless divisions within the societies, thus hindering their task of advancing Christian faith and practice. He called for suppression of the enthusiastic tendencies being encouraged by Whitefield.[5] Tristram Land also expressed concern about Methodist infiltration of the religious societies. In 1739 he published an open letter to Whitefield, to which he appended a circular he had previously written to members of the societies. Land commended the societies for the role they had played in promoting loyalty to the Church but cautioned them against allowing the Methodists to gain control. If they did get control, he believed, both Church and state were threatened:

> Considering the religious sentiments and political principles of some of the chief leaders of these Methodists, it may concern our ecclesiastical and civil governors carefully to watch your behaviour, lest in the end you should be artfully led into fatal mistakes and designs destructive of both parts of our constitution.[6]

William Berriman, rector of St. Andrew's, Undershaft, and fellow of Eton College, reiterated Land's concern in a sermon preached at the quarterly meeting of the religious societies, 21 March 1738–39. The sermon was a calm plea for caution, appealing to the members to obey the rules and regulations governing the societies. They should not force their own standards of religious duty on others, should be especially careful not to establish parties in the church based on personalities, should adhere to the doctrinal standards of the Church of England, and do nothing to create disesteem for the liturgy of the Church.[7]

---

5 005-Gr. [T. Gib], *Remarks on the Reverend Mr. Whitefield's journal*, 6.

6 009-Gr. Land, *A letter to the Rev. Mr. Whitefield*, 8.

7 048A-Ba. William Berriman, *A sermon preach'd to the religious societies* (London: John Carter, 1739). Berriman (1688–1750) was educated at Oriel College, Oxford, where he

Leonard Twells, in a sermon delivered before the religious societies in the early years of the revival, attacked the dangerous practices beginning to emerge. He was disturbed by the rejection of the standard expository commentaries and the growing custom of extempore exposition of the Scripture. Heresy and fanaticism, he thought, would be the inevitable outcomes if such practices were allowed to continue. Individual confession of sins before the whole society also disquieted him. The Methodists, Twells contended, had introduced these practices, and he urged the members of the societies to avoid them. Great care should be exercised in selecting spiritual directors to ensure that those chosen were "not only pious, but peaceable and modest." People such as the Methodists, who "break through the laws of the Church and State and defy the pastoral admonitions of their proper superiors," should not be chosen.[8] In 1744 Bishop Gibson noted that the Methodists had successfully infiltrated a number of the religious societies in London and Westminster. These, he said, had been "unhappily misled into . . . extravagances." The majority, however, had retained their allegiance to the Church of England and had "behaved with modesty and decency, and without any violation of publick order and regularity."[9] It is clear that both Anglican clergy and hierarchy thought that the combination of Methodists and religious societies was dangerous. A strong leader might unify and organize the societies and lead them to sever what tenuous ties they still retained to the Church. Left unchecked, Methodism might develop into a schismatic movement.

Anglican fears were heightened when Wesley assumed control of the Baldwin Street and Nicholas Street societies in Bristol and welded them into a unified society under his sole direction.[10] In mid-1738 he moved the "United Society," as they had begun to call themselves, into the unfinished New Room in the Horsefair, Bristol, Wesley's western headquarters. After returning to

---

earned his BA, MA, and DD degrees. He was ordained priest on December 12, 1712. *ODNB*.

8 Leonard Twells (?1684–1742), an Anglican priest and theologian, was rector of St. Matthew Street, London, from which he resigned some time before 1743, when he published some sermons in two volumes. *ODNB*. 154A-Ba. Leonard Twells, *Twenty–four sermons preach'd at the parish church of St. Mary le Bow*, 2 vols. (London: no printer, 1743), 363–64. Twells's sermon to the religious societies was probably preached in 1739 or 1740, but not published until it was placed in this collection of sermons. A second edition was published in one volume in 1755.

9 164-Gr. [Gibson], *Observations upon the conduct and behaviour of . . . Methodists*, 8.

10 See Baker, *JWCE*, chap. 5, "Societies, Preachers and Communion," 64–80.

London because of controversy in the Anglican Fetter Lane Society,[11] Wesley led out a minority of its members in November 1739 into a new society, which he set up in the Foundery, Upper Moorfields, the London headquarters of the nascent Methodist movement. He became the supreme authority in these societies. Members owed allegiance to Wesley, their spiritual director, rather than to the Church of England or its hierarchy. During the 1740s societies under Wesley's wing multiplied throughout England.

Methodist Societies

When the Methodists began to form their own societies, removed from all church control, Church of England clergy believed that their earlier fears were not unfounded—a schismatic movement was afoot. It was customary for religious societies to have a relationship to the Church of England, even if somewhat informal, but the Methodists began setting up societies outside the pale of Anglican supervision. While the Anglican societies had served the Church, the Methodist societies, critics complained, undermined it. Few Anglican clergy would have quarreled with Joseph Trapp's assessment—the effect, if not intent, of Methodism, he believed, was schism. As Methodists elevated the importance of their societies, the value they placed on the church diminished proportionately.

> The Church itself, as a regular, well-order'd society is by these irregularly upstart societies, even by the heat of them . . . greatly weaken'd and impair'd. By these extraordinaries they take off from the reverence due to the ordinary standing rules and laws of the Church. For tho' they do constantly attend divine service, as prescribed in the public offices; yet I appeal to all discerning and judicious persons, whether, in the nature of things, they are not likely to set a greater value upon their own particular meetings and exercises, set up purely by their own fancies . . . To be plain; if what I am inform'd of these meetings be true, they are schismatical, in their tendency at least, tho' not so designed.[12]

Thomas Church pressed the point further—the Methodists' societies did not

---

11   Richard P. Heitzenrater, *Wesley and the People Called Methodists* (Nashville: Abingdon, 1995), 10–12.

12   010-Gr. Trapp, *The nature, folly, sin and danger of being righteous over-much*, 37–38.

function as an arm of the Church, as previous religious societies had done, but were separate groups outside of, and pitted against, the establishment.[13]

Critics noted the differences between the Methodist and the Anglican societies. Bishop Gibson maintained that the former were harmful to the Church, while the latter, whose activities were carried out in "a private inoffensive way," were respectful of the Church. The latter's members attended the public services of the Church, and they met in the evening to "employ the remainder of the day in serious conversation, and in reading good books."[14] Church reiterated his diocesan's point: "Their [the Church's societies'] meetings are private ones, after having attended the publick assemblies of the Church. Yours [the Methodists'] are publick ones and have drawn people away from our churches."[15] In writing to Wesley, Church complained of the Methodists' establishment of "separate societies against the Church."[16] In 1746 he went so far as to allege that Wesley had set up what amounted to a series of nonconformist churches.[17] The author of *The Methodists: An humorous burlesque poem* opined that the Methodists wished to stay in the Anglican Church and, as a part of a satanic and popish plot, destroy it from within. Satan says:

> They with the church establish'd join.
> Its pow'r the more to undermine.
> By rule they eat, by rule they drink,
> Do all things else by rule but think,
> Accuse their priests of loose behaviour
> To get more in the laymen's favour,
> Method alone must guide 'em all,
> Whence Methodists themselves, they call,
> Here I my triumphs fix to come,
> And here shalt thou fix thine, O Rome![18]

---

13 185-Gr. Church, *Remarks on the Reverend Mr. John Wesley's last journal*, 14. Cf. 248A-Ba. A Lay-man, *A few queries concerning the growth of Methodism*, 73; 094-Gr. Bowman, *The imposture of Methodism display'd*, 73; 226A-Ki. Roche, *Moravian heresy*, 294.

14 164-Gr. [Gibson], *Observations upon the conduct and behaviour of . . . Methodists*, 8.

15 165-Gr. Church, *A serious and expostulatory letter to the Rev. Mr. George Whitefield*, 9.

16 185-Gr. Church, *Remarks on the Reverend Mr. John Wesley's last journal*, 14.

17 205-Gr. Church, *Some farther remarks on the Reverend Mr. John Wesley's last journal*, 13.

18 026-Gr. *The Methodists: An humorous burlesque poem*, 15.

An Emerging Methodist Structure

Wesley had no well thought-out, predetermined, or integrated structure to impose upon the Methodist movement. There was, as Frank Baker notes, "no master plan to form a new sect."[19] The structure that emerged piece by piece was pragmatic, functional, and responsive to the needs of the growing movement. To achieve what he believed was a "divine mission," Wesley was ready to use almost any method so long as it was in harmony with the Bible and the early church's teaching and practices.[20] Motivated by an overpowering sense of mission, Wesley began his bold and innovative experiments: the introduction of bands, select societies, classes, field preaching, itineration, and the use of lay preachers. Such ecclesiastical experiments in the emerging organization of Methodism provided ample fodder for controversy and vehement anti-Methodist attacks.

Bands

One of Wesley's most important innovations was the division of societies into small groups known as "bands" for intimate confession and exhortation. He had experimented with small groups in Oxford and Georgia and had supported the division of the Fetter Lane Society into two "companies"—married and single men—which met separately. It was after his visit to the Moravian settlement at Herrnhut in Saxony, however, that he began systematically to urge the religious societies to organize these small confessional cells consisting of four or five people, with the men separated from women, and the married from the single. On Christmas Day, 1738, Wesley drew up "Rules of the band-societies."[21] Intimate confession and penitential discipline were the marks of the Rules. Surprisingly, there was little criticism of the bands from outsiders. What attacks there were centered on three aspects—scurrilous charges concerning the bands for women, the secrecy surrounding what went on in the bands, and the similarity of the bands to the Catholic confessional.

---

19 Frank Baker, "The People Called Methodist—3. Polity," in *The History of the Methodist Church in Great Britain*, ed. Rupert Davies and Gordon Rupp (London: Epworth, 1965), 1:213.

20 Ibid., 214–15.

21 John Wesley, "Rules of the band societies drawn up Dec. 25, 1738," and "Directions given to the band societies, Dec. 25, 1744," in *BEWJW*, vol. 9, *The Methodist Societies: History, Nature, and Design*, ed. Rupert E. Davies (Nashville: Abingdon, 1989), 77–79.

The earliest attack in pamphlet form came in 1739 in an appendix added to *A compleat account of the conduct of that eminent enthusiast Mr. Whitefield*, entitled *A method of confession drawn up for the use of women Methodists. Taken from the original.* The author described it on the title page as "a most useful and entertaining catechism for the use of female Methodists." Basically, it was an amended, sexualized version of Wesley's band rules, with the following questions added:

> Are you in love?
>
> Do you take more pleasure in anybody than in God?
>
> Whom do you love just now, better than any other person in the world?
>
> Is not the person an idol?
>
> Does he not (especially in publick prayer) steal in between God and your soul?
>
> Does any court you?
>
> Is there any one whom you suspect to have any such design?
>
> Is there anyone who shews you more respect than to other women?
>
> Are you not pleased with that?
>
> How do you like him?
>
> How do you feel yourself, when he comes, when he stays, when he goes away?[22]

The alleged intimacy in the discussion of their love affairs made the bands for women a ready target. The former Methodist James Lackington spread the scurrilous rumor that some young Methodist men were known to disguise themselves as females to gain entry to the women's bands.[23]

The secrecy veiling what took place when these close-knit cells met worried critics. Antagonists disapproved of the public behavior of the Methodists and assumed that their private conduct could only be worse. If they

---

22 036-Gr. [Tucker], *A compleat account of the conduct of . . . Mr. Whitefield*, 19. "The method of confession" was also included in 040-Gr. An impartial hand [Josiah Tucker], *Life and particular proceedings of the Reverend Mr. George Whitefield*, 17–8. It had appeared earlier in the *Gentleman's Magazine* 9 (1739), 238–42.

23 560-Gr. Lackington, *Memoirs of . . . the life of James Lackington*, 120.

were so abusive to the clergy and the church in the open, what was taking place behind closed doors? John Roche wondered: "Men who vent so much bald scurrility, bitterness, nay hatred in print, what can escape them when among themselves in their private bands?"[24] One anti-Methodist sought to lift the veil of secrecy from the bands when in 1750 he printed a pirated edition of Wesley's band rules. Although accurately printed, the folio broadside carried unfriendly comment. By making these rules public, "which are kept by them [the Methodists] great secrecy," the opponent obviously hoped that the absurdity of how the bands operated would be exposed.[25]

It was the confessional nature of the bands that drew the strongest disapproval. Bishop Gibson sneered at the fact that the direction of the confessional cells was in the hands of "for the most part . . . common mechanicks and ignorant women."[26] Another author claimed that confessions from the women's bands were entered in a book by the band leader and passed on to Wesley.[27] The most vicious attack on the confessional aspects of the bands came from Bishop Lavington, who charged Wesley with having introduced the Roman Catholic confessional into his societies. The searching personal examination of the band meetings, he suggested, was akin to Jesuit interrogation in the confessional box. Lavington further accused Wesley of gathering reports of what was said in confidence in the bands, and of bringing delinquent members before himself to be confessed privately. Lavington asserted that practices such as gleaning personal secrets made the Jesuits powerful. This was Wesley's aim as well, he implied.[28] John Erskine, Presbyterian minister of Old Greyfriars Church, Edinburgh, issued similar charges. Wesley had gained ascendancy over his followers, he said, by gathering highly personal information from the bands to use as blackmail.[29] James Lackington claimed that the Methodists believed band confession was the only way to defeat the devil:

> [I]t is a maxim amongst them that exposing to one another what
> the devil has particularly tempted them to commit, will make the

---

24 226A-Ki. John Roche, *Moravian heresy* (Dublin: for the author, 1751), 288.

25 222A-Ba. *Rules for the band societies* (n.p.: no printer, 1750).

26 206-Gr. [Gibson], *The charge of the Right Reverend Father in God, Edmund, Lord Bishop of London . . . 1746 and 1747*, 6.

27 156-Gr. An Impartial Hand, *The progress of Methodism in Bristol*, 20–21.

28 213A-Ki. [Lavington], *The enthusiasm of Methodists and papist compar'd*, pt. 2, 167–70.

29 363-Gr. Erskine, *Mr. Wesley's principles detected*, 27.

old fellow more careful how he tempts, when he knows that all his secrets will be told the next meeting. This they call shaming the devil.[30]

Select Societies

In some of Wesley's larger societies there was another subdivision—the select society, later known as the select band.[31] Wesley first noted this category in his diary on May 20, 1741.[32] Originally membership of these groups was open to all who had evidenced consistent Christian lives and growth in grace. Later, they were regarded as designed for those who were acknowledged to be pressing on to perfection. This category gradually fell into abeyance, destroyed by spiritual pride. Surprisingly, there was little criticism of select societies. Augustus Toplady, however, noted them with scorn:

> You [Wesley] formed a scheme of collecting as many perfect ones as you could, to live together under one roof. A number of these followers were accordingly transplanted, from some of your nursery-beds to the hot-house. And what a hot-house it soon proved. For would we believe it? the sinless people quarrelled, in a short time, at so violent a rate that you found yourselves forced to disband the select regiment.[33]

Classes

The year 1742 saw the introduction of a new subdivision of the society—the class.[34] This grouping arose from a suggestion by Captain Foy that members of the Bristol society contribute a penny a week as a means to liquidate the debt on the New Room. To facilitate the collection of the contributions, the

---

30 560-Gr. Lackington, *Memoirs of . . . the life of James Lackington*, 119.

31 The Early Conferences Manuscript Minutes, Miscellaneous References, 1744–1764, MS Minutes, London Conference, June 1774, in *BEWJW*, vol. 10, *The Methodist Societies, the Minutes of Conference*, ed. Henry D. Rack (Nashville: Abingdon, 1976–), 123–46.

32 John Wesley, May 20, 1741, in *BEWJW*, vol. 19, *Journals and Diaries II (1738–1743)*, ed. W. Reginald Ward and Richard P. Heitzenrater (Nashville: Abingdon, 1976–), 461.

33 424-Gr. Augustus Montague Toplady, *A letter to the Rev. John Wesley relative to his pretended abridgement of Zanchius* (London: Joseph Gurney, 1770), 23.

34 See David Lowes Watson, *The Early Methodist Class Meeting: Its Origins and Significance* (Nashville: Discipleship Resources, 1985).

society was divided into classes of about twelve; each with a leader. Wesley was quick to appreciate the opportunities for pastoral oversight that such an arrangement offered. It was not long before groups of twelve or so people of both sexes and different ages and marital status were meeting together. Although the meetings were less searching than those of the bands, they were subject to much the same kind of criticism. The earliest attacks on classes concerned the tickets issued quarterly to members in good standing. The author of *The progress of Methodism in Bristol* satirized this practice in 1743 for engendering spiritual arrogance:

> All other comers then forbidden,
> Excepting those who, this priest-ridden,
> Believ'd, by virtue of this ticket.
> They'r separated from the wicked.[35]

Commenting on the custom of members to contribute a thank offering of a shilling when they received a new class ticket, Lackington suggested that "money seemed to be the principal end of issuing tickets."[36]

Anti-Methodists were astonished at the allegation that Wesley had distributed class tickets illustrated with a crucifix. This, critics claimed, was sure evidence of the Methodists' papist tendencies.[37] Moreover, since confession was a part of class meetings, opponents charged the Methodists with instituting Catholic auricular private confession in the classes, as well as in bands.[38] Fears were expressed regarding the information gleaned from disclosures of spiritual failings in the fellowship of the class. The spiritual scrutiny of classes often exposed "weaknesses in families and particular persons, which may be turned to the advantage of designing men." Could the Methodist leaders vouch for the integrity of all their class leaders? inquired Thomas Mortimer.[39] The author of *A plain and easy road to the land of bliss* suggested that one Methodist leader found that what he learned in confession was helpful in

---

35 156-Gr. An Impartial Hand, *The progress of Methodism in Bristol*, 15.

36 560-Gr. Lackington, *Memoirs of the . . . life of James Lackington*, 122.

37 174-Gr. Eusebius [Fleming], *A fine picture of enthusiasm*, 24–25. Cf. 194-Gr. An Impartial Hand, *An essay containing evident proofs against the Methodists*, 10.

38 194-Gr. An Impartial Hand, *An essay containing evident proofs against the Methodists*, 10.

39 268-Gr. [Mortimer], *Die and be damned*, 43–44. Mortimer (1730–1810) was the author of voluminous miscellaneous works, chiefly on economic issues. *ODNB*.

maintaining discipline: "As a shepherd, by his crook, has his sheep within his reach, and can pull them to this side, thrust them from him, or bring them back; so by dint of confession Mr. _____ has his followers under his thumb."[40] Confessional secrets confided by female devotees were found especially useful by lecherous male class leaders. Theodosia's spiritual adviser in *The story of the Methodist-lady* "was made master of her closest secrets, which he piously converted to his own purpose."[41] Combe dubbed class leaders "spiritual spies, who inform the principal teacher of what may be most essential to his wishes or his interest."[42] Combe warned of the danger, in confessing to the class leader, of trust betrayed:

> Ye sons of Loyola, now say, with tears
> Why sisters shou'd confess their sins and fears?
> Why ev'ry weakness to a knave reveal.
> Who keeps the key that he may freely steal.[43]

Class meetings were condemned as spiritual hothouses in which the worst traits of Methodism were propagated and nurtured—theological uncertainty was fostered, vicious rumours encouraged, spiritual pride engendered, self-depreciation promoted, and immorality advocated. John Erskine suggested that narrating doubts and scruples about the faith in small groups often excited similar uncertainty in the minds of others. If an individual found it difficult to keep a secret, Erskine was sure that confidences shared by twelve persons in a class could not be maintained. Vicious rumours would be spread by those who broke the trust among members.[44] Spiritual arrogance, John Kirkby believed, was the inevitable result of relating one's intimate spiritual experiences. He supposed that "these cabals" were established for no other purpose than "to afford them a freer opportunity without witnesses to please and gratify their pharisaical pride . . . in repeating their own supposed excellences to which their neighbours' foibles must always be their foil."[45] A former class member, James Lackington, disagreed with Kirkby, and claimed that rather than self-adulation, class meetings were marked by self-depreciation:

---

40 337-Gr. *A plain and easy road to the land of bliss*, 130.
41 238-Gr. *The story of the Methodist-lady*, 27.
42 516A-Ki. [Combe], *The fanatic saints*, 8n1.
43 517-Gr. [Combe], *Perfection: A poetical epistle*, 21–22.
44 363-Gr. [Erskine], *Mr. Wesley's principles detected*, 23.
45 217-Gr. Kirkby, *The impostor detected*, 52–53.

"the major part exclaiming against themselves, and declaring that they were the most vile abandoned wretches on this side of hell, that they wondered why the earth did not open and swallow them up alive."[46]

Combe made the scurrilous charge that immorality was condoned in classes—female class leaders acted as procuresses for the lecherous Wesley.[47] An anonymous author suggested that the physical attraction between male class leaders and female class members was irresistible:

> What maid wou'd not be holy kist?
> Or who her teacher can resist?
> Or when he tells her of her h——n
> What blessing thence to all are giv'n
> Which after death sh's sure to meet;
> The dear temptation is so sweet.[48]

It was no wonder the Methodists condemned the theater, another author said. They had no need for it. What went on in classes provided all the entertainment they needed: "[T]hey are every day hearing or seeing something new. When to this also we add a catalogue of anecdotes, experiences, visions, miraculous interpositions, &c. Nothing can be better calculated for amusing and entertaining weak and deluded men."[49]

Field Preaching

Since 1738 most Church of England pulpits in London and Bristol had been closed to Whitefield and the Wesley brothers. On February 23, 1739, Whitefield made an important break with ecclesiastical convention. Having sought and been denied access to the pulpits of Bristol, the young Anglican clergyman, following precedents set earlier by the Welsh layman Howell Harris and others, preached out of doors at Kingswood. John Wesley was not far behind. On April 2, 1739, he "submitted to be more vile" and began to preach in the open air.[50] Both men would have preferred to use a church, but they were

---

46 560-Gr. Lackington, *Memoirs of the . . . life of James Lackington*, 115–17.

47 523-Gr. [Combe], *Voltaire's ghost*, 27.

48 026-Gr. *The Methodists: An humorous burlesque poem*, 19.

49 555-Gr. *A review of the policy, doctrines and morals of the Methodists*, 1–8.

50 John Wesley, April 2, 1739, in *BEWJW*, vol. 19, *Journals and Diaries II (1738–43)*, ed. W. Reginald Ward and Richard P. Heitzenrater (Nashville: Abingdon, 1976–), 46–47.

forced from pulpit to field. From 1739 evangelical preaching out of doors became their norm.

The Anglican response was immediate and hostile. Ironically, the Methodists were rebuked for deserting the pulpits to preach in the open air. John Brownsword rushed into print in 1739 and reminded the Methodists that good ends may be pursued by bad means. Field preaching was not the appropriate means "ever to affect that end which is the glory of God, and the good of men, the purity of religion, and the peaceable fruits of righteousness."[51] Field-preaching was inimical to worship—sermons belonged in churches, the only appropriate places for the celebration of divine services. The willingness of Methodists to preach anywhere made the practice an easy target for attack: "Time, place, circumstance, &c. make no difference;" they will discourse "from a cart, a butcher's stall, or the brink of a draw well."[52]

The legality of Methodists assembling congregations outdoors was challenged in a sermon preached before the University of Oxford on August 5, 1739, by John Wilder, rector of St. Aldates, Oxford. He accused the Methodists of holding "illegal and tumultuous assemblies." Although he did not cite the specific civil and religious laws defied by the Methodists, he hinted broadly that they broke the provisions of the Act of Toleration. The actions of the Methodists, he opined, created "a breach of those laws which are enacted for the peace and quiet of the kingdom. And for the support of uniformity, decency, and order in the church."[53] If the early critics of the Methodists had been vague about which law was being broken by field preaching, Edmund Gibson, bishop of London, was not. In running afoul of Gibson, the Methodists came up against one who was universally acknowledged in his day to be the greatest authority on Anglican polity. Gibson attacked field preaching in his twenty-four-page pamphlet entitled *Observations upon the conduct and behaviour of a certain sect usually distinguished by the name of Methodist* (1744). The law of the land, he said, expressly forbade preaching in the field. Still on the statute books, Gibson reminded his readers, was the Conventicle Act of 1670, which proscribed crowds assembling in the open

---

51 043-Gr. Brownsword, *The case of the rich young man in the gospel*, 10.
52 337-Gr. *A plain and easy road to the land of bliss*, 27.
53 018-Gr. Wilder, *The trial of the spirits*, 3, 20.

air for worship.[54] Moreover, field preaching was in direct contravention of the provisions of the Toleration Act that permitted Dissenters to worship in places that had been duly certified by the bishop, archdeacon, or justice of the peace. The act made no provision for meetings in the open air:

> It would be a strange construction to give any other meaning to the word place in that clause of the Act, than a particular house opened for religious worship, and a fix'd place to be repaired-to by a congregation of dissenters; in which sense it has been universally understood. And, indeed, the Act of Toleration itself plainly leads to this meaning, when it forbids any assembly of persons, dissenting from the Church of England, to be had "in any place for religious worship, with the doors lock'd, barr'd, or bolted."[55]

The Methodists stoutly denied that the Conventicle Act applied to their outdoor gatherings. Whitefield, in answering Gibson, cited the act's title, which described it as "An Act to prevent and suppress seditious conventicles," and contended that the only field preaching prohibited was that which contrived insurrection.[56] Wesley also took refuge under the act's title and agreed with Whitefield that only seditious conventicles were intended. Numerous authors came to Gibson's defense—the Methodists were in error. All religious assemblies out of doors, not just those suspected of being seditious, were forbidden: "They are not only the field-assemblies levell'd at, that 'have contrived insurrections,' that have been disloyal but all, lest any 'may at their meetings contrive insurrections,' and shew their disloyalty."[57] Later in 1744 the arguments against the Methodist practice of holding outdoor services were stated succinctly and forcefully in a four-page pamphlet entitled, *The case of the Methodists briefly stated more particularly*

---

54 164-Gr. [Gibson], *Observations upon the conduct and behaviour of . . . Methodists,* 4. For a discussion of how the Conventicle Act applied to the Methodists, see John S. Simon, "The Conventicle Act and its Relation to the Early Methodists," *ProcWHS* 11 (December 1917): 82–93. Cf. David Neil Hempton, "Methodism and the Law, 1740–1820," *Bulletin of the John Rylands University Library* 70 (1988): 93–107.

55 164-Gr. [Gibson], *Observations upon the conduct and behaviour of . . . Methodists,* 4.

56 [George Whitefield], *An answer to the first part of an anonymous pamphlet entitled 'Observations. . .'* in *The Works of The Reverend George Whitefield,* 6 vols. (London: Edward and Charles Dilly, and Messrs. Kincaid and Creech, 1771–1772), 4:123–40).

57 166-Gr. J. B., *A letter to the Reverend Mr. Whitefield, occasion'd by his pretended answer to the first part of the 'Observations upon the conduct and behavior of the Methodists,'* 23.

in the point of field-preaching.[58] Undoubtedly, the author was Gibson. The attack is similar to that set out in *Observations* and cites the Conventicle Act as critical.

Antagonism toward field preaching was based on fear that it would provide opportunities for sedition, would poison parishioners against their regular clergy, would lead men and women to neglect their vocational and family responsibilities, and would expose the gospel to ridicule. Fear that field preaching would lead to riot and rebellion was expressed early.[59] This fear grew in the 1740s and reached its peak in Gibson's two-pronged attack on field preaching in 1744. The two tracts were published when the country was gripped with fear of an invasion by Charles Edward Stuart, aka Bonnie Prince Charlie (1720–1788), the Stuart Pretender.[60] It was only natural that those concerned about the nation's political stability would look upon the vast assemblies of the Methodists in the fields with apprehension. If the Methodists were allowed unlimited freedom to assemble out of doors, opportunities would be provided for those who had dangerous designs on the state to mingle among the crowd. Gibson was alarmed at reports in Whitefield's journals that he preached to crowds of between four thousand and eighty thousand people.[61] Such vast assemblies were potentially dangerous to the state. In the eyes of many of Methodism's opponents, field preaching and sedition were inextricably linked:

> For surely, persons of the most disloyal and seditious intentions, cannot desire a fairer opportunity getting together, in order to execute any private and sudden designs they may have formed than an unrestrain'd and unquestion'd liberty of assembling in those vast numbers which Mr. Whitefield's field-preaching, has by his

---

58 170-Gr. [Gibson], *The case of the Methodists briefly stated* (London: printed for Edward Owen, 1744).

59 010-Gr. Trapp, *The nature, folly, sin and danger of being righteous over-much*, 58.

60 Charles Edward Stuart (1720–1788), grandson of James II of England, claimed the right to the English crown, and was known as the Young Pretender. His father, Francis Edward (1688–1776), had claimed the right to the crown earlier and was known as the Old Pretender. He led a failed Jacobite uprising in 1715. See Basil Williams, *The Whig Supremacy: 1714–1760*, 2nd ed., rev. C. H. Stuart (Oxford: Clarendon, 1962), 252–57.

61 The estimated size of the crowd at Whitefield's field preaching was a matter of controversy during his lifetime. Late in life he revised his journal entries to exclude estimates larger than twenty thousand and wrote: "so many thousand that many went away because they could not hear."

own account been attended, from time to time.[62] Although fear
of insurrection was the overriding reason for hostility toward field
preaching, critics also claimed that it would deepen the spirit of
anticlericalism among the common people. The Methodists were
luring people out of their pews and onto the grass, away from
their duly appointed pastors.[63] Bishop Warburton questioned:
"What for instance, does field-preaching imply but a famine of
the word, occasioned by a total neglect in the spiritual pastors
appointed by law?"[64]

The precedent for field preaching, the Methodists argued, was to be found
in the willingness of Jesus and the apostles to preach in the open air. Opponents rejected this rationale—in apostolic times, they argued, field preaching
was the only method of spreading the gospel open to early Christians, but
with the close of the third century, when the church became established,
buildings were set aside for worship. In eighteenth-century England critics
could find no justification for outdoor preaching.[65] Anti-Methodists, however,
found precedents other than scriptural for field preaching. Trapp reminded
his readers that the Puritans in the seventeenth century had preached in the
fields and streets of the nation, and disorder had followed.[66] Others pointed
to the Scottish Covenanters of the seventeenth century and the national unrest
they had caused.[67] And, of course, Bishop Lavington found ample precedent
in Roman Catholic enthusiasts—Peter of Verona, Anthony of Padua, and
Ignatius of Loyola.[68]

Anti-Methodists wondered aloud why the Methodists took to the fields.
Certainly, they were not commissioned to do so by their bishops. How could
they prove they were directed to do so by the Holy Spirit, when there was

---

62 170-Gr. [Gibson], *The case of the Methodists briefly stated*, 2. For a fuller discussion of
   this aspect, see chapter 5, "Social Upheaval."
63 166-Gr. J. B., *A letter to the Reverend Mr. Whitefield*, 42.
64 342-Gr. [Warburton], *The doctrine of grace*, 169.
65 Ibid.
66 010-Gr. Trapp, *The nature, folly, sin and danger of being righteous over-much*, 57–58.
67 098-Gr. [Weller], *The trial of Mr. Whitefield's spirit*, 38; 110-Gr. [Grey], *The Quaker and
   Methodist compared*, 95–96. The Covenanters were Scottish Presbyterians in the late
   sixteenth and early seventeenth centuries who bound themselves by oaths to support
   Presbyterianism. *Oxford Dictionary of the Christian Church*, ed. F. L. Cross, second edition
   revised by F. L. Cross and E. A. Livingstone (Oxford: Oxford University Press, 1958, 1974).
68 213A-Ki. [Lavington], *The enthusiasm of Methodists and papists compar'd*, pt. 2.

no apparent necessity for the practice?[69] William Bowman dubbed them as successors to the Pharisees. Their motive, he suggested, was desire for adulation from the lower classes.[70] Lavington agreed:

> To be the head of a sect, distinguished by a peculiar denomination and notable singularities; — to frisk in the air of popularity, be hugged and followed with wishful looks . . . This is too sweet a morsel to be willingly cured of.[71]

As noted earlier, in the early days of the revival, the call was for suppression of field preaching because of its potential danger to church, society, and state.[72] But after the failure of the 1745 Jacobite rebellion, little further opposition to the practice was voiced. When it was, as in John Green's 1760 *The principles and practices of the Methodists considered*, it was a lament that field preaching was such an effective means of communication among the masses:

> [E]llocution from a stool, or vociferation from a hillock, whatever sort of religious information may be delivered from thence, will act with much more effect upon the multitude, than any kind of sober instruction, given in a plain way and from that old-fashion eminence, the pulpit.[73]

Itineration

Closely allied to field preaching was the practice of itineration. Claiming to obey God rather than human authority, the Methodists rejected parish boundaries and invaded other priest's parishes to preach the gospel. Wesley offered his rationale for the practice:

> I look upon the world as my parish: thus far I mean, that in whatever part of it I am I judge it meet, right, and my bounden duty to declare unto all that are willing to hear the glad tidings of salvation.

---

69 125-Gr. Inglefield, *An answer to a sermon preach'd at Rotherhith*, 11.
70 094-Gr. Bowman, *Imposture of Methodism display'd*, 65.
71 213A-Ki. [Lavington], *The enthusiasm of Methodists and papists compar'd*, xli.
72 018-Gr. Wilder, *The trial of the spirits*, 22.
73 294-Gr. Academicus [Green], *The principles and practices of Methodists considered*, 22.

> This is the work which I know God has called me to, and sure I
> am that his blessing attends it.[74]

George Whitefield, likewise claimed the world as his parish.[75] Both men, ignoring territorial boundaries, used itinerancy as an instrument for evangelism, thus enshrining it as one of the foundational practices of Methodism. Church of England clergy were quick to raise the alarm. As early as 1738, T. Gib requested that the bishops use their authority to prevent the young Methodist preachers from itinerating.[76] Adversaries pointed out that ordination was to a particular geographical location and did not provide the right to preach anywhere and everywhere an individual wished—the Church had wisely bound and limited the ministry of a priest to a parish. Gibson reminded the Methodist leaders that in the Church's ordination service it was clearly stated that a priest's duties were to be exercised in "the congregation whereunto he shall be lawfully appointed."[77] Notwithstanding this limitation, the Church of England authorized bishops and the universities to grant special licenses to certain clergy to preach. Such ministers could choose to itinerate. The fiftieth canon regulated this practice and required preachers to show their licenses to the minister or churchwarden where they were to preach. Since the Methodists did not possess the necessary authorization, their itineration directly contravened Anglican polity. Moreover, as England was already a Christian country, and priests were duly appointed to parishes all over the nation, critics could see no rationale for itineration. Yet the Methodists acted as if England were a pagan nation with no clergy but themselves. Thomas Green presented the case:

> The conversion of heathens and infidels is certainly a most charitable and good design; but those persons who generally travel from place to place in order to preach the Gospel where it is already sufficiently taught and established, and who think themselves above a stated or limited commission, act without any proper authority.[78]

---

74 Wesley, Journals and Diaries, in *BEWJW*, 11: 217–18.
75 Whitefield, *Works*, I: 105.
76 005-Gr. T. G. [Gib], *Remarks on the Reverend Mr. Whitefield's journal*, 19–20.
77 164-Gr. [Gibson], *Observations upon the conduct and behaviour of . . . Methodists*, 11.
78 249A-Fi. Green, *A dissertation on enthusiasm*, 93.

Various authors suggested reasons why the Methodists itinerated. John Brownsword opined in 1739 that in Whitefield's case it was due to a defect in his character. He had been cursed with a "roving temper" and could not stay long in any one place.[79] Fictional lay preacher Nathaniel Snip moved from town to town in order to find people suitable for him to convert. As he found difficulty in locating enough people who lived bad lives, he had to keep on the move to new towns where the soil might be more fertile.[80] One author believed itineration was a necessity because of the type of people converted to Methodism. They were "fickle," "giddy," and "weak," and required a diet of variety and novelty. Because of this they were

> constantly supported by a continual round of new preachers: someone or other of whom are perpetually entertaining them with something new. And no sooner do the charms of novelty begin to decay, than he is removed from his present round, to give place to a fresh successor. Thus the itching ears are perpetually tickled.[81]

That the Methodists came uninvited into their parishes and preached, against their wishes to their parishioners, disturbed the clergy. Such intrusion, Thomas Church said, was akin to burglary:

> The parochial clergy have a legal right to the care of their several districts, which may therefore with much . . . propriety be called their own houses . . . And yet, how have you and your brethren [Wesley and the Methodists] broke in upon them, endeavouring to supplant them, labouring to steal away the hearts of their people from them.[82]

An Anglican incumbent's pulpit in the eighteenth century was his freehold; it provided financial support for the appointed clergy. By preaching uninvited within another's parish, the Methodists were interfering with the priest's livelihood, and possibly endangering it. Some critics contended that itineration, if not checked, would eventually destroy the parish system, a

---

79 039-Gr. J. B. [Brownsword], *Remarks on the continuation of Mr. Whitefield's journal*, 12.

80 324-Gr. Snip *pseud. A journal of the travels of Nathaniel Snip*, 25–26.

81 555-Gr. *A review of the policy, doctrines and morals of the Methodists*, 6.

82 185-Gr. Church, *Remarks on the Reverend Mr. John Wesley's last journal*, 15.

system some thought to be as "old as Christianity."[83] Chaos would ensue if priests were allowed to preach wherever they pleased. Many parishes would be left untended, while others would be flooded by a surplus of preachers.[84] Even a Congregationalist joined the fray, opposing itineration because it would destroy a "settled ministry" and damage pastoral continuity.[85] Gibson contended that a settled ministry was more suited to the "instruction and edification of the people" than itinerancy, where preachers "run up and down from place to place, and from county to county drawing after them confused multitudes of people, and leading them into a disesteem of their own pastors."[86] The ideal clergyman, Gibson thought, was a scholar who sat "quietly at home," did "his duty in his own cure [appointed parish]," and kept "himself within his own station, and meddle[d] no further."[87]

The Circuit System

Itinerancy was based on two circles. The first was a grouping of societies within a given area, known initially as rounds, but later as circuits.[88] The circuit system became another distinguishing mark of Methodism. The preacher might spend a few days, including a weekend, in the chief town where he had lodgings, but would have to keep on the move the rest of the time visiting all of the societies in the circuit, often staying in the homes of society members. The job of the itinerant was to preach and shepherd the Methodist society members in their bands and classes and also to make sure they attended the local parish church for worship. The second circle in the itineracy involved the Methodist preacher moving from one circuit to another. Appointments to circuits were at Wesley's pleasure and were usually of short duration. In 1746 there were six circuits in England: London, Bristol, Newcastle, Cornwall, Evesham, and Yorkshire. A seventh circuit was

---

83 124-Gr. Mr. Whitefield's doctrines considered and confuted, 73; 200-Gr. B. A. [Stebbing], An earnest and affectionate address to the people called Methodists, 38.

84 205-Gr. Church, Some farther remarks on the Rev. Mr. John Wesley's last journal, 10.

85 385-Gr. An Independent [Newton], The causes and reasons of the present declension among the Congregationalist churches, 8.

86 164-Gr. [Gibson], Observations upon the conduct and behaviour of . . . Methodists, 164.

87 206-Gr. [Gibson], The charge of the Right Reverend Father in God, Edmund, Lord Bishop of London . . . 1746 and 1747, 5.

88 See Frank Baker, Riding the Rounds with John Wesley, MH, 23:3 (April 1985), 163–67.

Wales. By 1765 the number had grown to twenty-five circuits.[89] The circuit system was made possible by the growing number of lay preachers ready to join Wesley in the revival. In 1765 there were 71 preachers appointed to circuits. By 1791 there were more than 200 preachers stationed in 78 circuits in England.[90] With Scotland and Ireland included, the number of preachers was 285, stationed in 113 circuits.

Lay Preaching

At first only Wesley and his ordained Anglican co-evangelists itinerated, but within a few years Wesley began to utilize laity as preachers, and they, too, itinerated. In 1745 Henry Stebbing complained "Some of them [lay preachers] have since run about the country teaching and exhorting without any orders or authority, learning, or judgement."[91] The attack on lay preachers centered not only on their itineration, but upon their personal qualities, lack of training, and absence of ecclesiastical commission to preach. The use of laity was not something unique to eighteenth-century Methodism, but their employment scandalized conservative Anglicans. Even Wesley had been reluctant to accept laity as preachers. Initially he used them in emergency situations, but in the winter of 1740–41, he welcomed Thomas Maxfield as a "son of the gospel."[92] Later Wesley added other laity as full-time itinerant preachers.

Anglican clergy opposed the usurpation of the office of ordained preacher by those who were not ordained. Joseph Trapp was among the earliest to object. Trapp was offended even by the use of laity to read prayers anywhere but in the privacy of their own homes. Lay preaching was "an encroachment upon the office of those who are ordain'd to holy functions, and I fear takes off from the reverence and respect due to them." For "unletter'd laics to . . . expound or interpret the Scriptures [was] neither laudable, nor justifiable."[93]

---

89 Annual Minutes of Some Late Conversations, in *BEWJW*, vol. 10, *The Methodist Societies, The Minutes of Conference*, ed. Henry D. Rack (Nashville: Abingdon, 2011).

90 Ibid. The count of stationed preachers does not include Scotland, Ireland, or America.

91 200-Gr. B.A. [Stebbing], *An earnest and affectionate address to the people called Methodists*, 36.

92 Thomas Maxfield (d. 1784) was one of Wesley's early preachers. Wesley mentioned him at the Conference of 1766 as the first layman who helped him as a "son of the gospel." He was later ordained by the bishop of Derry, but left Wesley in 1763 and finally became an Independent minister in London.

93 010-Gr. Trapp, *The nature, folly, sin and danger of being righteous over-much*, 10–11.

Others echoed Trapp's sentiments. Some depicted what would happen if laity were permitted to preach. Warned James Bate, "It tends to make all priests and no religion."[94] Confusion and disorder would result if all who thought they should preach were allowed to do so. John Andrews cautioned the clergy of the deanery of Shoreham in 1743:

> There must be some to teach, as well as others to hear. If all
> were teachers where would be the hearers? and were all hearers,
> where would be the teachers? . . . The office of a preacher is great,
> and therefore not to be usurped by every pretender; is holy, and
> therefore not to be exercised by any but those, who are ordained
> and set apart to it.[95]

Gibson expressed the fear that the Methodists would be indiscriminate in their selection of laity as preachers and would thus encourage unfit people to choose preaching as a livelihood.[96]

The practice of lay preaching was attacked because those who had assumed preaching responsibilities had no commission from the Church to do so. Only those ordained by a bishop should preach:

> The governors and pastors must be lawful ones, that is, such as
> Christ hath commissioned to exercise those offices, because if
> they usurp the sacred offices of the Church, not being lawfully
> ordained to the same by the successors of Christ and his apostles,
> there will be very great danger of nullity in all their ministerial
> acts and offices.[97]

Critics could find no scriptural or early church precedent for the Methodist practice of lay preaching. There were examples, of course, of laity preaching in early Christendom, but "these did not run without being sent, nor thrust themselves into the work, without being approved of by those whom the great Master himself had appointed to be overseers of his vineyard."[98] Anglican

---

94 042-Gr. Bate, *Quakero-Methodism*, 10.

95 161D-Fi. John Andrews, *Of speaking as the oracles of God* (London: J. Tilly, 1744), 22–3.

96 164-Gr. [Gibson], *Observations upon the conduct and behaviour of . . . Methodists*, 24.

97 253B-Ki. Christophilus, *A serious enquiry whether a late epistle from . . . Charles Wesley . . . to John Wesley . . .* , 11.

98 524-Gr. Calvinisticus, *Calvinism defended and Arminianism refuted* (Leeds: Binns, 1780), 4.

theology on the call to ministry differentiated between an inward and an outward call. The inward call of the Holy Spirit to a person to preach had to be verified by an outward recognition of that call in a commission from the church. Laity might claim an inward call, said one author, but "no qualifications can empower any man to take upon him any office of ministration in the Church, till he has received a commission from those men who are authorized by God to give it. Can you not distinguish . . . between an inward motion to undertake an office, and an actual commission to execute it?"[99] Who verified the Methodist lay itinerants' calls to preach? asked antagonists. "When you call upon them for vouchers, they refer you to I know not what internal feelings, illapses, and illuminations, for the truth of which you are to take their own word."[100] Wesley was criticized for contravening Anglican law by sending out lay people to preach in his societies. No Anglican priest, critics complained, had authority to employ a body of laity as preachers. Indeed, the Twenty-third Article forbade it.[101]

The assumption of the office of preacher without ordination, anti-Methodists claimed, was dangerous to both Church and state. John Free was convinced it bordered on sedition:

> Whoever assumes the office of a preaching prophet or teacher not warranted by gospel ordinances or countenanced by the laws of the land; is, with respect to the gospel, [an] Antichristian teacher and false prophet, and with respect to the state, a mover of sedition, and a mutinous disturber of the publick peace, that acts in contempt and defiance of the laws established.[102]

James Penn agreed—lay preaching was a threat to the peace and order of society.[103] The most common charge against lay preachers was that they were unlearned; even illiterate. It was clear, opponents claimed, that lay preachers looked upon education as an unnecessary qualification for their task. Joseph

---

99 321-Gr. N. N., *Presbyters and deacons not commissioned to preach without the bishop's allowance* (London: N. Nicholl, 1761), 32.

100 346-Gr. William Backhouse, *The history of the man of God* (Cambridge: J. Bentham, 1763), 13.

101 See 248A-Ba. A Lay-man, *A few queries concerning the growth of Methodism*, 9; 208-Gr. George White, *A sermon against the Methodists* (Preston: for the author by James Stanley and John Moon, 1748), 13.

102 274-Gr. Free, *Rules for the discovery of false prophets*, 20.

103 338-Gr. Penn, *Various tracts*, 111.

Trapp had pointed out in 1739 that clergy needed to be skilled in languages and history if they were to expound the Scriptures rightly.[104] Thomas Green in 1755 rebuked the Methodists for allowing laity to preach without any formal preparation: "Persons cannot be properly qualified for the business of explaining the Scriptures, and preaching God's word in our days, without a sufficient stock of learning, and diligent study and labour . . . Why should this interpretation of the holy Scripture be looked upon . . . as so easy thing, that many undertake to teach what they never learned."[105] The author of a poem entitled *The enthusiast; or, Methodism display'd,* parodied the lay preachers' right to interpret scripture despite lacking an education:

> I'm full of zeal and inward light, Sir,
> Tho' I can hardly read or write, Sir.
> But what avails your men of letters?
> We lay-men know the scriptures better,
> Than all the students in the nation;
> Because it comes from inspiration.
> Saint Peter, sir, as I have read,
> To education ne'er was bred
> Yet, taught mankind the way to heav'n,
> As well as those whom more had giv'n;
> And why mayn't I, although a chandler,
> Of holy scriptures be a handler?[106]

Not only did lay preachers lack the appropriate kind of education; it was charged that they were illiterate—so illiterate, Nathaniel Fletcher claimed, that they could scarcely read a chapter of the Bible, or to write a page of English.[107] William Backhouse implied that some could not read at all.[108] Archdeacon Rutherforth complained that they were not even aware that the Bible was not written originally in English.[109] Their illiteracy was betrayed by their ungrammatical speech.[110] The anonymous author of a curious broadside

---

104 010-Gr. Trapp, *The nature, folly, sin and danger of being righteous over-much,* 12.
105 249A-Fi. Green, *A dissertation on enthusiasm,* 32.
106 248D-Fi. *The enthusiast; or, Methodism display'd* (Portsmouth: W. Horton for the author, 1753), 8.
107 210-Gr. Fletcher, *A Methodist dissected,* 1.
108 346-Gr. Backhouse, *The history of the man of God,* 15.
109 343-Gr. Rutherforth, *Four charges to the clergy of the archdeaconry of Essex,* 8.
110 268-Gr. [Mortimer], *Die and be damned,* 35.

entitled *The secret disclosed; or, The itinerant field orator's Methodist gibberish* presented what he claimed was a successful imitation of a typical Methodist sermon making use of the grossest metaphors:

> Do you know what trade Adam [followed]? If you don't I will tell you. Why Adam was a planter for he planted the beautiful Garden of Eden. Now, do you know the first thing he set in his garden? Ho! Ho! Ho! You don't, don't you. Then I will tell you. His foot. But he could not keep it there. No, no, no, no, no, no. He could not keep it there for Lucifer came behind him, tript up his heels and trundled him out again neck and shoulders.[111]

Evan Lloyd satirized the ignorance of lay preachers, and the absurdity of their claim to be able to explain the mysteries of religion:

> Evr'y blockhead, knave, and dunce
> Starts into preachers all at once
> Hence ignorance of ev'ry size,
> Of evr'y shape whit can devise,
> Altho' so dull it hardly knows,
> Which are its fingers, which its toes
> Which is the left hand, which the right,
> When it is day, or when 'tis night,
> Shall yet pretend to keep the key
> Of God's dark secrets and display
> His hidden mysteries, as free.[112]

The personal integrity of Methodist lay preachers was assailed—they were depicted as devoid of all principles. The Methodist itinerant in the farce *Methodism Display'd* was vilified as a pickpocket, opportunist, and counterfeit saint. The Newgate criminals, whom the Methodist lay preachers visited, recognized that the preachers were worse criminals than those who were incarcerated. One convict exclaimed, "Your new light is all hypocrisy . . . You preach only for interest . . . You are all a parcel of cheats

---

111 541-Gr. *The secret disclosed; or, the itinerant field orator's Methodist gibberish* ([Litchfield]: no printer, 1788) This item was originally a broadside, but was sent to the editor of the *Gentleman's Magazine,* who reprinted it in full in his columns: *Gentleman's Magazine,* May 1788, 488–89.

112 379-Gr. The author of *The powers of the pew* and *The curate* [Lloyd], *The Methodist: a poem,* 29–30.

and pickpockets."[113] For some lay preachers Methodism was just a passing fad. One friend asks the other what his motive was to move from "Churchism to Methodism" and why he now has "turned his backside upon Methodism, that once lovely, if not lucrative, faith." He further asks "whether he will not tack about hereafter to a different point of the compass." With so much "inconsistency and self-contradiction" will he be able to sleep in peace?[114] Others portrayed lay preachers as callous and inhuman. Fictional preacher Nathaniel Snip, having decided to become a Methodist lay preacher, rejected the needs of his family in obeying his calling to go and preach. Just as Snip was setting out to itinerate, his son fell down the stairs of the family home and broke his forehead. The would-be preacher noted in his journal: "I turned my back on him . . . and obeyed the call of the Spirit."[115]

Lay preachers were portrayed as avaricious rouges intent on their own financial gain. In Foote's play *The Devil on two Sticks*, a young couple, eloping with the assistance of the Devil, ask his help on finding a good vocation. The Devil, suggesting that they engage in "spiritual quackery," confesses that if he weren't the Devil, he would become a Methodist preacher.[116] George White claimed that the "underhand lay-preachers" were "in a better way of living than the generality of our vicars and curates."[117] Others confirmed White's charges. The purses of lay preachers were filled by "large contributions," and their bellies were filled by the "best of viands."[118] Richard Hardy asserted that some of the lay preachers were well-known thieves.[119] Another author assessed them as "keen, rapacious and scarcely honest in their dealings, with their eyes lifted up towards a heavenly inheritance they will hold a considerable reversion in this earth."[120] In Samuel Johnson's *A Curious letter from a mountebank doctor to a Methodist preacher*, the mountebank suggested that, as Methodist teachers and mountebank doctors were both charlatans,

---

113 154-Gr. [Este], *Methodism display'd: a farce*, 13–14.

114 458B-Ba. *Curse ye Meroz . . . to which is added a letter from a cobbler to a collier of high renown* (Hallifax: for the editor, [1773]), 34–36.

115 324-Gr. Snip *pseud., A journal of the travels of Nathaniel Snip*, 9.

116 Samuel Foote, *The devil on two sticks: a comedy in three acts* (London: no printer [1778]), 62.

117 208-Gr. White, *A sermon against the Methodists*, 10–11.

118 248A-Ba. A Lay-man, *A few queries concerning the growth of Methodism*, 5.

119 349-Gr. [Hardy], *A letter from a clergyman to one of his parishioners who was inclined to turn Methodist*, 3.

120 555-Gr. *A review of the policy, doctrines and morals of the Methodists*, 36–37.

they should engage in a reciprocal arrangement whereby mountebanks would release their dying patients to Methodist teachers who could convert them in their dying hour and have a will drawn up favoring Methodism. Methodist teachers, on the other hand, could send their members who were degenerating into madness to mountebanks to be purged, blistered, and dieted. "By these means," the mountebank suggested, "we shall reciprocally assist one another, and reap a plentiful harvest."[121] Two authors accused lay preachers of being involved in smuggling, despite Wesley's denunciation of the practice. "Lace and goods of easy, snug carriage," suggested William Combe, were carried in "packs" by lay itinerants.[122]

Obesity, it was claimed, was a mark of successful lay preachers. Although moderate in drinking habits, they habitually indulged in large quantities of food. "Their jolly faces, and plump carcasses proclaim, that they seldom sit down to a scanty table, or partake of a poor fare," avowed one author. Support of lay preachers, it was claimed, kept Methodist societies poor. The cost of entertaining itinerants was reckoned as "a very great sum." Lay preachers were well taken care of. The author of the satire *A journal of the travels of Nathaniel Snip*, commenting on Snip's commencing to preach because he had grown weary of his job, contended that laziness was "the usual motive to inspiration among our 'modern lay-preachers.'"[123] Not only did a circuit have to pay for the upkeep of preachers, but they were responsible, it was alleged, for 'convoys' of followers, which regularly accompanied them from town to town.[124]

Immorality of all kinds, especially sexual, was attributed to Methodist lay preachers.[125] Many, it was alleged, had been aspirants to the Anglican

---

121 577A-Fi. Hurlothrumbo [Samuel Johnson of Gawsworth, Cheshire], *A curious letter from a mountebank doctor to a Methodist preacher* ([Edinburgh]: printed for the booksellers, 1797). An almost verbatim account of the pamphlet is found, thirty-nine years earlier, in "A humorous letter from a mountebank to a Methodist teacher," *Gentleman's Magazine*, March 1758, 101–2. Johnson was music master, dancing master, poet, playwright, and jester. In fact, he was the last professional jester in England. He is best known for his play *Hurlothrumbo; Or, the Super-natural*, which opened at the New Theatre, Haymarket, London, April 1729. *ODNB*.

122 517-Gr. [Combe], *Perfection: a poetical epistle*, 17. See also 492A-Ba. A Gentleman of Northumberland, *A compleat answer to Mr. Wesley's Observations upon Dr. Price's essay on civil liberty*, 3.

123 324-Gr. Snip *pseud.*, *A journal of the travels of Nathaniel Snip*, 7.

124 555-Gr. *A review of the policy, doctrines and morals of the Methodists*, 33, 46.

125 See Gunter, *The Limits of 'Love Divine,'* chap. 12, "Wayward Preachers," especially the case of James Wheatley (184–86) and Wesley's polygamist brother–in–law, Westley Hall (187–202).

priesthood, but had been prevented from obtaining ordination by "early immoralities."[126] Among the Methodist preachers, hinted Combe, were fornicators, adulterers, and sexual predators:

> A sympathetic sigh, well tim'd,
> May win a wife or daughter to a favorite sin.[127]

"These men of God [lay preachers]," Combe noted, "are very watchful to steal in upon a lady's privacy and retirement whilst the husband (however much their friend) is absent, in order to insinuate ghostly comfort."[128] The author of *Preaching for bacon* advised husbands to keep an eye on their wives and their food supplies when the Methodist preacher visits:

> Come all you brave fellows who lead jovial lives,
> I'd leave you take care of your bacon and wives;
> For if you've got a vittle what pains will be taken
> They'l preach like be d—d where there's plenty of bacon.[129]

Some lay preachers took advantage of the brevity of circuit appointments, usually just a year or two, to sow their wild oats. They moved on to the next circuit, leaving behind a history of sexual misconduct, pregnant young women, and illegitimate children. Foote's play *The orators* relates the story of the fictional Shadrack Bodkin, a tailor by trade, who was compelled, he said, by the Holy Spirit to leave his trade, wife, and family and take up Methodism. Accused of sleeping with a number of women, Shadrack asserted he was compelled by the Spirit to sleep with other men's wives, with widows, and with maids. When charged with sleeping and impregnating a dozen women, he readily confessed to "only nine!"[130] Fictional reports of such sexual misconduct reinforced real claims about preachers' misbehavior.[131] The resulting damage to Methodism's reputation was considerable and far-reaching.

---

126 208-Gr. White, *A sermon against the Methodists*, v.

127 517-Gr. [Combe], *The fanatic saints*, 24.

128 Ibid.

129 607–Ki. (Formerly 009–Ba.) *Preaching for bacon* (n.p.: no printer, n.d.), broadside.

130 341D-Ki. Foote, *The orators*, 45.

131 The substance of the charge of wayward preachers first appeared in April 17, 1749, in a letter to the *Bath Journal*, no. 269, p. 13. In the late 1740s one of Wesley's preachers, James Wheatley, was found guilty of sexual misconduct with several young women in the Bristol circuit. In his defense he implied that a number of his fellow preachers were guilty of similar or worse improprieties. Wesley called ten accused preachers to account.

Wesley's control of lay preachers came under fire from Joanna Hawkins, a Quaker, who observed that they showed too great a deference to Wesley. The Holy Spirit's dictates ought to be heeded, rather than Wesley's, she advised the lay preachers in 1749: "You really are subject and subservient to John Wesley more than to Christ."[132] An Anglican critic believed exactly the opposite—that Wesley had lost control of his lay preachers. He had unleashed the laity and now did not know how to rein them in and command their loyalty. Wesley's brainchild, once so obedient, had become rebellious. Observed James Buller, "[T]hey are got quite headstrong . . . Should you thunder out your anathemas, your last reserve, and threaten them with eternal damnation upon non complyance you would find them to a man . . . setting up each for himself."[133]

Exorcism, Miraculous Cures, and Quack Remedies

Strange customs in dealing with sick people won the Methodists considerable notoriety. They were charged with reviving the ancient practice of exorcism, praying for miracles, and dispensing quack remedies. Bishops Lavington and Warburton combed Wesley's journals for incidents of exorcism.[134] The Methodists were accused of attributing all kinds of diseases to evil spirits, particularly epileptic fits, melancholia, and headaches. In order to expel devils, it was said, they hunted out people with such symptoms.[135] Wesley's right to exorcise was challenged. The twenty-second canon expressly forbade ministers from engaging in exorcism unless they were licensed by their diocesan.[136]

In 1788 four Methodist preachers were involved in the celebrated case of the exorcism of George Lukins, "the Yatton daemoniac."[137] They assisted

---

When Wheatley refused to repent, he was dismissed by Wesley. See Gunter, *The Limits of 'Love Divine,'* 187–202. See also William Gibson and Joanne Begiato, *Sex and the Church in the Long Eighteenth Century*, chap. 15.

132 214A-Ki. Hawkins, *Letter to John Wesley*, 11.

133 258-Gr. James Buller, *A reply to the Rev. Mr. Wesley's 'Address to the clergy'* (Bristol: S. Farley, 1756), 15.

134 225-Gr. [Lavington], *The enthusiasm of Methodists and papists compar'd*, pt. 3, 245–46; 342-Gr. [Warburton], *The doctrine of grace*, 123–24.

135 555-Gr. *A review of the policy, doctrines and morals of the Methodists*, 15.

136 See 156-Gr. An Impartial Hand, *The progress of Methodism in Bristol*, 12.

137 For a fuller account of the "Yatton daemoniac case" see Clive D. Field's annotation on item 542C*-Fi. *A Supplemental Bibliography*, 176–7.

Joseph Easterbrook, evangelical minister of Temple Church, Bristol, in driving the devils out of Lukins on June 13, 1788. Samuel Norman, a member of the Corporation of Surgeons in London, and surgeon at Yatton, published an exposé of the affair, claiming that Lukins was a fraud and that Easterbrook and Wesley's preachers had been duped.[138]

Wesley denied that he worked miracles, but his critics alleged that his journal accounts of praying for sick people, and then noting their speedy recovery, amounted to such a claim.[139] Commented Warburton, "[A]cute as well as chronical disorders fly before him."[140] Nathaniel Snip, satirizing entries in Whitefield's and Wesley's journals, where praying over the sick resulted in quick recovery, noted in his journal:

> April 5—This morning I visited a sister who lay dangerously ill of a fever. What increased her disorder was an inveterate costiveness which baffled all the art of the doctor: I prayed by her and sung an hymn, which was no sooner ended, than it pleased the Lord in the bowels of his compassion to open her bowels: On this she recovered so surprisingly as to be well in two days time—Oh, the great power of prayer.[141]

Wesley had a long interest in physical and spiritual health both for himself and others. His medical writings included *A Collection of Receipts for the Use of the Poor (1745)* and *Primitive Physick; or an Easy and Natural Method of Curing Most Diseases* (1747).[142] The *Primitive Physick*, which went through twenty-three editions in his lifetime, remained in print into the

---

138 542C-Ki. Samuel Norman, *Authentic anecdotes of G. Lukins* (Bristol: G. Routh, [1788]) and 542C*-Fi. *The great apostle unmask'd* (Bristol: printed for S. Johnson, 1788). Easterbrook's case appeared in his *Appeal to the public respecting G. Lukins* (Bristol, 1788), and *A narrative of the extraordinary case of Geo. Lukins*, 3rd ed. (Bristol: Bulgin and Rosser, 1788). It is interesting to note that Wesley had his doubts about Lukins's authenticity. Cf. Wesley, *Letters* (Telford), 8: 82.

139 See 185-Gr. Church, *Remarks on the Reverend Mr. John Wesley's last journal*, 71–72; 342-Gr. [Warburton], *The doctrine of grace*, 130.

140 342-Gr. [Warburton] *The doctrine of grace*, 138. See a similar comment in 387-Gr. [Lancaster], *Methodism triumphant*, 52.

141 324-Gr. Snip *pseud., A journal of the travels of Nathaniel Snip*, 21.

142 See John Wesley, *BEWJW*, vol. 32, *Medical and Health Writings*, ed. James G. Donat and Randy L. Maddox (Nashville: Abingdon, 2018). See also James G. Donat, "Empirical Medicine in the 18th Century: The Rev. John Wesley's Search for Remedies that Work," *MH* 44, no. 4 (July 2005): 216–26.

1880s.[143] Regardless, Wesley was branded as a charlatan and his medical writings ridiculed. What he could not cure by prayer, his opponents alleged, he attempted to cure with quack remedies.[144] William Combe poked fun at Wesley's prescriptions and cures:

Some cured for six pence, some at half a crown.
. . . .
Thus, at cheap rates, health and salvation sure;
Thus Christ's apostles now absolve and cure
With preaching, pray'r, drugs primitive, and Psalms;
But most of all with true perfection's balm.[145]

Evan Lloyd made Wesley's use of medication even more explicit:

Sickness of the soul? And in its state
With sin's disease grown desparate?
To divers quacks you may apply,
And special nostrums of them buy.
Tottenham's the best accustom'd place,
There Magnus squints men into grace.
Wesley sells powders, draughts, and pills
Sov'reign against all sorts of ills.[146]

If medication for some ailments was ineffective, Combe noted Wesley's use of his electric machine. Electric shock therapy, Wesley opined, rarely failed as a remedy for nervous conditions of every kind.[147] So popular was the procedure that Wesley set up a clinic in which to administer the treatment. Combe parodied the use of electricity as a cure-all, especially for sexual maladies:

---

143 Ibid.
144 342-Gr. [Warburton], *The doctrine of grace*, 251; 455-Gr. Richard Hill, *Logica Wesleiensis*, 46; 472-Gr. Augustus Montague Toplady, *The scheme of Christian and philosophical necessity asserted* (London: for Vallance and Simmons, 1775), vi; 488-Gr. Hawes, *An examination of Rev. Mr. John Wesley's 'Primitive Physic'*; 488A-Ki. Detester of Hypocrisy, *To that fanatical, political, physical, enthusiast* (London: no printer, 1776), broadside.
145 521-Gr. [Combe], *Fanatical Conversion*, 38–39.
146 379-Gr. [Lloyd], *The Methodist: A poem*, 35–36. In the poem Magnus is a pseudonym for George Whitefield. Because his eye was turned, Whitefield was nicknamed Dr. Squintum.
147 A Lover of Mankind and Common Sense [John Wesley], *The desideratum; or, Electricity made plain and useful* (London: Bailliere, Tindall, and Cox, 1760). See A. Hill, *John Wesley among the Physicians: A Study in Eighteenth-Century Medicine* (London: Epworth, 1958). R. A. Hunter, "A Brief Review of the Use of Electricity in Psychiatry with Special Reference to John Wesley," *British Journal of Physical Medicine* 20, no. 5 (1957): 99.

And, if perchance, th'electric force they feel,
Another glance they do not take but steal;
With thy perfection arm'd, in that they trust
They peep and peep again, but never lust.[148]

The most detailed attack on Wesley's *Primitive Physick* came from William Hawes (1736–1808), a young London physician and an elder in St. Thomas Presbyterian Church, pastored by Abraham Rees.[149] A Whig and advocate of the colonists in their revolt from English rule, Rees was highly critical of Wesley's support of the British ministry's actions. In his preface to *An examination of the Rev Mr. John Wesley's Primitive physic*, Hawes made it clear that he shared Rees's political views.[150] Hawes questioned Wesley's character and conduct, which he felt were "far . . . away from perfection, though that is a doctrine for which he [Wesley] is well known to be a zealous advocate." His open hostility to Wesley in some measure accounts for Hawes's level of rancor in his examination of *Primitive Physic*.[151]

Hawes characterized *Primitive Physic* as "an injudicious collection of pretended remedies for almost every disorder that can affect the human frame."[152] Numerous remedies prescribed by Wesley, Hawes claimed, were either absurd or dangerous to health. In wading into the waters of medicine Wesley, Hawes said, was out of his depth. He should stick to preaching and not dabble in medicine. Of interest is the fact, as Heitzenrater points out, that Hawes did not challenge Wesley's frequent prescription "to be electrified," except as a remedy for old age, nor did he comment on Wesley's suggestion of mouth-to-mouth resuscitation for drowning victims.[153]

---

148 517-Gr. [Combe], *Perfection: A poetical epistle*, 16.
149 William Hawes, *ODNB*. See also *BEWJW*, vol. 32, *Medical and Health Writings*, 61.
150 488-Gr. Hawes, *An examination of the Rev. Mr. John Wesley's Primitive Physic*, iii–iv, 59–61.
151 Ibid., iv.
152 Ibid., i.
153 See "Directions with respect to drowned persons" in *BEWJW*, vol. 32, *Medical and Health Writings*, ed. James G. Donat and Randy L. Maddox (Nashville: Abingdon, 2018), 514–16. See also "The Pretending Physician, William Hawes' Critique," in Richard P. Heitzenrater, *The Elusive Mr. Wesley: John Wesley as Seen by Contemporaries and Biographers* (Nashville: Abingdon, 1984), 2:128–38.

Diaries and Journals

From his Oxford days John Wesley kept a diary as a means of "spiritual pulse taking."[154] When he began to use lay preachers, he advised them to follow his example and regularly record their spiritual condition as a matter of discipline. John Free depicted the custom as ludicrous. He ridiculed the Methodists for keeping

> a diary of the most insignificant and trivial actions of their lives; such perhaps as how many slices of bread and butter they eat with their tea, and how many dishes of tea they drank, how many country dances they called at their dancing club; or after a fast, the number of pounds of mutton they might devour of a leg of mutton.[155]

The Methodists did not keep the accounts of their personal lives to themselves but published them for all to read.[156] Both Wesley and Whitefield issued extracts of their journals, and others released edited accounts of their religious pilgrimages. Critics recoiled at the excessive subjectivity of these narratives. John Roche contended that it was a sign of weakness in the Methodists

> to let the world know in puffing print when we fasted, when we prayed . . . when we had a ray of revelation, when the Lord conversed with us, promised his special blessing, directed particular people to receive and assist us, which are scarcely to be believed.[157]

In a pamphlet that purported to be a Methodist lay preacher's journal, one anonymous author parodied the custom. A section of the title proclaimed that it was "an account of the many marvelous adventures which befell him in his way from the town of Kingston upon Hull to the city of York."[158]

The printed journal extracts of Whitefield and Wesley provided much

---

154 Richard P. Heitzenrater, "Diaries and Methodists," in chapter 4, "The Quest of the First Methodist: Oxford Methodism Reconsidered," in *Mirror and Memory: Reflections on Early Methodism* (Nashville: Abingdon, 1989), 66–68.

155 274-Gr. Free, *Rules for the discovery of false prophets*, vi.

156 W. Reginald Ward, "The Nature of Wesley's Journal," in *BEWJW*, vol. 18, *Journals and Diaries (1735–38)*, ed. W. Reginald Ward and Richard P. Heitzenrater (Nashville: Abingdon, 1988).

157 226A-Ki. Roche, *Moravian heresy*, 296.

158 324-Gr. Snip *pseud., A journal of the travels of Nathaniel Snip.*

fuel for the anti-Methodist fire, giving critics evidence to prove their charges. One author contended that Wesley's motives in publishing his journal were unworthy of him. The Methodist leader contrived to ensnare the credulous: "Honesty, good sense, knowledge, and character are sacrificed to this end . . . You see there a man of good sense and knowledge, retailing stories and anecdotes full of falsehood and absurdity, which no man of common understanding can possibly swallow: but they are all so calculated as to suit the understanding of his followers."[159]

Jail Visitation

Visiting jail inmates, an activity in which Methodists engaged, began as an outreach ministry of the Oxford Holy Club. When they left university, the Wesleys and Whitefield continued the practice and developed it as a characteristic ministry of the revival. The Methodists even assumed the role of unofficial chaplain to condemned criminals, reading them the scriptures and praying with them as they rode on the death cart to the place of execution. English satirical caricaturist William Hogarth has sympathetically depicted the practice in his "The Idle Prentice Executed at Tyburn."[160] While the Anglican chaplain rides safely through the large and boisterous crowd in a carriage, the Methodist lay preacher, Silas Told, heedless of the crowd, is in the death cart with a convicted felon, heading to Tyburn for the hanging. With an open Bible in one hand, the other upraised, Told exhorts the condemned man to repent. Antagonists found such behavior worthy of ridicule. Complained one author:

> Next round the jails they hov'ring fly
> To plague the wretches e'er they die.[161]

Anti-Methodists found the offer of salvation to condemned criminals on their way to the gallows offensive—heaven was a reward for a virtuous

---

159 449-Gr. The author of P. O. [Hill], *A review of the policy, doctrines and morals of the Methodists*, 51.

160 *The effects of industry and idleness . . . being an explanation . . . of twelve . . . prints lately published and designed . . . by Mr. Hogarth* (London: for C. Corbett, [1847]). See Plate 11, "The Idle Prentice Executed at Tyburn," depicts Silas Told, a Methodist, riding in the prison cart with a condemned felon. Told's experiences in prison ministries are recorded in his *An account of the life and dealings of God with Silas Told* (London: 1785). For Wesley's assessment of Told's ministry, see Wesley, *Journal and Diaries VI*, December 20, 1778, 115.

161 026-Gr. *The Methodists: An humorous burlesque poem*, 23.

life. How, they asked, could notorious lawbreakers, in a moment of prayer, suddenly be transformed into saints? Commenting on Wesley's dealings with criminals about to be executed, Nathaniel Lancaster wrote:

> These, then adjudg'd unfit on earth to live,
> He (pious priest!) would gladly have consign'd,
> To realms ordain'd for virtue's proper need.[162]

"Fanatical conversation, visionary hymns, bold and impious applications of the scriptures"—with such means, alleged James Lackington, the Methodists whipped up the emotions of condemned criminals. The joy with which the convicts died was falsely based. They went "in such raptures, as would better become martyrs innocently suffering in a glorious cause [rather] than criminals of the first magnitude."[163]

John Green believed that by exalting criminals Whitefield condoned crime. He referred to Whitefield's association with "coachman T. hanged at Tyburn." This was, no doubt, Robert Tilling (coachman to Samuel Lloyd, Esq.) who was hanged at Tyburn on April 28, 1760. After the execution Tilling's body was taken to the Tabernacle, where the public was allowed to view the corpse before burial in Bunhill Fields Burying Ground.[164] Green commented: "[Y]ou, it seems, can cancel at once all the guilt and infamy of an execution and enroll a man into the list of the saints, who a week before was condemned and hang'd as a felon. Is this a likely way of improving the morals of the people . . . to re-judge in effect the most solemn acts of public justice, that the decisions of the tabernacle should thus tend to defeat . . . the proceedings of Tyburn?"[165]

Methodist practices—particularly bands, classes, field preaching and itineration, lay preaching—were ready-made targets for attack. Despite strong criticism of the methods Wesley employed to win converts and nurture them, he continued to embrace them. His only question was a pragmatic one—did they work?

---

162 387-Gr. [Lancaster], *Methodism triumphant*, 11.
163 560-Gr. Lackington, *Memoirs of the . . . life of James Lackington*, 291–292.
164 See Tyerman, *The Life and Times of the Rev. George Whitefield*, 1:426.
165 294-Gr. Academicus [John Green], *The principles and practices of the Methodists further considered*, 73–74.

CHAPTER 5

Social Upheaval

The eighteenth century in England, in contrast to the seventeenth century, was marked by stability and complacency, with little or no social discontent. With the English Civil War and Interregnum in the past, a sense of security pervaded the nation. The evils of fanatical Puritanism were vanquished, and order and stability restored. Society, once again, rested firmly upon a hierarchical class structure. At the apex of the society was the wealthy and influential nobility. Peers and their close family all but monopolized major political appointments. The senior positions in the army and the navy, and the wealthiest ecclesiastical preferments, were in the main filled from the ranks of the upper class. Beneath the nobility were the gentry, those closely connected with the land, from whom came justices of the peace and numerous members of Parliament. Their relatives secured commissions in the armed services, sought church preferments, went into trade, or swelled the developing professional class. Next in social importance came "the middling sort": substantial tenant farmers, smaller freeholders, innkeepers, traders, shopkeepers, apothecaries, schoolmasters, clerks, and civil servants. Next on the social class ladder were the mass of manual workers: blacksmiths, tailors, shoemakers, bakers, carpenters. Below them were the poor.

Social distinctions were undisputed. A person's place in eighteenth-century English society was determined by birth and wealth. Characteristic of the age was the cleavage between the upper class well-to-do and the lower-class poor. The upper classes considered those beneath them as members of a different order. The lower classes knew, and did not question, their place in society.[1] The teaching of the church provided a sanction to class structure. Each person's station was appointed by God, and the expectation was that an individual would remain for life in his or her appointed station.[2]

Many historians today depict Methodism in eighteenth-century England

---

1 For a fuller discussion of English society in the eighteenth century, see Dorothy Marshall, *Eighteenth Century England* (New York: David McKay, 1962), 29–37; Basil Williams, *The Whig Supremacy 1714–1760* (Oxford: Clarendon, 1939), 123–43; J. Steven Watson, *The Reign of George III, 1760–1815* (Oxford: Clarendon, 1960), 36–40.

2 Roland N. Stromberg, *Religious Liberalism in Eighteenth-Century England* (Oxford: Oxford University Press, 1954), 139.

as a counterrevolutionary force, intent on maintaining the status quo.[3] This, however, was not how many contemporary critics of the revival viewed it. Methodism, they claimed, threatened the social equilibrium, and the very continuance of the social order. Anti-Methodists sketched an alarming picture of individuals neglecting their responsibilities in order to engage in Methodist religious activities. Industry and trade, they claimed, were adversely affected and led to increased vagrancy and idleness throughout the nation.

The riots that accompanied the introduction and growth of Methodism in many localities fanned the fear that general disorder and confusion were an inevitable consequence of the spread of Methodism. The Methodist doctrine of renunciation sounded to opponents strangely like the leveling principle of the Puritans. Furthermore, in the evangelicals' practices critics believed they saw the beginning of the dismantling of England's class structure. While the Methodists spoke of burgeoning religious revival, their opponents spoke of imminent social revolution. Rather than cementing society together, the Methodists were deliberately tearing it apart.

Vocational Responsibilities Neglected

As noted earlier, it was commonly believed in eighteenth-century England that a person's position in society and his or her vocation were determined and appointed by God. Inherent in each station were certain responsibilities and functions that individuals were expected to know and to faithfully perform. The traditional Anglican view was expressed by Bishop Gibson in his 1739 pastoral letter:

> The several stations in life, together with the duties belonging to them, are to be considered as God's appointment; and a willing acquiescence in the station wherein his providence hath placed you, and a diligent attendance on the duties belonging to it as

---

3 Bernard Semmel, trans. and ed., Elie Halévy, "Methodism and Revolution," introductory chapter in Elie Halévy, *The Birth of Methodism in England* (Chicago: Chicago University Press, 1971), 1–29; Bernard Semmel, *The Methodist Revolution* (New York: Basic Books, 1973). Halévy's hypothesis was that England was spared the kind of revolution experienced by the French because of the stabilizing influence of evangelical religion, especially Methodism. Halévy's thesis was embraced by many Methodist historians and popularized in Robert F. Wearmouth, *Methodism and the Common People of the Eighteenth Century* (London: Epworth, 1945). E. P. Thompson challenged the prevailing view in *The Making of the English Working Class* (New York: Pantheon Books, 1964). Thompson depicts Methodism crushing rather than elevating the spirit of the rising proletariat.

appointed by him, is in the strictest sense the serving . . . of God. The care that the Gospel has taken to inculcate the general duty of diligence in our stations, and to acquaint us with the particular duties belonging to the chief relations in life, of husband and wife, of parents and children, of masters and servants, is a sufficient intimation to us, how great a part of the Christian life consists in regular and conscientious discharge of those duties.[4]

The best way for people to serve God, Gibson maintained, was through the fulfilling of their social and vocational responsibilities. God was pleased, Gibson wrote some years later in his 1746–47 *Charge*, with "diligent attendance on the business of . . . [a person's] station, out of a sense of duty to God."[5] The author of *Dr. Codex's pastoral letter versified* echoed Gibson:

> Next in your station 'mongst mankind
> To whatever part confin'd,
> Be't yours, the pow'r divine t'obey,
> And to his will submission pay;
> Be careful to discharge your trust;
> To th' duty of that station just.
> And tho' your mind is oft perplex'd,
> By various duties to't annex'd,
> Know in this life our trial is
> To fit our souls for future bliss;
> And still the more we suffer here,
> We shall be better thought on there.[6]

Numerous critics expressed the fear that Methodism did not recognize people's social responsibility.[7] It was alleged that the Methodists were teaching that people could neglect their callings in order to perform religious duties. Stebbing cautioned the Methodists in 1739:

> We may be with God, you see, and in our calling too; yea, if we abide not in our callings we cannot serve God as we ought to

---

4 029-Gr. [Gibson], *The bishop of London's pastoral letter*, 6–7.

5 206-Gr. [Gibson], *The charge of the Right Reverend Father in God, Edmund, Lord Bishop of London*, 26.

6 030-Gr. *Dr. Codex's pastoral letter versified* (London: for J. Brett, 1739), 14–15.

7 For example, 137-Gr. *A letter from a gentleman in the country to his friend in Edinburgh*, 30–31.

serve him. We may pray, and fast, and do many other such like things; but this will not be serving God, if we neglect the duties of our callings. The station in which every man is placed by the providence of God, shows him his duty as plainly as any written law can do; and when religious duties fall in with these and help them forward, they are acceptable to God. But what think you? If a man should refuse to maintain his aged and indigent parents; would it be a justification to say that he gives away his money in charity? . . . It would be the same case if a servant should neglect to do his master's business, or the husband or wife to take care of their families upon whatever religious pretense it is done: For God cannot disannul the eternal laws of his own government.[8]

The excessive piety of the Methodists, antagonists claimed, caused neglect of their social obligations. People were not only religious beings, who must learn the way to heaven through spiritual discipline, but, critics reminded the Methodists, they were also social beings, responsible for the welfare of society as well as for their own souls:

By an honest industry in tilling and cultivating the earth, in carrying on trade and commerce, in the improvement of knowledge, arts, and sciences [an individual] is to promote the mutual benefit and advantage of society, without which [humanity] would be destitute of all necessaries and conveniences of life and be in reality the most miserable of all the creation.[9]

The Methodists, critics contended, spent too much time in prayer, Bible reading, fasting, and attending their society meetings.[10] Thomas Church urged moderation in things religious: "It is bad to be always engaged in spiritual exercises."[11] Another author suggested sardonically that the Methodists were so busy preparing for the life hereafter that they had little time to be involved with the obligations of this world.[12] As the revival progressed, opponents

---

8 017-Gr. Stebbing, *A caution against religious delusion*, 21.

9 117-Gr. A friend to true religion [Joseph Nicoll], *The sentiments of Archbishop Tillotson and Sharp on regeneration* (London: printed and sold by C. Corbett, [1741]), 3.

10 017-Gr. Stebbing, *A caution against religious delusion*, 14. See also 117-Gr. A friend to true religion [Nicoll], *The sentiments of Archbishop Tillotson and Sharp on regeneration*, 3.

11 049-Gr. Church, *An explanation and defence of the doctrine of regeneration*, 55.

12 316-Gr. *An address to the Right Honourable—* (London: W. Sandby, 1761), 2–3.

continued to be alarmed by the Methodists' attitude to their place in society and to their vocations. Henry Stebbing had voiced strong criticism of the aspect in 1739, and he repeated it in 1745 in his anonymously published *An earnest and affectionate address to the people called Methodists*.[13] Again he urged that men and women should not, on any account, even because of religious exercises, neglect their social and vocational responsibilities: "There is no sort of necessity or occasion, that this should set aside a just and prudent application to our respective trades and callings."[14] Critics blamed field preaching for inducing many to disregard their social duties. Ralph Skerret asked the "laborious and meckanick part" of society

> to consider how greatly they break in upon all relative duties
> and the benefits of social life by daily assembling themselves in
> troops upon the hills and the neighboring commons under a vain
> pretense of serving God more acceptably; who requires no such
> extraordinary service at their hands: Because all such service is
> contrary to common decency, unanimity and good order."[15]

John Wilder agreed. Attendance at Methodist services in the field went hand in hand with the neglect of duties and business.[16] What worried critics of the revival was the Methodists' practice of holding preaching services every day of the week. In contrast the Church of England set aside one day for the worship of God, Sunday. All that was required of a Christian, opponents of Methodism said, was the attendance of divine service on that one day. The Methodists were accused of failing to heed the implication of the fourth commandment: enjoining the use of one day in seven for worship, the commandment suggested that one engage in work in the intervening six.[17] A writer in 1739 chided the Methodists for drawing "the people from their necessary employments, and leading them miles from home to hear a sermon."[18] John Thorold, writing in 1745, complained that the Methodists "should have

---

13 200-Gr. A. B. [Stebbing], *An earnest and affectionate address to the people called Methodists*.

14 Ibid., 41.

15 008-Gr. Skerret, *The nature and proper evidence of regeneration*, vii–viii.

16 018-Gr. Wilder, *The trial of the spirits*, 18.

17 117-Gr. A Friend to True Religion [Nicoll], *The sentiments of Archbishop Tillotson and Sharp on regeneration*, 3–4; 142-Gr. Gib, *A warning against countenancing the ministrations of . . . Whitefield*, 18; 205C-Ki. W. D. [Dowars], *Errors in part discovered*, 26.

18 031-Gr. *An earnest appeal to the publick* (London: sold by J. Roberts, 1739), 10.

been at their respective trades and employments," instead of traveling vast distances to their religious meetings.[19] Methodists wasted two or three hours a day, it was estimated by some, in traveling to and from services, waiting for the preacher to arrive, and listening to sermons. The economic impact of this practice ought not to be overlooked—there was not only a loss of working hours and productivity, but a loss of revenue as well. Complaints were made of the Methodists "stopping trade, dragging poor servants from their work . . . hurting their masters and impoverishing their families."[20] One country curate reported that he had received numerous complaints from parish officers and masters that servants had neglected their duties to attend Methodist services.[21] George White predicted the ruin of industry in Yorkshire if the Methodists continued to hold weekday services.[22]

Idleness and Vagrancy

Several opponents complained that Methodism was promoting idleness. Because Methodist preaching services on Sundays were held very early in the morning in some places, people were encouraged to be idle for the rest of the day. Rather than returning to their homes, or going to the parish church for morning prayer, many, it was said, were guilty of disorderly behavior.[23] In other places where Methodist congregations met later in the day, it was reported that they waited "publickly (and very indecently too)" for the appearance of their preacher.[24] Idleness was not just a Sunday phenomenon. Methodism was blamed for the general indolence observable in some localities. William Bowman bewailed: "How many useless hands are now found in every corner of your parish . . . How trade droops and decays."[25]

Methodists were blamed for exacerbating the growing problem of vagrancy throughout England. Some converts not only neglected their vocations,

---

19 197-Gr. A Layman [Thorold], *Extracts of letters relating to Methodists and Moravians* (London: for B. Dod, 1745), 20–21.

20 009-Gr. Land, *A letter to the Rev. Mr. Whitefield*, 22.

21 032-Gr. A Curate in the Country, *Observations on the Reverend Mr. Whitefield's answer*, 26–27.

22 208-Gr. White, *A sermon against the Methodists*, 21.

23 117-Gr. A Friend to True Religion [Nicoll], *The sentiments of Archbishop Tillotson and Sharp on regeneration*, 4–5.

24 142-Gr. Gib, *A warning against countenancing the ministrations of . . . Whitefield*, 20.

25 094-Gr. Bowman, *The imposture of Methodism display'd*, 51.

critics said, but actually quit their employment, becoming vagrants, and thus a burden on their parish for poor relief. One critic called for the suppression of Whitefield because his doctrine encouraged vagrancy:

> Can nothing shew his doctrine flagrant;
> Yet have an act against the vagrant
> Who makes for cobblers quit their stalls,
> And leave behind their ends and awls;
> And on the parish leave their wives,
> To follow where the Devil drives.[26]

Wesley, likewise, faced the accusation of promoting vagrancy:

> Fathers and mothers, widows, wives, till death,
> May rue the minute when you drew your breath.
> How many idle vagrants hast thou made,
> Who else had liv'd upon a wholesome trade
> who now their industry shall use no more.[27]

A number of opponents believed there was a causal connection between the growth of Methodism and the increasing number of people swelling the ranks of the poor. Several critics reported that those who were becoming a burden on their parishes for poor relief were Methodists.[28] Others cautioned that if Methodism continued to spread, poverty would increase.[29] In 1791 one author suggested that an analysis should be undertaken of the growth of the poor and its correlation with the growth of Methodism:

> Have the poor rates increased with the increase of Methodism? Perhaps upon examination they will be found to have kept pace with the progress of the religion. And it would give this opinion some weight, if the rates, in particular places, have corresponded with the prevalence of Methodism.[30]

---

26 048-Gr. A Muggletonian, *The amorous humours, and audacious adventures of one Whd* (London: for the author, [1739], 23.

27 488A-Ki. Detester of Hypocrisy, *To that fanatical, political, physical, enthusiast.* Broadside.

28 032-Gr. A Curate in the Country, *Observations on the Reverend Mr. Whitefield's answer,* 26–27; 555-Gr. *A review of the policy, doctrines and morals of the Methodists,* 50.

29 205C-Ki. W. D. [Dowars], *Errors in part discovered,* 30; 008-Gr. Skerret, *The nature and proper evidence of regeneration,* vii–viii.

30 555-Gr. *A review of the policy, doctrines and morals of the Methodists,* 50.

Lay preachers Ignore Their God-Ordained Station

A further disruptive influence on society was the Methodists' use of lay preachers. In order to take up preaching, they left their proper trade. What was to become of society, critics wondered, if tradesmen were to lay down their tools, forsake their trades, and go off preaching just because they felt an inner urge to do so? Theophilus Evans accused lay preachers of trying to rise above their God-given stations: "In the particular trade any of these was brought up, taylor, tinker, weaver, &c. he might be useful, and earn his bread in an honest way; but growing idle and self-conceited, the general method is to turn exhorter."[31] Satirists scorned laity who deserted their trade to be itinerant preachers:

> The bricklay'r throws his trowel by,
> And now builds mansions in the sky;
> The cobbler, touch'd with holy pride,
> Flings his old shoes and lasts aside.
> And now devoutly sets about
> Cobbling of souls that ne'er wear out;
> The baker, now a preacher grown,
> Finds men live not by bread alone,
> And now his customers he feeds
> With pray'rs, with sermons, groans and creeds;
> Barbers unreap'd will leave the chin,
> To trim, and shave the man within
> The brewer, bit by phrenzy's grub,
> The mashing for the preaching tub
> Resigns, those waters to explore,
> Which if you drink, you thirst no more.[32]

Once a tradesman, always a tradesman. Anti-Methodists believed that training for a trade made deep impressions on lay preachers—marks too deep to be erased simply by assuming a new role of preacher.[33]

---

31 235-Gr. [Evans], *The history of modern enthusiasm*, 116.

32 379-Gr. The author of *The powers of the pew* and *The curate* [Lloyd], *The Methodist: a poem*, 32–33.

33 324-Gr. Snip *pseud.*, *The journal of the travels of Nathaniel Snip*, 17–18.

Family Life Disrupted

Not only were individuals neglecting their vocational responsibilities, but the revival appeared to many to be disrupting the basic social unit, the family. Anti-Methodists reported that families were being divided by the new sect, pitting wife against husband and vice versa. Women were misusing family income to support the revival, husbands and wives alike were rejecting family and domestic responsibilities, and the health and education of children in Methodist homes were being neglected. Should families all over England begin to disintegrate, anti-Methodists feared the collapse of the nation in the future.

Jesus had prophesied that following him could cause disruption in the family (Luke 12:51–53). To the revival's critics this prophecy appeared to be literally fulfilled in Methodism. Wesley conceded that it was. It was inevitable, he thought, that when some members of a family became disciplined Christians tensions within the home might emerge: "For is it to be supposed that a heathen parent would long endure a Christian child, or that a heathen husband would agree with a Christian wife?"[34]

The harmony of the home was sometimes torn by bitter fighting when a member converted to Methodism. Families fragmented as husband turned against wife, wife turned against husband, parents were divided against their children, and children against their parents, noted one author in 1741 as he commented on the social effects of the revival:

> 'Tis notorious what dismal feuds the Methodists have raised in
> private families, by alienating the affections of husbands and wives
> from each other, by rendering parents unnatural to their children
> and children undutiful to their parents.[35]

An occasional critic complained of the deleterious effect on families caused by the conversion of men to Methodism.[36] More frequent, however, were complaints against wives and mothers who became Methodists. Once converted, it was alleged, many women refused to obey their husbands, became alienated from them, and even deserted them. This was said to have been one of the contributory causes of the Wednesbury riots. The wife of a

---

34 John Wesley, *A Farther Appeal to Men of Reason and Religion*, pt. 1 (1745), in *BEWJW*, 11:188.

35 118-Gr. J. Trevor, *A short history of the Donatists*, 44.

36 124-Gr. *Mr. Whitefield's doctrines considered and confuted*, 24.

local collier had been missing for several days, sometime before Christmas 1743. After finding her at a class meeting with a Methodist preacher, the husband took her back home. Several days later, she again absented herself, and the distraught husband once more had to retrieve her.[37]

Evan Lloyd hinted that family divisions could be beneficial to lecherous Methodists:

> The closest union can divide,
> Take husbands from their spouses' side,
> But if it turns out better use,
> Wives from their husbands to seduce.[38]

Ex-Methodist James Lackington reported that he knew of some women in Wesley's London society who had refused, after their conversion, to have sexual relations with their husbands. He also reported the case of a "Mrs. G_____" who had deserted her husband and children (one of whom she had been breast-feeding) when she came from Ireland to London to join Wesley's society.[39]

The process of marital disruption is satirized in *The story of the Methodist-lady: or, the injur'd husband's revenge*.[40] The central figure, Theodosia, a middle-class woman, had been happily married for ten years. Theodosia first went to hear Whitefield out of curiosity but was converted. Her conversion had disastrous effects on her family life. She neglected her domestic duties, and a rift developed in her marriage. Rejecting her husband as a heathen, she concentrated her affections on a handsome young rake who, feigning conversion to Methodism in order to seduce her, had become her spiritual adviser. The story ends with Theodosia pregnant by her "Methodist" confidant, the miscarriage of a five-month baby, being thrown out of the house by her husband, an impending divorce, and the castration of her lover in revenge.[41]

Adults were not the only ones to be won into the Methodist fold: young

---

37 173-Gr. *Some papers giving an account of Methodism at Wednesbury* (London: for J. Roberts, 1744), 21–23.

38 379-Gr. The author of *The powers of the pew* and *The curate* [Lloyd], *The Methodist: A poem*, 28.

39 560-Gr. Lackington, *The memoirs of the life . . . of James Lackington*, 234.

40 238-Gr. *The story of the Methodist-lady* (London: for John Doughty, [1752]).

41 Ibid., 48–51.

people were converted, often contrary to their parents' wishes. Noting this, Evan Lloyd complained of the alienation of children from their parents.

> Domestic peace he [the Methodist preacher] can destroy,
> And the confusion view with joy,
> Children from parents he can draw,
> What's conscience?—he is safe from law.[42]

Rumors that female converts to Methodism were misusing money and goods designated by the head of the household for the support of the family, kindled the indignation of anti-Methodists. Instead of purchasing food and clothing for the family, Methodist women, it was alleged, diverted their husbands' money to religious causes. Itinerants were supported and preaching houses were erected with money that should have fed and clothed the family. Children starved and wore rags, but preachers feasted sumptuously and were finely arrayed.

The allegation that gullible women were giving their families' substance to the Methodist leaders was noted in the 1739 farce *The mock-preacher*. A cobbler's wife who had given away all the family's earnings to Whitefield, was beaten by her husband to teach her a lesson.[43] *The story of the Methodist-lady* (1752) raised the same criticism. Theodosia had no sooner been converted than "she gave away profusely more than her husband could afford, but not to the poor directly, but to this saint [Whitefield] to be disposed of as he should think meet."[44] Another author, writing about the same time (1753), suggested that Methodist women even robbed their husbands in order to be able to support the new sect.[45] In soliciting and accepting such contributions, wrote the author of *The notions of the Methodists farther disprov'd*, the Methodist leaders were in effect picking people's pockets and robbing them of what they needed to sustain their families.[46] It was the children who suffered most. Two satirical poets, the first in 1743, the second in 1778, drove the point home. A couplet in *The progress of Methodism in Bristol* reads:

---

42 379-Gr. The author of *The powers of the pew* and *The curate* [Lloyd], *The Methodist: a poem*, 27.

43 025-Gr. *The mock-preacher* (London: C. Corbett, 1739), 17.

44 238-Gr. *The story of the Methodist-lady*, 11.

45 248A-Ba. A Lay-man, *A few queries concerning the growth of Methodism*, 5.

46 160B-Ba. [Smith], *The notions of the Methodists farther disprov'd*, 61.

> And some 'tis said, who thither [to the New Room] come,
> Their children want for bread at home.[47]

William Combe, addressing Wesley, drew even harsher criticism:

> Creep into houses, blast domestic life,
> Sow false religion, and eternal strife.
> Tempt weaker vessels to betray their head,
> And with your dogs divide the children's bread
> Industrious trade with contributions crush,
> And plunder poverty without a blush.[48]

Although financial contributions were at the center of the storm, critics complained that gifts in kind also impoverished families.[49] In Thomas Este's farce *Methodism display'd*, Padwell, a prisoner, complained to Vizard, the Methodist preacher, that his family had suffered because of his wife's association with Methodism: "We had but three blankets in the world, and two of them she gave to some of your crew; by which means, two of my bairns caught their deaths with cold, and soon dy'd of the chin cough."[50]

Domestic Responsibilities Neglected

A common charge made against the Methodists was neglect of domestic responsibilities. Parents left their homes untended as one or both of them went off to society meetings. As early as 1739 it was alleged that hundreds of homes were in a deplorable state because Methodism was siphoning off those whose duty it was to maintain them.[51] In 1739 Weller ridiculed women for attending society meetings. They were out of place at society meetings, he opined; their right place was in the home.[52] Such denunciations of the Methodists' domestic irresponsibility continued throughout the eighteenth century. In 1755 Thomas Green alluded to it.[53] W. Penrice circulated the

---

47 156-Gr. An Impartial hand, *The progress of Methodism in Bristol*, 17.
48 415-Gr. [Combe], *Perfection: a poetical epistle*, 13.
49 160B-Ba. [Smith], *The notions of the Methodists farther disproved*, 61.
50 154-Gr. Este, *Methodism display'd: A farce*, 13.
51 031-Gr. *An earnest appeal to the publick*, 9.
52 098-Gr. [Weller], *The trial of Mr. Whitefield's spirit*, 35–36.
53 249A-Fi. Green, *A dissertation on enthusiasm*, 87.

accusation in 1771.[54] Religious duties, some opponents reported, were placed above care of the family. The cobbler in the 1739 farce the *Mock-preacher* complains to his wife:

> And so you must dance about after this mock-preacher [White-
> field], Must you? And leave me to nurse your children? . . . I have
> had no dinner—You know you went to Moorfields in the morning
> and to Kensington-Commons at night—where you have been all
> the rest of the day, you know best.[55]

James Buller indicted Wesley for keeping the women in his Bristol society so busy with religious duties, during a time of high prices in 1740, that they could not work to earn cash to supplement their husbands' income and so help sustain their families. "The husbands," Buller said, "loudly repeated, ye are idle, ye are idle, but were as often answer'd with, we must serve the Lord and save our souls."[56] The author of *A plain and easy road to the land of bliss* alleged satirically that Methodist women were actively encouraged as a matter of faith to neglect their homes and families: "[S]o far from being an infidel, if you refuse to work for your own and their living . . . it is the greatest argument of your faith; and you'll certainly be duly rewarded if you leave them to shift for themselves."[57]

Children Neglected

Not only were children deprived of sustenance; they remained uneducated, noted William Bowman, because of their mothers' frequent and long absences from their homes.[58] George White believed that Methodism would thus usher in a generation of widespread illiteracy.[59] James Penn believed that Methodist children, robbed of a strong family relationship, would grow up undisciplined, becoming "a prey to idle and loose company."[60] The anonymous author who

---

54 446A-Ki. W. Penrice, *The causes of Methodism set forth* (London: no printer, 1771), 3–4.
55 025-Gr. *The mock–preacher*, 15–16.
56 258-Gr. Buller, *A reply to the Rev. Mr. Wesley's 'Address to the clergy,'* 25.
57 337-Gr. *A plain and easy road to the land of bliss*, 65.
58 094-Gr. Bowman, *The imposture of Methodism display'd*, 51.
59 208-Gr. White, *A sermon against the Methodists*, 21.
60 338-Gr. Penn, *Various tracts*, 91.

in 1791 issued *A review of the policy, doctrines and morals of the Methodists,* summed up the fears that had been expressed:

> No children are so much neglected in their articles of education, of religious instruction, in a proper attention to their moral conduct, in providing for them a decent maintenance, and in instilling into them habits of diligence and industry, as are the children of the Methodists. Their members are so occupied, and have their time so filled up with attending on prayers and preaching, that they have but little time left to attend to more important concerns of their families; and many of the poorer sort of this society, thinking it their duty to attend upon worship at hours unreasonably early and late at such times leave their helpless off-spring to shift for themselves, in the best manner, that they can. . . . No children are so wild, so brutish and untractable, none more base in their morals, than the children of the Methodists.[61]

Society's Peace and Order Threatened

In the late 1730s and early 1740s, the cry of the anti-Methodist was "Society in danger!" Like the early Christians, the Methodists were accused of turning the world upside down. Wherever the Methodists went, Joseph Trapp complained in 1739, they have "thrown whole neighbourhoods and parishes into confusion."[62] Opponents could not reconcile Methodism with eighteenth-century Christianity. In 1740 Daniel Waterland defined Christianity in terms of social stability. It "is an humble, quiet, peaceable, and orderly religion: not noisy, or ostentatious, not assuming or censorious, not factious or tumultuous."[63] Methodism did all the things that Christianity, by Waterland's definition, was not supposed to do. When the Wesleys and Whitefield, in contravention of the laws of the land, took to the out-of-doors to preach, gathered huge crowds, censured the regular clergy with harsh epithets, and invaded their parishes uninvited, their contemporaries could not believe the Methodists had the good of society in mind.[64] Henry Stebbing described how the Methodists

---

61 555-Gr. *A review of the policy, doctrines and morals of the Methodists,* 39.
62 010-Gr. Trapp, *The nature, folly, sin and danger of being righteous over-much,* 37.
63 107-Gr. Waterland, *Regeneration stated and explained,* 40.
64 See chapter 4, "Innovative Practices," and chapter 6 "The Church in Danger."

disregarded order and peace: "rash uncharitable censures, damning all that do not feel what they feel; . . . gathering tumultuous assemblies to the disturbance of the publick peace; . . . setting at nought all rule and authority; . . . intruding into other men's labours."[65] The message of Saint Paul was that all things should "be done decently and in order" (1 Corinthians 14:40), but the Methodists did not do things in decency and order, Joseph Trapp complained. In promoting "tumult and confusion" the Methodists were breaking scriptural admonitions.[66] If the Methodists went unchecked, cautioned Samuel Weller and John Wilder, the safety and peace of the nation were at stake.[67]

Mob Violence

In many localities where Methodism was introduced, violence erupted. Houses belonging to society members were wrecked or ransacked; preaching houses were damaged or pulled down; men, women, and children were beaten, with many severely injured. Although, as John Walsh has pointed out, mob violence in eighteenth-century England was "an almost traditional means of group expression," opponents blamed the Methodists for the riots that occurred.[68] William Bowman contended that Benjamin Ingham and the Methodists were responsible for the riots in Dewsbury in 1740. The disturbances had been hatched in their "infernal assemblies."[69] The riot at Minchin Hampton, Gloucestershire (1743), was said to have resulted from the Methodists' attempt to disrupt trade and impoverish families by encouraging men and women to neglect their work in order to hear evangelical preachers.[70] Another author, examining the riots at Wednesbury in Staffordshire (1743), alleged that they arose out of protest to the Methodists' shattering of the peace of society: "Instead of that peace, charity, and goodwill, which their

---

65 017-Gr. Stebbing, *A caution against religious delusion*, 14.

66 010-Gr. Trapp, *The nature, folly, sin and danger of being righteous over-much*, 20.

67 098-Gr. [Weller], *The trial of Mr. Whitefield's spirit*, 4; 018-Gr. Wilder, *The trial of the spirits*, 20.

68 See John Walsh, "Methodism and the Mob in the Eighteenth Century," in *Popular Belief and Practice*, ed. C.J. Cuming and Derek Baker, 215. See also Clive Field, "A Revised Bibliography," 165. Field has identified descriptions of anti-Methodist riots in pamphlets 169-Gr., 173-Gr., 187-Gr., 188-Gr., 242-Gr., and 243A-Ba.

69 094-Gr. Bowman, *The imposture of Methodism display'd*, 75, 79.

70 166-Gr. J. B./A Gentleman of Pembroke College, Oxon, *A letter to the Reverend Mr. Whitefield occasioned by his pretended answer to the first part of the 'Observations on the conduct and behaviour of the Methodists,'* 22.

preachers boasted to be the fruits there of their [preaching]; malice, spleen, and endless feuds sprang up in their room."[71] The immediate cause of the Wednesbury riots, the author claimed, was anger at the division Methodism caused in families.[72] Disruption of family life was said also to have been the cause of the riots in Exeter (1745). There was no doubt that Methodist doctrine and practice were "injurious to society."[73] Richard Hurd, in the preface to his sermon at the Norwich Assizes on July 29, 1752, praised the magistracy for suppressing Methodism in that city.[74] The printing of his sermon commended the prudent endeavors of the magistracy and the clergy of Norwich to restore that peace and charity that had suffered so greatly from the public dissentions of the Methodists.

Social Anarchy

Methodism and social anarchy became synonymous in the minds of some gentry and church leaders. The disorders of the seventeenth century were a popular topic of pamphleteers in 1739 and the early 1740s. With innuendo as their weapon, pamphleteers highlighted the similarities between the Methodists and the Puritans, and then reminded their readers of the disorder and confusion that English society had experienced under the Puritan ascendancy.[75] Other critics, such as the author of *A compleat account of the conduct of . . . Mr. Whitefield*, stated the charge more boldly. History was repeating itself:

> I . . . venture to affirm that the present enthusiasts have made a much quicker progress since their first publick appearance than their predecessors [the Puritans] did in the same compass of time, and that the nation is now more disposed to receive any ill impression . . . to despise authority, and to run into disorders of any kind than it was at the beginning of those times of confusion.[76]

John Wilder claimed that Whitefield was an anarchist bent on the de-

---

71 173-Gr. *Some papers giving an account of . . . Methodism at Wednesbury*, 12, 21–22.
72 Ibid.
73 188A-Ki. A Layman of the Church of England, *Remarks on a late pamphlet intitled 'A brief account of the late persecution . . . at Exeter,'* 6, 13–24.
74 237-Gr. Hurd, *The mischiefs of enthusiasm and bigotry*, vi.
75 029-Gr. [Gibson], *The bishop of London's pastoral letter*, 29. See also the anonymously issued 031-Gr. *An earnest appeal to the publick*, 31.
76 036-Gr. [Tucker], *A compleat account of the conduct of . . . Mr. Whitefield*, 11.

struction of English society: "He [Whitefield] is resolved to make his voice the trumpet of the war; and reduce, if possible, this Church and State to anarchy and confusion."[77] Opponents, even into the 1750s and 1760s, continued to compare Methodists and Puritans, and suggested that the evangelical revival was rekindling the flames of seventeenth-century anarchy. By then, however, the charge was recognized as unfounded and had lost most of is force.[78]

Levelers

Methodists, it was feared, were a new generation of Levelers who were quietly engineering a proletarian revolution. Methodists were charged with preaching the radical doctrine of obligatory renunciation of this world's goods, whereas Christianity taught voluntary renunciation. The charge of linking the Christian doctrine of renunciation to "leveling principles" was made first by John Brownsword in 1739.[79] He accused the Methodists of wanting to bring the rich down to the level of the poor—society would have no gradations according to wealth if the Methodists had their way. Alexander Jephson, writing twenty years later, reiterated the charge—the Methodists were eighteenth-century Robin Hoods intent on removing distinctions between wealth and poverty by establishing "an equality of fortune."[80]

The Methodists, William Bowman claimed in 1740, were espousing community of goods. Bowman took offence at the thought of the indolent sharing the fruits of the industrious and frugal. It would rob people of their incentive to work. But even more disastrous effects were in store if the Methodists continued with this practice:

> Mutinies, riots, robberies, and disorders of every kind are the natural consequences of a leveling scheme and a community of goods; And when men have once ruined and reduced themselves to beggary, it is very easy to imagine, they will soon fall upon the

77 018-Gr. Wilder, *The trial of the spirits*, 21.

78 240-Gr. *Candid remarks on some particular passages in . . . Mr. Whitefield's . . . sermons;* 342-Gr. [Warburton], *The doctrine of grace,* 184; 360-Gr. A. T. Blacksmith [Witherspoon], *A defence of Christianity against the power of enthusiasm* (Bristol: for the author, [1764]), 14; 378-Gr. Peter Paragraph *pseud.* [Adair], *The Methodist and mimick,* 19.

79 043-Gr. Brownsword, *The case of the rich young man in the gospel.*

80 297-Gr. Jephson, *Friendly and compassionate address to all serious . . . Methodists,* 76.

opulence of their neighbour, when they think they have the same
right to it, and as justifiable a property as he.[81]

Opponents found evidence of the leveling principle in the extraordinary
practices the Methodists employed. Their primary example was the use
of laity as preachers. This disrupted the stability of society by ignoring the
time-honored division between clergy and laity. "No sooner does a person
commence Methodist; than he may hope to rise through all the different
gradations of the society and may even aspire to become in time a travelling
preacher," an anonymous author complained.[82] Critics also saw the leveling
principle operating in the Methodists' alleged blurring of class distinctions.
The Methodists lacked proper respect for their betters. The Methodist doctrine
of perfection was destroying social distinctions, Bishop Gibson contended,
as it led lower-class people to think themselves better than their superiors:

> The exalted strains and notions . . . tend to weaken the natural and
> civil relations among men, by leading the inferiors, into whose heads
> those notions are infused, to a disesteem of their superiors; while
> they consider them as in a much lower dispensation than them-
> selves; though those superiors are otherwise sober and good men.[83]

George Croft, writing in 1786, more than forty years after Gibson, observed in the Methodists' behavior "an entire renunciation of terms importing
respect and courteousness."[84]

Methodist preachers were accused numerous times of being disrespectful
to their Anglican ecclesiastical superiors. Such insubordination was further
example of the Methodists ignoring social distinctions.[85]

The Dangerous Poor

Methodism, from the beginning, was known for its work among the poor.[86]
The fact that Methodism appeared to address itself primarily to the poor

---

81 094-Gr. Bowman, *The imposture of Methodism display'd*, 6.

82 555-Gr. *A review of the policy, doctrines and morals of the Methodists*, 8.

83 164-Gr. [Gibson], *Observations upon the conduct and behaviour of . . . Methodists*, 10.

84 536A-Ki. Croft, *Eight sermons preached before the University of Oxford*, 184.

85 See chapter 6, "The Church in Danger."

86 See Richard P. Heitzenrater, ed., *The Poor and the People Called Methodists, 1729–1999*,
(Nashville: Kingswood Books, 2002), esp. chap. 1 (15–38). See also Theodore W. Jennings

generated much suspicion. The words of stanza 5 of Charles Wesley's hymn "Where shall my wondering soul begin" confirmed the Methodists' avowed interests in working with the lower ranks of society:

> Outcasts of men, to you I call,
> Harlots and publicans, and thieves!
> He spreads his arms t'embrace you all;
> Sinners alone his grace receives.[87]

By 1740, authors were expressing general apprehension about the grip Methodism had upon "the dregs and refuse of the people, the weak, unsteady mob."[88] "J. B." expressed fear in 1744 that the Methodist leaders at the head of "a set of creatures of the lowest rank, most of them illiterate, and of desperate fortunes; cursing, reviling, and shewing their teeth at everyone that does not approve of their frenzy and extravagance," could not be trusted if a national emergency arose.[89] Methodism was one of the causes of the increase of poverty instigated by people leaving their trades to engage in Methodist preaching services and society meetings:

> For them the shuttle's left by lazy weavers;
> And butchers drop their marrow-bones and cleavers;
> And, while the weaver's wife forsakes the loom,
> Susan leaves half mop'd the dining-room;
> These are the dregs, the rubbish of mankind,
> Sightless themselves, and guided by the blind,
> Strangers to virtue, as unknown to schools:
> As ev'ry like its like, fools cherish fools.[90]

Anglican leaders remained apprehensive of Methodism's success among the poor. The lower classes were easy prey for Methodism, Lavington contended,

---

Jr., *Good News for the Poor: John Wesley's Evangelical Economics* (Nashville: Abingdon, 1990).

87 Frank Baker, ed., *Representative Verse of Charles Wesley* (New York and Nashville: Abingdon, 1962), no. 1, st. 5, p. 4. See *A Collection of Hymns, for the Use of the People called Methodists*, ed. Franz Hilderbrandt and Oliver A. Beckerlegge, in *BEWJW* (Nashville: Abingdon, 1983), no. 29, st. 5, 7:117.

88 094-Gr. Bowman, *The imposture of Methodism display'd*, 2.

89 166-Gr. J. B./ A Gentleman of Pembroke College, Oxon, *A letter to the Reverend Mr. Whitefield occasioned by his pretended answer to the first part of the 'Observations on the conduct and behaviour of the Methodists,'* 18.

90 092–Fi. [Thomas] Cooke, *The mournful nuptials* (London: for T. Cooper, 1739), 73.

because a large proportion of them were unlearned and unstable.[91] John Douglas feared Methodist preachers because they had "acquired such authority amongst crouds of persons in the lower stations of life, whose ignorance maketh them fit tools for designing men to work upon."[92] The numbers of poor who flocked to the Methodists alarmed John Free. He bemoaned the fact that the "vulgar in the capital cities, and the body of artisans in the most populous trading towns are mostly in the hands of these people."[93]

The Methodists' success with the poor was dangerous, Gibson thought, because it was propagating "peculiar notions and doctrines . . . among the lower sort, who are least able to judge of them."[94] Writing in 1789, Richard Price maintained that Methodism's influence had been deleterious: "[T]he lower orders of people . . . are sinking into a barbarism in religion lately revived by Methodism."[95]

Some antagonists feared Methodism because it organized the poor into well-disciplined cells, known as bands and classes, that owed allegiance to leaders who were not part of the authority structure in society. Though most anti-Methodists expressed only vague apprehension about Methodism's organization of the lower classes into close-knit cadres, a sinister motive was directly imputed by William Bowman. The Methodists, he warned, were plotting in "these secret conventicles to destroy the peace and welfare of the public."[96]

Social Distinction between Men and Women Erased

The revival's appeal to women gave some critics cause for concern. A number of authors scorned the fact that Methodist societies seemed to consist mainly of women. Noted early in the revival, such disdain recurred from time to time throughout the century. William Fleetwood, in 1741, observed that "for

---

91 213A-Ki. [Lavington], *The enthusiasm of Methodists and papists compar'd*, pt. 2, 1–2.

92 237-Gr. [Douglas], *An apology for the clergy, with a view to expose the groundless assertions of a late commentator*, 29; 384-Gr. [Tottie], *Two charges delivered to the clergy of the diocese of Worcester*, 360; 531-Gr. Muirhead, *A review of the principles of such Methodists as are under the direction of . . . John Wesley*, v.

93 274-Gr. Free, *Rules for the discovery of false prophets*, ii.

94 206-Gr. [Gibson], *The charge of the Right Reverend Father in God, Edmund Lord Bishop of London . . . 1746 and 1747*, 7.

95 549A-Ba. Richard Price, *A discourse on the love of our country* (London: T. Cadell, 1789), 16.

96 094-Gr. Bowman, *The imposture of Methodism display'd*, 79.

the most part, their attendants are silly women."[97] In 1743 one pamphleteer ventured to estimate that three-quarters of the members of Methodist societies were women.[98] Nathaniel Lancaster, writing in 1767, asserted that of the twenty-four thousand converts of Wesley, the great majority were women.[99] The issue had not changed by century's end, when James Lackington wrote of his former spiritual leader, "I believe that by far the greatest part of his people are females; and not a few of them sour, disappointed old maids, with some others of a less prudish disposition."[100]

In concentrating on converting women, their adversaries maintained, the Methodists were attacking society at its weakest point—women were particularly susceptible to the emotional appeal of Methodist enthusiasm.[101] The vulnerability of women, it was claimed, was a gift to the Methodists; women were easily won to the cause and eagerly helped advance it:

> Since they do seldom dispute
> Or argue, cavil, or confute,
> And yet whate'er they think is good
> Have wond'rous tongues to spread abroad.
> . . . .
> To move by rule and pious seem
> Fixes at once their frail esteem.[102]

The author of *Lucifer's lectures* echoed that sentiment as he addressed the Methodist leaders:

> I play my arts upon with advantage, especially the female kind, who make up the more numerous parts of your societies, their weak heads being unable to withstand the speciousness of your doctrine; I deceive then with visions, dreams, &c. puff them up with pride and vanity, make them all ill-natured, mean, selfish, and indolent, spurring them on to be exceeding liberal to you.[103]

---

97 131-Gr. Fleetwood, *The perfectionists examin'd*, 2.
98 156-Gr. An Impartial Hand, *The progress of Methodism in Bristol*, 20.
99 387-Gr. Lancaster, *Methodism triumphant*, 91.
100 560-Gr. Lackington, *Memoirs of the life . . . of James Lackington*, 123.
101 238-Gr. *The story of the Methodist-lady*, 3–4; 274-Gr. Free, *Rules for the discovery of false prophets*, 27.
102 026-Gr. *The Methodists: An humorous burlesque poem*, 19.
103 575D-Fi. *Lucifer's lectures; or, the infernal tribune*, 28.

The very continuance of English society was at stake if Methodists continued to convert so many women. One early satirist suggested that the Methodists deliberately sought out women to convert so that there should be a supply of new Methodists for future generations.[104] John Oswald, author of *Ranae comicae evangelizantes,* wrote satirically of the dire social consequences of Methodists converting women. Noting the effects of a Methodist preacher on his female converts, he commented, "Several of them communicated . . . to the fruit of their womb, the dire contagion of superstition, and stamp'd th'unhappy foetus a fanatic for life."[105]

The social distinction between male and female seemed threatened by the Methodists. Opponents believed that Saint Paul's injunction that women should keep their place in the church, and that wives should obey their husbands, was to be strictly obeyed. It was not a woman's place, thought Samuel Weller, to attend religious society meetings:

> Christian women can never frequent such unscriptural assemblies, without contemning the rule of their Lord and Master. From their fathers, their husbands, their masters, or their respective heads of those families wherein they live, are these persons, by God's express commands to seek for instruction in the doctrines of Christ.[106]

It was not just that the Methodist women attended religious meetings to discuss the faith that caused concern. There were horrified reports that the Methodists accorded equality to women in many religious duties. Women were being allowed to assume functions the society had always reserved for men—they were praying in public, visiting the sick, and worst of all, they were even preaching.[107]

Dull Puritan Sundays Revived

The ardent commitment of the Methodists to piety, opponents recognized, had manifested social repercussions. The strict and sober Methodist society

---

104 040-Gr. An Impartial Hand [Tucker], *The life and particular proceedings of the Rev. George Whitefield,* 80.

105 535-Gr. [Oswald], *Ranae comicae evangelizantes,* 43.

106 098-Gr. [Weller], *The trial of Mr. Whitefield's spirit,* 35–36.

107 Ibid., 30; 094-Gr. Bowman, *The imposture of Methodism display'd,* 27; 555-Gr. *A review of the policy, doctrines and morals of the Methodists,* 9; 213A-Ki. [Lavington], *The enthusiasm of Methodists and papists compar'd,* pt. 2, 124.

members reminded their contemporaries of the seventeenth-century Puritans, and they feared an attempt by the Methodists to regulate communal life, just as the Puritans had done. If the Methodists were allowed to have their way, a revolution in leisure activities would ensue. Traditional pastimes would have to be abandoned, innocent customs would have to be renounced, and everything joyous would be prohibited. George Whitefield's denunciations of horse racing, dancing, and wrestling (all common amusements of the day) as inherently sinful caused alarm. The Methodists were killjoys. Anti-Methodist pamphleteers reminded their readers that

> relaxation, amusement or diversion of one kind or another is ab-
> solutely necessary to the human mind, as indispensably requisite
> to the health of the body. Piety will direct us to such sort of diver-
> sions, as are innocent and safe. . .The Holy Spirit has nowhere in
> Scripture descended so low . . . as to forbid men, this or that sort
> of entertainment; nor been pleased to be so particular as these
> modern casuists in making out precisely what exercise, amuse-
> ment, like eating and drinking are hurtful only in the excess, but
> [are] innocent in their nature.[108]

There was no need to forgo simple pleasure and pastimes, antagonists maintained. Such renunciation made dull and uninteresting people. One woman, it was reported with scorn, had, because of her conversion to Methodism, even given up singing.[109] John Oswald, author of the satire *Ranae comicae evangelizantes*, parodied a Methodist preacher damning all who "waste" their time in recreation:

> Pastimes! sports! . . . time killing, soul damning, God-hating pas-
> times and sports! Where be all those who rejoiced in the profane
> pastimes of this world? In hell, my brethren, broiling on the hottest
> gridirons in the deepest pits of hell.[110]

Methodism's antipathy towards the theater did not pass without criticism either. Its condemnation of the stage was considered intemperate and un-justified. Not only did plays provide innocent amusements, but some were

---

108 098-Gr. [Weller], *The trial of Mr. Whitefield's spirit*, 44–50.

109 335-Gr. John Langhorne, *Letters on religious retirement* (London: for H. Payne and W. Cropley, 1762), 57.

110 535-Gr. [Oswald], *Ranae comicae evangelizantes*, 21.

designed to help "reform men's manners and bring into subjection their unruly passions and vicious appetites," wrote one author in defense of the theater.[111]

Lastly, critics of Methodism were angered by the movement's strict sabbatarian principles. The Methodists had revived the dull Puritan Sunday. No longer was it a day of amusement and mirth. It was a day of long religious services. Oswald called on cities, towns, and villages to sponsor music and drama on Sundays. He hoped that the "national habit of melancholy would give place to habitual gaiety of mind; Sunday Schools would be deserted; hungry Methodists might whine to uncompassionate walls as the rest of the populace enjoyed themselves in leisure activities."[112] James Lackington believed that the sabbatarian principles enforced by Wesley had brought economic ruin to some Methodists. They had to work on Sundays to make a living, but Wesley forbade it.[113]

The fear expressed by such critics as William Warburton, that the revival was a harbinger of social revolution, though unfounded, was real. History, however, confirms that the influence of Methodism was not destructive to English society but acted as a stabilizing social force in the eighteenth and early nineteenth centuries.

---

111 124-Gr. *Mr. Whitefield's doctrines considered and confuted*, 14.
112 535-Gr. [Oswald], *Ranae comicae evangelizantes*, 46.
113 560-Gr. Lackington, *Memoirs of the life . . . of James Lackington*, 268.

CHAPTER 6

The Church in Danger

Complacency marked the Hanoverian Church of England. Eighteenth-century divines eulogized the perfections of England's established church. Typical was Archbishop John Sharp of York (1646–1714), who pronounced confidently at the beginning of the century that it was "undoubtedly, both as to doctrine and worship, the purest church . . . in the world; the most orthodox in faith, and the freest on the one hand from idolatry and superstition; and on the other hand from freakishness and enthusiasm of any now extant."[1] The majority of the Church of England at the onset of the revival, clergy and laity alike, would have willingly seconded the archbishop's assessment—they entertained no doubts concerning the Church of England's virtues.[2] In like manner Thomas Mortimer, writing in 1758, offered adulatory testimony to the orthodoxy and apostolicity of the Church of England—it was a church in which "the rites and ceremonies of the Christian religion, as well as its doctrines seem to be preserved in that purity and simplicity in which they were first taught and observed, and most agreeable to the plain impartial interpretation of Scripture."[3] It was a church devoid of extremes:

> The English Church too mod'rate seems,
> She laughs at and avoids extremes.
> Too honest to imbibe my schooling
> Too solid to be caught by fooling;
> Yet from this good I'll draw this ill;
> Her charity shall hurt her still.[4]

Given the prevailing view of the state of the church, it is no wonder the emergent evangelical revival encountered such strong resistance.

---

1 John Sharp, *The Works of John Sharp* (London: for the Executrix of Mary Kettilby, 1738), 1:268. See also Thomas Sharp, *The Life of Archbishop John Sharp*, 2 vols. (London: printed for C. and J. Rivington, 1825), 1:354–56.

2 See Norman Sykes, "The Church," in *Johnson's England*, ed. A. S. Turberville, 2 vols. (Oxford: Clarendon, 1933), 1:15.

3 268-Gr. [Mortimer], *Die and be damned*, 15. Mortimer usually wrote on trade and finance. *ODNB*.

4 026-Gr. *The Methodists: An humorous burlesque poem*, 11.

Divergent Views of the State of the Church of England

In contrast to the bright picture of the state of the Anglican Church, a church in no need of further reform, the Methodists depicted a church with faults crying for remedy. Anglican theology had drifted from its Reformation moorings, and there were places where Anglican clergy neglected their ministry. Charles Wesley's poetic epistle to his brother John captured the attitude of many Methodists to the Church of England:

> Yet vainly of our ancestors we boast,
> We, who their faith and purity have lost,
> Degenerate branches from a noble seed,
> Corrupt, apostatiz'd, and doubly dead.
> . . . .
> Shall man presume to say, 'There is no hope:
> God must forsake, for we have giv'n her up
> To save a Church so near the gates of hell,
> This is a thing—with God impossible!'
> And yet this thing impossible is done,
> The Lord hath made his pow'r and mercy known,
> Strangely reviv'd our long forgotten hope,
> And brought out of their graves his people up.[5]

Opponents of Methodism found such statements extremely repugnant. Equally offensive were those instances, gleaned from the writings of Whitefield and the Wesleys, of Methodism's self-identification as God's agent to rekindle the fire of the church from the smoldering, almost extinguished, ashes of the Hanoverian church.[6]

Pamphleteers rallying to the defense of the Church of England extolled its virtues in phrases strongly reminiscent of those used almost a half a century earlier by Sharp. It was a "very noble and excellent" church, the "best of churches," indeed, "one of the purest branches of the Christian

---

5 Charles Wesley, "An Epistle to the Reverend John Wesley. By Charles Wesley, Presbyter of the Church of England" (1755), in Baker, ed., *Representative Verse of Charles Wesley*, 291–92 (see chap. 5, n. 87).

6 Hymn no. 209, *A Collection of Hymns for the Use of the People Called Methodists*, in *BEWJW*, vol. 7, ed. Franz Hilderbrandt and Oliver A. Beckerlegge with the assistance of James Dale, 341–42. Stanzas 1 and 2 can be read as a description of Methodism's growth from tiny beginnings.

Church."[7] Purged of popish corruptions, it was a church thoroughly reformed. In its pristine purity, it could stand beside the primitive church as a worthy successor to the apostles' ministry. Conservative controversialist Zachary Grey exulted in the happy state of the Church:

> Her doctrines are the same they were near 180 years ago, when reform'd and purg'd from the dregs and corruptions of Romish superstition: nay, just the same they were in the first and purest ages of Christianity. Her discipline, tho' we wish yearly that it was better, is in reality much better than is to be met with in any of those pretended churches which separate from her.[8]

Evangelicals misrepresented the Church of England, wrote Henry Stebbing: "Believe me, it is a very great injustice to insinuate that any necessary doctrines or duties of Christianity are neglected to be inculcated and taught in our Church . . .You need not go elsewhere for necessary instruction and exhortations to a life of piety and virtue."[9] Anglicans scorned the Methodists for engaging in redressing "imaginary errors while . . . broach[ing] real ones of their own, contrary to the doctrines of Christ and his apostles."[10]

Puritanism Reborn

John Free expressed the common fear that Methodism threatened the Church of England with "general alteration or total subversion."[11] Memories of how the Puritans had toppled the Church of England in the seventeenth century were still fresh. A chorus of voices shouted that the Methodists were a new brand of Puritanism, with doctrines and practices replete with enthusiasm. Would not the Methodists' enthusiasm, as it had with the Puritans,' end in

---

7 194-Gr. An Impartial Hand, *An essay containing evident proofs against the Methodists*, 6; 208-Gr. White, *A sermon against the Methodists*, iii; 253B-Ki. Christophilus, *Serious enquiry whether a late epistle from . . . Charles Wesley . . . to John Wesley . . .* , 13. This tract was a response to Charles Wesley's poetical epistle to his brother John. Throughout the pamphlet the author took offence at the Methodists' claim that they were God's human agents of a new reformation.

8 186-Gr. A Sincere Protestant [Grey], *A serious address to lay Methodists*, 6–7.

9 200-Gr. A. B. [Stebbing], *An earnest and affectionate address to the people called Methodists*, 5–6.

10 253B-Ki. Christophilus, *A serious enquiry whether a late epistle from . . .Charles Wesley . . . to John Wesley . . .* , 14.

11 274-Gr. Free, *Rules for the discovery of false prophets*, 3rd ed., ii.

disaster for the Church of England? And if the Church fell, was not the state endangered again? Chief among those who raised such questions was Bishop Edmund Gibson.[12]

Secured by acts of Parliament—the Corporation Act (1661), the Act of Uniformity (1662), the Conventicles Act (1664), and the Toleration Act (1689)—the alliance between church and state rested, eighteenth-century divines contended, on an "unassailable basis."[13] When the Methodists made accusations of deficiencies in the Church, it seemed to many that national security was endangered. The Stuart axiom, "no bishop, no king," had not been forgotten. The anonymous author of a 1741 tract drew parallels between seventeenth-century Puritans and eighteenth-century Methodists:

> The Methodists say they want to make Christianity shine in its original brightness . . . But we may remember that this was the language of our reformers, in the late rebellion; they, good people! only wanted to regulate church exorbitances, as they were pleased to style it, but episcopacy was the thing they aimed at; when that order of men was abolished, monarchy found but little mercy.[14]

This sentiment was echoed in 1767 in James Makittrick Adair's lines:

> Cromwell like you did first pretend
> Religion was his only end;
> But soon the mask away did fling,
> Pull'd down the church and killed the king.[15]

Further support for the charge came from Bishop Warburton's pen. He traced the Methodists' political and religious ancestry to the seventeenth century regicides—"Both [were] of the same stock," he averred.[16]

---

12 164-Gr. [Gibson], *Observations upon the conduct and behaviour of . . . Methodists*, 24; 176A-Ba. [Gibson], *Directions given to the clergy of the diocese of London*, 87–88; 316-Gr. *An address to the Right Honourable—*, 6; 522-Gr. *Methodism and popery dissected and compared*, 2; 378-Gr. Peter Paragraph *pseud.* [Adair], *The Methodist and mimick*, 19.

13 Sykes, *Church and State in England in the XVIIIth Century* (Cambridge: Cambridge University Press, 1934), 284.

14 124-Gr. *Mr. Whitefield's doctrines considered and confuted*, 5.

15 378-Gr. Peter Paragraph *pseud.* [Adair], *The Methodist and mimick*, 19.

16 342-Gr. [Warburton], *The doctrine of grace*, 186.

Contemptuous Attitude Toward the Clergy

While professing loyalty to the Anglican Church, Methodist preachers, it was said, publicly vilified its divines.[17] George Whitefield reveled in issuing general charges of doctrinal unorthodoxy, neglect of pastoral responsibility, and moral laxity on the part of his clergy colleagues.[18] If Whitefield was particularly at fault for his rash censure of the clergy, Wesley and some of his lay preachers, though more moderate, were not entirely innocent of the practice. Wesley occasionally recorded harsh comments on particular sermons and ministers who preached them, but refrained from general railing at the clergy, realizing that it never helped, but often hindered, the revival.[19] He laid down the general rule: "No contempt, no bitterness to the clergy." Some of Wesley's preachers did not always, however, follow his maxim.[20]

Understandably, Anglican clergy took exception to the scathing criticism of their persons and ministry coming from some evangelical quarters. Whitefield's attacks, it was alleged, were without distinction or respect to person. Joseph Trapp noted in 1740 that the young evangelist Whitefield divided his ordained brethren into three categories: "profligates," "Methodists," and "those neither righteous enough to have an habitual desire of improving virtue to its perfection, nor quite so flagitious [shameful] as to give into self-destroying Vices."[21] Only the Methodists and his close associates were safe from Whitefield's unrelenting castigation. Samuel Weller complained, "Hypocrites, Pharisees, and such like appellations are what this gentleman [Whitefield] gives undistinguishedly to all who are not of his party."[22] If Whitefield's uncomplimentary remarks about the clergy in his

---

17 For a discussion of the anticlericalism of the Methodists, see W. Stephen Gunter, 'The Limits of Love Divine': John Wesley's Response to Antinomianism and Enthusiasm (Nashville: Kingswood Books, 1989), chap. 2, "Anticlericalism," 27–34.

18 See Whitefield, sermon 19, "The Folly and Danger of Being Not Righteous Enough," in WGW, 5:129. Cf. "The Method of Grace," Fifteen sermons preached on various important subjects (Philadelphia: Joseph Smith, 1794), 278.

19 For an example of Wesley's comments on antagonistic clergy, see Wesley, BEWJW, vol. 19, Journals and Diaries II, April 17, 1743 (322–23); and BEWJW, vol. 20, Journals and Diaries III, April 20, 1745 (62–63).

20 See John Wesley, A Farther Appeal to Men of Reason and Religion, pt. 3, in BEWJW, 11:304–5.

21 093-Gr. [Trapp], The true spirit of the Methodists and their allies, 11.

22 098-Gr. [Weller], The trial of Mr. Whitefield's spirit, 10; 093-Gr. [Trapp], The true spirit of the Methodists and their allies, 3.

preaching ruffled some feathers, vituperative comments concerning them in his published journals aroused their ire. Thomas Church alleged that "a great part of his [Whitefield's] journals is taken up with abusive reflections on his brethren the clergy of the Church of England."[23] Indeed, Whitefield's rash labels helped polarize the Church. "We cannot but look upon you as our most inveterate and bitter enemy, who have taken all opportunities, and used all methods of vilifying us," Church protested.[24] Though Wesley's criticism of his fellow priests was more moderate, as noted earlier, opponents charged him also with fostering disrespect of the Church of England's clergy. The author of an anonymous tract of 1744 accused Wesley of being the "ringleader of dissension . . . spreading abroad through the nation . . . vile calumny against your brethren."[25] James Buller, writing twelve years later in response to Wesley's *Address to the Clergy*, branded the Methodist leader as a "principal agitator" in stirring up anticlericalism.[26] Wesley, Thomas Church complained, was at fault for failing to reprimand Whitefield's censure of the clergy.[27]

All Methodists preachers, critics claimed, rashly censured Anglican clergy in the harshest of terms.[28] Evangelical Anglicans vilified their non-evangelical colleagues.[29]

Thus assailed, Anglican clergy naturally retaliated in kind. The Methodists were proscribed under every term of opprobrium imaginable. Trapp branded Whitefield a "notorious slanderer and liar, who said what he pleased to abuse the clergy with all the malice of hell; without alleging the least appearance of one single proof."[30] Bishop Gibson found the Methodists guilty of "slander . . . in a very unworthy and licentious

---

23 049-Gr. Church, *An explanation and defence of the doctrine of regeneration*, 49.
24 165-Gr. Church, *A serious and expostulatory letter to the Rev. Mr. George Whitefield*, 23.
25 160A-Ba. [Smith], *The notions of the Methodists fully disprov'd*, 20.
26 258-Gr. Buller, *A reply to the Rev. Mr. Wesley's 'Address to the clergy,'* 18. See John Wesley, "Address to the Clergy," (1756), *Works* (Jackson), 10:480–500.
27 205-Gr. Church, *Some farther remarks on the Rev. Mr. John Wesley's late journal*, 105–7.
28 173-Gr. *Some papers giving an account of . . . Methodism at Wednesbury*, 12.
29 See criticism of William Romaine in 237-Gr. [Douglas], *An apology for the clergy with a view to expose the groundless assertions of a late commentator*, 9. Berridge was the target of a similar criticism in 249-Gr. Academicus [Green], *The principles and practices of the Methodists considered*, 5.
30 093-Gr. [Trapp], *The true spirit of the Methodists*, 29.

manner."[31] Others applied execratory adjectives to the Methodists—they were abusive, unchristian, defamatory, censorious, rancorous, and fanatical.[32]

Many clergy were offended that they were tarred with the same brush with which the Methodists blackened irresponsible clergy. The guilt of a few, they said, was transferred to the many. One anonymous author expressed the clergy's anger at the use of the tactic of guilt by association: "To . . . reproach them as if they were the devils; and on account of a few careless members to reflect on the whole body indiscriminately . . . betrays amazing illiberality, rancor, and devilism."[33] Numerous writers rallied to defend the clergy's good name. Zachary Grey's picture of the clergy, for instance, was in marked contrast to Whitefield's:

> The lives and manners of the generality of them are not only blameless and unexceptionable, but highly exemplary. Their preaching [is] . . . grave and serious, and pathetic, without fanatical flights. They preach the pure doctrines of the gospel, without putting any false glosses or misinterpretations upon them.[34]

Most opponents of Methodism did not claim that Anglican clergy were perfect. Priests, they admitted, were human and subject to human frailty, but the Methodists magnified out of all proportion the weaknesses they saw in other clergy. This contention, although stated in earlier writings, was best expressed in a 1764 pamphlet:

> They [the Methodists] fall unmercifully upon the rural character of their ministers and aggravate every little blemish . . . into such stupendous faults . . . and I have heard ministers described by

---

31 176A-Ba. [Gibson], *Directions given to the clergy of the diocese of London*, 85–86.

32 See 018-Gr. Wilder, *The trial of the spirits*, 9; 166-Gr. J.B./A Gentleman of Pembroke College, Oxon., *A letter to the Reverend Mr. Whitefield, occasion'd by his pretended answer to the first part of the 'Observations on the conduct and behaviour of the Methodists,'* 42; 226A-Ki. Roche, *Moravian Heresy*, 292; 487-Gr. A Member of the Church of England, *Naked thoughts on some of the peculiarities of the field-preaching clergy* (London: for J. Pridden [1776]), 15–17.

33 487-Gr. Ibid., 15–17.

34 186-Gr. A Sincere Protestant [Grey], *A serious address to lay Methodists*, 6–7. See similar defense in 355-Gr. Philagathus Cantabrigiensis, *The Methodist instructed*, 5.

some of these virulent people, in such opprobrious terms that one would really take them for monsters of impiety, when upon enquiry they have been found to deserve a very good character.[35]

If Methodists complained that their Anglican opponents caricatured them, the clergy accused the revivalists of resorting to a similar practice:

Is any of a free cheerful and sociable disposition and does not wholly abstain from appearing in company, then he is a drunkard. Is he frugal, and not given to profuse living, then he is covetous. Is he conscientious in maintaining the dues of his church, and will not suffer them to be invaded by the sacrilege of covetous world-lings, then he is litigious and given to law; he is covetous, &c. So exceedingly industrious are Satan and his agents to blacken the reputation of ministers of true religion.[36]

The Methodist caricature of the Georgian divine was so pervasive by mid-century that John Maud devoted his eight-page *Apology for the clergy* to a demonstration of the injustice of the distorted picture. Maud defended the clergy against charges of greed, pride, contentiousness, loose living, and neglect of pastoral responsibilities.[37]

Confuting unfair charges was not enough. Bishop Gibson counseled the priests of his diocese to become conscientious models in the discharge of their duties, particularly in visiting the sick, private admonition of the wayward, and catechizing the youth: "These being the most undeniable evidence to their flock how undeservedly they are reproached by these noisy itinerant leaders."[38]

Deleterious Effects of Methodism's Anticlericalism

Opponents imputed base motives for the Methodists' censure of their brethren. They denigrated the clergy, suggested John Roche, to make themselves

---

35 354-Gr. An Enemy to Pious Fraud, *A sovereign remedy for the cure of hypocrisy and blind zeal*, 5. See similar statements in 190-Gr. *The question whether it be right to turn Methodist, considered*, 53; 253B-Ki. Christophilus, *A serious enquiry whether a late epistle from . . . Charles Wesley . . . to John Wesley . . .*, 12.

36 354-Gr. Ibid., 18.

37 191-Gr. Maud, *An apology for the clergy, in a letter to a gentleman of fortune*.

38 206-Gr. [Gibson], *The charge of the Right Reverend Father in God, Edmund, Lord Bishop of London . . . 1746 and 1747*, 25.

appear in a better light.[39] Two London preachers, John Free and John Downes, suggested that Methodist denunciation of Anglican divines was a smoke screen behind which to hide their own deceitful actions.[40] An anonymous author implied that the Methodists resorted to denunciations because they could not confute the arguments of their opposers.[41] Early critics of the revival observed the deleterious effects the Methodists' censure of the clergy was having upon the Church. Whitefield's reproofs, said Joseph Trapp in 1739, were ridiculous, and would invite laughter, were they "not so deplorable and detestable as to create the greatest grief and abhorrence."[42] The following year Trapp elaborated on the charge. He accused the Methodists of being in league with Rome in an effort to exterminate Anglican divines.[43] Most opponents couched their charge in milder terms. Tristram Land claimed that the Methodists' contempt for the clergy fostered anticlericalism.[44] Archbishop Secker believed that Methodists had prejudiced multitudes against their parish ministers.[45] James Buller and others applied the charge directly to Wesley. Because of his attacks on the clergy, "some that would . . . have been contented even to pluck out their own eyes to give them to their pastors . . . now as readily stigmatize them as blind leaders."[46] Anticlericalism was rampant because Methodists encouraged "people to despise and rebel against those pastors and governors whom God hath set over them."[47] In London, John Free claimed, anticlericalism assumed ugly proportions. Clergy dreaded walking the city's streets:

> To such a pitch of insolence are they arrived, that your clergy are

---

39 226A-Ki. Roche, *Moravian heresy*, 292.

40 174-Gr. Free, *Rules for the discovery of false prophets*, 23; 282-Gr. Downes, *Methodism examined and exposed*, 55–56.

41 354-Gr. An Enemy to Pious Fraud, *A sovereign remedy for the cure of hypocrisy and blind zeal*, 3.

42 010-Gr. Trapp, *The nature, folly, sin and danger of being righteous over-much*, 12.

43 093-Gr. [Trapp], *The true spirit of the Methodists and their allies*, 33–34.

44 009-Gr. Land, *A letter to the Rev. Mr. Whitefield*, 4–5.

45 341A-Ki. Secker, *The charge designed to have been delivered by the Archbishop of Canterbury to the clergy of his diocese* (London: no printer, 1762). The charge is also in the *Works of Thomas Secker*, new ed., 4 vols. (Edinburgh: J. Dickinson and W. Laing, 1792), 4:187.

46 258-Gr. Buller, *A reply to the Rev. Mr. Wesley's 'Address to the clergy,'* 19. See also 160A-Ba. [Smith], *The notions of the Methodists fully disprov'd*, 20.

47 253B-Ki. Christophilus, *A serious enquiry whether a late epistle from . . . Charles Wesley . . . to John Wesley . . .* , 6.

often interrupted by these enthusiasts as they pass the streets and are told to their faces by the lowest and most ignorant wretches, that they know nothing of the true gospel; and what still shews a greater contempt of our establishment, we are the most subject to these indignities and disturbances when we appear in that dress, which the laws and customs of this country assigns us.[48]

Critics claimed that the clergy's authority in civil and religious matters had been undermined by the Methodists and jeopardized the success of their ministry. Bishop Gibson was the spokesman for many early opponents when he cautioned the Methodists in 1739:

The success of ministers in the discharge of their duty, depends greatly upon the esteem and good opinion of their people; and they who go about to represent the parochial clergy as unable or unwilling to teach their people aright, are so far answerable for defending the good effects that their ministry might otherwise have.[49]

At the same time the Methodists undercut the clergy's prestige and influence, they lured Anglicans to join Methodist societies. This action, some said, was part of the Methodists' plan for schism.[50]

Opponents contended that attacks on the clergy were a prelude to other kinds of assault. The St. Margaret's affair of February 4, 1739, confirmed their fears.[51] The regular Sunday lecturer of St. Margaret's, Westminster, the Reverend Mr. Morgan, arranged for John James Majendie to substitute for him on the first Sunday in February. Members of the religious society, however, engaged George Whitefield as their preacher. When the time for the sermon arrived, Majendie was prevented from preaching and Whitefield was ushered into the pulpit. Whitefield was accused of unlawful intrusion into another's

---

48 274-Gr. Free, *Rules for the discovery of false prophets*, ii.

49 028-Gr. [Gibson], *The bishop of London's pastoral letter*, 24. See similar comments in later pamphlets: 253B-Ki. Christophilus, *A serious enquiry whether a late epistle from . . . Charles Wesley . . . to John Wesley . . .* , 6; 528E-Fi. [Shute Barrington], *A charge delivered to the clergy of the diocese of Sarum*, 11–12; 049-Gr. Thomas Church, *An explanation and defence of the doctrine of the Church of England,* 49.

50 206-Gr. [Gibson], *The charge of the Right Reverend Father in God, Edmund, Lord Bishop of London . . . 1746 and 1747*; 253B-Ki. Christophilus, *A serious enquiry whether a late epistle from . . . Charles Wesley . . . to John Wesley . . .* , 18; 528D-Ki. Thomas Moorhouse, *A view of practical Methodism* (Oxford: no printer, 1783), 12.

51 Luke Tyerman, *The Life of the Rev. George Whitefield*, 2 vols. (New York: Anson D. F. Randolph, 1877), 1:172–75.

pulpit and of employing force in doing so. No doubt Whitefield felt justified in claiming what he thought was his right, as the preacher invited by the society, to preach that Sunday. But it was a pyrrhic victory. It became the occasion for much hostile criticism. Methodists, following the St. Margaret's incident, were stigmatized as pulpit stealers.[52] Whitefield was denounced in articles and letters in the February 1739 issues of the *Weekly Miscellany*. Extracts were widely circulated in a 1739 tract, *The life and particular proceedings of the Rev. Mr. George Whitefield*.[53]

John Free complained of personal threats made by the Methodists. They attempted to intimidate him by threatening to have the income of his lectureship at Newington cut off.[54] A second charge was more serious—Free alleged that while preaching in the parish church of St. Mary Magdalene, Bermondsey, on Sunday, April 29, 1759, he had been "in continual and most imminent danger of being murdered by the Methodists." His opponents, he said, made repeated, but unsuccessful attempts to get into the pulpit during the service. Harassment continued until Free reached safety inside the rectory.[55]

Methodist Rejection of the Church of England

The Methodists, it seemed to many, besieged the Church on all sides—doctrine, liturgy, and discipline. Methodists vigorously contended that the doctrine of the revival was deeply rooted in the Anglican tradition, but clerical opponents denied the claim with equal fervor—the Methodists' tenets were aberrations of the Church's theological heritage and thus endangered the Church.[56]

Methodists were accused of neglecting some of the rubrics of the Book of Common Prayer, particularly those concerning the celebration of Holy Communion. The rubric that enjoined parishioners to notify their parish priest a day in advance of their intention to receive communion was totally ignored

---

52 See 118-Gr. Trevor, *A short history of the Donatists*, 36; 200-Gr. A. B. [Stebbing], *An earnest and affectionate address to the people called Methodists*, 34.

53 040-Gr. An Impartial Hand [Tucker], *The life and particular proceedings of the Rev. Mr. George Whitefield*. For a fuller discussion of the incident, see Tyerman, *The Life of the Rev. George Whitefield*, 1:172–75.

54 276-Gr. Free, *Dr. Free's edition of the Rev. Mr. John Wesley's second letter*, 26.

55 278-Gr. Free, *The whole speech which was delivered to the reverend clergy . . . of London*, iii–iv.

56 For a fuller account of attacks on Anglican theology, see chapter 3, "Doctrinal Deviation."

by the Methodists.[57] Moreover, it was alleged that they were contemptuous of the rubric for distribution of the communion elements, in that they omitted more than half of what was prescribed to be said.[58] It was not just a matter of rubrics being ignored, however; it was fear that the Methodists were setting aside the beloved Book of Common Prayer as they experimented with extempore experiences of worship. If the Book of Common Prayer was jettisoned, the very existence of the Church was at stake. Even when Wesley used the Prayer Book service, as he did in the City Road Chapel and elsewhere, opponents found his motive suspect. William Combe alleged that it was to cover up his preferred worship style:

> Temples bring gain—that act no saint can bear—
> Hence you adopt, at last, the Common-Pray'r.
> Basely you'll drudge thro' an ungrateful task,
> And use a liturgy by way of mask.
> When interest calls, to gain a ready pass,
> You'd mumble o'er a Pray'r-Book or a mass.[59]

The charge was made that the Methodists were undermining the Church of England by rejecting its discipline. Even if the Methodists preached soundly, and duly administered the sacraments, more was required of those who claimed loyalty to the Church. Thomas Church reminded Wesley that respect for, and observance of, the laws of the Church was required:

> It will be requisite in order to approve yourself as such [a Church of England priest] that you follow her rules and orders at least in matters of moment and consequence; that you constantly conform to the method of worship she has prescribed; and study to promote her peace.[60]

Accusations that the Methodists disregarded the canons of the Church were common in the early years at the revival. Usually the charge was couched in general terms; no specific infractions being cited. Typical was

---

57 164-Gr. [Gibson], *Observations upon the conduct and behaviour of . . . Methodists*, 5–6.

58 200-Gr. [Stebbing], *An earnest and affectionate address to the people called Methodists*, 35.

59 517-Gr. [Combe], *Perfection: A poetical epistle*, 30. For a fuller discussion see chapter 8, "Methodists at Worship."

60 205-Gr. Church, *Some farther remarks on the Rev. Mr. John Wesley's last Journal*, 5.

James Bate's observation that the Methodists engaged in "perfidious trampling upon those canons of [their] Church to which [their] obedience is due."[61] Only a few pamphleteers accused the Methodists of violation of specific church laws. They invoked the almost forgotten, certainly completely neglected, regulations from the *Constitutions and Canons Ecclesiastical* (1603). Bishop Gibson remarked that the Methodists' behavior was "in contempt of those wise rules of government, discipline and worship, which were judged by our pious ancestors to be the best and most effectual means for preserving and maintaining religion."[62] Gibson cited the Methodists' contempt of the twenty-eighth canon in that they encouraged men and women to receive Holy Communion in parishes other than their own.

Methodism's practice of itineration was a more important bone of contention. Gibson was joined by others in pointing out that the fiftieth canon regulated preachers coming from outside the parish. The Methodists completely disregarded the canonical requirement to obtain a license from the bishop or the universities when they presided over the Eucharist in another priest's church.[63] Canons 71–73, John Thomas believed, were disregarded by the Methodists. He contended that Thomas Coke exceeded his canonical responsibilities in "appointing a fast and exercises; or what comes nearly to the same thing, preaching or reading lectures on week days which are not holy days in the parish church . . . without express authority." Such a practice, he claimed, was forbidden by canon seventy-two. The establishment of Methodist religious societies, which met in barns and houses, was, Thomas added, an infringement of the seventy-first and seventy-third canons.[64] An anonymous author pointed out that the Methodists disregarded the twenty-second canon, which expressly forbade ministers to engage in exorcism unless they

---

61 034-Gr. Bate, *Methodism displayed; or, remarks upon Mr. Whitefield's answer*, 28. See other general accusations in 166-Gr. J. B./A Gentleman of Pembroke College, Oxon, *A letter to the Reverend Mr. Whitefield*, 15; 010-Gr. Trapp, *The nature, folly, sin and danger of being righteous over-much*, 37–38; 190-Gr. *The question whether it be right to turn Methodist, considered*, 65.

62 164-Gr. [Gibson], *Observations upon the conduct and behaviour of . . . Methodists*, 5–6, 11, 20.

63 160A-Ba. [Smith], *The notions of the Methodists fully disprov'd*, 20; 273-Gr. Free, *A display of bad principles of the Methodists*, 13; 321-Gr. N. N., *Presbyters and deacons not commissioned to preach without the bishop's allowance*, 34–35. Canon 50, it should be noted, was one of a series (47–50) that regulated the practice of licensing preachers.

64 502-Gr. John Thomas, *Two letters to the Rev. Thomas Coke* (London: sold by G. Robinson, 1777), 3–6.

were licensed by their diocesan bishop.[65] The employment of lay preachers, several opponents pointed out, contravened the twenty-third article, which expressly forbade taking up preaching unless under the Church's authority.[66]

Setting aside some of the vows in the Anglican Ordinal was another charge leveled at the Methodists. First, the evangelicals' itineration was in direct violation of the wording of the ordinal, which limited the exercise of a priest's ministry to the parish to which he was appointed. Second, Methodists disregarded their sacred ordination vows to obey their ecclesiastical governors.[67]

Disrespect and Disobedience toward the Hierarchy

Disrespect for the Church's hierarchy among the leaders of the revival disturbed critics of Methodism. Whitefield's replies to Gibson's *Observations* shocked his clerical colleagues, who found his attitude to the bishop "insolent," "impudent," and "petulant." James Bate's rebuke is characteristic of others:

> You . . . fly in the face of [your] diocesan, with such unparallel'd
> pride and impudence! Were he wrong does not the character he
> is invested with entitle him to a more decent treatment? Is this
> the respect due from such a priest to such a bishop? Is it thus you
> return the glorious stands my Lord of London has made in every
> gap, through which any danger has ever threatened the peace or
> welfare of the Church?[68]

Whitefield was not alone in feeling the brunt of criticism for lack of respect to his ecclesiastical superiors. A chorus of critics claimed that disrespect for church leaders characterized Methodists in general. John Maud expressed

---

65 156-Gr. [Impartial Hand], *The progress of Methodism in Bristol,* 12.

66 208-Gr. White, *A sermon against the Methodists,* 13; 248A-Ba. A Lay-Man, *A few queries concerning the growth of Methodism,* 9; 502-Gr. Thomas, *Two letters to the Rev. Thomas Coke,* 5–6; 276-Gr. Free, *Dr. Free's edition of Wesley's second letter,* 11.

67 012-Gr. Scrub, *A letter to Robert Seagrave, M.A.,* 44; 037-Gr. *A plain address to the followers and favourers of the Methodists* (London: for H. Whitridge, [1739]), 6; 164-Gr. [Gibson], *Observations upon the conduct and behaviour of . . . Methodists,* 11.

68 034-Gr. Bate, *Methodism displayed; or, Remarks upon Mr. Whitefield's answer,* 36; 098-Gr. [Weller] *The trial of Mr. Whitefield's spirit,* 20; 049-Gr. Church, *An explanation and defence of the doctrine of the Church of England,* 5; 165-Gr. Church, *A serious and expostulatory letter to the Rev. Mr. George Whitefield,* 10.

dismay that "vigilant and faithful . . . [bishops were] promiscuously treated with rudeness and contempt" by the Methodists.[69] James Buller instanced a direct affront by the Methodists to the bishop of Bristol. Members of Wesley's Bristol society went to church to hear an evangelical preacher. Unbeknownst to them, arrangements had been made for the diocesan bishop to fill the pulpit. As he mounted the pulpit steps, the Methodists noisily left the church "as tho' his sermon would have actually poison'd them or the whole fabrick had been falling about their ears."[70] Such an insolent attitude, opponents warned, undermined episcopal status and authority, and could only end in the disintegration of the Church. John Roche pressed the point, "What more certain remedy can be taken to destroy any community on earth, than to ridicule the acting chiefs, and rendering them insignificant to the people, by lessening them in their esteem?"[71]

Not only did the Methodists fail to respect their superiors; they actually disobeyed them. The Methodists were reminded that those ordained promised in their ordination vows to submit to their lawful governors. In disregarding their superiors' admonitions to cease preaching dangerous doctrines and engaging in certain practices, the Methodists were guilty of rank insubordination:

> Now the bishops and chiefs of this Church, the bishop of London especially in his excellent pastoral letter have publickly declared themselves against your doctrines and practices, and yet you stiffly disobey their directions, and with unparallel'd obstinacy withstand and reject all their admonitions.[72]

There is no doubt that the Methodists disregarded episcopal exhortations to reject their evangelical practices and doctrines. Wesley, in his *Earnest Appeal to Men of Reason and Religion*, firmly stated the principle that God, rather

---

69 191-Gr. Maud, *An apology for the clergy, in a letter to a gentleman of fortune*, 4; 185-Gr. Church, *Remarks on the Reverend Mr. John Wesley's last journal*, 14–15.

70 258-Gr. Buller, *A reply to the Rev. Mr. Wesley's 'Address to the clergy,'* 19.

71 226A-Ki. Roche, *Moravian heresy*, 290.

72 160A-Ba. [Smith] *The notions of the Methodists fully disprov'd*, 19–20; 190-Gr. *The question whether it be right to turn Methodist considered*, 14; 037-Gr. *A plain address to the followers and favourers of the Methodists*, 7; 040-Gr. An Impartial Hand, *The life and particular proceedings of the Rev. Mr. George Whitefield*, 3–4; 381-Gr. Jean Henri Formey, *An ecclesiastical history from the birth of Christ*, 2 vols. (London: for R. Davis, J. Newberry, and C. Reymers, 1766), 2:269–70; 332-Ba. Dodd, *A conference between a mystic, a Hutchinsonian, a Calvinist, a Methodist, a member of the Church of England, and others*, 60–61.

than bishops, must be obeyed. There could be no unqualified submission to ecclesiastical superiors. The Methodists would not "obey 'such' injunctions as . . . 'are contrary to the Word of God.'"[73] Wesley's principle evoked a predictable reaction. Thomas Church wanted to know which laws of God the Anglican hierarchy had commanded Wesley to transgress.[74] Thomas Sharp pointed out that the very existence of the Church depended on the lesser clergy being obedient to those in authority. Discipline ensured order in the Church—if each minister followed what he believed was a divine mandate in disobeying his ordinary, the Church would be destroyed:

> I always thought governors had a right to obedience in things for the good order and discipline of the Church: and it seems a matter of some nicety with me how far a man may contradict those orders or be free from an engagement he has solemnly resolved to perform. Be not rash in your determination. If men may be thus at liberty, and have this dispensing power within themselves, farewell all order, discipline, and government.[75]

Another author believed that, despite their protestations of love for and loyalty to the institution of church, the Methodists' flagrant disregard of their ecclesiastical governors amounted to a renunciation of the Church of England: "I do not tax you with schism, because you take the people from buildings called churches, but by taking them from their bishop, the principle of unity to them."[76]

Not only did the Methodists ignore their bishops' advice and instruction; they usurped episcopal authority. Faithful Anglicans were affronted by tales of Wesley's actions during his sojourn as missionary in Georgia. Citing the colonial grand jury's accusation that Wesley had called himself "Ordinary of Savannah,"[77] Thomas Church noted the Methodist leader's "long inclination to be independent and uncontrolled." This had become even more evident in England since 1739. By appointing preachers, and by "excommunicating"

---

73 Wesley, *An Earnest Appeal to Men of Reason and Religion* (1743), §83 in *BEWJW*, 11:81.

74 205-Gr. Church, *Some farther remarks on the Rev. Mr. John Wesley's last journal*, 6–7.

75 161-Gr. [Sharp], *Remarks on a book entitled, 'An earnest appeal to men of reason,'* 5.

76 212-Gr. A Clergyman of the Church of England, *An answer to a late pamphlet, entitled, 'A plain account of the people called Methodist'* (London: for E. Withers, 1749), 13–14.

77 *Ordinary* was a term used to denote diocesan bishops who exercised ecclesiastical authority over, and were accountable within, a designated area.

backsliders from Methodist societies, Wesley had begun to function as a self-styled bishop.[78] Church's accusation was reasserted by Bishop Lavington in 1749. Lavington viewed the Methodists' commissioning and assignment of preachers, and the expulsion of those who did not meet their standards, as "usurpation of the powers wherewith their superiors are legally invested."[79] Another author found further evidence of the usurpation of episcopal authority in Wesley's *Address to the Clergy* (1756).[80] It was the height of presumption, thought James Buller, for a presbyter to issue what amounted to an episcopal pastoral letter.[81]

Methodists as Schismatics

Repeatedly throughout the eighteenth century, Methodists were branded schismatics. The charge originated in the early years of the revival and was widely circulated in hostile pamphlets. Both Whitefield and Wesley were accused of creating a breach in the Church because they taught novel doctrines. James Makittrick Adair summarized the charge in verse:

> [The Methodists] set new doctrines afloat
> And rend to rags Christ's seamless coat,
> Viler than pilot's [sic] soldiers were,
> They'd not the holy garment tear;
> That the great emblem seem'd to be,
> Of Christian churches unity.[82]

Methodist practices made the breach even wider. Field preaching, the use of extempore prayers and sermons, itinerancy, the establishment of societies, the formation of bands and classes, the use of lay preachers, the erection of preaching houses, the innovation of love feasts and watch night services—the list was long and frightening. Taken individually, none of these practices could

---

78 205-Gr. Church, *Some farther remarks on the Rev. Mr. John Wesley's last journal*, 14–15.
79 213–Ki. [Lavington], *The enthusiasm of Methodists and papists compar'd*, pt. 2, 124, 126–27.
80 Wesley, "An Address to the Clergy," *Works* (Jackson), 10:480–500. Wesley examines the gifts and grace that clergy should exhibit in their lives.
81 258-Gr. Buller, *A reply to the Rev. Mr. Wesley's 'Address to the clergy,'* 3.
82 378-Gr. Peter Paragraph *pseud.* [Adair], *The Methodist and mimick*, 15. Cf. 005-Gr. T. G. [Gib], *Remarks on the Reverend Mr. Whitefield's journal*, 23; 009-Gr. Land, *A letter to the Rev. Mr. Whitefield*, 5–6; 237-Gr. [Douglas], *An apology to the clergy, with a view to expose the groundless assertions of a late commentator*, 2–3.

be regarded as creating a rupture with the Church of England, but viewed collectively, they appeared to augur schism. By "tearing out the bowels of the Church," Methodists had begun "a schismatic rebellion."[83]

Although the Methodists frequently voiced their love for the Church, critics of the revival found such professions of loyalty insincere. How, they asked, could one love the Church and yet at the same time draw people away from it? While protesting that their aim was to make their converts better people, they lured them from the Church into Methodist societies. An anonymous author expressed the sense of rage felt by many. The Methodists made

> proselytes, not to the Church but to themselves, not to the unity and peace, but to separation and division . . . [their] conversions were, in truth, no other than inlisting so many enemies, to oppose and fight against her. . . Instead of reducing the Dissenters, and those who reject her communion, they encouraged them into separation: Instead of confirming the serious part of her members to continue in her bosom, they have laboured, with all their might, to draw them away from her; and the last visible thinness of our congregations is too melancholy proof of their success.[84]

Answering such allegations, the Methodists claimed to encourage people to retain their ties with the Church of England and to attend its services regularly. But opponents believed this amounted to practicing deceit. The Methodists engaged in underhanded methods of gathering churches out of churches:

> Hurried on by violence or zeal, they have stolen in upon prejudices, and without alarming, have insinuated themselves into the hearts of mankind. They are taught never to desert (at least nominally) their original profession: they frequent the ordinances of their respective original societies; they adhere to all their forms; hence living upon good terms with their former brethren, they

---

83 160A-Ba. [Smith], *The notions of the Methodists fully disprov'd*, 22–23. Cf. 208-Gr. White, *A sermon against the Methodists*, iii.

84 190-Gr. *The question whether it is right to turn Methodist considered*, 60. See also 049-Gr. Church, *An explanation and defence of the doctrine of the Church of England*, iv; 094-Gr. Bowman, *The imposture of Methodism display'd*, 18; 226A-Ki. Roche, *Moravian heresy*, 287; 164-Gr. [Gibson], *Observations upon the conduct and behaviours of . . . Methodists*, 8; 297-Gr. Jephson, *Friendly and compassionate address to all . . . serious Methodists*, 48–49.

have a free intercourse and communion with all their members; they have an opportunity of insinuating themselves into their favour and good graces . . . By a professed adherence to original principles, they make the attack, without creating the suspicion of their design; and hence the new converts became insensibly transformed, without feeling the shock that an immediate rupture would produce.[85]

Some anti-Methodist authors saw evidence in the erection of Methodist preaching houses that the spirit of the evangelical movement was not revival, but schism. In 1744 Bishop Gibson first hinted that the Methodists, by erecting buildings for preaching and worship, were moving into Dissent.[86] For almost a decade, no one pursued this charge against the Methodists. In the mid-1750s and early 1760s, however, no doubt spurred by an increase in building activity among the Methodists, a number of attacks broadly hinted at schism. John Douglas informed his readers that the act of erecting preaching houses had removed the Church of England's "mask" from the face of Methodism. Methodists were revealed as they really were—Dissenters.[87] John Free and William Dodd agreed that Wesley's Foundery and Whitefield's Tabernacle and other Methodist preaching houses were, in reality, Dissenting meeting houses and should be so licensed immediately.[88] Other opponents believed that the rate at which Methodist buildings were being erected in the 1760s was an indication that Methodism had become de facto a separatist movement. John Penn thought that Methodism would "soon have its spacious tabernacles in every city and county," and that Anglican churches would be deserted as a consequence.[89] An anonymous author warned that by 1771, if the Methodist movement continued, there might be as many Methodist preaching houses as Anglican churches.[90] Clearly preaching house and parish church were seen as competing institutions.

As well as erecting ecclesiastical edifices, several critics noted that the

---

85 555-Gr. *A review of the folly, doctrines and morals of the Methodists*, 2–4. See also 248A-Ba. A Lay-Man, *A few queries concerning the growth of Methodism*, 3.

86 164-Gr. [Gibson], *Observations upon the conduct and behaviour of . . . Methodists*, 4.

87 237-Gr. Douglas, *An apology for the clergy, in a letter to a gentleman of fortune*, 2–3.

88 276-Gr. Free, *Dr. Free's edition of the Rev. Mr. John Wesley's second letter*, 50. See also 332A-Ba. [Dodd], *A conference between a mystic . . .* , 60–61.

89 338-Gr. Penn, *Various tracts*, 65.

90 320A-Ba. *Memoirs of the life of a modern saint*, 87.

Methodists had established the organization for a new church. In 1744 Bishop Gibson sketched what he believed was the outline of the new structure.

- Bands had been formed.
- Superintendents and exhorters supervised the bands.
- Associations and meetings had been established at set times and set places.
- Moderators for these gatherings had been selected.
- A system of the visitation of societies had been instituted.

Gibson believed this amounted to a "new church-constitution upon a foreign plan."[91] Writing five years later, another of Methodism's episcopal opponents, George Lavington, indicted the Methodists for setting up "an Independency" and establishing (echoing Gibson) "a new independent government: appointing bands and societies, with superintendents, exhorters, moderators, and visitors."[92] Lavington's branding the Methodists as "Independents" stuck. From this time forward the Methodists were accused of forsaking Anglican polity in favor of congregational organization.[93]

One of the strongest attacks on this issue came from Thomas Church, who saw in Wesley's emerging connection an independent church being birthed: the Methodist leader's unauthorized itinerancy, uninvited entry into other ministers' parishes, gathering together of congregations, establishment of preaching houses, procedures for issuing society membership tickets, removal of backsliders from society membership, and employment of laity to preach—all these were proof positive, for Church, that Wesley had set up his own ecclesiastical organization. In summarizing the charge Church did not mince words:

> Does not everyone see in all this a separate ecclesiastical society or communion formed, over which you had appointed yourself as governor, and accordingly took upon you all the spiritual authority which the very highest church governor could claim?

---

91 164-Gr. [Gibson], *Observations upon the conduct and behaviours of . . . Methodists,* 20–22.

92 213A-Ki. [Lavington], *The enthusiasm of Methodists and papists compar'd,* pt. 2, 126–27.

93 355-Gr. Philagathus Cantabrigiensis, *The Methodist instructed* (London: for R. Withy and C. Marsh, 1764), 4.

Can you pretend, that you received this authority from our
Church? or that you experienced it in subjection or subordination
to her lawful governors? How then will you vindicate all these
powers? What could any Independent deserve or claim more?
You cannot say that this was only a private friendly meeting.
According to your account "after fifty-two were withdrawn, you
had still upwards of ninety left." Here is a manifest congregation.
Either it belonged to the Church of England or not. If it did, shew
where the Church gave you such authority of controlling and reg-
ulating it . . . If you say, your society did not belong to the Church,
you . . . accuse yourself of setting up a separate communion
against her."[94]

Even nonconformists were convinced that Methodism was moving into
Dissent. In 1770 Gilbert Boyce questioned Wesley pointedly: "If you are not
forming a church . . . what are you doing[,] . . . sir?"[95]

During Wesley's lifetime the Methodists insisted they had not separated
from the established church, and never would unless forced out. If the Methodists protested vigorously that they remained firmly within the Anglican
fold, churchmen contended just as forcibly that separation had occurred. The
Methodists might refuse to formally separate, but they were reproached time
and again for having done so, their claims of loyalty and unity dismissed as
dishonest. An Irish author asked in 1753, "Is it not a contradiction to say that
they continue members of a church, which they have renounced by their
own voluntary departure from it?"[96] Anglicans took offense at the Methodists'
refusal to admit that a separation had taken place. William Dodd remained
unimpressed by Wesley's denial that Methodists had broken away from the
Church, commenting: "[Methodist] reasoning is much of a piece with that of
the Society of Jesus."[97] Dodd wanted the Methodists to admit that Methodism
existed as a fully orbed, distinct, ecclesiastical institution in competition with
the established church:

---

94 205-Gr. Church, *Some farther remarks on the Rev. Mr. John Wesley's last journal*, 13.

95 428-Gr. Boyce, *A serious reply to the Rev. Mr. John Wesley*, 74.

96 248A-Ba. A Lay-Man, *A few queries concerning the growth of Methodism*, 8. See also
094-Gr. Bowman, *The imposture of Methodism display'd*, 73; 226-Ki. Roche, *Moravian
heresy*, 290; 528E-Fi. [Barrington], *A charge delivered to the clergy of the diocese of
Sarum*, 12.

97 280-Gr. Dodd, *Cautions against Methodism*, 11–12.

> I cannot for my own part conceive, what sophistry of argument
> can be sufficient to disprove their separation, who have broken
> loose from all obedience to their ordinary; entirely leaped over
> all parochial unity and communion; have built and continue to
> preach in conventicle, under a licence, as Dissenters; who diffuse
> the liturgy of the Church of England; and who preach in all places,
> without reserve; who employ, and send forth laymen of the most
> unlettered sort, to preach the gospel, without any authority or
> commission from God or man . . . And, after all this, to hear such
> men exhorting to union, and disclaiming separation has something
> in it so double and so offensive, that it must raise the indignation
> of every serious and reasonable Christian.[98]

Despite such comments, no admission of the facts came from the Methodists, and the issue remained unresolved. In his Bampton Lectures at Oxford in 1786, George Croft gave evidence that the issue still troubled Anglican divines: "The Church of England might entertain a more favourable opinion of them [the Methodists] if they did not appropriate to themselves the appellation of true members or pretend to be faithful auxiliaries."[99]

Steps toward Separation

The year 1784 was momentous for Methodism. Wesley took steps to ensure the continuation of the movement after his death. Methodism was clearly on the path to separation from the Church of England. What had been evident to "all but the most blind or prejudiced" now became undeniable.[100] The first two of three steps Wesley took dealt with the needs of the movement in America. First, Wesley revised and abridged the Book of Common Prayer to form the *Sunday Service of the Methodists in North America*.[101] Second, to provide clergy for the Methodists in America, Wesley ordained Thomas Coke as superintendent for America and ordained two elders, Thomas Vasey and Richard Whatcoat, also for service in America.[102] The

---

98 332A-Ba. [Dodd], *A conference between a mystic . . .* , 60–61.

99 536A-Ki. Croft, *Eight sermons preached before the University of Oxford*, 181–82.

100 Baker, *JWCE*, 218.

101 John Wesley, *BEWJW*, vol. 23, *Journals and Diaries VI (1776–1786)*, September 1, 1784 (329–30). See Baker, *JWCE*, 234–55.

102 Baker, *JWCE*, 256–82.

third step dealt with the establishment and registration of the Deed of Declaration, which, in designating and defining the Methodist Conference as his successor, had in effect established a distinct denomination in the British Isles.[103]

Strangely, particularly in the light of earlier criticism that the Methodists were "mangling" the Prayer Book, there were no pamphlet attacks on Wesley's revision of the Book of Common Prayer.[104] It was the second step, ordination for America, that raised the alarm for some anti- Methodists. The result was, Bishop George Horne thought, the establishment of "a spurious episcopacy without [apostolic] succession." He scoffed at Wesley's pleading "necessity" to justify the action and warned that if it should be followed, it would be a fatal precedent.[105]

> For if a presbyter can consecrate a bishop, we admit that a man
> may confer a power, of which he is not himself possessed; instead
> of "the less being blessed of the greater," the "greater is blessed of
> the less," and the order of all things is inverted.[106]

In 1785 an anonymous twelve-page pamphlet entitled *Strictures on the substance of a sermon preached at Baltimore . . . at the ordination of the Rev. Francis Asbury to the office of Superintendent,* by Thomas Coke was published. Scholars attribute the pamphlet to Charles Wesley.[107] This attribution of author-ship to Charles Wesley is generally accepted, but proof positive is lacking. Certainly, there are phrases in the pamphlet that echo Charles's other statements on ordination, such as: "Does not ordination necessarily imply separation?"[108] The pamphlet was a stinging rebuke of Thomas Coke, and by extension, John Wesley, for defending and carrying out ordination by presbyters. By doing

---

103 Ibid., 218–33.

104 See chapter 8, "Methodists at Worship."

105 556-Ki. George Horne, *A charge intended to have been delivered to the clergy of the diocese of Norwich* (Norwich: Yarington and Bacon, 1791), 23–24.

106 Ibid., 24.

107 533-Gr. A Methodist of the Church of England [Charles Wesley], *Strictures on the substance of a sermon preached at Baltimore.* Field attributes the pamphlet to Charles Wesley. Field, "A Revised Bibliography," 237. Field's attribution is based on a comment from Charles Boone, one of Wesley's preachers, to Samuel Bardsley. See Gareth Lloyd, *Charles Wesley and the Struggle for Methodist Identity* (Oxford: Oxford University Press, 2007), 207; and John A. Vickers, *Thomas Coke: Apostle of Methodism* (Nashville and New York: Abingdon, 1969), 102.

108 Ibid., 4.

so, Charles claimed, Coke became a Dissenter. Moreover, Coke's "ambitious views and worldly designs" had driven him to "usurp the title of Bishop."[109]

The Deed of Declaration legally incorporated Methodism in the British Isles. It furnished a legal definition of the term "Conference" to secure the preaching houses for the preachers loyal to Wesleyan doctrine. In 1784 there were almost four hundred preaching houses in Methodism and roughly two hundred preachers in the connection. Wesley chose and named one hundred of the preachers, without regard to age or seniority. He seems to have wanted to provide a balance—a cross-section, including youth and inexperience with age and experience. The one hundred preachers became known as the "legal hundred" and the Methodist societies were incorporated through their names as the Conference. Not all the preachers approved—there was a handful of disgruntled assistants who were not named. Several resigned; while others quietly nursed their wounds.

One of the disappointed preachers was John Hampson. His simmering disaffection with Wesley came to a head in 1784 with his exclusion from the "legal hundred." Hampson's response was the anonymously issued *Appeal to the Reverend John and Charles Wesley,* a clarion call to all Wesley's preachers, especially the "excluded 91," to attend the ensuing Methodist Conference and vote for the rejection of the Deed.[110] When the Deed was passed at Conference, both Hampson and his father, John Sr., along with a handful of other itinerants, withdrew in 1785. On Wesley's death Hampson's *Memoirs of the late Rev. John Wesley,* the first full biography of Wesley, appeared in June 1791.[111] Bitterness over his grievance with Wesley colored his appraisal of the Methodist leader. Hampson found Wesley's exercise of authority arbitrary, his distinctive doctrines to be "not true, or dubious, or indifferent."[112]

Suggested Means of Dealing with Methodism

Few Georgian divines observing the effects of the evangelical revival upon the established church remained impartial. The Methodist movement elicited

---

109 Ibid., 5.

110 531A-Ba. [Hampson], *An appeal to the Reverend John and Charles Wesley* (n.p.: no printer, 1784).

111 560B-Ba. Hampson, *Memoirs of the late Rev. John Wesley,* 3 vols., (Sunderland: James Graham, 1791). See Heitzenrater, chap. 2, "Images of Power: The Controversial Early Biographies," in *The Elusive Mr. Wesley: John Wesley as Seen by His Contemporaries and Biographers,* 168–70.

112 560B-Ba. Hampson, *Memoirs of the late Rev. John Wesley,* 3:121.

strongly felt responses. The clergy either viewed Methodism favorably, in some cases cooperating with its leaders, or they were wholly antagonistic toward it. Those sympathetic to the revival were in the minority; those who assisted, but a handful. The majority believed that the revival endangered the Church. Confronting them was the problem of formulating the Church's response. Opposition was expressed in a variety of forms, but there was no concerted or coordinated effort to quash the revival or prevent the growth of Methodism. Numerous anti-Methodist pamphlets contained counsel on how Methodism and its leaders should be handled. The suggestions ranged between two extremes: noninterference and suppression by secular authorities.

As recorded in the Acts of the Apostles (5:34–39) Gamaliel's advice to the Jerusalem Sanhedrin concerning Christianity was to refrain from interfering with the young movement: If it was of divine origin, it would prosper; if it was not of God, it would disappear. Just as first-century Jews had found Christianity hard to ignore, eighteenth-century divines found it difficult to turn a blind eye to Methodism. There were clergy, nevertheless, who argued that the Church should not meddle with Methodism. Among them was James Penn, who argued that the movement ought not to be persecuted, because it "would not lessen but increase the number [of Methodists]; opposition always rendering the propagation of error successful."[113] This view found support in the highest ranks of the Church. Warburton, despite his scurrilous pamphlet attacks on Wesley and the movement, contended that persecution would help Methodism prosper rather than prevent its continuing growth.[114] Fellow Bishop Horsley concurred: "The propagation of Methodism hath been less owing to its own powers than to the injudicious manner in which it hath been resisted."[115]

If Methodism were left alone to run its course without persecution, would it be ignored? Few clergy thought so. Penn suggested, "Ridicule will succeed the best in putting a stop to it."[116] This course of action proved to be immensely popular. From the outset the revival was derided by pamphleteers.

---

113 338-Gr. Penn, *Various tracts*, 198–99.
114 342-Gr. [Warburton], *The doctrine of grace*, 260–66.
115 561-Ki. Samuel [Horsley], *The charge of Samuel, Lord Bishop of St. David's to the clergy of his diocese* (Gloucester: Raines, 1791), 28.
116 338-Gr. Penn, *Various tracts*, 198–99.

Nor did they let up throughout the second half of the century—tracts that held Methodism up to ridicule continued to pour into print.

Some advocated more direct action against Methodism. Beginning in 1738 most Church of England pulpits were closed to the Wesleys and Whitefield, despite efforts by some sympathetic divines (such as George Stonehouse, curate of St. Mary's, London) to keep them open. Pamphleteers encouraged clergy to refuse evangelicals permission to preach in their churches. Henry Stebbing in a 1739 tract reminded readers that the Church of England's constitution knew of "no necessity to yield . . . [the pulpit] to every stranger who would usurp it."[117] William Bowman's words in 1740 echoed the sentiment: "1 know of no law that obliges an incumbent whatsoever to leave his pulpit open to every saucy intruder, or to let it out as a stage for mountebanks and Jack-puddings to play their tricks upon."[118] To ban the Methodists from Anglican pulpits, opponents believed, was the most effective way of checking the spread of the revival's dangerous tenets.[119]

Pamphleteers reminded the Methodists that they broke the fifteenth canon if they preached in parishes without an episcopal license. Here, opponents boasted, was a neat and legal method to get rid of pesky evangelicals. Strict observance of the fifteenth canon had been effective in London in 1739 and 1740. For more than twenty years the barring of Methodists from Anglican pulpits was employed as a device to stanch the revival's growth. As late as the 1760s, clergy were still advising their brethren against permitting evangelicals to preach in Church of England pulpits.[120] It was only in Wesley's old age that the principle of exclusion began to be relaxed and he was welcome once more to preach from Anglican pulpits.

Prohibition of Methodists preaching in Church of England pulpits, however, was only effective to a degree in preventing the Church's "contagion" from the revival. Since Whitefield and the Wesley brothers had circumvented Anglican pulpits by moving to the out-of-doors to preach, gathering congregations that consisted of Dissenters as well as Anglicans, clearly a broader strategy was called for. Church members needed to be warned of the dangers

---

117 200-Gr. A. B. [Stebbing], *An earnest and affectionate address to the people called Methodists*, 19–20.

118 094-Gr. Bowman, *The imposture of Methodism display'd*, 26.

119 197-Gr. A Layman [Thorold], *Extracts of letters relating to Methodists and Moravians*, 20–21.

120 282-Gr. Downes, *Methodism examined and exposed*, 87.

of the movement, encouraged to stay clear of Methodist preachers and meetings, and exhorted to remain loyal to the mother Church. The weapon of choice for Anglicans was the coordination of "pulpit and pamphlet." Preached and printed sermons attacking the doctrines of the revival were common in 1739 and through the 1740s. Twenty years later their usefulness in combating Methodism was still being advocated. John Free urged his clerical colleagues in London to enter into an agreement never to admit a Methodist into their pulpits.[121] John Downes urged his fellow preachers to controvert Methodist doctrine from the pulpit: "Was this done in the constant course of our preaching, it could not but have very good effects. For sure I am, there were many who are inclined to think more favourably of the errors of the Methodists, or rather not to think them in error at all, purely for the want of better information."[122] Downes also believed the pulpit should be used to inculcate loyalty to the establishment. Sermons should impress upon parishioners the need for constant attendance at the services of the Church, and loyalty toward their own parish. Henry Stebbing's stated aim in publishing his *Earnest and affectionate address* was typical: "to draw you from the principles and practices of the Methodists and from your attendance on such teachers, as I am persuaded have hitherto misled you."[123]

Although the printing of sermons ensured circulation of the message, they had a somewhat limited appeal for the general public. Pamphlets in other literary forms, such as satires, plays, poems, open letters, and addresses attracted a wider and different kind of audience.

Formalizing the Break

For those clergy who contended that Methodism had already engaged in de facto separation from the Church of England, the question of what to do about the movement was answered simply. The Methodists should he forced to formalize the break. They should be compelled to quit the church and be legally recognized as Dissenters. Early pamphlets delighted in bringing to people's notice Whitefield's cooperation with Dissenting clergy. Because

---

121 278-Gr. Free, *The whole speech which was delivered to the reverend the clergy of . . . London*, 31.

122 282-Gr. Downes, *Methodism examined and exposed*, 74.

123 200-Gr. [Stebbing], *An earnest and affectionate address to the people called Methodists*, 5.

Methodist practices, some pamphleteers claimed, had more in common with those of the nonconformists, critics urged Methodists to go where they really belonged. Typical was the remark, "Let them go over to their proper companions, their favourites, the Dissenters, and utter their extemporary effusions in a conventicle, but not be suffer'd in our churches hypocritically to use our forms which they despise."[124] Joseph Trapp wished the Methodists would get out of the Church, there being "more danger to the church from a kind of half-Dissenter in it, than those who are total Dissenters from it."[125] Other writers hoped that Dissenters would initiate the move and induce Whitefield and the Methodists to join them.[126] Advice to get out continued to be offered to the Methodists. Thomas Balguy in 1769 put it bluntly: "If they cannot lawfully comply with the terms of communion, let them make an open separation; let them not profess to continue members of a Church, which they conscientiously disobey."[127]

There were those who advised taking deliberate steps to force the Methodists out of the Church. An anonymous Irish author, writing in 1753, contended that Methodists had "forfeit[ed] all the benefits, and advantages the members of a spiritual polity may be entitled to; as rebels and traytors do those in the temporal [sphere]." Since Methodists no longer ought to be considered members of the established church, the clergy ought to refuse to admit them to communion. The Church should take every step to completely disassociate itself from Methodism.[128]

John Wesley addressed the issue of schism with the preachers at the 1744 Conference: "I exhorted them to keep to the Church, observing that this was our peculiar glory not to form any new sect, but abiding in our own Church to do to all men all the good we could possibly do."[129] In 1755, with the growing number of dissenters in Methodist societies bringing their own prejudices against the Anglican Church, Wesley saw the need to fully

---

124 036-Gr. An Impartial Hand [Tucker], *A compleat account of the conduct of . . . Mr. Whitefield*, 9.

125 010-Gr. Trapp, *The nature, folly, sin and danger of being righteous over-much*, 38.

126 014-Gr. *Observations and remarks on Mr. Seagrave's conduct*, 33.

127 423A-Ki. Balguy, *A sermon preached at Lambeth Chapel on the consecration of the bishop of Llandaff*, 18.

128 248A-Ba. A Lay-man, *A few queries concerning the growth of Methodism*, 7.

129 Wesley, "Farther Thoughts on Separation from the Church" (1789), in *BEWJW*, vol. 9, *The Methodist Societies: History, Nature, and Design*, ed. Rupert E. Davies, 34, 538–40. This tract was initially published in the *Arminian Magazine*, April 1790, 214–16.

discuss whether the Methodists should leave the Church.[130] The need was heightened by concerns about the use of lay preachers. At issue was the request of many lay preachers to be permitted to preside at celebrations of the Lord's Supper. In October 1754 two preachers, Charles Perronet in London[131] and Thomas Walsh in Reading,[132] took matters into their own hands and celebrated Holy Communion in their circuits. Charles Wesley feared that John, in order to increase the availability of the sacrament, might be prepared to permit the practice. To Charles, whose loyalty to the Church of England was of paramount importance, this move was dangerous—a further step toward schism. Charles could no longer remain silent and, in preparation for the 1755 Conference, wrote his concerns in a poetic epistle to John.[133] To give the epistle wider circulation, he published it and read it to a number of Methodist societies. The epistle restates his abiding affection for John and reaffirms the nature of Methodism as a movement to revive the church and not establish a new church:

> Yet still the Methodists the Church are not:
> A single faculty is not the soul,
> A limb the body, or a part the whole.[134]
> When first sent forth to minister the word,
> Say, did we preach ourselves, or Christ the Lord?
> Was it our aim disciples to collect,
> To raise a party, or to found a sect? [135]

Charles pleads that John remain loyally within the Church of England:

---

130 Wesley called for a general discussion of the issue in 1755, not 1758, as he wrote in the text of "Farther Thoughts on Separation."

131 Charles Perronet and his brother, Edward, sons of Anglican priest Vincent Perronet, pushed for wider acceptance of Methodist preachers presiding at celebrations of the Lord's Supper.

132 Former Irish Roman Catholic Thomas Walsh agreed to cease conducting services of Holy Communion after the decision of the 1755 Conference.

133 Charles Wesley, Presbyter of the Church of England, *An Epistle to the Reverend Mr. John Wesley*, 2nd ed. (London: [Strahan] for J. Robinson, 1755). A transcript of the *Epistle* is printed in Baker, *Representative verse*, 288–94 (see chap. 5, n. 87). See also *Epistle to John Wesley*, 1755, produced by the Duke Center for Studies in the Wesleyan Tradition, ed. Randy L. Maddox and Aileen F. Maddox. While strictly not within Green's original parameters (a work in opposition to Methodism), Charles's epistle to John provides a valuable critique of the path the Methodist movement was taking. From the inside Charles was saying what those outside were saying—Methodism was heading toward schism.

134 Wesley, *An Epistle to the Reverend Mr. John Wesley*, line 54ff.

135 Ibid., 252ff.

> Wilt thou with me in the Old Church remain,
> And share her weal or woe, her loss, her gain,
> Spend in her service thy last drop of blood,
> And die—to build the temple of our God.[136]

When the 1755 Conference met, the arguments on both sides went on for several days and culminated in an agreement that it was by no means expedient that the Methodists should leave the Church of England.[137]

Suppression of Methodism

Throughout the early years of the revival, there were calls for the suppression of Methodism from various quarters in the Church. The ecclesiastical machinery, however, that could have achieved the desired suppression of the movement was no longer operative. Convocation, although it met on a few occasions in the eighteenth century, was willing to undertake no more than minor changes to the existing ecclesiastical system. Thus, it became virtually impossible for the Church of England as a whole to have any policy on Methodism. The lack of an effective Convocation was deplored by some pamphleteers. One of the characters of The mock-preacher (1739) lamented, "What a glorious cause was lost, when Queen Anne . . . was snatch'd away from us? Had she liv'd, the Convocation could have taken these affairs in hand."[138] Tristram Land feared that without decisive action from the Church, the cancerous spread of Methodism could not be contained. "The want of discipline," he wrote in 1741, ". . . 'tis likely, encourages these persons to turn faith into faction."[139]

An anonymous author, writing in 1744, bemoaned the fact that "the greatest protestant reformed church . . . [did] not have all necessary assistance for the suppressing" Methodism.[140] In the late 1750s, since the episcopacy seemed reluctant to initiate action, John Free made a plea for calling Convocation a

---

136 Ibid., line 232ff.
137 Wesley, "Farther Thoughts on Separation," in BEWJW, 9:538–40. See also: John Wesley, "Reasons against a Separation from the Church of England" (1758), in BEWJW, 9:334–49; and sermons number 74 ("Of the Church") and 75 ("On Schism") in BEWJW, vol. 3, Sermons III, 45–69, ed. Albert C. Outler (Nashville: Abingdon, 1986), 45–69.
138 025-Gr. The mock-preacher, 21–22.
139 133-Gr. Land, A second letter to the Rev. Mr. Whitefield, 32.
140 194-Gr. An Impartial Hand, An essay containing evident proofs against the Methodists, 6.

matter of urgency, since "the Church of England [was] now in great danger from licentious enthusiasts under the direction of certain malignant preachers distinguished by the name of Methodists."[141]

The plea for a convocation was echoed in James Makittrick Adair's verse:

> But if each Church of England's brother,
> Who'd wisely stick by one another.
> And call a general convocation,
> Of all true church men in the nation;
> And on this article insist,
> That none should deal with Methodist
> Nor the fat—ar—s ever grease,
> Of separated swine like these;
> . . . .
>
> This scheme would from their kennels rout 'em,
> And make the prick-ears [converts] look about 'em;
> They'd soon leave . . . [Methodism] in the lurch,
> And glide like snakes again to church.[142]

Free lamented that Gibson, due to his age and infirmity, was unable to provide the kind of episcopal leadership needed to quash Methodism. To halt the growth of the evangelical movement, Free called for the formation of a "public association" of the clergy of the city of London. The Methodists, he thought, would "stand more in awe of a collected force, and decline, through fear or prudence, many an attack, to which they might be invited by the weakness of single combatants."[143]

While some pamphleteers requested that the Church take steps to prevent Methodism's growth, others thought it was a matter for the secular authorities.[144] The concern of many authors that the Methodists engaged in illegal practices has been noted earlier. As early as 1739 there were requests for the magistracy to take appropriate steps to enforce the law of the land

---

141 278-Gr. Free, *The whole speech which was delivered to the reverend the clergy of . . . London*, 26.

142 378-Gr. Peter Paragraph *pseud.* [Adair], *The Methodist and mimick*, 19–20.

143 278-Gr. Free, *The whole speech which was delivered to the reverend the clergy of . . . London*, 26–31.

144 For a discussion on the magistracy and Methodism, see David Hempton, "Methodism and the Law, 1740–1820," *Bulletin of the John Rylands Library of Manchester* 70, no. 3 (1988): 93–108.

against Methodism and thus suppress the new sect. Timothy Scrub supported this proposal. The activities and preaching of the Methodists, he said, "very properly fall under the cognizance of the civil magistrates."[145] John Wilder agreed—it was high time the magistrates should "restrain and put a stop to the proceedings of these spiritual champions."[146] An anonymous author also pleaded in 1739:

> If our Christian magistrates, as they most certainly may and should do, will oblige them [the Methodists] to preach in some certain licenced place, agreeably to the Act of Toleration, or silence them if they refuse to comply with the laws, the number of their followers will soon be lessen'd, and their power of doing mischief greatly weaken'd.[147]

William Bowman suggested another duty for the magistracy: it should keep the Methodist meetings under surveillance, so that "faith be not turn'd into faction, nor religion into rebellion."[148]

On at least two occasions rumors circulated that Parliament would pass an act to hinder Methodism's progress. Whitefield believed the purpose of Gibson's *Observations* was "to represent . . . the Methodists as dangerous to the Church and State, in order to procure an Act of Parliament against them."[149] An author who signed his answer to Whitefield "J. B." lamented that the government had taken no decisive action.[150] Some pamphleteers only hinted at the need for parliamentary intervention, but John Free made the request openly: "We must apply to Parliament."[151] A report that just such a move had been made to the House of Commons circulated in the 1750s and early 1760s. Howell Harris noted in 1762 that he had been informed that Archbishop Secker presented "a

---

145 012-Gr. Scrub, *A letter to Robert Seagrave, M.A.*, 22.
146 018-Gr. Wilder, *The trial of the spirits*, 22.
147 036-Gr. [Tucker], *A compleat account of the conduct of . . . Mr. Whitefield*, 13.
148 094-Gr. Bowman, *The imposture of Methodism display'd*, 80.
149 Whitefield, *A letter to the Right Reverend the Bishop of London* (London: J. Robinson, 1744), 7.
150 166-Gr. J. B./ A Gentleman of Pembroke College, Oxon, *A letter to the Reverend Mr. Whitefield occasioned by his pretended answer to the first part of the 'Observations upon the conduct and behaviour of the Methodists,'* 16–17.
151 274-Gr. Free, *Rules for the discovery of false prophets*, v–vi.

scheme against the Methodists" to the speaker of the House of Commons.[152] Secker's involvement in such a scheme is highly unlikely. Where some voices called for efforts to drive the Methodists out of the Church of England, others, like Secker, entreated the Church to bring them back into the fold. Permeating Secker's 1762 *Visitation Charge* was an irenic and winsome spirit. Reconciliation, not persecution, he urged, was the approach the Church of England should take toward Methodism. Not only should the Church not drive the Methodists into Dissent; it should win back those who had been alienated:

> Now it should not only be injurious, but profane, to brand, with an opprobrious name, Christians remarkably serious, merely for being such, and equally imprudent to disclaim them as not belonging to us, to let a sect gain the credit of them, and labour to drive them into it. Surely, we should take even were they wavering, or actually gone from us, this most respectful and persuasive means of recalling such, and fixing them with us. Nay, supposing any person irretrievably gone, we should not be hasty to condemn, even in our thoughts, either them or their party, as enthusiasts or hypocrites . . . when we are undoubtedly well informed of any extraordinary things which they have assorted or done, it may be useful to speak strongly of them, but not with anger and exaggeration . . . Nor will ridicule become our character or serve our cause better than invective . . . Therefore we must guard every word that we utter, against misrepresentation: be sure to express, in public and private our firm belief of whatever evangelical truths recommend ourselves to them by our mildness, our seriousness and diligence.[153]

There were pamphleteers who believed the Church's response to Methodism ought to take the form of a reawakening. They listed the establishment's faults—the clergy neglected their pastoral responsibilities, sermons in parish churches were unintelligible to the masses, nonresidence among the senior clergy meant that some parishes were not adequately served, affairs of state kept bishops away from proper supervision of their dioceses—and called for

---

152 Howell Harris, *Howell Harris, Reformer and soldier, transcribed and edited by Tom Benyon* (Caernarvon, UK: Calvinistic Methodist Bookroom, 1958), 139.

153 Thomas Secker, A charge (1762) in the *Works of Thomas Secker*, new ed., 4 vols., 4:187.

the Church to shake off its lethargy.[154] If the Church awoke, these authors were convinced, Methodism, losing its reason for existence, would dwindle away. John Tottie was optimistic:

> If we are constant in the discharge both of the publick and private duties that belong to it [the parish ministry], and if we show an earnest and affectionate care for the spiritual welfare of our flock, striving to promote it upon all occasions by instruction, admonition, persuasion, and example—the instances, I am convinced, will be very rare where any of our people will forsake us to run after new teachers.[155]

Richard Hardy, writing in 1763, believed Methodism had revived the English church:

> First, in quickening the more lukewarm and lethargic among the people, by their well-timed and passionate zeal and address; and secondly, by introducing a kind of necessity upon divines, to make some abatement in their defenses of Christianity, and to turn unto, to dwell and insist more frequently and particularly upon the doctrines of it.[156]

Since Methodism's task had been completed, Hardy believed, there was no need for its further existence. It should begin to make every move to close the schism that had developed. The first step, he suggested, would be the suppression of lay preachers.

With such variation in advice on how Methodism was to be treated, it was impossible for any concerted attack to be mounted. The leadership of the Church avoided clear and decisive action. Things were allowed to take their own course. In the long run it was a stance like that of Gamaliel in the book of Acts that was followed—Methodism, if it was of God, would flourish. If it was not of God, it would fade away.

---

154 446A-Ki. Penrice, *The causes of Methodism set forth*, 4–10; 295-Gr. Edward Goldney, *Scriptural remedies for healing the unhappy divisions in the church* (London: for the author, 1760); 384-Gr. Tottie, *Two charges delivered to the clergy of the diocese of Worcester . . . 1763 and 1766*, 363–64.

155 384-Gr. Tottie, *Two charges*, 363–64.

156 349-Gr. Hardy, *A letter from a clergyman to one of his parishioners who was inclined to turn Methodist*, 82.

CHAPTER 7

Methodism and Politics

O pponents of Methodism viewed the movement with alarm—it was a political menace to both Church and society. There were two main periods in which grave concerns were raised about Methodism's political stance and its potentially disastrous influence. In the first, 1739 and the 1740s, numerous anti-Methodist authors alleged kinship both between Methodism and seventeenth-century Puritanism, and Methodism and Roman Catholicism. In the second, the 1770s and 1780s, it was John Wesley's own political writings that sparked hostility.[1]

A Culture of Fear

During 1739 and 1740 vague charges circulated that the Methodists were bent on undermining the political foundations of the state. Their infiltration of religious societies and their preaching out of doors raised a red flag. Pamphleteers questioned whether Methodism's purposes were solely religious. Tristram Land strongly advised people to avoid society meetings where Methodists had assumed leadership. The "political principles" of the Methodists, he cautioned, might lead the unwary into "designs destructive of both parts of our Constitution."[2] Some early pamphleteers alleged that George Whitefield headed a subversive movement whose aim was to overthrow the government. John Wilder branded Whitefield an anarchist, "resolved to make his voice the trumpet of war; and reduce, if possible, this Church and State, to anarchy and confusion."[3] Another author depicted Whitefield as "artfully compounding churchmen and dissenters, people of all sorts and

---

1 For a discussion of the political and social consequences of Methodism in its first century, see David Hempton, *Methodism and Politics in British Society, 1750–1850* (London: Hutchinson, 1984), chap. 2, "The Wesleyan Heritage," 20–54. See also Theodore R. Webber, *Politics in the Order of Salvation: Transforming Wesleyan Political Ethics* (Nashville: Kingswood Books, 2001), esp. chap. 3, "Public Political Controversies I: John Wesley and the '45 Rebellion" (69–86). Cf. "Introduction," in *BEWJW*, vol. 11, *The Appeals to Men of Religion and Reason and Certain Related Open Letters*, ed. Gerald R. Cragg, 1–42.

2 009-Gr. Land, *A letter to the Rev. Mr. Whitefield*, 8.

3 018-Gr. Wilder, *The trial of the spirits*, 21.

denominations to bring about his design of ruining the present constitution."[4]

By 1744, when the nation was in the grip of fear that an invasion by Bonnie Prince Charlie, the young Stuart Pretender to the British crown, would bring the prospect of open war with France, critics of Methodism exploited the alleged similarities between Methodism and Catholicism.[5]

Revived Puritanism

Methodism and insurrection became interchangeable in the vocabulary of those who opposed the revival. Memories of the English Civil War (1641–51) and the Commonwealth (1649–1660), which followed it, were still fresh in the minds of many. Fearing a disastrous repetition of that history, numerous pamphleteers set out to remind any who might have forgotten that history had lessons to teach—Puritans had destroyed the state. Perhaps the Methodist revival would complete the unfinished work of the Puritan Revolution. In 1739 and the early 1740s, pamphleteers haunted their readers with the specter of chaos caused by the Puritan ascendancy during the Interregnum (1649–1660). In his 1739 *Pastoral Letter*, Bishop Edmund Gibson drew the parallel between the Methodists and the Puritans, and then reminded his diocese of the legacy of civil strife the Puritans had left. The implication was clear—encouragement of Methodism would end in political disaster and a return of seventeenth-century sectarianism.[6] Gibson, in his 1741–42 visitation charge, cautioned his diocese to take care lest Methodist enthusiasm usher in a recurrence of the disaster of the Commonwealth.[7] Other critics stated the point even more directly. History, said the author of *A compleat account of the conduct of that eminent enthusiast Mr. Whitefield*, was repeating itself in Methodism:

> Whoever will be at the trouble of comparing the first rise of those troubles which at last overturn'd the constitution and ruin'd the nation, will see too great a similitude between them and the present risings of the enthusiastick rant not to apprehend great danger that, unless proper precautions be taken in time, the remote

---

4 166-Gr. J. B. /A Gentleman of Pembroke College, *A letter to the Reverend Mr. Whitefield occasioned by his pretended answer to the first part of the 'Observations on the conduct and behaviour of the Methodists,'* 22.

5 Charles Edward Stuart (1720–1788). See chap. 4, n. 60.

6 029-Gr. [Gibson], *The bishop of London's pastoral letter*, 29.

7 176A-Gr. [Gibson], *Directions given to the clergy of the diocese of London*, 87–88.

consequences of them may be fatal . . . Your modern ones [the
Methodists] do not come behind any of their predecessors [the
Puritans] for heat and boldness, and it is justly to be feared that
they will not if suffered to take their course, stop short of their
madness and wickedness.[8]

John Wilder echoed the concern that the Methodists aimed to destroy the
government just "as it was effected . . . in the last century by the like spiritual
enthusiasts."[9] The Methodists might protest that their intentions were not
political, that they were not insurrectionists, and that they loved the crown,
but such protestations of loyalty fell on deaf ears. History, wrote "J. B.," taught
that people like the Puritans and the Methodists were not to be trusted:

Supposing your intentions at this time are not levell'd at the subversion of our constitution—yet does not our history of the saints in
the last century teach us—that such lengths may be run by spiritual
superintendents, as to retreat or retract would be unsafe; when to
go on and make sure work with the constitution, may tickle their
ambition, and spur 'em on to pernicious views they never before
dream't of! For these reasons . . . their Lordships, and the zealous
adherers to our present constitution may well be afraid to trust
you; since you're already trampling on the laws that are to secure
us from confusion, does not betray the present jealousy in you for
the interest of the national constitution.[10]

Even though by mid-century the charge had begun to lose its force, there
were occasionally pamphleteers who continued to compare the Methodists
and the Puritans, suggesting that the revival was rekindling the flames of
seventeenth-century anarchy. In 1752 one author pointed to the Puritan skeleton in the Methodist closet. The Puritans had instituted a "purer reformation
with axes and hammers," and the Methodists, he believed, were following in
their predecessors' steps.[11] An anonymous writer in 1761 urged his readers
to take precautions lest the Methodists "bring on the dismal scene exhibited

---

8 036-Gr. [Tucker], *A compleat account of the conduct of . . . Mr. Whitefield,* 11.

9 018-Gr. Wilder, *The trial of the spirits,* 21.

10 166-Gr. J. B. /A Gentleman of Pembroke College, *A letter to the Reverend Mr. Whitefield
occasioned by his pretended answer to the first part of the 'Observations on the conduct
and behaviour of the Methodists,'* 27.

11 240-Gr. *Candid remarks on some particular passages in . . . Mr. Whitefield' s . . . Sermons,*
47.

in the middle of the last century."[12] Bishop William Warburton in 1763 went to particular pains to describe the Methodists' Puritan ancestry. The blood of regicides flowed in Methodist veins:

> They who now go under the name of Methodists were in the days of our fore-fathers, called Precisians; terms of similar and almost equal import . . . Whoever reads the large accounts of the spiritual state of the regicides while under condemnation . . . and compares them with the circumstantial Journals of the Methodists, will find so exact a conformity in the frenzy of sentiment . . . as may fully satisfy him, that they are both of the same stock; and ready on a return of the like season, to produce the same fruits.[13]

"A. T. Blacksmith" described, in 1764, the relationship between Methodists and Puritans as "moderns copy[ing] their old masters."[14] James Makittrick Adair put into verse in 1767 what the English feared about Methodism—the destruction of the monarchy.

> Cromwell like you did first pretend,
> Religion was his only end.
> But soon the mask away did fling
> Pull'd down the church and kill'd the King.[15]

The charge that Methodism was a revival of Puritanism was rooted in the fear of the resurgence of enthusiasm. The failure to distinguish rightly between the ordinary and the extraordinary gifts of the Holy Spirit led the Methodists, like the Puritans before them, to profess divine inspiration in thought, word, and deed. If enthusiasm had led the Puritans to destroy the monarchy in the previous century, surely, critics claimed, it would lead Methodism to a similar end.

To add fuel to the fire, opponents drew parallels between Methodist practices and doctrines and Puritan practices and doctrines. Theophilus Evans stated it bluntly: "There is no attending the progress of Methodism without

---

12 316-Gr. *An address to the right honourable—*, 6.
13 342-Gr. [Warburton], *The doctrine of grace,* 184–86.
14 360-Gr. A. T. Blacksmith [Witherspoon], *A defence of Christianity against the power of enthusiasm,* 14.
15 378-Gr. Peter Paragraph *pseud.* [Adair], *The Methodist and mimick,* 19. See 018-Gr. Wilder, *The trial of the spirits,* 21.

raking into the shocking and horrible things belonging to the history of this strange sect, which is indeed but the revival of several enthusiastick notions and mad pranks, among the several sectaries of the last century."[16] Because contemporary church leaders associated extempore prayer and sermons, field preaching, itinerancy, and lay preaching with the Puritans, these practices adopted by the Methodists were branded as pernicious in consequence. The title of one tract in 1739 spelled out the charge: *Enthusiasm no novelty; or, the spirit of the Methodists in the year 1641 and 1642.* The stated purpose of this work was to

> present the reader with a specimen of that enthusiasm, which in 1641 and the following years, pour'd forth a deluge of misery and confusion over the whole kingdom; tho', at its first appearance the marks of a new regeneration were, at least, equally visible in the extempore prayers and sermons of those times, as they are in the field-meetings on Kensington-Common, &c. in these our days.[17]

Rebellion against the government, it was believed, was an inevitable consequence of field preaching. Samuel Weller contended that "some evil consequences, some riot, and rebellion is naturally to be expected from these disorderly proceedings . . . It [will] indeed be nothing less than a miracle should there not soon arise from these licentious people, preachers inciting them to overturn the civil and religious establishments."[18]

Methodist itinerancy reminded Bishop Gibson of Puritan itinerancy that he thought had contributed greatly to the downfall of both Church and state in the previous century. This, he wrote, should be "a sufficient warning to all who have . . . a just regard to publick peace and order in the Church and State, to use their best endeavours to oppose and suppress that spirit of enthusiasm, which is gone out."[19]

Theophilus Evans noted that Methodists, like the enthusiastic sects of the century before, fostered connections with the lower social classes and had welcomed them into the ranks of lay preachers. Evans complained, "It is in fact the revival of the enormities and licentiousness of the last age, now

---

16 235-Gr. [Evans], *The history of modern enthusiasm*, 128–29.
17 024-Gr. *Enthusiasm no novelty*, iii.
18 098-Gr. [Weller], *The trial of Mr. Whitefield's spirit*, 40.
19 176A-Ba. [Gibson], *Directions given to the clergy of the diocese of London*, 88.

above a century ago, when it was free for any silly mechanick and illiterate pretender to vent his nonsense, not only with impunity, but with applause and reverence."[20]

The doctrines of the evangelical revival, it was noted, echoed Puritan doctrines. The tenet of justification by faith had produced antinomianism among the Puritans and contributed to the "confusion one hundred years ago," and, said the critics, it was beginning to have the same effect upon the Methodists and the state.[21] The Methodist doctrine of renunciation was, some believed, merely the doctrine of the Levelers in a new guise. Other writers found the flame of Puritanism rekindled in the adoption of Calvinist tenets by Whitefield and his followers.[22] The formula used by many opponents was a simple one—Methodist principles and practices were Puritanism revived. Methodism, opponents claimed, was bent on the realization of a similar end.

Association with Roman Catholicism

The oft-reiterated charge that the Methodists were associated with Roman Catholics also bore political undertones. During the first half of the eighteenth century, there were a number of plots by the supporters of the Stuart dynasty, who had been driven out of England in 1688, to return and unseat the Hanoverian line. Those who advocated and worked for the return of the Stuarts to the British throne were known as "Jacobites." In the popular mind they were identified with Roman Catholicism and opprobriously nicknamed "papists" and their practices "popery." No doubt the accusation that Wesley was a Catholic was due in part to the circulation as a broadside in Bristol, probably in 1740, of Captain Robert Williams's affidavit concerning Wesley's behavior during his missionary sojourn in Georgia. Among other things, the affidavit charged Wesley with High-Churchmanship.[23] Patrick Tailfer provided

---

20 235-Gr. [Evans], *The history of modern enthusiasm*, 122.

21 031-Gr. *An earnest appeal to the publick*, 31.

22 240-Gr. *Candid remarks on some particular passages in . . . Mr. Whitefield's . . . Sermons*, 47.

23 152A-Ba. Robert Williams, *The life and conversation of that holy man Mr. John Wesley, during his abode in Georgia* ([Bristol]: no printer, 1739). Wesley engaged in what he believed were genuine apostolic procedures: baptizing by immersion, mixing water with the wine at communion, praying for the dead. See Baker, *JWCE*, notes to pages 40–41.

support for this charge in his *True and historical narrative of the colony of Georgia*.[24] Tailfer dubbed Wesley a papist because his ritualistic procedures smacked of High Church and laid out evidence in support of this charge:

1st. Under an affected strict adherence to the Church of England he most unmercifuly damned all Dissenters . . .

2ndly. . . Persons suspected to be Roman Catholics were received and caressed by him as his first-rate saints.

3rdly . . . Confirmation of this suspicion arose from his endeavours to establish confession, penance, mortification, mixing wine with water in the sacrament . . . ; saying no more than, 'The body of Christ; the blood of Christ' . . . , by appointing deaconesses, with sundry other innovations, which he called Apostolic constitutions.[25]

Fanned by such accusations, rumors that the Methodists were papists in disguise spread throughout England. The author of the long satiric poem *The Methodists* (1739) fostered the association of Methodism and popery in the popular imagination by depicting the Methodist movement as a satanic and popish plot to re-subjugate England to Rome's authority. Satan advises Rome that Whitefield is his agent for the task:

On him ye Catholicks rely,
He'll do your business bye and bye.
To him prepare a new-form'd shrine
Let W—d 'mong your legends shine.[26]

Since Methodists were perceived as papists, it was only natural that the association between Methodist and Jacobite was made. Tales spread that the evangelicals were a part of an underground movement supporting the Stuart

---

24 Patrick Tailfer, author of *A true and historical narrative*, originally printed in Charles Town, South Carolina, in 1741, was a Scottish-born physician and disgruntled colonist involved in importing slaves and liquor into the colonies. See *BEWJW*, vol. 18, *Journals and Diaries*, 164–165n12. See also the section in the narrative dealing with John Wesley, which was reprinted in 156-Gr. An Impartial Hand, *The progress of Methodism in Bristol*, 65–71, and received wide circulation throughout England.

25 156-Gr. An Impartial Hand, *The progress of Methodism in Bristol*, 41–44, esp., 42–43. Section also reprinted in *The Journal of John Wesley*, ed. Nehemiah Curnock, Standard ed. (London: Charles H. Kelly, 1916), 8:304–7.

26 070-Gr. T. H., *The Methodists: A satirical poem* (London: Sold by C. Corbett, 1739), 16.

cause. Some anti-Methodists believed that if Methodism were successful, the Pretender would return to England and Roman Catholicism would be reinstated as the established religion of the state. William Bowman expressed the fear that the Methodists were engaging in subversive activities in their society meetings, and that they had become puppets of the great Roman Catholic powers Spain and France.

> I imagine I see, behind the curtain, the hand that plays the puppets and gives them their borrow'd voice and action. I fancy I behold the proud Iberian, impotent in deed, and almighty in gasconade [boasting], vainly attempting, by their means . . . to raise discontents and divisions among us . . . I think I discern something of the Gallic policy and the horrid councils of the conclave, in these factious and seditious doctrines calculated for the destruction of this nation.[27]

Later in the pamphlet, Bowman harshly denounced the Methodists as "traytors and rebels . . . sap[ping] the foundations of our civil constitution, to deliver up our King and country to ruin!"[28] An anonymous author in 1741 agreed with Bowman; people should be wary of the Methodists. They were subversive and dangerous agents: "A secret enemy is always more dangerous than a professed one; if therefore we are not upon our guard Mr. Whitefield may effect . . . the utter subversion of our government."[29] Samuel Weller, also writing in 1741, suggested that the papists had infiltrated Methodist ranks for the purpose of using them to whip up insurrection.[30]

In early 1744, when it seemed that an invasion by the Pretender was imminent, the pamphlet *The case of the Methodists briefly stated, more particularly in the point of field-preaching* was issued. The author, probably Edmund Gibson, enunciated the fear that the vast assemblies of the Methodists out of doors provided ample opportunities for those who planned sedition to mingle among the crowd in order to carry out their nefarious purposes. Gatherings of the size noted in Whitefield's journals (from four thousand to eighty thousand people) were believed to be seedbeds of sedition.[31] In

---

27 094-Gr. Bowman, *The imposture of Methodism display'd*, 62.
28 Ibid., 81.
29 124-Gr. *Mr. Whitefield's doctrines considered and confuted*, 4.
30 098-Gr. [Weller], *The trial of Mr. Whitefield's spirit*, 41.
31 170-Gr. [Gibson], *The case of the Methodists briefly stated*, 2.

1744 hearsay that the Methodists were active supporters of the Pretender found acceptance in various parts of England.[32] One pamphlet attributed the riots at Wednesbury, Staffordshire, to the pervasive rumor that the Methodists met on purpose to promote the interests of popery, and to usher in the Pretender.

> And when some neighbouring gentlemen, who had been so-licited to quell the mob, were endeavouring to affect the same, the mob told the said gentlemen, that they were doing what the soldiers shortly would do; and that if they endeavour'd to stop them they were enemies of his Majesty, and friends of the Pretender.[33]

With the defeat of the rebellion, the specific charge of Jacobitism gradually disappeared, but the notion that the Methodists were papists and were involved in sedition lingered. Nathaniel Fletcher, writing in 1750, circulated the common belief that Methodism was still suspect of planning insurrection.[34] A couplet in Samuel Bowden's *The mechanic inspir'd* kept alive the association of Methodism and popery. Methodist preachers were

> By Jesuits deluded, with pious commission,
> To kindle the schismatic coals of sedition.[35]

By 1766 the charge that the Methodists were a political threat was recognized by most people as specious, but there remained a handful of pamphleteers who cautioned the state to keep the evangelicals under surveillance because of their dangerous tendencies. One such author, John Free, who

---

32 Wesley was so vexed by the misunderstanding that the Methodists were Jacobites that he wrote to King George II on March 5, 1744, professing their loyalty to the Crown: "The Humble Address of the Societies in England and Wales in Derision Called Methodists." See Wesley, March 5, 1744, *Journal and Diaries III (1743–1754)* in *BEWJW* 20:16; and John Wesley, "Letter to His Majesty King George II," March 5, 1744, *Letters II (1740–1755)* in *BEWJW* 26:104–8. Wesley wished to publish the "Address," but was persuaded from doing so by his brother Charles, who feared that if it was published, it would be seen as a sign by many that Methodism constituted a distinct sect, apart from the Church of England. See Charles Wesley, March 5, 1744, in *Journal of Charles Wesley, M.A.*, introduction and occasional notes by Thomas Jackson, 2 vols. (London: John Mason, 1849), 1:354–55; repr., Baker Book House, 1980.

33 173-Gr. *Some papers giving an account of . . . Methodism at Wednesbury*, 23.

34 217A-Ki. Fletcher, *A vindication of the 'Methodist dissected,'* 9.

35 249-Gr. Bowden, "The Mechanic inspir'd," in *Poems on various subjects*, 213.

although he shied away from calling them rebels, thought Methodists must remain suspect:

> A rebel is a traitor, who appears in arms—I never yet laid such a thing as this to the charge of the Methodists. They never, that I know of, appeared in arms; though if the government have not a watchful eye upon them, as their turbulence and numbers go on to increase it is not so unlikely but they may: If there should happen to be a confusion in the state, what so probable a course for a foreign enemy to take, as to gain over; or if an invasion succeeds, command their leaders to join their party?[36]

Free expressed the common belief that church and state in the eighteenth century were so inextricably intertwined that to attack the church was tantamount to attacking the state. To undermine the clergy, furthermore, was to undermine not only ecclesiastical authority but civil as well. The Methodists alleged assault upon the church was, therefore, aggression against the state.[37]

The Wilkes Affair

Beginning in 1770 Wesley wrote a number of political tracts.[38] Most had to do with his reflections on liberty arising from the Wilkes affair, the American colonies' move toward independence, and the issue of slavery. None of them made an original contribution to political theory; it was not their intent. They were written as responses to specific political issues. In all of them, with the exception of *Thoughts on slavery*, Wesley's Tory sympathies emerge.

The first political writing of Wesley to draw hostile criticism was his conservative defense of the king, ministers, and parliament over the Wilkes Affair. The House of Commons had expelled John Wilkes, a radical journalist and politician, from Parliament on February 3, 1769, on the grounds that he was an outlaw at the time of his election to Parliament from Middlesex.[39] He

---

36 276-Gr. Free, *Dr. Free's edition of the Rev. Mr. Wesley's second letter*, 21–22.

37 274-Gr. Free, *Rules for the discovery of false prophets*, 2.

38 For a summary of Wesley's political tracts, see the section titled "Wesley and British Politics" in Kenneth J. Collins, *John Wesley: A Theological Journey* (Nashville: Abingdon, 2003), 206–14. See also Ronald H. Stone, *John Wesley's Life and Ethics* (Nashville: Abingdon, 2001), 172–97.

39 For a discussion of the Wilkes affair in British politics see J. Steven Watson, *The Reign of George III, 1760–1815* (Oxford: Oxford University Press, 1960), 131–145.

was elected on three occasions by substantial margins, but Parliament refused each time to seat him. When his opponent, Henry Luttrell, was seated, despite that fact that Wilkes had been elected overwhelmingly, the lower and middle classes of London erupted in riots. In the midst of the unrest and controversy surrounding Wilkes, a number of pamphlets were published. Wesley, at the urging of a friend, reluctantly entered the fray with a pamphlet entitled *Free thoughts on the present state of public affairs.*[40] Despite his opening disclaimer that he was not a politician, and that politics was "quite out of [his] province," Wesley jumped into the middle of the controversy and firmly defended the House of Common's right to exclude John Wilkes.[41] He went on to examine the "causes and consequence of the present commotions." The causes of national unrest were not due to politics, Wesley wrote, but to moral faults in human beings—covetousness, ambition, envy, pride, and resentment.[42]

In 1771, Joseph Towers, printer, bookseller, biographer, and later Dissenting minister, issued a strong rebuke to Wesley in an anonymously printed tract, *A letter to the Rev. Mr. John Wesley.*[43] In 1775, a second pamphlet, issued under the pseudonym "Juniolus" and entitled *Fallacy detected*, took Wesley to task for his *Free thoughts.*[44] Both authors impugned Wesley's motives for becoming involved in politics, contending that he had written his tract in order to win political favors. "I presume," wrote Joseph Towers, "from your present situation and connexions, that you have no aspirations after a miter; and you are only desirous of venting the effusions of your extreme loyalty. Your character of the K___g nevertheless, certainly deserves some reward; so ample an eulogium ought to be well paid for."[45] Juniolus satirically praised Wesley for achieving his aim of gaining support for his views from "some of the most virulent Tories . . . who before held [him] . . . in contempt."[46]

Both critics argued that Wesley was an enemy to freedom in general and to the rights of the common people in particular. Wesley's *Free thoughts*, said Towers, was nothing more or less than "a studied insult upon all who

---

40 John Wesley, *Free Thoughts on the Present State of Public Affairs, Works* (Jackson), 11:14–33.

41 Ibid., 14.

42 Ibid., 28.

43 446-Gr. [Joseph Towers], *A letter to the Rev. Mr. John Wesley in answer to his late pamphlet entitled 'Free thoughts on the present state of public affairs'* (London: J. Towers, 1771).

44 483A-Ba. Juniolus, *Fallacy detected* ([London]: no printer, 1775).

45 446-Gr. [Towers], *A letter to the Rev. Mr. John Wesley . . .* , 4.

46 483A-Ba. Juniolus, *Fallacy detected,* 6.

have asserted the cause of public freedom." Wesley was pessimistic about the general public's ability to make critical assessments of national affairs. By contrast Towers articulated an optimistic view:

> You [Wesley] attempt to ridicule the propensity of the English nation to political disquisitions, and seem to think . . . that it is an absurdity for common people to meddle in such matters . . . The bulk of the people, I believe, seldom judge amiss in points of importance to the interests and welfare of the state . . . The people, in general, are sufficient judges whether their own rights and privileges are attacked or preserved inviolate and whether the honour and dignity of the nation is maintained abroad.[47]

Wesley rejected any notion that Wilkes's exclusion had national implications. If any wrongs had been committed, only the electors of Middlesex had been affected. By contrast, Towers saw far-reaching implications—the principle of representation was at stake:

> By decision, therefore, which in a single instance deprives the County of Middlesex of the right of election, the possession of that right in every other part of the kingdom is rendered precarious . . . If the House of Commons has a right to incapacitate one man, it has the same right to incapacitate two, three, or any number.[48]

Wesley had been critical of the petitions that had been collected between May 1769 and January 1770 in support of Wilkes and in protest to Luttrell's admission to the House of Commons. Claiming that the vast majority of those who signed the petitions had not read what they put their names to, Wesley asserted that the petitions did not reflect "the sense of the nation."[49] Towers denied Wesley's contention. People had been apprised of the contents of the petitions prior to their signing, and the large number of signatures collected made the petitions "truly declarative of the sense of the nation."[50]

---

47 446-Gr. [Towers], *A letter to the Rev. Mr. John Wesley* . . . , 4, 9–10. Cf. 483A-Ba. Juniolus, *Fallacy detected*, 4, 19.

48 446-Gr. [Towers], *A letter to the Rev. Mr. John Wesley* . . . , 24–25.

49 Wesley, *Free Thoughts on the Present State of Public Affairs*, in *Works* (Jackson) 11:18–19.

50 Ibid., 15.

Juniolus attributed base motives to Wesley's attack on the petitions. The Methodist leader deliberately misrepresented the purpose of the petitions. The intent was not to inflame the people against the ministry, as Wesley had claimed, but to inform the king of public sentiment. Wesley had "join[ed] the herd of ministerial bullies full tilt" in order to win their favor.[51] Juniolus castigated Wesley for supporting the wrong side in the struggle. Wesley had accused the organizers of the petitions of being ambitious and greedy. But were not the supporters of the ministry corrupted by similar motives? Why had Wesley not condemned them?

> Not a word here of the devouring leeches, who share so many millions of the people's money, not a word of the dirty mungoes who betray the people for reward, not a word of the public default-ers of unaccounted millions, not a syllable about placemen and pensioners and hireling S____t____rs: all exculpated as having no share in the people's wrongs . . . [You] acquit the criminal and blame the prosecutor.[52]

Both Juniolus and Towers were convinced that religion and politics did not mix. "I am sorry to see you, at this advanced period of your life [Wesley was in his late sixties], going out of the proper business of your character and profession," wrote Towers.[53] The critics' advice: Wesley should stick to religion and not meddle in politics. Wesley did not take the advice. In February 1772 he published *Thoughts upon liberty*, in which he developed similar arguments to those he had written earlier.[54] The same year he released *A calm address to the inhabitants of England*, in which he defended his Tory sentiments from any connection with Jacobitism.[55] Surprisingly there were no anti-Methodist attacks on these pamphlets.

Slavery

In the latter part of 1736, while visiting Charles Town, South Carolina (now Charleston), Wesley encountered for the first time the brutal reality of

---

51   483A-Ba. Juniolus, *Fallacy detected*, 10.
52   Ibid., 16–17.
53   446-Gr. [Towers], *A letter to the Rev. Mr. John Wesley . . .* , 56.
54   Wesley, *Thoughts upon Liberty*, in *Works* (Jackson), 11:34–46.
55   Wesley, *A Calm Address to the Inhabitants of England*, in *Works* (Jackson), 11:129–40.

slavery.[56] Over the next thirty or so years, Wesley came to view the slave trade as morally indefensible.[57] In 1772 he was moved by reading Anthony Benezet's antislavery tract, *Some historical account of Guinea*, first printed in 1771,[58] to publish *Thoughts upon slavery*, his own attack on the inhumane and immoral trade.[59] Thirty percent of the text of this pamphlet Wesley borrowed from Benezet; Wesley appealed, not to the members of Parliament to initiate legislation, but to all those who were connected with the lucrative industry to abolish it. The grounds of his appeal were moral—slavery was unchristian. Those involved in the trade should not risk eternal damnation for financial gain.

Following on the heels of Wesley's *Thoughts*, came a critical pamphlet from an anonymous author: *A supplement to Mr. Wesley's pamphlet entitled Thoughts upon slavery*.[60] In a critique almost twice as long as Wesley's tract, the critic did his utmost to make Wesley's *Thoughts* appear ridiculous by arguing that the picture the Methodist leader had drawn was greatly exaggerated. "All my efforts will be to reduce and soften his colours," wrote the critic.[61] Wesley sketched an idyllic picture of black people in their natural state living a peaceful, industrious, and prosperous existence in well-organized and governed African villages. In contrast, he described the brutal manner in

---

56 John Warren Smith, *John Wesley and Slavery* (Nashville: Abingdon, 1986). Utilizing Wesley's letters and other writings, Smith chronicles Wesley's developing views on slavery from his first encounter in America until the publication of his *Thoughts upon slavery*. See also Stone, *John Wesley's Life and Ethics*, 187–97.

57 For the influences on Wesley in developing his own tract on slavery, see Frank Baker, "The Origins, Character and Influence of John Wesley's 'Thoughts on Slavery,'" in *MH* 2 (January 1984): 75–86.

58 Anthony Benezet (1713–1784), *Some historical account of Guinea, its situation, produce, and general disposition of its inhabitants with an inquiry into the rise and progress of the slave-trade, its nature and lamentable effects* (Philadelphia: John Cruikshank, 1771). Wesley was also acquainted with three earlier pamphlets by Benezet: *Observations on the enslaving, importing, and purchasing of Negroes* (Germantown, 1759); *A short account of that part of Africa, inhabited by the Negroes* (Philadelphia, 1762); and *A caution and warning to Great Britain and her colonies, in a short representation of the calamitous state of the enslaved Negroes in the British dominions* (Philadelphia, 1766). In addition, Baker recognized the influence of Nathaniel Gilbert and his brother Francis upon Wesley's efforts to help the slaves. They were a significant influence "in promoting a gradual change of emphasis in Wesley from Christianization to emancipation." Baker, "The Origins, Character and Influence of John Wesley's 'Thoughts upon slavery,'" in *MH* 22 (January 1984): 75–86.

59 Wesley, *Thoughts upon Slavery*, in *Works* (Jackson), 11:59–79.

60 470-Gr. *A supplement to Mr. Wesley's pamphlet entitled 'Thoughts upon slavery'* (London: H. Reynell, 1774).

61 Ibid., 3.

which slaves were procured, transported, sold, and treated by their owners. *Thoughts upon slavery* purported to be based on facts. Indeed, the *Monthly Review* praised Wesley for the accuracy of his facts,[62] but the author of *A supplement to Mr. Wesley's pamphlet entitled Thoughts upon slavery* criticized him for being generally misinformed.[63] Indeed, Wesley lacked firsthand knowledge. He was a victim of credulity and his own vivid imagination. The critic suggested that Wesley's conception of African life before the encounter with white people was wholly mistaken. Wesley had painted "a picture of the very great happiness enjoyed by the natives of Africa, heightened with colours far beyond anything we would possibly have conceived." But, the critic argued, such a view of primitive African culture was closer to fantasy than to fact. Wesley totally ignored such vicious tribal practices as child-eating and leaving old people to die. African life before the coming of the white man had not been so idyllic as Wesley had depicted.[64]

Furthermore, Wesley's critic attacked him for his overgenerous assessment of black people's capabilities. In Wesley's concept of the "noble savage" corrupted by white civilization, there was something of the spirit of Rousseau. Hand in hand with Christianity, said Wesley, Europeans had introduced "every vice" of white people. The author of *A supplement* strongly disagreed. Blacks had not been corrupted by whites; they were by nature inferior: "Whatever imperfections are . . . found in the negroes transported to the colonies ought not to be ascribed to any other cause . . . than an original defect in the manners and customs of their natale solum."[65]

Wesley had defended the natural intelligence of the black slaves. If they were slow-witted, it was because their masters provided no opportunity for them to develop their intellects. Such assertions, Wesley's critic bluntly denied: "Stupidity is really natural to these classes of men [and women]."[66]

Wesley's picture of the horrors of slave life had also been overdrawn, the anonymous critic argued. Wesley had contrasted the former happy life of the African tribesman with the miserable existence of the black slave. He had depicted the defenseless slave as subject to inhuman treatment by his or

---

62 *Monthly Review* 51 (1774): 234.
63 470-Gr. *A supplement to Mr. Wesley's pamphlet entitled 'Thoughts upon slavery,'* 50–51, 69.
64 Ibid., 50.
65 Ibid., 95–96.
66 Ibid., 89–90.

her owners. In doing so, the critic argued, Wesley had credulously accepted stories of general harsh treatment of slaves. Instances of individual slave owners mistreating or neglecting their slaves were not to be denied, said the critic, but Wesley was guilty of generalizing from these particular cases. Harsh treatment was not universal:

> Mr. Wesley has certainly (in his Accounts) overstepped the line of probability, and passed a censure much too general to be consistent with justice, I had almost said, with truth—The slave-holders (as Mr. Wesley terms them) have certainly very large and unlimited powers over their slaves, but is it not ungenerous to infer from thence, that they have inclinations to exercise these powers in cruelty and injustice? Mr. Wesley appeals to facts; if these facts are founded in truth, he should have told us in what particular islands they were perpetrated, and under what governments, and have pointed out a remedy more likely to reform such disorders.[67]

Over the next thirty years, *Thoughts upon slavery* went through thirteen editions in America and continued to have an impact on the issue.[68] Wesley's interest in slavery did not stop with *Thoughts upon slavery*—he took numerous opportunities to keep the issue before the public.[69] Of note is his caustic reference to slavery in *A calm address to our American colonies:*

> Who then is a slave? Look into America and you may easily see; See that Negro fainting under the load, bleeding under the lash! He is a slave. And is there 'no difference' between him and his master? Yes; the one is screaming, 'Murder! Slavery!' The other silently bleeds and dies! But wherein then consists the difference between liberty and slavery. Herein: you and I, and the English in general, go where we will, and enjoy the fruit of our labours: This is liberty. The Negro does not. This is slavery.[70]

Wesley's final thrust against slavery was his well-known and oft-quoted

---

67 Ibid., 97–98.
68 Warren Thomas Smith, *John Wesley and Slavery*, 101.
69 Ibid., 101–3.
70 Wesley, *A Calm Address to our American Colonies*, in *Works* (Jackson), 11:81.

deathbed letter to William Wilberforce, February 27, 1791, urging him to continue to advocate the abolition of the slave trade by act of Parliament, which finally occurred in 1807.

Roman Catholic Relief

Despite Wesley's olive branch to Roman Catholics in his open *Letter to a Roman Catholic* and his sermon, *Catholic spirit,* both of which imply an openness by Wesley to work with Roman Catholics, Wesley shared the typical prejudice against Catholicism held by English people of his time.[71] The prejudice was based on fear of Rome as a foreign power with designs for reconverting England and destroying cherished English liberties. Apprehension concerning the menace of "popery" mushroomed again in the late 1770s. If nervous Protestants were disturbed in 1774 when the English government, by means of the Quebec Act, granted official recognition to the Roman Catholic Church in Canada, they were greatly alarmed by the Saville Act of 1778, which brought the problem home by providing a measure of relief to Catholics in England. In 1779 extremist Protestants, imitating the Scottish Presbyterians who had dissuaded the British ministry from extending the moderate toleration to Scotland, formed an alliance known as the Protestant Association, with Lord George Gordon (1751–1793), politician and religious agitator, at its head.

Indicative of Wesley's growing apprehension was his publication in 1779 of *Popery calmly considered,* a twenty-five page denunciation of what he considered to be the errors of Rome.[72] On January 18, 1780 Wesley recorded that "receiving more and more accounts of the increase of popery," he felt obligated to comment publicly about it.[73] This comment took the form of *A Letter to the printer of the 'Public Advertiser' occasioned by the late Act passed in favour of popery,* dated City Road, January 21, 1780.[74] As well as being printed in the *Public Advertiser,* this letter was disseminated to papers throughout England, and was later issued as a broadside. In this letter Wesley

71 Wesley, *A letter to a Roman Catholic,* in *Works* (Jackson), 10:80–86. John Wesley, Sermon 39, *Catholic Spirit,* in *BEWJW,* 2:79–95.

72 Wesley, *Popery calmly considered,* in *Works* (Jackson), 10:140–58.

73 Wesley, January 18, 1780, in *BEWJW* vol. 23, *Journals and Diaries VI (1776–1786),* ed. W. Reginald Ward and Richard P. Heitzenrater, 159.

74 Wesley, *A letter to the printer of the 'Public Advertiser,'* in *Works* (Jackson), 10:159–61.

lent support to the Protestant Association by means of commending a recent pamphlet, *An appeal from the Protestant Association,* for containing "strong and conclusive" reasoning.[75] The argument he developed against Roman Catholicism rested on his conviction that it was a potential national threat. He set forth two main propositions: First, Catholics were not to be trusted, because the decree of the Council of Constance that "no faith is to be kept with heretics" remained binding on every Roman Catholic. Second, every Roman Catholic, by virtue of allegiance to the pope, was unable to render total loyalty to a temporal ruler, treason and rebellion being pardonable sins for Rome. Wesley's attitude was unequivocal: "No government ought to tolerate men who cannot give any security to that government for their allegiance and peaceable behaviour."[76]

It was to be expected that reactions to the *Letter* would be sharply divided. On the one hand, Protestant groups applauded Wesley; the intolerant Protestant Association voted its thanks unanimously, and Wesley's erstwhile Calvinist foes, who had branded his theology as "popery," offered him warm commendation in the February 1780 issue of the *Gospel Magazine.*[77] On the other hand, Roman Catholics raised cries of protest. Chief among the antagonists was Arthur O'Leary (1729–1802), a Capuchin friar of Dublin and an avid controversialist, who wrote six letters to the *Freeman's Journal,* Dublin, attacking Wesley's letter. These he then published as an eighty-eight page tract, *Mr. O'Leary's remarks on the Rev. Mr. Wesley's letters in defence of the Protestant Associations in England*—a witty assault replete with ridicule.[78] Wesley replied to the letters in the *Freeman's Journal* (before their publication in the tract) with two letters to the editor.[79] O'Leary closed the

---

75 *An appeal from the Protestant Association to the people of Great Britain* (London: J. Pasham, 1779). Many English Protestants had misgivings about the Catholic Relief Act of 1778, which proposed relaxing some social, economic, and political restrictions against Roman Catholics. Out of this concern the Protestant Association formed to protest the Act. Lord George Gordon assumed leadership of the association in 1779. On May 29, 1780, Gordon called a meeting of the association and subsequently led a march to the House of Commons to deliver a petition against the Act.

76 Ibid., 159–61.

77 See Luke Tyerman, *The Life and Times of John Wesley,* 3rd ed. (London: Hodder and Stoughton, 1876), 3:320. *Gospel Magazine,* February 1780, 86–89.

78 525C-Ki. Arthur O'Leary, *Mr. O'Leary's remarks on the Rev. Mr. Wesley's letters. ODNB.*

79 Wesley later published these in 1781 together with his original letter to the *Public Advertiser.* See John Wesley, *A letter to the printer of the 'Public Advertiser,'* in *Works* (Jackson), 10:162–63.

debate with *A rejoinder to Mr. Wesley's reply*.[80] A lesser antagonist was John Whittingham, apparently a seedsman in Coventry, and convert to Roman Catholicism. Using the pseudonym "Old Fashion Farmer," Whittingham inveighed in two broadsides against those (Wesley in particular) who attacked his faith.[81]

Both O'Leary and Whittingham decried the effects of Wesley's *Letter* upon the general populace. Whittingham declared that Wesley's views had been "very industriously dispersed throughout the kingdom with a design to inflame the people against Roman Catholics," and this aim had been achieved.[82] Its effectiveness was attested, O'Leary claimed, by the success of the Protestant Association's organizers in obtaining large numbers of signatures for their petitions against Roman Catholic relief. Wesley might claim to be the apostle of peace, but he was in reality the trumpeter of war.[83] This assessment was echoed in Whittingham's characterization of Wesley as "a pretended charitable preacher."[84]

Wesley's chief contention was that Catholics were not to be trusted because the Council of Constance had decreed that no faith was to be kept with heretics.[85] No such principle had been authorized by the Council, claimed O'Leary. In fact, just the opposite: "the fathers of that council condemned lies, frauds, perjury, and those horrors which Mr. Wesley would fain fix upon Roman Catholics." Wesley, the Irish priest asserted, had cruelly caricatured Catholics as "a set of perjurers authorized to commit all kinds of crimes with impunity."[86]

John Whittingham attacked Wesley for challenging the integrity and loyalty of Roman Catholics. Oaths of loyalty to the state were as binding on

---

80 527-Gr. Arthur O'Leary, *Miscellaneous tracts . . . containing: V. Rejoinder to Mr. Wesley's reply to the above remarks* (Dublin: Tho. McDonnel, 1781), 289–312.

81 525B-Ki. The Old Fashion Farmer [John Whittingham], *To the public* (Coventry: no printer, 1780). A manuscript note on the Bodleian Library's copy states that John Whittingham, a seedsman and convert to Rome, used the pseudonym "Old Fashion Farmer." Wesley replied to Whittingham with a broadside, entitled *A letter to Mr. John Whittingham* (London: T. Luckman, July 1780).

82 525B-Ki. The Old Fashion Farmer [Whittingham], *To the public*.

83 525C-Ki. Arthur O'Leary, *Mr. O'Leary's remarks*, 13.

84 525B-Ki. Whittingham, *To the public*.

85 The Council of Constance (1414–17) was convoked to end the Great Schism, reform the church, and combat heresy. *Oxford Dictionary of the Christian Church*, 2nd ed., ed. F. L. Cross and E. A. Livingstone (Oxford: Oxford University Press, 1977), 336–37.

86 525C-Ki. Arthur O'Leary, *Mr. O'Leary's remarks*, 37, 56.

Catholics as they were on anyone else: "We [Catholics] are bound to pay allegiance to our lawful Sovereigns let their religion be what it will." Surely the loyal, virtuous, and peaceful behavior of English Catholics proved beyond any doubt that they were no danger to the state, Whittingham contended.[87] Indeed, Catholics were better patriots than Protestants were, he asserted: "No religion upon earth teaches men to be better Christians or better subjects to their lawful princes, than the Roman Catholic religion does."[88]

Wesley had made much of the pope's authority over the mind and behavior of the individual Catholic. O'Leary countered that Wesley exercised more power over his followers than the pope did over his.[89] The central error in the Methodist leader's argument, O'Leary suggested, was his condemnation of eighteenth-century Catholics for the alleged faults of their ancestors:

> On the wide theatres spread by the revolutions of time, new characters daily appear and different circumstances are productive of different events. It is vain to ransack old councils, imperial constitutions, and ecclesiastical canons, whether genuine or spurious, against heretics, in order to brand the present generations of Catholics . . . from the opinions of men, or the actions of popes, or the disciplinary canons of councils, or the proceedings of bishops who composed them, in one age, there is no arguing to the belief of men in another.[90]

From June 2 to 12, 1780, following an attempt to present to the House of Commons the anti-Catholic petitions gathered by the Protestant Association, ugly riots occurred in London. After the disaster, one author, who called himself "A Consistent Whig," speculated on the causes of the disturbance, fixing some of the blame for its occurrence on Wesley and his followers. Both the leader of Methodism and his disciples had agitated the common people against the Catholics, the opponent charged. The Protestant petition was "an instrument originating from Methodist preachers," he contended, and the majority of the signers were drawn from "frequenters of the tabernacles,

---

87 525B-Ki. John Whittingham, *To the public.*
88 Ibid.
89 525C-Ki. O'Leary, *Mr. O'Leary's remarks,* 46–47.
90 Ibid., 73.

and nightly conventicles, from the fanatic followers of Wesley and others like him."[91]

The American Revolution

Controversy over the British government's handling of American affairs had raged in the press for some time before John Wesley's *A calm address to our American colonies* appeared in print in 1775.[92] Already, sheaves of political tracts, including Samuel Johnson's *Taxation no tyranny*, debating the ministry's policy, had been published.[93] In spite of the fact that the dispute over the colonies had reached fever pitch before Wesley entered the fray, the *Calm Address* caused an immediate furor. Indignant partisans of the American cause issued hostile attacks upon Wesley and his political views. Wesley was, of course, no stranger to pamphlet attack during his long career as an evangelist, author, and publisher, but no single publication he issued created such an intense storm or was attacked with more severity. From October to December 1775, an avalanche of criticism almost buried the aging Methodist leader. Unfavorable reviews, comments, and letters appeared in the *London Magazine*, the *Gentleman's Magazine*, *Lloyd's Evening Post*, the *Public Ledger*, the *London Chronicle*, the *Gazetteer*, the *Public Advertiser*, the *Morning Chronicle*, and the *Monthly Review*. Hostile attacks were not limited to those contained in periodicals. Of greater significance here were the critical pamphlets. Although Samuel Johnson was apparently disappointed with the response to his *Taxation no tyranny*, Wesley could never make the same claim about his abridgment of Johnson's tract under the title *A calm address*.[94] In the last three months of 1775, no fewer than

---

91 525D-Ki. A Consistent Whig, *Considerations on the late disturbance* (London: J. Almon, 1788), 13–14.

92 This section was published with the title "John Wesley's Calm address: The Response of the Critics," in *MH* 14, no. 1 (October 1975): 13–23. It is used here by permission of *Methodist History*.

93 See monthly lists of publications in the *London Magazine*, the *Monthly Review*, and *Gentleman's Magazine*. Albert M. Lyles, "The Hostile Reactions to the American Views of Johnson and Wesley," *Journal of the Rutgers University Library* 24 (December 1960): 3, lists a number of titles, randomly selected, indicative of the opinion in the publications.

94 William P. Courtney, *A Bibliography of Samuel Johnson*, rev. David N. Smith (Oxford: Oxford University Press, 1915), 125–27, lists ten replies to *Taxation no tyranny*. *Boswell's Life of Johnson*, ed. G. B. Hill, rev. ed. by L. F. Powell (Oxford: Oxford University Press, 1934), 2:335, records, in April 1775, Johnson's dissatisfaction with the lack of response.

fifteen tracts and numerous letters to London magazines were directed at Wesley or his able defender John Fletcher.[95] By 1776 the furor had largely subsided—only six antagonistic tracts appeared.[96] Wesley's support of the British government against the colonists was not immediately forgotten, however. As late as 1779, Wesley's Calvinistic critics took pleasure on occasion in preventing the wounds of 1775 from healing by rubbing salt into them.[97]

Since most of the controversialists preferred anonymity, they delighted in pseudonyms such as: "A Lover of Truth and the British Constitution," "A Friend of the People and Their Liberties," and "Americanus." Among the authors whose names we know are Augustus Toplady, an evangelical Anglican minister and theological foe of Wesley; James Murray, Dissenting minister of High Bridge Chapel of Newcastle-upon-Tyne; Caleb Evans, Baptist minister in Bristol; John Towers (younger brother of the better-known controversialist Joseph Towers), an Independent preacher in London. It was to be expected that most of those who crossed swords with Wesley on the American question

---

95 473-Gr. J. T. [Towers], *Elihu's reply*; 475-Gr. Americus, *A letter to Mr. John Wesley*; 479-Gr. A Hanoverian [Augustus Montague Toplady], *An old fox tarr'd and feather'd* (London: J. French, 1775); 480-Gr. *A constitutional answer to the Rev. Mr. John Wesley's 'Calm address'* (London: E. and C. Dilly, 1775); 480A-Ki. A Gentleman of Northumberland [James Murray], *A grave answer to Mr. Wesley's 'Calm address.'* I have not been able to locate this item, but it is noted in *ProcWHS* 12:191; 481-Gr. T. S., *A cool reply to a 'Calm address'* (London: by the author, 1775); 482-Gr. Americanus [Caleb Evans], *A letter to the Rev. Mr. John Wesley, occasioned by his 'Calm address'* (Bristol: William Pine, 1775); 483-Gr. Caleb Evans, *A reply to the Rev. Mr. Fletcher's Vindication* (Bristol: W. Pine, 1775); 483A-Ba. Juniolus, *Fallacy detected*; 483C-Ba. W. Y., *A serious answer to Mr. Wesley's 'Calm address'* (Bristol: no printer, 1775); 483D-Ki. *Resistance no rebellion* (London: for N. Maud, 1775); 484-Gr. W. D., *A second answer to Mr. John Wesley* (London: Wallis and Stonehouse, 1775); 485-Gr. A Lover of Truth and the British Constitution [Titus Hibbert], *A letter to the Rev. Mr. John Wesley on his 'Calm address'* (Manchester: no printer, 1775); 485A-Ba. [Dr. Sutcliff of Settle], *Political propositions* ([Leeds]: no printer, [1775]); 485C-Fi. Civis, *A letter to the Reverend John Wesley* (London: no printer, 1775).

96 486-Gr. *Political empiricism* (London: J. Johnson, 1776); 486A-Ki, A Friend to the People and Their Liberties, *A full and impartial examination of the Rev. Mr. John Wesley's address* (n.p.: no printer, 1776); 488A-Ki. Detester of Hypocrisy, *To that fanatical, political, physical, enthusiast*; 492-Gr. Caleb Evans, *Political sophistry detected* (Bristol: W. Pine, 1776); 491B-Fi. Member of the Rev. Mr. Wesley's Society, *The Rev. John Fletcher's arguments . . . considered* (Bristol: W. Pine, 1776); 492D-Fi. William Moore, *The address for blood and devastation* (London: for the author by T. W. Shaw, [1776]).

97 See, particularly, 496-Gr. Rowland Hill, *Imposture detected and the dead vindicated* (London: T. Vallance, 1777), 7, 33–34. The seven satirical poems of 1778–79: 516-Gr. [Combe], *The saints*; 517-Gr. [Combe], *Perfection: A poetical epistle*; 518-Gr. [Combe], *The temple of imposture*; 519-Gr. [Combe], *The love-feast*; 520-Gr. Combe, *Sketches for tabernacle-frames*; 521-Gr. [Combe], *Fanatical conversion*; 523-Gr. [Combe], *Voltaire's ghost.* Combe's seven poems rehearsed with obvious relish all the old charges of 1775.

were English nonconformist clergy since they were in the main loyal Whigs politically and Calvinists theologically. Fervent in their support of the ideals of liberty, the right of resistance to tyranny, the power of the people, and freedom of expression, English Dissenters were outspoken in their defense of the American cause. They believed in the colonists' case and became strong critics of the British ministry's stand.[98]

Wesley's earliest antagonist, Caleb Evans, was also his prime opponent. His *Letter to the Rev. Mr. John Wesley* became the center of continuing controversy.[99] Due mainly to the controversy with each other, Evans and Wesley perfected the successive editions of their respective pamphlets. In addition to Wesley's counterattack, Evans's *Letter* drew John Fletcher, the Methodist leader's able lieutenant, into the battle. Evans and Fletcher traded shots in a series of pamphlets. To Fletcher's *Vindication* [of Wesley],[100] Evans responded angrily with *A reply.*[101] Fletcher's rejoinder, *American patriotism,*[102] was in turn answered by Evans in *Political sophistry.*[103] Lesser Methodist sympathizers also joined in the debate. An anonymous author came to Wesley's side with an eight-page *Defence.*[104] Wesley appended the pseudonymous author's *A Native of America, A calm address to Americanus* to his December 16 revised edition of *Calm address.*[105] Finally, Thomas Olivers, one of Wesley's preachers, came to his leader's side with *A full defence*, a response to the new edition of Evans's *Letter.*[106]

It was Evans who raised most of the principal objections to the arguments espoused in Wesley's *Calm address*. Although only two other pamphleteers acknowledged their indebtedness to Evans, others appear to have been

---

98 See Russell E. Richey, "Counter-Insurgency," *Drew Gateway* 41 (Winter 1971): 82–83.

99 482-Gr. Americanus [Caleb Evans], *A letter to the Rev. Mr. John Wesley, occasioned by his 'Calm address'* (1775). It was reissued in London by E. and C. Dilly the same year, 1775. Pine published this second edition. A "new edition" prefixed by Evans's "Observations on the Rev. Mr. Wesley's late reply" was issued by E. and C. Dilly, 1775.

100 John Fletcher, *A vindication of the Rev. Mr. Wesley's 'Calm address to our American colonies:' in some letters to Mr. Caleb Evans* (Dublin: Whitestone, 1776).

101 483-Gr. Caleb Evans, *A reply to the Rev. Mr. Fletcher's vindication of Mr. Wesley's 'Calm address.'*

102 John Fletcher, *American patriotism* (Shrewsbury, 1776).

103 492-Gr. Caleb Evans, *Political sophistry detected.*

104 *A Defence*, 2nd ed. (n.p.: no printer, 1775).

105 *A calm address to Americanus by a native of America* (London: R. Hawes, 1775).

106 Thomas Olivers, *A full defence of the Rev. John Wesley, in answer to the several personal reflections cast on that gentleman by the Rev. Caleb Evans in his observations on Mr. Wesley's later reply prefixed to his Calm address* (London: no printer, 1776 [1775]).

familiar with his *Letter* and were content to reiterate the issues he had raised.[107]

Some of the critical replies were serious attempts at logical and historical refutation of Wesley's central arguments, but most directed the weapon of satire at his propositions and reasoning, impugning his motives for printing the tract. Usually the pamphlet title set the tone for the attack. Some were, by and large, free from personal invective, the critique being clearly focused on the arguments.[108] Others were, however, neither cool nor impartial, but full of vituperation and satire.[109] A few published elaborate satiric attacks on Wesley's motives.[110] Even pamphlets that were not primarily satiric descended to invective and ridicule when discussing Wesley's person and purpose.[111] Calumny, name-calling, and scurrilous innuendo (bordering on libel) abounded. Wesley was denounced as a wolf in sheep's clothing, a madman, a chaplain in ordinary to the Furies, a cunning fox, a Jesuit in disguise, and a Jacobite traitor.[112]

Out of the mass of specific vilifications, five general accusations may be discerned: Wesley had plagiarized Johnson's tract, he was a turncoat, his motivation was suspect, his purpose was doubtful, and his dabbling in politics was unwelcome. Wesley's failure to acknowledge his indebtedness to Johnson in his first edition of *A Calm address* left him open to easy criticism. The discovery of plagiarism had been noted with scorn by Wesley's earliest pamphlet opponent, Caleb Evans.[113] Practically every succeeding critic joined Evans in a chorus of disapproval of Wesley's passing off whole sections of Johnson as his own. Various terms were used to describe the close

---

107   484-Gr. W. D. [W. Denham], *A [s]econd answer to Mr. John Wesley* (London: Wallace and Stonehouse, 1775). The author contended that Evans had "completely" answered Wesley. Nevertheless, in twenty–two pages he rehearsed the same charges that Evans had made. The author of *Political empiricism* in several places borrowed heavily from Evans.

108   483C-Ba. W.Y., *A serious answer to Mr. Wesley's 'Calm address'*; 485A-Ba. [Sutcliff], *Political propositions*; 483A-Ba. Juniolus, *Fallacy detected.*

109   481-Gr. T. S., *A cool reply to 'A calm address'*; 486A-Ki. A Friend to the People and Their Liberties, *A full and impartial examination of the Rev. Mr. John Wesley's address.*

110   479-Gr. A Hanoverian [Toplady], *An old fox tarr'd and feather'd*; 493-Gr. Bull, *A wolf in sheep's cloathing; or An old Jesuit unmasked* (London: Mary Trickett, [1777]).

111   480-Gr. *A constitutional answer to the Rev. Mr. John Wesley's 'Calm address'*; 482-Gr. Americanus [Evans], *A letter to the Rev. Mr. John Wesley.*

112   493-Gr. Bull, *A wolf in sheep's cloathing*, 6, 11; 479-Gr. A Hanoverian [Toplady], *An old fox tarr'd and feather'd*, where Wesley is depicted on the title page as a grinning fox in clerical gown and bands; 473-Gr. [Towers], *Elihu's reply*, 19; 485-Ba. [Sutcliff], *Political propositions*, 28–29.

113   482-Gr. [Evans], *A letter to the Rev. Mr. John Wesley, occasioned by his 'Calm address,'* 2.

relationship between the two tracts. Wesley had "borrowed" from Johnson; he was guilty of "literary theft"; he was a "dealer in stolen wares"; he had "pirated Johnson's tract."[114]

The most elaborate attack on Wesley's plagiarism came in Toplady's *An old fox tarr'd and feather'd,* which appeared in November 1775. Half the tract is devoted to setting out passages from Johnson and Wesley side by side to demonstrate that Johnson's pamphlet was "the very hole of the pit, from which Mr. Wesley has dug and fetch'd up his own."[115] The pseudonymous Patrick Bull, in his imaginative satire, accounted for the similarities between the two tracts by creating the fiction that both had been written by the ghost of Father Petre, the Jesuit confessor of James II.[116]

If there were those opponents who were convinced that Wesley, in extracting *Taxation no tyranny,* had ruined its grandiloquent style, there were others who correctly perceived that what Wesley had done in simplifying the language of the original tract and abbreviating it was to provide the pamphlet with a wider reading public and increase its influence.[117] Indeed, the author of *Political empiricism* believed that Johnson's tract, had Wesley not "undertook to lop off its luxuriant branches . . . and to condense its diffuse and flowing periods," would have been destined to oblivion. By editing it Wesley had brought it within "the reach of the weaker brethren."[118] Such opponents attacked Wesley for his uncritical dissemination of Johnson's arguments, swallowing, as Toplady complained, "the pamphlet by wholesale, errors and all."[119]

Opponents believed that the plagiarist was without principles. Toplady depicted Wesley musing to himself after purchasing a copy of Johnson's tract: "What a man buys and pays for is certainly his own, therefore, this tract is no longer its author's but mine. Consequently, I shall do no evil if I gut the

---

114 479-Gr. A Hanoverian [Toplady], *An old fox tarr'd and feather'd,* 31; 486-Gr. *Political empiricism,* 4; 496-Gr. Hill, *Imposture detected and the dead vindicated,* 7; 483D-Ki. *Resistance no rebellion,* 2; 480-Gr. *A constitutional answer to the Rev. Mr. John Wesley's Calm address,* 3.

115 479-Gr. A Hanoverian [Toplady], *An old fox tarr'd and feather'd,* 2, 8–19.

116 493-Gr. Bull, *A wolf in sheep's cloathing; or, An old Jesuit unmasked,* 8–9.

117 To the Reverend Mr. W———, *London Magazine,* December 1775; 496-Gr. Hill, *Imposture detected and the dead vindicated,* 7; 520-Gr. [Combe], *Sketches for tabernacle-frames,* 20.

118 486-Gr. *Political empiricism,* 7, 13; 493-Gr. Bull. *A wolf in sheep's cloathing; or, An old Jesuit unmasked,* 8–9.

119 479-Gr. [Toplady], *An old fox tarr'd and feather'd,* 15.

substance of it and republish it under my own name."[120] Another author satirically praised Wesley's wisdom in not acknowledging Johnson, thereby being able not only to accept what commendation the *Address* received, but also to shift the blame, if criticism eventuated, by a quick announcement that it was really the doctor's work.[121]

The consistency of Wesley's political principles also came under heavy fire. Again it was Caleb Evans who first noted Wesley's sudden and dramatic change of attitude toward the American colonists by lifting out passages from Wesley's 1770 tract *Free thoughts* and comparing them with the sentiments expressed in the *A calm address*.[122] Evans pointed out that Wesley had not only recommended Parker's *Argument* to several of his followers but had on a number of occasions spoken favorably of the colonists, urging Bristol Methodists to vote in the parliamentary elections of 1771 for candidates who favored conciliation with the colonies. Unable to reconcile Wesley's new views with his former actions, Evans concluded that the Methodist leader had feigned his earlier support of the colonies in an attempt to infiltrate the ranks of those who dissented from the ministry's position.[123]

Wesley's alleged political inconsistency became a repeated target. Toplady flung the epithet "turn-coat" at Wesley, implying that by changing sides he had betrayed a noble cause. The Anglican evangelical expressed no surprise at Wesley's shift in loyalties, suggesting that the Methodist leader was, after all, a weathercock, easily moved by changing winds.[124] The author of *Political empiricism* was likewise not surprised by Wesley's altered political stance. If the Methodist leader believed in instantaneous religious conversion, why not sudden political conversion?[125] Patrick Bull satirically suggested that Wesley was "so inconsistent in his principles, that we may in a few days, expect from him a vindication of the Americans and a satire upon the administration."[126] The charge of political instability continued to plague Wesley. The author of

---

120 Ibid., 4.
121 486-Gr. *Political empiricism*, 8.
122 482-Gr. [Evans], *A letter to the Rev. Mr. John Wesley, occasioned by his 'Calm Address,'* 2.
123 Ibid., 23.
124 479-Gr. A Hanoverian [Toplady], *An old fox tarr'd and feather'd*, 2, 21.
125 486-Gr. *Political empiricism*, 9.
126 493-Gr. Bull, *A wolf in sheep's cloathing*, 10.

Methodism and popery dissected wrote in 1779 that Wesley "never stuck close to one [political] opinion forty hours."[127]

In attempting to understand Wesley's political reorientation in the *Calm address*, most opponents sought motives that would provide an easy explanation for the change. Almost all disputants implied that Wesley did not really believe the arguments he espoused but printed them for reasons of personal gain. Another suggestion was that Wesley feared the expulsion of Methodists from America if the colonies won independence. The only way to ensure that his societies would continue across the Atlantic was to support the government in its efforts to crush the colonists.[128] A further suggestion was that, by serving the government as a political pamphleteer, Wesley was attempting to atone for past seditious statements.[129]

Two base motives were attributed by numerous critics—financial gain and episcopal aspiration. The writer of *Political empiricism* suggested that Wesley was out for a quick penny. Wesley deliberately set the price for his tract at two pence so that it might have a large sale among his multitudinous followers. The same author went on to imply that Wesley was on the government's payroll, arrangements for which had been made by the Earl of Dartmouth, friend of the Countess of Huntingdon, and patron of the evangelical clergy.[130] If some writers hinted broadly that there had been a financial arrangement between Wesley and the British Ministry, others stated it as a fact. Toplady, and the author of *A constitutional answer to the Rev. Mr. John Wesley's 'Calm address,'* labeled Wesley a "court sycophant."[131] The author of *Resistance no rebellion* contended that Wesley, having "bartered a fair reputation and a good conscience for a bribe," was one of a "number of mercenary writers" employed by the Ministry.[132] The accusation that Wesley's political dealings were corrupted by financial motivation persisted. The satiric poet Combe suggested that Wesley's political wavering in the 1770s had been "check'd

---

127 522-Gr. *Methodism and popery dissected and compared,* 58. See also 520-Gr. [Combe], *Sketches for tabernacle-frames,* 14.

128 486-Gr. *Political empiricism,* 25.

129 496-Gr. Hill, *Imposture detected and the dead vindicated,* 33–34.

130 486-Gr. *Political empiricism,* 20, 31; cf. 475-Gr. Americus, "Letter to Mr. John Wesley," *Gentleman's Magazine,* December 1775, 564.

131 479-Gr. A Hanoverian [Toplady], *An old fox tarr'd and feather'd,* 5; 480-Gr. *A constitutional answer to the Rev. Mr. John Wesley's 'Calm address,'* 22.

132 483D-Ki. *Resistance no rebellion,* 3.

by the canker of a courtly bribe" in 1775.[133] A critic who signed his name "Americus" accused Wesley of having "one eye upon a pension and the other upon heaven; one had stretched out to the K—g and the other raised up to God. I pray the first may reward you and that the last may forgive you."[134]

The second major motive Wesley's opponents attributed to him was his alleged insatiable desire for elevation to the episcopate. Augustus Toplady was the first to stigmatize Wesley as an unprincipled preferment seeker, hoping to "slip into an English Cathedral or (at least) be appointed to the first American Bishoprick."[135] The author of *A full and impartial examination* believed that Wesley had his eye on a particular episcopal see in America—Boston.[136] Another author thought that a Canadian diocese might be more appropriate, since Methodism was a "species of popery" and Parliament had passed (in 1774) the Quebec Act, permitting a measure of freedom to the Roman Catholic Church in Canada.[137] Patrick Bull agreed that Wesley had chosen Canada, but satirically suggested that instead of a miter, Wesley deserved a nightcap "which in justice ought to be drawn over his eyes."[138]

Wesley's adversaries, claiming that his intention was to stir up the English public against the colonies, delighted in a play on the title of his tract. By contrast with the title, they pointed out, the contents of the *calm address* were far from being calm. It was impossible, said Americus, for an inveterate enthusiast to be calm about anything.[139] John Towers depicted Wesley, "olive branch in mouth, stir[ring] up the people of England to shed the blood of their brethren."[140] Instead of attempting to reconcile differences between the ministry and the Americans, Wesley had become, said another, an "incendiary" inflaming the populace.[141] Others were certain that the *Calm address* was

---

133 520-Gr. [Combe], *Sketches for tabernacle-frames*, 4.
134 475-Gr. Americus, "A letter to Mr. John Wesley on his Address to the Americans," 1775. It appeared in *Gentleman's Magazine*, 1775, 564.
135 479-Gr. A Hanoverian [Toplady], *An old fox tarr'd and feather'd*, 3–5.
136 486A-Ki. A Friend to the People and Their Liberties, *A full and impartial examination of the Rev. Mr. John Wesley's address*, 29–30.
137 481-Gr. T. S., *A cool reply to a 'Calm Address,'* 4–5.
138 493-Gr. Bull, *A wolf in sheep's cloathing*, 22–23.
139 Americus, "A letter to Mr. John Wesley on his Address to the Americans," *Gentleman's Magazine*, December 1775, 564.
140 473-Gr. [Towers], *Elihu's reply*, 19.
141 486A-Ki. A Friend to the People and their Liberties, *A full and impartial examination of the Rev. Mr. John Wesley's address*, 29.

among the most inflammatory political tracts ever composed.[142] The author of *Political empiricism* conceded that Wesley's aim might have been reconciliation, but the *Calm address* was ill suited to achieving this end. If Wesley had wanted to quench a fire, he ought to have poured water on the flames, rather than oil.[143] Satiric criticism of the pamphlet's title haunted Wesley. Combe played upon the title in three of his seven satires.[144]

A number of critics joined in censuring Wesley for turning politician. Caleb Evans, reminding Wesley of his earlier statements in his 1770 *Free thoughts*: "I am no politician: politics lie quite out of my province," posed the question: "How comes Mr. John Wesley, who was then no politician, to commence one now?"[145] Toplady, with characteristic virulence, likened Wesley to "a low and puny tadpole in divinity which proudly seeks to dis-embowel an high and mighty whale in politics."[146] Another author suggested that Wesley was too old (he was seventy-two) to suddenly become embroiled in politics.[147] Others expressed disappointment in the Methodist leader for not sticking to his religious duties, where he had done some good.[148]

Wesley's dabbling in politics was not forgotten. The anonymous satirist suggested, in *Tyranny the worst taxation*, that Wesley's role in extracting Johnson's pamphlet was to provide religious sanction to the corrupt political theories of an eighteenth-century Machiavelli.[149] Combe depicted Wesley "beating his drum for murd'rers to enlist."[150] In another of his poems, he elaborated the theme that Wesley was a ruthless and merciless priestly politician akin to Samuel and Innocent III.[151] In a third poem, refusing to let the

---

142 493-Gr. Bull, *A wolf in sheep's cloathing*, 11; 475-Gr. Americus, *A letter to the Rev. Mr. John Wesley on his address to the Americans*, 6.

143 486-Gr. *Political empiricism*, 16.

144 Part of the title of 517-Gr. *Perfection* read, "*Calmly addressed to the greatest hypocrite in England.*" In the text of the satire (page 36), the author accused Wesley of a "Massacre of Mankind with 'Calm address.'" Cf. 519-Gr. [Combe], *The love-feast*; 323-Gr. [Combe], *Voltaire's ghost*, 45.

145 482-Gr. Americanus [Evans], *A letter to the Rev. Mr. John Wesley, occasioned by his 'Calm address,'* reissued ed. by Edward and Charles Dilly, advertisement, 2. See John Wesley, *Free Thoughts on the Present State of Public Affairs*, in *Works* (Jackson), 11:14.

146 479-Gr. A Hanoverian [Toplady], *An old fox tarr'd and feather'd*, 3.

147 481-Gr. T. S., *A cool reply to a Calm address*, 3.

148 480-Gr. *A constitutional answer to the Rev. Mr. John Wesley's 'Calm address,'* 22; 485-Gr. A Lover of Truth, *A letter to the Rev. Mr. John Wesley on his 'Calm address,'* 1.

149 505A-Ki, The author of *Royal perseverance, Tyranny the worst taxation*, 22.

150 516-Gr. [Combe], *The saints*, 28.

151 518-Gr. [Combe], *The temple of imposture*, 32.

caricature fade, the author put Wesley at the head of a parade, beating a "martial drum" and whining "church militant!"[152] Though most opponents chose to call names, accusing Wesley and his able defender John Fletcher of sophistry, rather than refute the arguments laid out in the *Calm address*, some sought to refute its chief propositions.

Wesley's critics defended the colonists' cry, "No taxation without representation," as vigorously as he had opposed it. They rejected the comparison Wesley had drawn between the Americans and the English who did not have a vote. Evans pointed out that the majority of nonvoters in England were women, minors, leaseholders, or poor. The Americans who sought representation, however, did not fit into these categories.[153] An author who signed his pamphlet "W. Y." contested Wesley's argument that those who left England to settle the colonies thereby had given up their right to representation. If they had lost their freehold in England, surely, they had gained another in America.[154] At stake, the critics believed, was a fundamental principle of English government—the right of people to grant their taxes. The ministry's policy of taxing the colonies without their consent, insisted the author of *A full and impartial examination,* was antithetical to the British constitution:

> The taking of people's money without their consent is treating them, I think, inconsistently with the spirit of the British Constitution. If the Americans are to be deemed a part of the British subjects they ought in all reason to enjoy the privileges of such[;] i.e. they ought to grant their own money and consent to their own laws.[155]

Taxation without representation amounted to taxation without consent, and taxation without consent was tantamount to slavery.[156]

---

152 525F-Ki. [William Combe], *A sketch of the times* (London: J. Bew, 1780), 30–31.

153 492-Gr. Evans, *Political sophistry detected,* 4; 482-Gr. Americanus [Evans], *A letter to the Rev. Mr. John Wesley occasioned by his 'Calm address,'* 12–13; 485-Gr. A Lover of Truth [Hibbert], *A letter to the Rev. Mr. John Wesley on his 'Calm address to the American colonies,'* 11.

154 483C-Ba. W. Y., *A serious answer to Mr. Wesley's 'Calm address,'* 11.

155 486A-Ki. A Friend to the People and their Liberties, *A full and impartial examination of the Rev. Mr. John Wesley's Address,* 10; 481-Gr. T. S., *A cool reply to 'A calm address,'* 27.

156 482-Gr. Americanus [Evans], *A letter to the Rev. Mr. John Wesley, occasioned by his 'Calm address,'* 3–4, 8; 481-Gr. T. S., *A cool reply to 'A calm address,'* 27.

Having refused to accept Wesley's parallel between the colonists and unenfranchised English people, the critics suggested an analogy: Were not the American colonies much like Ireland? If the Irish parliament had been allowed to raise its own taxes, why should not the colonial assemblies have the same right? [157]

From the question of the legality of the government's policy, Wesley's opponents moved to a critique of the morality of the ministry's position. Four specific questions were raised: (1) If England had neglected the colonies for more than a century, giving them little or no assistance until the war against the French, did she now have the moral right to impose taxation upon them?[158] (2) Had not the colonies paid their fair share in the war against the French by raising money and troops?[159] (3) Was not taxation of the colonies unfair, when Britain's trade monopoly with America brought into England a large revenue, more than enough to pay their share of their protection?[160] (4) Would American taxes be used for the defense of the colonies, or would they be squandered in England upon placemen and pensioners?[161]

To Johnson's arguments, Wesley had added his own explanation of the causes leading to the unrest in England and the colonies. Both at home and in America, Wesley contended, those who hated the monarchy had stirred up others in order to bring about the separation of the colonies from the mother country. With England's troops across the Atlantic absorbed in the crisis in the colonies, republican agitators at home, Wesley feared, might engineer a

---

157 482-Gr. Americanus [Evans], *A letter to the Rev. Mr. John Wesley, occasioned by his 'Calm address,'* 15–16; 483C-Ba. W. Y., *A serious answer to Mr. Wesley's 'Calm address,'* 16; 485-Gr. Lover of Truth, *A letter to the Rev. Mr. John Wesley,* 4–5.

158 480-Gr. *A constitutional answer to the Rev. Mr. John Wesley's 'Calm address,'* 4, 16; 482-Gr. Americanus [Evans], *A letter to the Rev. Mr. John Wesley, occasioned by his 'Calm address,'* 18–19; 483C-Ba. W. Y., *A serious answer to Mr. Wesley's 'Calm address,'* 17.

159 486A-Ki. A Friend to the People and their Liberties, *A full and impartial examination of the Rev. Mr. John Wesley's Address,* 18; 481-Gr. T. S., *A cool reply to 'A calm address,'* 28–9; 485-Gr. A Lover of Truth [Hibbert], *A letter to the Rev. Mr. John Wesley on his 'Calm address,'* 3.

160 482-Gr. Americanus [Evans], *A letter to the Rev. Mr. John Wesley, occasioned by his 'Calm address,'* 19–20; 485D-Ki. *Resistance no rebellion,* 28–29; 485-Gr. A Lover of Truth [Hibbert], *A Letter to the Rev. Mr. John Wesley, on his 'Calm address to the American Colonies,'* 9–10; 486A-Ki. A Friend to the People and their Liberties, *A full and impartial examination of the Rev. Mr. John Wesley's Address,* 10.

161 481-Gr. T. S., *A cool reply to 'A calm address,'* 10–12; 486A-Ki. A Friend to the People and their Liberties, *A full and impartial examination of the Rev. Mr. John Wesley's Address,* 71; 485-Gr. A Lover of Truth [Hibbert], *A letter to the Rev. Mr. John Wesley, on his 'Calm address,'* 9–10.

successful revolution, removing the monarch.[162] This impugning of the patriotism and loyalty to the monarchy of those who supported the colonists' cause resulted in furor and was, no doubt, the reason for the large number of pamphlets attacking Wesley's tract. Critics hurriedly and heatedly denied that pro-American Englishmen were anti-monarchists. Wesley's accusation was labeled scandalous, and he was called upon to verify it and provide names.[163] Others ridiculed it:

> It is wonderful indeed, that a few men, at a distance of more than 2000 miles, should have been capable of raising a general spirit of discontent in so many colonies—That they should have armed an hundred thousand men on the other side of the Atlantic, and have stirred up new thousands at home even to madness that they should be using them as their tools to change the whole system of government, and that not one of their deluded followers either in America or England should have been able to penetrate their grand design: I would by all means advise this wonder-working gentleman to add a few embellishments to his story, and send it as a curious manuscript to the Vatican: It will cut a glorious figure amongst the numerous legends already laid up in that precious treasury.[164]

Supporters of the American colonists, the critics insisted, were the true patriots and lovers of the monarchy. Those like Wesley and Johnson who argued against the American cause were the real enemies of the English constitution, for they supported arbitrary rule. Such men were Jesuits and Jacobites; they were friends to the pope and the Stuart Pretender, and thus adversaries of the Hanoverians.[165] Wesley, then, was hailed by his critics as the defender of tyranny and the arch foe of the principles of the Glorious Revolution. His *Calm address* was caricatured as a feeble attempt to revive the Stuart doctrines of the divine right of kings, and nonresistance to the sovereign's arbitrary power. "W. Y." summed up the charge:

---

162 Wesley, *Works* (Jackson), XI: 86–88.

163 485-Gr. A Lover of Truth [Hibbert], *A letter to the Rev. Mr. John Wesley, on his 'Calm address,'* 6; 480-Gr. *A constitutional answer to the Rev. Mr. John Wesley's 'Calm address,'* 19–20; 484-Gr. W. D. [Denham], *A second answer to Mr. John Wesley,* 18.

164 486A-Ki. A Friend to the People and their Liberties, *A full and impartial examination of the Rev. Mr. John Wesley's Address,* 27. Cf. 493-Gr. Bull, *A wolf in sheep's cloathing,* 23–24.

165 481-Gr. T. S., *A cool reply to 'A calm address,'* 30; 483D-Ki. *Resistance no rebellion,* 32–33.

Our author's ill-tim'd zeal against a commonwealth may be easily and justly accounted for. He is a warm friend to absolute and hereditary monarchy and a bitter enemy to our present form of government by law established . . . [He supports] making the King of England as arbitrary as any prince in Europe: and giving him that illegal and unlimited power, which was claimed by the unhappy House of Stuarts.[166]

Patrick Bull suggested that the *Calm address* was a seditious treatise, written "in favor of the Pretender's title to prove that the present family has no right to the crown." A loyal subject, such as Wesley, could not have written it. The author, Bull alleged satirically, must have been the ghost of Father Edward Petre—James II's spiritual advisor. Only he could have advanced such a diabolical doctrine that "our lives, liberties, and property are all dependent on the Sovereign's will."[167] Nor did the *Calm address* stand alone. During the six years of the American Revolution, Wesley published no fewer than seven royalist pamphlets.[168] Unfavorable response to these, however, was slight—none evoked as much hostility as did the *Calm address*.[169]

There can be no doubt that the *Calm address* was one of the most significant pamphlets in the controversy that surrounded the government's conduct of American affairs. Coming as it did in the middle of an already-heated debate, it did much to fan the fires. Its effectiveness in setting forth the government's arguments in a clear and concise form that could be easily

---

166 483C-Ba. W. Y., *A serious answer to Mr. Wesley's 'Calm address,'* 18. Cf. 483D-Ki. *Resistance no rebellion,* 8, 12; 485A-Ba. [Sutcliff], *Political propositions,* 28–29; 485-Gr. A Lover of Truth and the British Constitution [Hibbert], *A letter to the Rev. Mr. John Wesley,* 7. Hibbert was a Manchester merchant and Unitarian.

167 493-Gr. Bull, *A wolf in sheep's cloathing,* 5, 18.

168 *A sermon preached at St. Matthew's Bethnal–Green on Sunday November 12, 1775, for the benefit of widows and orphans of the soldiers who lately fell near Boston* (1775); *Some observations on liberty* (1776); *A seasonable address to the more serious part of the inhabitants of Great Britain respecting the unhappy context between us and our American brethren* (1776); *A calm address to the inhabitants of England* (1777); *A serious address to the people of England with regard to the state of the nation* (1778); *An account of the conduct of the war in the middle colonies* (1780); *Reflections on the rise and progress of the American rebellion* (1780).

169 A hostile response to Wesley's *Some observations on liberty* (1776) came from James Murray in 492A-Ba. A Gentleman of Northumberland [Murray], *A compleat answer to Mr. Wesley's observations upon Dr. Price's essay on civil liberty.* To Wesley's *Calm address to the inhabitants of England* there were three rejoinders: 504A-Ba. W. J. [W. Jordon], *W. J. against J. W.* (n.p.: by the author, 1777); 505-Gr. Murray, *The finishing stroke to Mr. Wesley's 'Calm address;'* 504-Gr. Lofft, *Observations on Mr. Wesley's second calm address.*

assimilated by the reader led to its wide distribution in cheap editions, thus popularizing the ministry's position throughout the length and breadth of the land. Such a powerful pamphlet so extensively circulated could not go unchecked. Opponents of the government made every attempt in print to discredit Wesley and weaken his arguments.

CHAPTER 8

Methodists at Worship

M ost eighteenth-century Anglican divines would have nodded with approval at Thomas Church's use of the adjective *excellent* to describe
the Book of Common Prayer.[1] Along with the Thirty-nine Articles and the
Book of Homilies, the Prayer Book[2] was recognized by the church as one of
the three cardinal documents of the English Reformation. Not only was the
Prayer Book loved for the cadence of its phrases, but it stood as a theological
bulwark for the Church of England—a wall to protect it from heresy. Conformity to its use was established by an act of Parliament in 1662 that required
Anglican clergy, at the time of their ordination, to vow to use the liturgy in
the Church's services of worship.[3]

John Wesley held the Book of Common Prayer in high esteem—he
valued it only slightly less than the Bible.[4] The extent to which he revered it
is seen in his statement

> I believe there is no liturgy in the world, either in ancient or mod-
> ern language, which breathes more of a solid, scriptural, rational
> piety, than the [Book of] Common Prayer of the Church of England.
> And though the main of it was completed considerably more than
> two hundred years ago, yet is the language of it, not only pure,
> but strong and elegant in the highest degree.[5]

Throughout his ministry Wesley urged his lay preachers to read parts of
the service of Morning Prayer when neither he nor Charles was able to be
present. From the outset Wesley strongly discouraged his preachers from

---

1 165-Gr. Church, *A serious and expostulatory letter to the Rev. Mr. George Whitefield*, 17.
2 The Book of Common Prayer was often referred to informally as the Prayer Book.
3 The Parliamentary Act of Uniformity of 1662 prescribed the form of public prayers, the
  administration of the sacraments, and other rites of the Church of England as established
  in the Book of Common Prayer. See *Statutes of the Realm*, vol. 5, 1628–80, ed. John
  Raithby (s.l, 1819), 364–70. *British History Online*.
4 John Wesley, "A letter to Mr. Somebody, alias Philodemus, alias T. H.," December 1, 1760,
  in *BEWJW*, vol. 27, *Letters III*, ed. Ted A. Campbell, 220–23. Source: Public Transcription:
  'Lloyd's Evening Post,' December 1–3, 1760, 530.
5 See a notice dated at Bristol, September 9, 1784, appended to *John Wesley's Sunday Service
  of the Methodists in North America*, with an introduction by James F. White, *Methodist
  Bicentennial Commemorative Reprint* (Nashville: United Methodist Publishing House, 1984).

holding services during church hours—indeed, in 1766 he ordered a stop to such a practice and declared that Methodist worship on Sunday was to be held at 5 a.m. and 5 p.m. so as not to conflict with Anglican services.[6] Love for the Book of Common Prayer did not prevent Wesley, however, from establishing such innovative practices as extempore prayer and preaching, and ancillary worship experiences such as love feasts, watch nights, and covenant services, none of which superseded Anglican services but presupposed them.[7]

Denigration and Neglect of the Book of Common Prayer

Methodists, opponents believed, were either "curtailing and mangling" the Prayer Book, or totally setting it aside.[8] Such practices, they contended, fostered a depreciation of the liturgy, which inexorably led to the denigration of the Church itself. Bishop Horne noted that the practice of weekly prayers in parish churches was being neglected. At fault, he opined, was the Methodists' overemphasis on preaching—they attended church only to hear a sermon and were "indifferent, even on Sunday, to the prayers of the church."[9]

Fear that the Book of Common Prayer was being neglected lay behind Bishop Gibson's advice in his 1746–47 *Charge* to the diocese of London:

> The more active they [the Methodists] are in perswading the people, that the establish'd worship and service, with regular attendance upon it is not sufficient to answer the ends of devotion . . . the more diligent must the clergy be to inculcate into their people, on the one hand, the excellences of our liturgy, as a wise, grave, and serious service, wisely calculated for all the ends of devotion; and on the other hand, the folly of depreciating that, and a preferring to it the wild and indigested effusions of enthusiastical teachers.[10]

---

6 "Annual Minutes of some late conversations 1766," Question 28, in *BEWJW*, 10:326.

7 Ibid.

8 200-Gr. [Stebbing], *An earnest and affectionate address to the people called Methodists*, 35–36. By 1815 seventeen editions had been printed; 029-Gr. [Gibson], *The bishop of London's pastoral letter*, 15; 332A-Ba. [Dodd], *A conference between a mystic . . .*, 60–61.

9 556-Ki. George [Horne], *A charge intended to have been delivered to the clergy of the diocese of Norwich* (Norwich: Yarington and Bacon, 1791), 39.

10 206-Gr. [Gibson], *The charge of the Right Reverend Father in God, Edmund, Lord Bishop of London . . .1746 and 1747*, 24. An earlier expression of this fear is found in 043-Gr. Brownsword, *The case of the rich young man in the gospel*, 9.

Anti-Methodists maintained that the existence of the Church of England depended on conformity to the Prayer Book.[11] John Thomas spelled out the disastrous effect of not enforcing conformity: "There would soon, in all probability, be as many forms of public devotion as there are parish churches in this realm; and, probably, as little real vital Christianity, as is found in a journey to Mecca."[12]

Communion Practices

Throughout his life Wesley stressed the importance of frequent communion, but for many years Wesley resisted celebrating communion in Methodist preaching houses. In the early years of the revival, Wesley led large groups of his followers to parish churches in Bristol and London for Morning Prayer and the Lord's Supper. In 1743 Wesley began celebrating Holy Communion for his London societies in the old Huguenot Chapel in West Street, Seven Dials, London. Elsewhere, the practice of attending the parish church for communion continued. Wesley's procedure angered some clergy. Gibson claimed that it contravened Anglican Church law and thus technically disqualified the Methodists from communicating in this manner. In support of his claim, Gibson cited the rubric that enjoined parishioners to inform their intention to communicate a day in advance. Moreover, the twenty-eighth canon, which set out the duties of churchwardens, expressly forbade those from other parishes to receive the communion elements (bread and wine) except in their own parish churches. Occasional exceptions were permissible, but the Methodists, openly contemptuous of the regulations, made the exception the rule.

Gibson accused the Methodists of seeking "the vain pleasure of appearing together in a body and as a distinct sect."[13] Gibson's charge was seconded by one who signed his pamphlet "J. B." The Methodists left their own churches and "march[ed] openly in droves to others."[14] The author of *A short history of the Donatists* was not offended by the Methodists attending parish churches

---

11 037-Gr. *A plain address to the followers and favourers of the Methodists*, 7–8.
12 502-Gr. Thomas, *Two letters to the Rev. Thomas Coke*, 23.
13 164-Gr. [Gibson], *Observations upon the conduct and behaviour of . . . Methodists*, 5–6.
14 166-Gr. J. B./A Gentleman of Pembroke College, Oxon, *A letter to the Reverend Mr. Whitefield occasioned by his pretended answer to the first part of the 'Observations on the conduct and behaviour of the Methodists,'* 36.

for the sacrament, but by the practice of their receiving communion "now and then in Court-Houses instead of churches."[15]

Antagonists contended that the Methodists taught that preparation on the part of the communicant was not necessary before participating in the Lord's Supper. Wesley had written in his fourth journal: "There is no previous preparation indispensably necessary, but a desire to receive whatsoever He pleases to give . . . No fitness is required at the time of communicating, but a sense of our state of our utter sinfulness and helplessness; everyone who knows he [or she] is fit for hell being just fit to come to Christ."[16] Bishop Gibson suggested that these words could be interpreted to mean that self-examination, repentance for past sins, and a resolution to live a better life were unnecessary before the communicant came to the Lord's table. This would be contrary to the Prayer Book's exhortations. In ordinary circumstances, Gibson noted, "where there is leasure and opportunity for it, a previous preparation is necessary." As Wesley's statement stood, Gibson believed, it assumed that the communicant was purely passive. This "makes the sacrament and the benefits convey'd by it to look more like a charm than a reasonable service, and a truly spiritual performance on our part."[17] George Lavington pushed the issue even farther. The passivity of the communicant, he said, was a popish doctrine: "[T]he efficacy of the sacrament is produced; as it were by charm, ex opere operato, i.e. from the mere doing of the work, without any regard to the fitness of the receiver."[18]

Wesley believed that the sacrament could be a converting ordinance, that communicants did not have to possess assurance of faith before they partook of the elements. Thomas Church found this tenet exceedingly dangerous—the Church of England communion ritual presupposed the communicant to have faith. By rejecting the prerequisite of faith, Wesley had opened the table to the worst of sinners, who could come without any repentance or resolve to amend their lives.[19] The Baptist Gilbert Boyce agreed and took Wesley to task on this issue: "The persons for whom the Lord's Supper was ordained, are all those who are renewed in the image

---

15 118-Gr. Trevor, *A short history of the Donatists*, 34.

16 Wesley, June 28, 1740, *Journal and Diaries II* (1738–1743) in *BEWJW*, 19:52.

17 206-Gr. [Gibson], *The charge, of the Right Reverend Father in God, Edmund Lord Bishop of London*, 19.

18 213-Gr. [Lavington], *The enthusiasm of the Methodists and papists compar'd*, pt. 2, 153.

19 185-Gr. Church, *Remarks on the Rev. Mr. John Wesley's last journal*, 56–57.

of God, whose sins are forgiven, and who are restrained from sin by the grace of God."[20]

A further criticism alleged that Wesley altered the liturgy when celebrating the sacrament. Henry Stebbing claimed that the Methodists omitted part of the sentences for distributing the elements. They customarily pronounced only the words "The Body of our Lord Jesus Christ" and "The Blood of our Lord Jesus Christ."[21] Stebbing implied that the Methodists, in leaving out the remainder of what was prescribed in the rubric, practiced the Roman Catholic doctrine of transubstantiation.[22] From the Calvinist wing of Methodism came the allegation that Wesley omitted the prayer of general confession from the communion service, since it was "so ill suiting so angelic a company."[23]

The Methodist behavior at communion services was not beyond reproach. Lavington complained about bizarre occurrences. Although the majority of communicants were serious and devout, there were some who carried their devotion to extremes by falling into ecstasy at the communion rail.[24] Some interrupted the services by calling out to the minister or by stomping out of the church. Others would slip the bread into their pockets if they were not watched. Lavington claimed he spoke from "personal knowledge" of such irreverent behavior.[25]

Extempore Prayer

Serious critics reported that Methodists not only altered the liturgy and disregarded certain parts of the rubrics but rejected the Book of Common Prayer in

---

20 428-Gr. Boyce, *A serious reply to the Rev. Mr. John Wesley*, 100–101.

21 The full text in the Book of Common Prayer for the distribution of the elements read, "The Body of our Lord Jesus Christ, which was given for thee, preserve thy body and soul unto everlasting life. Take and eat this in remembrance that Christ died for thee, and feed on him in thy heart by faith, with thanksgiving. The Blood of our Lord Jesus Christ, which was shed for thee, preserve thy body and soul unto everlasting life. Drink this in remembrance that Christ's blood was shed for thee and be thankful."

22 200-Gr. [Stebbing], *An earnest and affectionate address to the people called Methodists*, 35.

23 449-Gr. The author of *P. O.* [Hill], *A review of all the doctrines taught by Mr. Wesley*, 60. See also 591C-Fi. Richard Polwhele, *A third letter on the itinerancy and non-conformity of the vicar of Charles, Plymouth* (London: printed for Cadell and Davies, and Chapple, 1800).

24 Bizarre behavior in Methodist preaching services will be dealt with later in this chapter.

25 213-Gr. [Lavington], *The enthusiasm of the Methodists and papists compar'd*, pt. 2, 127–28.

their ordinary services in favor of extempore prayer.[26] Wesley and Whitefield were reminded that the Prayer Book service was, by law, the liturgy of the Church and were bound by their ordination vows to use it and no other.[27]

Antagonists believed that extempore prayer was a manifestation of enthusiasm. The Methodists presumed, it was alleged, when praying extempore, to be open to the immediate dictates of the Holy Spirit. Furthermore, they claimed, the Methodists eschewed all preparation for praying in public services except "purging their minds of all thought and reason," so that "the impulses of the Spirit may be the more energetic."[28] Extempore prayer was not the result of the Holy Spirit's dictation, anti-Methodists averred; it was an acquired skill.[29] Theophilus Evans explained it as an "accomplished ability . . . gained by study and imitation, the effect of nature and art, a good memory, and a voluble tongue, improved by a right method of digesting their thoughts, a stock of Scripture phrases, a natural warmth of temper, and a convenient boldness and presence of mind."[30] Thomas Green seconded Evans's explanation. The Methodists were blessed with good memories and fluent utterance.[31]

Because the early church had practiced extempore prayer was no justification for its contemporary use, critics argued. By the close of the apostolic age, the Christian church had composed its liturgies and the need for extempore prayer had passed.[32] The primitive church had good reasons for establishing set forms of prayer. One was to prevent heretical statements that could creep into extempore prayers through ignorance or haste.[33] Another was to maintain due reverence in worship. Extempore prayer destroyed the beauty and dignity of religious services. It was an impious affront to the Almighty, Thomas Green opined: "[W]hen persons appear before God in public to offer whatever comes into their mind, this is, I think, making too

---

26 049-Gr. Church, *An explanation and defence of the doctrine of the Church of England*, 60; 165-Gr. Thomas Church, *A serious and expostulatory letter to the Rev. Mr. George Whitefield* (London: for M. Cooper, 1774), 17; 029-Gr. [Gibson], *The bishop of London's pastoral letter*, 15; 167-Gr. [Smalbroke], *A charge deliver'd to the. . . clergy in . . . the diocese of Lichfield, 1741*, 19–20; 200-Gr. A. B. [Stebbing], *An earnest and affectionate address to the people called Methodists*, 35–36.

27 200-Gr., 35–36.

28 398-Gr. W.C., *Remarks on the Reverend Mr. Whitefield's letter to the vice-chancellor*, 29.

29 029-Gr. [Gibson], *The bishop of London's pastoral letter*, 15.

30 235-Gr. [Evans], *The history of modern enthusiasm*, xv.

31 249A-Fi. Green, *A dissertation on enthusiasm*, 15.

32 034-Gr. Bate, *Methodism displayed or remarks on Mr. Whitefield's answer*.

33 249A-Fi. Green, *A dissertation on enthusiasm*, 31.

free with the divine majesty."[34] The length, repetitiousness, and arrogance of the extempore prayers uttered by the Methodists, and the fact that they often prayed in the open air before large crowds, reminded some critics of the New Testament Pharisees. As Jesus had condemned the prayers of the Pharisees, antagonists believed that the extempore effusions of the Methodists would similarly meet with divine disapprobation.[35] The length of extempore prayers was often a target. In Lucifer's satirical lectures, Lucifer urged the Methodists to continue the practice of extempore prayer:

> Let your prayers be of an extraordinary length, that so the younger folks may be laid to sleep, and the rest be forced to turn their eyes and thoughts upon some new objects, in order to keep themselves awake. You need not be much concerned for materials to prolong your prayers, there are some phrases and expressions which you may repeat twenty times over, with a little variation; it will help to cheat those-over-religious persons, who think that a great deal of devotion lies in speaking over those and such-like words; and those of more discernment will be offended and they will entirely neglect your house of worship; thus will my interest be promoted.[36]

The character of the petitions in extempore prayer was cause for ridicule. One author, reminding his readers of the similarities between the extempore prayers of the Methodists and those of the Puritans, published what he claimed was a record of a Puritan's daily conversation with God. It was full of petitions for such mundane matters as a good price for the cattle he was selling, the cure of two animals that were ill, the settling of a dispute over the division of a deceased friend's estate, and rain in a time of drought.[37] Extempore prayer, James Buller claimed, was ephemeral. The Book of Common Prayer would endure, while the use of extempore prayer would disappear:

> A little novelty is well pleasing to most, but more especially to the vulgar. A fricasy or a minc'd pye may please squeamish stomachs,

---

34 Ibid. See also 536A-Ki. Croft, *Eight sermons preached before the University of Oxford*, 166.
35 See 037-Gr. *A plain address to the followers and favourers of the Methodists*, 10–12; 360A-Fi. John Harman, *Remarks upon the life, character and behaviour of the Rev. George Whitefield* (London: by the author, 1764), 44–45.
36 575D-Fi. *Lucifer's lectures; or, the infernal tribune*, 25.
37 024-Gr. *Enthusiasm no novelty* (London: T. Cooper, 1739), 3–45.

better than a good piece of beef; but I hope the latter, as well as our most excellent liturgy will remain two standing dishes, never out of fashion in these dominions.[38]

Extempore Preaching

Another innovative practice anti-Methodists condemned was extempore preaching. Again, enthusiasm was seen as the source: "[Y]our off-hand harangues [are] a mere enthusiastick rant, a wild rhapsody of non-sense, the foam of an over-heated imagination, like old wives' fables, or profane and vain babblings."[39] The Methodists were alleged to claim immediate inspiration as the genesis of their sermons. One critic contended that he had read that Whitefield spent no time in preparing his sermons, as other clergy did, but preached what was dictated to him by the Holy Spirit. Inspiration "flowed upon him as fast as he could utter it."[40] John Greenwood parodied "spiritual" preachers:

> Their spiritual and powerful way of preaching and praying . . . is but a nauseous, or at best a vicious pronunciation, and mere counterfeit eloquence . . .The most ignorant, unbred and unthinking people, who think, yea, are assured in their own giddy, weak minds, that they hear a most able, powerful and spiritual-gifted preacher if his voice be sharp, quavering, as tho' he sung, if he draw out some of his words with a mournful accent, or hideous tones, if he strains his sides and lungs, din and rave . . . distort his mouth and lips . . . beat on his breast and pulpit as tho' he was in fits.[41]

Robert Potter attacked the Methodists for "profaning the sacred character of a prophet by their wretched mimicries [and laying] claim to a particular and immediate inspiration in those nauseous effusions wherewith they harangue their infatuated followers."[42]

---

38 258-Gr. Buller, *A reply to the Rev. Mr. Wesley's 'Address to the clergy,'* 22, 166.

39 398-Gr. W.C., *Remarks on the Reverend Mr. Whitefield's letter to the vice chancellor,* 32.

40 148-Gr. A True Lover of the Church and Country, *Some observations upon the conduct of the famous Mr. W____field,* 4.

41 491-Ki. John Cox Greenwood, *Remarks on a wild oration, or funeral sermon, in memory of William Austin, late a Methodist preacher at Bledlow . . . September 11, 1776 . . . Also some remarks . . . delivered at Thame, by the irreverend Mr. Well* [sic] (London: no printer, [1776]), 10–11.

42 272-Gr. Potter, *On the pretended inspiration of the Methodists,* 22–23.

Most critics of Methodism believed that the sole aim of preaching was edification—to shed light, not to generate heat.[43] They doubted if Methodist extempore expositions of the Scriptures could be very instructive. If homilies were to be informative, they needed to be well prepared and carefully preached from manuscript: "Scriptures must be properly applied, the difficulties of it explained, several texts carefully compared with one another to find out their true meaning and be so interpreted as to keep up a consistency in the whole."[44]

Although Wesley and Whitefield continued to prepare manuscript sermons on specific topics and texts, they looked upon extempore preaching as an invaluable tool for evangelism. John Douglas challenged the Methodists' insistence that the object of preaching was evangelism: "Now, I think, a preacher should take it for granted, that every one of his hearers is a sincere believer in Jesus Christ. The pulpit never was intended, and never can with any success, be made the place to instruct those who are ignorant of Christianity and its fundamental doctrines."[45] The author of *Lucifer's Lectures* urged the Methodist preachers to let their zeal exceed the bounds of moderation in order to manipulate their hearers' emotions:

> So long as it partakes of enthusiasm; I will allow you to strike the passion of those you preach to: but take care, and do not address yourselves to their understandings, nor rectify their judgments, nor purify the affections; be careful that your voices are well modelled; let them be nervous, raising them by degrees, as you see the people affected; let your sermons be full of raptures, and numberless O's!—let Christ!—'and the love of Christ!' be often repeated with an extraordinary emphasis . . . Then exalting your voice still more, shooting out your hands, and by other violent motions wind them up, by quick advances to the highest pitch of transport till . . . they sink down with a groan, which runs through the whole assembly; just like rattling thunder with cracks and breaks within all quarters.[46]

---

43 249A-Fi. Green, *A dissertation on enthusiasm*, 35–36.

44 Ibid., 24.

45 237-Gr. [Douglas], *An apology for the clergy, with a view to expose the groundless assertions of a late commentator,* 31.

46 575D-Fi. *Lucifer's lectures; or, the infernal tribune,* 27.

There was much about extempore preaching that disturbed more conventional pulpiteers. They claimed that sermons delivered extemporaneously lacked internal organization—there was a beginning and an end, but in between Methodist preachers wandered randomly from one subject to another. A purported example of a Methodist lay sermon is found in *A sermon upon turf*, a rambling, incoherent address. Exhortations, denunciations, personal reminiscences, and unrelated facts were all jumbled together.[47] One critic cited a Methodist preacher who "in the middle of exhorting the people to piety and works of salvation . . . start[ed] wide of his subject, and [told] how victorious Alexander was, and that the Great Mogul was the richest potentate in the world."[48] Two satirists ridiculed the practice by publishing what they claimed were extempore sermons copied down exactly as they had been spoken by Methodist preachers. Not only were their sermons disorganized; critics claimed that they were interminably long:

> 'Twas after a long lecture given.
> From which all gospel was quite driven
> and in its room were wond'rous tales,
> of storms, of providence, and whales;
> of saints made out of wicked sinners,
> 'till hearers' guts grumbled for dinners.[49]

Anti-Methodists were offended by the crude illustrations used in extempore sermons. John Harman attributed the following to George Whitefield:

> Where do you put your money for safety? Why in the bank (say you) to be sure: And what do you have for it? Bank notes. But what are those notes in comparison to these? Here's a book of God Almighty's bank notes; (holding up the Bible) who has got any money to put in? Here's a book filled with notes, which you may have given you for it this moment if you desire it. This bank is always open.[50]

Methodist preachers were accused of lacing their extemporaneous discourses with large doses of fear. An author writing in 1744 deplored the fact

---

47 469-Gr. A saint from the Tabernacle, *A sermon upon the turf*, passim.

48 154-Gr. Este, *Methodism display'd: a farce*, 15.

49 378-Gr. Paragraph *pseud.* [Adair], *The Methodist and mimick*, 6.

50 319-Gr. Harman, *The crooked disciple's remarks on the blind guide's method of preaching*, 33.

that "they thunder out from the pulpit threatenings, damnation, and frightening denounciations to the audience."[51] Moreover they allowed their imaginations to run riot in depicting in elaborate detail the horrors of hell to terrify their congregations. Helme quotes the Methodist preacher pleading with God to frighten sinners:

> Shake them, Lord, shake them over hell-fire in a sack, and if they will not repent of their unbelief and evil ways before the sack is burnt, then Lord let them fall in.[52]

Opponents attacked Whitefield's use of theatrical mannerisms while preaching extemporaneously—he used a voice loud enough to wake the dead; resorted to all kinds of flamboyant gestures to hide his lack of content; pounded the pulpit cushion, laughed, wept, waved his arms about in the air, and shook his head up and down.[53] John Harman described Whitefield in action "in an attitude similar to that of Ajax in Ovid's *Metamorphoses*":

> His body erect—his hands extended,—his face thrown upwards, with his eyes gazing towards the stars. Torvo vultu, tendens ad sidera palmas, alternately changing from his theatrical astonishments into violent enthusiastical agitations and distortions, accompanied with weeping, wailing and gnashing of teeth: Strange vicissitudes! which he strictly keeps up to throughout the whole of his preaching.[54]

Methodist preachers, John Brownsword claimed, encouraged attendance on their sermons so that they could show off their talents.[55] Harmon even suggested that Whitefield hired "hummers, sighers, and weepers" at two shillings and sixpence a week to respond audibly to his sermons.[56]

---

51 194-Gr. An Impartial Hand, *An essay containing evident proofs against the Methodists*, 17.

52 341C-Fi. Helme, *A specimen of preaching*, 12. See also 294-Gr. Academicus [Green], *The principles and practices of the Methodists considered*, 28–29; 560-Gr. Lackington, *Memoirs of the life . . . of James Lackington*, 84, 87–89.

53 487-Gr. A Member of the Church of England, *Naked thoughts on some of the peculiarities of the field-preaching clergy*, 2–7.

54 319-Gr. Harman, *The crooked disciple's remarks upon the blind guide's method of preaching*, 1.

55 043-Gr. Brownsword, *The case of the rich young man in the gospel*, 10.

56 319-Gr. Harman, *The crooked disciple's remarks upon the blind guide's method of preaching*, 44.

Ecstatic and Physical Reactions in Preaching Services

Few aspects of Methodist worship, in the early years of the revival, offended opponents' propriety as much as the bizarre physical agitations that accompanied Methodist conversions during preaching services.[57] Rational Anglicans were astonished by the accounts of conversion Wesley published in his *Journal*. In Wesley's description of Thomas Maxfield's conversion on May 21, 1739, they found ample material for objection:

> In the evening I was interrupted at Nicholas Street, almost as soon as I had begun to speak, by the cries of one who was 'pricked at the heart,' and strongly groaned for pardon and peace. Yet I went on to declare what God had already done, in proof of that important truth that 'he is not willing that any should perish, by that all should come to repentance.' Another person dropped down, close to one who was a strong asserter of the contrary doctrine. While she stood astonished at the sight, a little boy near him was seized in the same manner. A young man who stood behind fixed his eyes on him and sunk down himself as one dead, but soon began to roar out and beat himself against the ground, so that six men could scarcely hold him. His name was Thomas Maxfield. Except J[oh]n H[aydo]n, I never saw one so torn of the evil one. Meanwhile many others began to cry out to 'the Saviour of all,' that he would come and help them, in so much that all the house (and indeed all the street for some space) was in uproar. But we continued in prayer, and before ten the greater part found rest to their souls.[58]

Methodists referred to happenings like these as "pangs of the new birth." Opponents found such talk strange and unscriptural. The Bible nowhere recorded that violent physical convulsions or screaming fits were the usual accompaniment of conversion. "God is a God of order[,] not confusion," reminded one author.[59] Warburton, noting that Wesley sometimes attributed

---

57 Similar behavior occurred in the Great Awakening in America and elsewhere during the eighteenth century.

58 Wesley, May 21, 1739, in *BEWJW*, vol. 19, *Journal and Diaries II (1738–1743)*, 61. Maxfield's experience was just one of the 234 cases enumerated by Sydney Diamond in *The Psychology of the Methodist Revival: An Empirical and Descriptive Study* (London: Oxford University Press, 1926), 126–27. Diamond claims that these phenomena occurred only between 1739 and 1742. No glossolalia is recorded in Wesley's journals.

59 205C-Ki. [Dowars], *Errors in part discovered*, 9; 009-Gr. Land, *A letter to the Rev. Mr.*

the paroxysms accompanying conversion to God and sometimes to Satan, ridiculed the Methodists' apparent inability to distinguish between the work of the devil and that of the Holy Spirit.[60] Anti-Methodists could not accept the imputation of physical agitations to the agency of the Holy Spirit. Gibson suggested that "those sudden agonies, roarings and screamings, tremblings, droppings-down, ravings, and madnesses," recorded as a part of conversion in Wesley's journals, were not an indication that the Holy Spirit was present in them.[61] Thirty years later John Tottie echoed Gibson's sentiments:

> The operations of the Spirit are not violent and tempestuous, ag-
> itating the whole human frame and throwing it into convulsions,
> like the dispossession of a demoniac; nor are they ever attended
> with such derelictions, terrors, despairings, struggles and pangs,
> as are almost equal to the torments of hell—but they are so gentle
> and peaceable in their nature as they are in their effects, and . . .
> they cannot with certainty be discovered any other way than by
> the fruits which they produce.[62]

Anti-Methodists believed the convulsions had natural causes. Theophi-lus Evans argued that it was the content and means of delivery of Methodist sermons that raised "a ferment in the passions, often attended with screaming and trembling of the body."[63] An anonymous author suggested that the con-vulsions were staged.[64] Lavington agreed, satirically suggesting that Wesley trained accomplices to go into counterfeit convulsions when he preached.[65] William Combe believed there was another explanation—Wesley was drug-ging his converts:

Whitefield, 5; 249A-Fi. Green, A dissertation on enthusiasm, 118; 235-Gr. [Evans], The history of modern enthusiasm, 130.

60 342-Gr. [Warburton], The doctrine of grace, 231–32. Cf. 343-Gr. Rutherforth, Four charges to the clergy of the archdeaconry of Essex (Cambridge: printed for J. Bentham, 1763), 33–34.

61 164-Gr. [Gibson], Observations upon the conduct and behaviour of . . . Methodists, 10. Cf. The list of the "shocking and horrible" physical manifestations enumerated in 235-Gr. [Evans], The history of modern enthusiasm, 107: "crying out, screamings, roaring, groanings, trembling, yellings, convulsions, swooning, blasphemies, curses, despairing agonies, and variety of tortures in body and mind."

62 384-Gr. [Tottie], Two charges delivered to the clergy in the diocese of Worcester . . . 1763 and 1766, 356.

63 235-Gr. [Evans], The history of modern enthusiasm, 119.

64 174-Gr. Eusebius [Fleming], A fine picture of enthusiasm, 20–21.

65 213A-Ki. [Lavington], The enthusiasm of Methodists and papist compar'd, pt. 2, 170–90.

> . . . whence come these agitations,
> These frantic spasms in heaven's choice congregations?
> Why such is ev'ry convert's sad condition?
> I answer—'John's priest, wizard, and physician.
> Starved bodies with apt nostrums he controls,
> And with worse physic stupifies their souls.[66]

The Methodist insistence that conversion was necessary caused some to despair or go mad. One anti-Methodist author complained:

> Modern enthusiasts carry their fancies of instantaneous and irre-
> sistible grace so far as to suffer all religion to rest upon this one
> point, and poor pious, melancholy Christians, who cannot work
> themselves up into such heights, are delivered either to despair
> or madness.[67]

Bedlam, London's insane asylum, it was claimed, was filled with Method-ists. One author, noting that Methodists were beginning to erect buildings, suggested they build insane asylums instead of preaching houses, and so accommodate their converts who had gone mad: "I would recommend . . . the plan of a certain edifice founded by Dr. Swift which, if considerably augmented, may accommodate many of the religious mad in this country."[68]

Hymnody

The singing of hymns was one of the cardinal innovations of the Methodist revival. In 1737 John Wesley edited and published *A Collection of Psalms and Hymns.*[69] Before this collection there was no hymnbook specifically designed for congregational singing in Anglican churches.[70] In 1739 John Wesley began to share the responsibility of publishing with Charles, and

---

66 521-Gr. [Combe], *Fanatical conversion*, 28–29.

67 349-Gr. Hardy, *A letter from a clergyman to one of his parishioners who was inclined to turn Methodist*, 5.

68 232B-Ba. A Country Gentleman [William Evans], *A letter to the Rev. Mr. —re B—k—r*, 18–19. See also 222E-Fi. *A letter from the deists to the chief rulers amongst the Methodists*, 12–13.

69 *John Wesley's First Hymn–Book, A Facsimile with Additional Materials*, ed. Frank Baker and George Williams (Charleston: Dalcho Historical Society, and London: *WHS*, 1964).

70 Wilfred Douglas, *Church Music in History and Practice* (New York: Charles Scribner, 1937), 235.

accordingly Charles's name was added to an altered title page. From this beginning the two brothers continued to write and publish their hymns and encourage their converts to sing them. In the Wesleys' hymns the Methodists imprinted their theology on their hearts and minds. The hymns not only became an important way of teaching and informing the distinctive Methodist doctrinal emphases in those who sang them, but also of confirming and explaining their spiritual experiences by providing a context for their emotions[71] Wesley succinctly summed up the role of hymns in Methodism in his preface to *A Collection of Hymns for the Use of the People Called Methodist*: "This Book is, in effect, a little body of experimental and practical divinity."[72] The hymns addressed both head and heart, as seen in Joanna Cruickshank's examination of the role of suffering in Charles Wesley's hymns. She argues the hymns helped make sense of the physical, emotional, and spiritual pains the Methodists encountered and to see these experiences as a part of the divine plan of salvation.[73]

The practice of singing hymns received its share of censure. Both words and music came under fire as artistically and religiously inappropriate for corporate worship. The author of *A fine picture of enthusiasm* characterized the hymns as overly sentimental, and the relationship between the singer and God too familiar. Methodist hymns, the critic continued, present God as "much more friendly and compassionate to human beings than God the Father ever was." Many critics agreed; Methodist hymns were overemotional: "[T]heir singing is calculated to engage the passions by nothing more than words and the melody of the sounds or voices."[74]

Critics pointed to Charles Wesley's incomparable "Wrestling Jacob" as a pointed example of the Methodists' overfamiliarity with the Divine:

> In hymns they take th' Almighty by the nose;
> Ev'n of his oath upbraid him with a breach;

---

71 Teresa Berger, *Theology in Hymns? A Study of the Relationship of Doxology and Theology According to a Collection of Hymns for the use of the People Called Methodist (1780)*, trans. Timothy E. Kimbrough. (Nashville: Kingswood Books, 1995). See also Brett C. McInelly, *Textual Warfare and the Making of Methodism*, chap. 4, "Hymn Singing, the Anti-Methodist Response, and the Revival," 120–45.

72 Preface, in *BEWJW*, vol. 7, *A Collection of Hymns for the Use of the People called Methodists*, 74.

73 Joanna Cruickshank, *Pain, Passion and Faith: Revisiting the Place of Charles Wesley in Early Methodism* (Lanham, MD: Scarecrow Press, 2009).

74 174-Gr. Eusebius [Fleming], *A fine picture of enthusiasm*, 24.

Omniscience daringly presume to teach;
Make a full stand, and with their God contest
Till they wring from him ev'ry pert request.[75]

John Kirkby complained that the brothers Wesley lacked poetic skill. They were "just about as fitly cut out for poets as a lame horse would be for a rope-dancer." To hide their ineptitude as poets, they printed their doggerel side by side with hymns of good quality stolen from other authors.[76]

The music the Methodists used as hymn tunes was roundly criticized in William Riley's *Parochial Music Corrected* (1762). The Methodists, Riley protested, ignoring distinctions between church, theater, and chamber music, selected music that was unfit for use as hymn tunes. The Methodists, he added, wed sacred words to "light airy melodies usually adapted to ballads." He was scandalized at the use of such tunes as "My bliss too long my bride denies," "Sure Jacky was the bonniest swain," and "Tell me, lovely shepherd, where." By singing God's praise to the accompaniment of "lascivious music," Methodists, it was said, degraded the Almighty. Although they may have catchy melodies, Riley thought the ballad tunes were too difficult for congregations to master. The tunes set to the metrical version of the psalms were more suitable for congregational use, he opined, because they were easier to learn and sing.[77]

The way evangelical clergy introduced Methodist hymns whenever they had the opportunity was roundly criticized. Riley noted with displeasure that evangelical clergy introduced hymn-singing at morning and evening lectures and encouraged members of the congregation to pay the clerk and organist to be absent in order to substitute others who would provide music to the evangelical taste.[78] John Thomas depicted the strife that occurred when Thomas Coke forced the singing of Wesley's hymns on an unwilling congregation on the final Sunday of 1776. Part of the congregation wished to retain the use of Sternhold and Hopkins's psalms.[79] While Coke and his Methodist supporters sang a hymn, conservative members of the congregation sang

---

75 519-Gr. [Combe], *The love-feast,* 22.
76 217-Gr. Kirkby, *The impostor detected,* 44–55.
77 340-Gr. William Riley, *Parochial music corrected* (London: for the author, 1762), 3, 48.
78 Ibid., 3.
79 Sternhold and Hopkins's metrical Psalter was commonly used in Anglican churches in the eighteenth century.

Psalm 95. Coke, furious, berated the recalcitrant congregation, calling them "Devil's trumpeters, Satan's agents."[80]

Opposition to hymn singing came not only from Anglicans, who were affronted by the unsuitability of Methodist hymns, but from Baptists, who dismissed the singing of hymns as "another instance of will-worship of which the New Testament is altogether silent."[81] Gilbert Boyce voiced a similar concern. He could find no scriptural precedent for "singing in a promiscuous manner, good and bad, holy and unholy, men and women, boys and girls, all mixed together." He then asked, "May poor ignorant boys and girls and profane men and women be allowed to sing high praises of God?"[82]

Love Feasts

Three special worship experiences introduced by the Methodists fostered a sense of community and increased their self-identity. From the Moravians they borrowed the revived form of the ancient Christian love feast, from the early church's vigils they developed the watch night, and from English Puritanism they appropriated material for the covenant service. The last mentioned drew no unfavorable printed comment, watch nights received occasional criticism, but the introduction of love feasts was severely ridiculed. Wesley had begun to celebrate love feasts in the Fetter Lane Society in 1738.[83] Quickly they became a normal feature of the evangelical revival.[84] Accusations that the Methodists had sexualized spirituality were circulating as early as 1739 and 1740 and continued sporadically throughout most of the century,[85] culminating in the scurrilous and obscene satirical poem *The love-feast* (1778).[86] The Methodists

---

80 502-Gr. Thomas, *Two letters to the Rev. Thomas Coke*, 18.

81 216B-Ki. *A plain and familiar dialogue*, 20.

82 428-Gr. Boyce, *A serious reply to the Rev. Mr. John Wesley*, 92.

83 Frank Baker, *Methodism and the Love-Feast* (London: Epworth, 1957), 10–11.

84 Ibid.

85 519-Gr. [Combe], *The love-feast*. For instances of sexualized spirituality, see 312B-Fi. *Miss Kitty F—h—r's miscellany, with a dramatic sermon by two Methodist Preachers* (London: for H. Ranger, 1760). The title is an allusion to Catherine Maria (Kitty) Fisher, a prominent eighteenth-century courtesan. See Field's annotation on the pamphlet: The whole content is highly sexualized. Reference, as is expected, is made to Methodist love feasts, 49.

86 519-Gr. [Combe], *The love-feast*. See also 048-Gr. A Muggletonian, *The amorous humours and audacious adventures of one Whd.*, 7; Brett C. McInelly, *Textual Warfare and the Making of Methodism*, chap. 5, "Sexualized Spirituality, Sexual Politics, and the Revival," 146–79; Henry Abelove, *The Evangelist of Desire: John Wesley and the Methodists* (Stanford: Stanford University Press, 1990, 49–73).

were reprimanded for reintroducing and attempting to establish, as a regular service of the church, the love feast—a service that had been discredited in early Christendom. Samuel Weller noted that love feasts had hardly been introduced into the early church before they had to be suppressed because of "irregularities."[87] Bishop Gibson in 1744 echoed Weller's point. He asked whether it was helpful to the church to revive a service of worship that had fallen into disrepute and had long been discontinued.[88]

Satirists found the origin of love feasts outside the Christian tradition. Methodist love feasts derived from pagan festivals, suggested William Combe, author of *The love-feast*.[89] Another author insinuated that Whitefield had gained the idea of holding love feasts during a wild, erotic dream in 1736.[90] The very name *love-feast*, and the fact that the service was held at night, invited scurrilous attacks. A satirist in 1743 wrote:

> This loving feast (if that be right)
> Is celebrated, too, by night;
> Which time, and thing, they much admire.
> For why? it suits with their desire,
> Their ghostly father to revere.
> when he and all his sons draw near
> The pious sisters, wives, and misses,
> And greet them, well with holy kisses.[91]

Lavington, true to form, heaped scorn upon the Methodists for holding their love feasts at night:

> such nocturnal pranks, mysteries at dead of night, when regular and sober persons would chuse to be in their beds. Mr. *Wesley* had better have prescribed a sleeping draught, or good feather bed, than have encouraged such irregular cabals: when darkness, watchings, and enthusiasms concurring, would naturally draw on those ominous dreams, and mad consequences.[92]

---

87 098-Gr. [Weller], *The trial of Mr. Whitefield's spirit*, 37.
88 165-Gr. [Gibson], *Observations upon the conduct and behaviour of . . . Methodists*, 24.
89 519-Gr. [Combe], *The love-feast*. The frontispiece depicts the Consecration of 'Reynardo' [Wesley] by 'the Goddess Murcia' [Venus].
90 337-Gr. *A plain and easy road to the land of bliss*, 100–110.
91 156-Gr. An Impartial Hand, *The progress of Methodism in Bristol*, 23.
92 225-Gr. [Lavington], *The enthusiasm of Methodists and papists compar'd*, pt. 3, 158–59.

While some authors only hinted at sexual irregularity, others, fixated on assumptions about what Methodists did in private, boldly made their accusations public—the love feast was indeed a sex orgy.[93] Unrestrained licentiousness reigned: fornication, adultery, even incest were practiced:

> Together wanton pairs promiscuous run,
> Brothers with sisters, mothers with a son:
> Fathers, perhaps with yielding daughters meet,
> Pure souls are fir'd by love's divinest spark
> And paradise is open'd in the dark.[94]

The religious ritual, opponents argued, was mere show; a formality to be hurried through.

> Ev'n whilst they kneel their vicious passions glow
> Clear proofs that such religion is but show.
> . . . .
> E'n whilst the chalice to his lips is put,
> One eye thanks heav'n and t'other marks a slut.[95]

One author hinted that love feast celebrations gave the Methodists the opportunity to remove their "troublesome disguises" of sanctity for a time and enjoy the pleasures of the flesh:

> — So passed they naked on . . .
> Thus taking hand in hand alone
> — Into their inmost bower . . . they went;
> And eased the putting off
> These troublesome disguises which we wear,
> Strait side by side were laid;
> Nor Eve the rites mysterious
> Of congenial love refused.[96]

---

93 048-Gr. A Muggletonian, *Amorous humours, and audacious adventures of one Whd*, 7. See also 166-Gr. J.B./ A Gentleman of Pembroke College, Oxon, *A letter to the Reverend Mr. Whitefield*, 44; 248A-Ba. *A few queries concerning the growth of Methodism*, 5; 324-Gr. Snip *pseud.*, *The journal of the travels of Nathaniel Snip*, 23; 555-Gr. *A review of the policy, doctrines and morals of the Methodists*, 35; 366-Gr. A Presbyter of the Church of England, *The doctrines of Methodism examined and confuted*, 11–12.

94 519-Gr. [Combe], *The love-feast*, 28.

95 Ibid., 13–14.

96 312B-Fi. *Miss Kitty F—h—r's miscellany*, 50–51.

Both Whitefield and Wesley were portrayed as lechers who reveled in opportunities to satiate their lust:

> A pure and spotless virgin sister,
> 'Till you and W—ly, finely kissed her;
> Then took her under your tuition;
> So now she's in a fine condition! *
> Your love for her, poor girl, was such,
> You made her righteous over-much!
> . . . .
> So when for God of lust she burns,
> You both inflame her— by turns:
> Both nature and your God abuse
> With vilest arts that man can use![97]

One author alleged that Whitefield had contracted venereal disease from being indiscriminate in his choice of partners at love feasts.[98] Malicious rumors circulated that Wesley placed drugs in the loving cup to facilitate the release of people's inhibitions. Bishop Lavington gave wide currency to this rumor, as did William Combe, author of the satirical poems *Perfection, Fanatical conversion*, and *The love-feast*, who stated that the beverage for Methodist love feast celebrations was drugged with love potions.[99]

Watch Nights

The peculiar Methodist practice of holding watch night services was begun by a group of converted Kingswood colliers who spent the nights they had formerly spent in drunkenness in prayer and praise. Wesley approved the practice and set aside the Friday night nearest the full moon for these meetings, so participants would have enough light to return home after midnight. Monthly services were established in Bristol, London, and Newcastle. Methodists could not hope to escape criticism of these midnight services. Yet on the whole, fewer attacks were directed specifically at this practice than might have been

---

97 048-Gr. A Muggletonian, *The amorous humours and audacious adventures of one Whd.*, 10.

98 320A-Ba. *Memoirs of the life of a modern saint*, 77.

99 225-Gr. [Lavington], *The enthusiasm of Methodists and papists compar'd*, pt. 3, 163–64; 517-Gr. [Combe], *Perfection: A poetical epistle*, 13; 521-Gr. [Combe], *Fanatical conversion*, 45; 519-Gr. [Combe], *The love-feast*, 28.

expected. Often, opponents lumped them together with love feasts in their abuse.[100] It was the fact that watch nights went so long into the evenings that raised their adversaries' suspicions:

> To join together —What to do?
> 'Tis to be hop'd, no evil thing,
> But those, who in the night, thus roam,
> But watch them out and watch them home.[101]

Although they concluded their services at midnight, because some participants came from Bristol to Kingswood for the watch night celebrations, they could be seen walking home in the early hours of the morning:

> Men, boys, and girls, and women too
> Come strolling home at morning two.[102]

In his *Fanatical conversion* and *Perfection*, Combe alleged, as he had done concerning love feasts, that watch night services acted as screens behind which the Methodists engaged in sexual irregularities. The watch night service was deliberately lengthened to sharpen the participants' sexual appetite. At midnight young virgins stretched on the ground in front of frenzied lovers:

> Celestial impregnation to receive
> And share those gifts which all who feel believe.[103]

In *Perfection* Combe noted the ardor with which awkward, clumsy preachers entered into watch night services:

> When preaching lubbers [awkward, clumsy men], who have dropped
>   their pack;
> In watchnight labours prove themselves not slack,
> 'Thro' calls of love to tender scenes advance,
> And slide into adult'ry in a trance.[104]

---

100 525C-Ki. O'Leary, *Mr. O'Leary's Remarks on the Rev. Mr. Wesley's letters*, 31.
101 156-Gr. An Impartial Hand, *The progress of Methodism in Bristol*, 22.
102 156-Gr. Ibid.
103 521-Gr. [Combe], *Fanatical conversion*, 13; 517-Gr. [Combe], *Perfection: A poetical epistle*, 17.
104 517-Gr. Ibid.

By contrast, former Methodist James Lackington depicted the atmosphere at watch nights as melancholic—in preparation, Methodists fasted, and the activities in which they participated during the evening heightened the air of depression: "the hymns which they sing on those nights are wrote for such occasions, and abound with gloomy ideas, which are increased by the time of night."[105] Irish Catholic priest Arthur O'Leary linked watch night services in Ireland to civil disorder.[106]

Preaching Houses

Anti-Methodists were, in the main, strangely silent in opposing in print the establishment of Methodist preaching houses. It might have been expected that there would have been a hue and cry raised about their being built, and the refusal of the Methodists, initially, to have them licensed under the Toleration Act. This, however, does not seem to have been an important issue for literary critics of Methodism. Bishop Gibson noted in 1744 that the Methodists had begun to open "publick places of religious worship, with the same freedom, as if they were warranted by the Act of Toleration," but he did not press the point further.[107]

There was criticism of the construction of the New Room in Bristol, the Orphan House at Newcastle, and the City Road Chapel in London, but only passing notice of Wesley's Foundery in London and Whitefield's Tabernacle on Tottenham Court Road. Satirists gleefully noted the proximity of the Foundery to Bedlam, the London insane asylum,[108] and nicknamed Whitefield's chapel "Squintum's Schism Shop."[109]

The major criticism concerning the New Room and the Orphan House was the way they were financed. The members of the Methodist societies in Bristol contributed to the mortgage payments. There were broad hints that some of the money collected was not being used for reduction of the debt, but instead was lining the pockets of the Methodist leaders. It was suggested, furthermore, that some society members were donating so much money that

---

105 560-Gr. Lackington, *Memoirs of the life. . . of James Lackington,* 114.
106 525C-Ki. O'Leary, *Mr. O'Leary's Remarks,* 31.
107 164-Gr. [Gibson], *Observations on the conduct and behaviour of . . . Methodists,* 4.
108 517-Gr. [Combe], *Perfection: A poetical epistle,* 25.
109 378-Gr. Peter Paragraph *pseud.* [Adair], *The Methodist and mimick,* 5.

they were being reduced to poverty.[110] While Methodist families suffered, their leaders prospered. Wesley's decision to hold the deed of the New Room in his own name was satirized:

> But John, more cunning than them all,
> Obedient to an inward call,
> Secur'd the title of this room
> Unto himself, and heirs to come.
> Now, who can say he acted odd?
> their souls they trust within his hands,
> Why mayn't they trust him with their lands? [111]

Henceforth these charges dogged Wesley's footsteps. From Newcastle came a repetition of the accusation that Wesley's seeking subscriptions to build preaching houses was putting too great a burden on the poor.[112] When the City Road Chapel was built, Combe indicted Wesley for taking money from the pockets of the poor to erect edifices to his own glory:

> For their soul's good—by knaves with fears beset,
> They drain that purse which shou'd have paid a debt;
> . . . .
> While temples thus arise to one man's praise,
> How many families with herds must graze?
> Filch'd by imposture, can such fabrics stand?
> A temple rais'd by fraud is built on sand.
> A temple pilfer'd is no house for God
> Such splendid traps the eyes of men may catch,
> But heav'n prefers integrity and thatch.[113]

The author of *A review of the policy, doctrines and morals of the Methodists* claimed that the Methodists erected "very elegant and highly finished preaching houses." The total value of Methodist property in 1791, he estimated, was almost £1,500,000. Annual operating costs, he thought, would be almost £500,000. Because they were such expensive buildings and were

---

110 200C-Fi. Katharine Pimm, *A true and faithful account of some transactions . . . of Doctor Westley.*

111 156-Gr. An Impartial Hand, *The progress of' Methodism in Bristol*, 15, 16–17.

112 160B-Ba. [Smith], *The notions of the Methodists farther disprov'd*, 51.

113 517-Gr. [Combe], *Perfection: A poetical epistle*, 27–29.

paid for entirely by men and women from the lower classes, the author contended that Methodism was "one of the severest taxes that ever was laid upon the laboring part of the people."[114]

Some of the strongest criticism of Wesley's erection of the City Road Chapel came from Rowland Hill. On the title page of his *Imposture detected and the dead vindicated* (1777), he noted that Wesley laid "the first stone of his new Dissenting meeting-house near City-Road." In the text of his pamphlet, he further noted that Wesley now licensed many of his preaching houses under the Act of Toleration. Since in some of his preaching houses he made "no scruple to administer the Sacraments, from time to time," Hill claimed that Wesley could no longer maintain the fiction that they were not Dissenting meeting houses.[115]

Collections

Without tithes or endowments, the Methodists built and sustained their buildings and met their itinerant preachers' needs.[116] The work of the revival was supported entirely by voluntary collections. Critics found much in this practice to attack. Samuel Martin alleged that Methodist preachers were guilty of "a concerted scheme of dissimulation." Whenever they began work in a new area, they disclaimed all intentions of asking for financial support, Martin said. Yet in a little while they asked unfailingly for "a very small matter for a tent, a little collection for four walls and a roof, and then regular collections, pennies a week, and tickets."[117]

Some opponents found the methods used to solicit contributions unethical. Preachers, they said, played on the emotions of congregations or used threats when entreaties did not result in liberal gifts. Ralph Jephson, tongue in cheek, suggested that Whitefield could improve his methods of collection by employing two sturdy off-siders, one with a sack, the other with a club,

---

114 555-Gr. *A review of the policy, doctrines and morals of the Methodists*, 44.

115 496-Gr. Rowland Hill, *Imposture detected and the dead vindicated* (London: T. Vallance, 1777), see title page and 18.

116 See Samuel Rogal, *Studies in the History of Missions,* vol. 21, *The Financial Aspects of John Wesley's Methodism (1720–1791)* (Lewiston, Queenston, Lampeter: Edwin Mellen Press, 2002), 19–20.

117 376-Gr. [Martin], *A few thoughts and matters of fact concerning Methodism*, 4.

with orders to knock down any not disposed to be charitable.[118] The reasons for Methodist collections were frequently challenged. Whitefield's tireless solicitation of funds for "Bethesda," his orphanage in Savannah, Georgia, was attacked many times. So, too, was Wesley's raising money to build preaching houses. Satirists depicted Methodist congregations as sheep being fleeced by both leaders:

> Those orphans' cases George espouses
> Whilst John erects religious houses!
> Good shepherds always take that care
> To fold their sheep as well as shear.[119]

The leaders never missed an opportunity to gather in a harvest:

> And frequently, both here and there.
> sums great, and, small, collected were.
> As oft' were those collections made;
> And all collectors acted right.
> They ne'er refus'd the widow's mite
> But what was gather'd first and last
> Into the treasury was cast. [120]

Suspicion that the money raised by the Methodists had been misused led to calls for the public disclosure of all funds collected and an accounting of how the money was spent.[121] Some satirists hinted that the Methodist leaders were accumulating fortunes. One of the preachers in the farce *The mock-preacher* claimed the Methodists' success in raising money came from base motives:

> The scheme is well carried on and succeeds even beyond our
> utmost expectations. Who would be a poor curate under a lazy
> vicar, when by taking a little pains to gull the public, I have two
> tides of money flow in a day?[122]

---

118 006A-Ba. A Gentleman of Oxford [Jephson], *Methodism and enthusiasm fully display'd*, 63. This is the second edition of *The Methodists dissected*.

119 156-Gr. An Impartial Hand, *The progress of Methodism in Bristol*, 8.

120 Ibid., 9.

121 208-Gr. White, *A sermon against the Methodists*, 10–11; 272C-Fi. J. D. [Dove], *Remarks on the Reverend Mr. John Wesley's 'Sufficient answer*,' vi–vii.

122 025-Gr. *The mock–preacher*, 13.

In 1739 Joseph Trapp estimated Whitefield was gaining in one year more money than an average Anglican priest earned in twenty.[123] In 1775 another author alleged Whitefield had amassed £10,000 by the time of his death in 1770.[124] It was alleged that John Wesley had a better income than most Anglican bishops.[125] Mr. Baily of Cork calculated that Wesley was earning the princely sum of two thousand pence a week from band and class tickets.[126]

Critics were scandalized that Methodist leaders allegedly became wealthy at the expense of the poor.[127] Samuel Martin computed that belonging to a Methodist society cost between thirteen and fourteen shillings a year—an amount, he thought, a poor family could not afford.[128] Children, one satirist alleged, often starved because of their parents' ill-conceived generosity to Methodism:

> There peasants gull'd by many a tortur'd text,
> Throw in their last-week's-mite, to starve the next;
> There fascinated parents cry "Divine!"
> And giving all, forget their child must dine.[129]

The generosity of some Methodists caused family divisions. Katharine Pimm, the wife of Joseph Pimm, a Quaker and London Methodist, was angered by her husband's substantial contribution of £100 in 1742 for the erection of the Newcastle Orphan House. In a four-page pamphlet entitled *A true and faithful account of some of the transactions and horrid impositions of Doctor Westley* [sic], Katharine denounced John Wesley, claiming that her husband was "tricked out of several hundred pounds of their dear-earn'd

---

123 093-Gr. [Trapp], *The true spirit of the Methodists and their allies*, 53.

124 476-Gr. *A letter to a friend on the subject of Methodism*, 23.

125 208-Gr. White, *A sermon against the Methodists*, 25.

126 See 219-Gr. Philalethes [John Bailey], *A second letter to the Rev. Mr. Wesley* (Cork: no printer, 1750). No copy of this work has survived. For a partial reconstruction, see Wesley, "A Letter to the Rev. Mr. Bailey of Cork," in *BEWJW*, vol. 9: *The Methodist Societies, Histories, Nature and Design*, ed. Rupert E. Davies, 565–56.

127 160B-Ba. [Smith], *The notions of the Methodists farther disprov'd*, 61; 025-Gr. *The mock-preacher*, 11; 154-Gr. [Este], *Methodism display'd*, 13; 274-Gr. Free, *Rules for the discovery of false prophets*, 26; 205C-Ki. W. D. [Dowars], *Errors in part discovered*, 26.

128 376-Gr. [Martin], *A few thoughts and matters of fact concerning Methodism* (Edinburgh: sold by W. Gray, 1766), 9–10.

129 516-Gr. [Combe], *The fanatic saints*, 15.

reward [for] their sweat and labour . . . acquired by their honest industry."[130] The loss of their savings resulted in the "ruin of himself and family. . . entirely destroy'd her substance, . . . and caused a total separation between her and her husband."[131] To Wesley's relief Joseph repudiated his wife's assertions in a pamphlet entitled *A letter from Mr. Joseph Pimm to the Rev. Mr. Broughton* (1754). He confided his relief to Elizabeth Hutton, a London supporter.[132]

Despite strong opposition to their worship methods and practices, such as extempore prayer and preaching, use of hymnody, celebration of love feasts and watch nights, Methodists continued to employ them and enshrined them as distinguishing marks of the movement.

130 200C-Fi. Pimm, *A true and faithful account of some of the transactions . . . of Doctor Westley,* full title page.
131 Ibid., title page.
132 Wesley to Elizabeth Hutton, January 18, 1746, in Frank Baker, ed., *BEWJW,* vol. 26, *Letters II,* 1740–1755, 96, 184.

CHAPTER 9

Calvinist "Elect" and Arminian "Saint" at War

In its early years, no sharp theological lines partitioned the evangelical revival. This, however, did not last long. The conflict between Wesley and Whitefield over predestination polarized Methodism into two main camps, later labeled *Arminian* and *Calvinist*.[1] The debate between the two sides was the longest and most visible theological controversy in the eighteenth-century religious revival in England.[2]

During the half century 1741–91 there were four major periods of conflict with minor disputes in between. At the center of each was one of Wesley's publications. In 1739 his sermon *Free Grace* initiated a heated debate concerning predestination. A printed attack on James Hervey's *Theron and Aspasio* in 1758 touched off the second major battle. Controversy over predestination was rekindled in 1770, when Wesley published a rejoinder to Augustus Toplady's treatise on that subject and the third battle ensued. The fourth, final, and bitterest struggle of all over the role of works in justification was occasioned by a doctrinal section in the *Minutes* of Wesley's 1770 Conference.

---

1 It should be noted at the outset that the terms "Arminian" and "Calvinist" were used as loosely in the eighteenth century as was the term "Methodist." The Arminianism of Wesley and his followers is neither the high Anglican Arminianism of the seventeenth century, with its interest in high church ceremony and ritual, nor Dutch Arminianism, based on the theology of Jacob Arminius (1560–1609), Dutch Reformed theologian. The distinguishing mark of Methodist Arminianism was the universality of grace. "Calvinism" was an imprecise term used to describe the theology of many of those evangelicals who disagreed with Wesley on matters of doctrine. In that they taught the sovereignty of God, predestination, perseverance of saints, imputed righteousness, and other tenets usually associated with Calvinism, many of Wesley's evangelical opponents were described as Calvinists. But they were not Calvinists in the sense that they adhered closely to the teachings of John Calvin. Mostly they looked to the Anglican Thirty–nine Articles for support rather than Calvin's writings. Indeed, Whitefield confessed that he had never read anything by Calvin, and only a few of the "Calvinists"—Romaine and Toplady, for example—had ever studied Calvin's *Institutes of Religion* in depth. See Whitefield, *Works*, 1:205, and S. C. Carpenter, *Eighteenth Century Church and People* (London: John Murray, 1959), 221.

2 See Alan P. F. Sell, *The Great Debate: Calvinism, Arminianism, and Salvation* (Worthing: H. E. Walter, 1982).

The Free Grace Dispute

Although Wesley had been advised by friends at the outset of his evangelical preaching to avoid disputes concerning predestination, by early April 1739 he had become anxious about what seemed to him the pernicious antinomian tendencies of the doctrine of predestination. On April 26, unable to remain silent any longer, Wesley spoke "strongly and explicitly" against predestination while preaching at Newgate.[3] His hearers' response buttressed his belief that in the future he ought not to refrain from the subject. In order to obtain further confirmation from God, he cast lots to decide whether to "preach and print" his views opposing the tenet. After receiving an affirmative answer, he wrote and published his sermon *Free grace*.[4]

In *Free grace*, more a controversial treatise than a homily, Wesley issued a scathing denunciation of predestination. Convinced that there was no such thing as single predestination, he insisted that the election of some to eternal salvation implied the reprobation of the remainder to eternal damnation. It was a blasphemous doctrine, he maintained, that caricatured the nature of God, representing "the most holy God as worse than the devil, and both more false, more cruel, and more unjust."[5] It was, moreover, unscriptural and disfigured the message of the gospel that God is a God of love and mercy. Finally, and most importantly, Wesley contended that predestination destroyed zeal for good works.

In deference to Whitefield, Wesley refrained from issuing a second edition for more than a year, and may have also, for a time, suppressed sales of the 1739 Bristol edition. Events in June 1740 in London—the Fetter Lane Society's disruption by "quietism" and "predestinarianism"— prompted Wesley to issue a new edition of *Free grace*. It was this action that released the floodgate of controversial pamphlets, the only known attack of the first

---

3 John Wesley to James Hutton and the Fetter Lane Society, April 30, 1739, in *Letters I, BEWJW*, 25:637–41; Wesley, April 30, 1739, in *Journals and Diaries II (1738–1743)* in *BEWJW*, 19:52–53, 387.

4 John Wesley, Sermon 110, "Free Grace," in *BEWJW*, vol. 3 *Sermons III*, ed. Albert C. Outler, 544–63. Although Wesley did not include "Free Grace" in his early collection of sermons, he continued to reprint it. He included it, however, in his collected *Works* (1771–74), placing it among his controversial publications. An excellent discussion of the origins of this sermon and the ensuing clash between the two Methodist leaders, George Whitefield and John Wesley, may be found in Frank Baker's "Whitefield's Break with the Wesleys," *Church Quarterly* 3 (October 1970):103–13.

5 Wesley, "Free Grace," *BEWJW*, 3:555.

edition being an anonymous tract with a title that parodied Wesley's—*Free grace indeed!*[6]

No fewer than eight pamphlets were printed in opposition to *Free grace*. The most damaging attack was from Wesley's old pupil, friend, and fellow evangelist, George Whitefield, who fired off a thirty-one-page volley in the form of an open letter to Wesley.[7] Others with Calvinist leanings joined Whitefield in assaulting Wesley in print. Among the detractors were Joseph Hart, ultra-Calvinist hymn writer and Independent preacher, of London;[8] Samuel Blair, Presbyterian minister of Londonderry, Pennsylvania, and friend and colleague of Whitefield in America;[9] William Birt, who described himself as "an illiterate mechanick;"[10] John Oulton, Baptist minister of Liverpool (formerly of Leominster) and early supporter of the revival;[11] Edward Ridgway, an author with pronounced Calvinistic leanings;[12] and one who signed his tract "Christianus."[13]

Debate with Wesley, though in earnest, was marked by restraint in contrast to their opponents in 1770. Personal abuse, characteristic of the later period, was absent. Mild rebukes were the order of the day. Typical was Christianus's reprimand of Wesley for his "mistaken zeal and fondness for . . . [his] own opinion."[14] Whitefield, too, although leveling charges of "carnal reasoning" and "sophistry" at Wesley, refrained from invective. His pamphlet, a capable attack upon his erstwhile friend's sermon, was courteous

---

6　100-Gr. *Free grace indeed! A letter to the Reverend Mr. John Wesley* (London: H. Kent, 1740). The tract was reprinted in Philadelphia and Boston in 1741, appearing before Wesley's second edition. See the note to Wesley's preface in the second edition.

7　116-Gr. George Whitefield, *A letter to the Reverend Mr. John Wesley, in answer to his sermon entituled 'Free–grace'* (London: W. Strahan 1741).

8　127-Gr. Hart, *The unreasonableness of religion.*

9　248B-Ba. Samuel Blair, *The doctrine of predestination truly and fairly stated* (Belfast: reprinted for Robert Johnston, 1753). The tract was originally published in Philadelphia in 1742.

10　205A-Ba. William Birt, *The doctrine of predestination defended* (London: by the author, 1746).

11　291-Gr. John Oulton, *A vindication of the seventeenth article of the Church of England* (London: Aaron Ward, 1760).

12　137A-Ki. Edward Ridgway, *Truth defended; or, the awful sovereignty and righteousness of God* (London: J. Wilson, 1741).

13　101-Gr. Christianus, *A letter to the Reverend Mr. John Westley, occasion'd by his sermon against predestination* (London: printed for D. Midwinter and A. Ward, 1741).

14　Ibid., 4. Cf. Similar comments appear in 127-Gr. Hart, *The unreasonableness of religion,* 17; 137A-Ki. Ridgway, *Truth defended; or, the awful sovereignty and righteousness of God,* iii; 100-Gr. *Free grace indeed! A letter to the Reverend Mr. John Wesley,* 4.

throughout.[15] Although early opponents refrained from personal abuse, Joseph Hart disparagingly designated Wesley and his fellow workers "Arminian"—a label that would stick to them for the rest of the century and later be embraced by Wesley and his followers much the same way they had adopted the epithet "Methodist."[16]

The 1741 controversy was not theologically profound. None of the lesser disputants was a skilled theologian. Although somewhat more intent on denying Wesley's statements than affirming their own position, they all defended the doctrine of predestination with tenacity. They were convinced that it rested on sound bases—the mass and weight of Scripture supported it, and the seventeenth article of the Church buttressed it. Wesley's quarrel with predestination was, they said, not with them but with Scripture and Anglican doctrinal standards.[17] Wesley had been led into error by appealing to "carnal" reason as his authority for judging doctrine. He rejected predestination because it seemed to him to be "unreasonable." His critics insisted that God is not circumscribed by the limits of the human mind. God's ways are inscrutable—beyond human capacity to grasp intellectually. Ridgway questioned Wesley: "Will you censure the decrees of God? Will you arraign the Almighty at your bar, because they comport not with your carnal reason, with your proud imaginations?"[18]

Underlying the predestinarians' statements were two major premises: the first was God's sovereign freedom;[19] the second, based on observation, was that the majority of humankind appeared to reject God's provisions of salvation. From these convictions the Calvinists concluded that God elected some to salvation while the remainder were reprobated to eternal damnation.

If Wesley contended that predestination dishonored God, the Calvinists

---

15 116-Gr. Whitefield, *A letter to the Reverend Mr. John Wesley, in answer to his sermon entituled 'Free Grace,'* 26.

16 127-Gr. Hart, *The unreasonableness of religion,* 14.

17 100-Gr. *Free grace indeed! A letter to the Rev. Mr. John Wesley,* 4; 116-Gr. George Whitefield, *A letter to the Reverend Mr. John Wesley, in answer to his sermon entituled 'Free grace,'* 10; 101-Gr. Christianus, *A letter to the Rev. Mr. John Westley, occasion'd by his sermon against predestination,* 12; 291-Gr. Oulton, *A vindication of the seventeenth article of the Church of England,* 10.

18 137–Ki. Ridgway, *Truth defended; or, The awful sovereignty and righteousness of God,* 3, 13. Cf. 127-Gr. Hart, *The unreasonableness of religion,* 22.

19 291-Gr. Oulton, *A vindication of the seventeenth article of the Church of England,* 40–41; 100-Gr. *Free grace indeed,* 12–13; 137–Ki. Ridgway, *Truth defended; or, The awful sovereignty and righteousness of God,* 41.

hurled the charge back at him—Wesley's doctrine of redemption demeaned the Almighty. John Oulton complained that "Mr. Wesley's scheme appears too narrow a representation of the Divine Being."[20] In Wesley's scheme God was no longer sovereign. Whereas they emphasized God's grace and human humility, Wesley, they said, like Pelagius, reversed the order, emphasizing works above grace. Thus, wrote the author of *Free grace indeed!*: "The Creator depends on the creature; the creature [is] introduced as more absolute than the Creator; and the Creator [is] traduc'd as the weak creature."[21]

Whitefield dismissed Wesley's horror at the injustice of reprobation as unfounded:

> As all humans sinned in Adam, explained Whitefield, God might justly have passed them all by, without sending his own Son to be a Saviour for any one . . . For if God might justly impute Adam's sin to all, and afterwards have passed by all, then he might justly pass by some.[22]

Wesley's predestinarian opponents vigorously denied that the doctrines of election led to antinomianism. They did not neglect good works; they were conscientious in the performance of their Christian duty. "Holiness," Whitefield reminded Wesley, "[is] made a mark of our election by all that preach it."[23]

Wesley depicted predestination, because it implied reprobation, as a "horrible decree;" a source of fear.[24] In complete contrast the Calvinists presented it, because it spoke of sure election, as a "comfortable doctrine," a source of strength for the Christian. Whitefield witnessed to the comfort it brought to his life:

> This doctrine is my daily support. I should utterly sink under a

---

20 291-Gr. Oulton, *A vindication of the seventeenth article of the Church of England*, 40–41.

21 100-Gr. *Free grace indeed! A letter to the Reverend Mr. John Wesley*, 12–13. Cf. 291-Gr. Oulton, *A vindication of the seventeenth article of the Church of England*, 4; 116-Gr. Whitefield, *A letter to the Reverend Mr. John Wesley entituled 'Free grace,'* 20–21.

22 116-Gr. Whitefield, *A letter to the Reverend Mr. John Wesley*, 20–21.

23 Ibid., 12, 15. Cf. 127-Gr. Hart, *The unreasonableness of religion*, 50–51; 101-Gr. Christianus, *A letter to the Rev. Mr. John Westley*, 11; 100-Gr. *Free grace indeed! A letter to the Rev. Mr. John Wesley*, 26.

24 For the phrase "horrible decree," see John Calvin, *Institutes of the Christian Religion*, Library of Christian Classics, 2 vols., ed. John T. McNeill, bk. 3, chap. 23, sec. 7. The Wesley brothers took the phrase out of Calvin's context and used it derogatorily.

> dread of my impending trials, was I not firmly persuaded that God
> has chosen me in Christ from before the foundation of the world,
> and that now being effectually called, he will suffer none to pluck
> me out of his Almighty hand.[25]

Whitefield had prefaced his attack with a statement expressing the wish that the controversy not polarize the revival: "I desire that they who hold election would not triumph or make a party [be divisive] on the one hand (for I detest any such thing) and that they who are prejudiced against that doctrine be not too concerned or offended on the other."[26] But his words were in vain, the damage had been done, and Methodism had been divided into two opposing camps. The battle standards of the two wings had been raised. Increasingly leaders and members rallied to one or the other. Although within a few months Wesley and Whitefield achieved personal reconciliation, and some evangelicals (William Grimshaw and Howell Harris in particular) continued to move freely behind the lines of both camps, the battle lines had been drawn and theological trenches dug. Suspicion between the two camps existed for the next fifty years. Despite the absence of any permanent reconciliation, at times the relationship was cordial enough to allow a measure of cooperation. At other times, however, the embers of theological disagreement were fanned into flames of bitterness.

Minor Skirmishes 1741–1758

From 1741 to 1758, when the next major battle between the two wings occurred, Arminians and Calvinists traded numerous shots, occasionally engaging in minor conflicts. Wesley's opponents in this period were, in the main, not from the Calvinist wing of the revival, but from other denominations with Calvinist leanings.

Wesley's 1739 sermon *Free grace* was but the first shot from the Arminian side. Convinced that the inevitable consequence of the doctrine of predestination would be manifest in antinomianism and quietism, Wesley released during the 1740s (particularly in 1741) and early 1750s a barrage of anti-Calvinist publications. His aim was not to convert those wholly indoctrinated with

---

25 116-Gr. Whitefield, *A letter to the Reverend John Wesley*, 15. Cf. 127-Gr. Hart, *The unreasonableness of religion*, 36–37.

26 116-Gr. Whitefield, *A letter to the Reverend Mr. John Wesley*, iii.

Calvinism to the Arminian side but to preserve the members of his societies from being swayed by the dialectics of his opponents. By means of these anti-Calvinist pamphlets, Wesley provided his followers with both armor and ammunition to defend themselves from theological onslaught from the other side. The list of these tracts between 1741 and 1752 is impressive. Wesley's extract of a tract by Isaac Watts (1642–1748), *Ruin and recovery of mankind*, appeared in 1740 under the title *Serious considerations concerning the doctrines of election and reprobation*.[27] The following year he published *Serious considerations on absolute predestination*.[28] Charles prepared *Hymns on God's everlasting love*, which John published in 1741.[29] Whereas the earlier *Hymns and sacred poems* (1740) struck a mild blow to Calvinism, the new book of hymns, particularly the poem "The horrible decree," initiated a powerful attack. Also, in 1741, Wesley prepared a further assault on predestination, adapting a work by Thomas Grantham (1664–1692), entitled *A dialogue between the Presbyterian and the Baptist*, and publishing it under the title *A dialogue between a predestinarian and his friend*.[30] This he followed, the same year, with *The Scripture doctrine concerning predestination, election and reprobation*, an extract of Henry Haggar's *Order of causes*.[31] In 1745 he attacked antinomianism in two dialogues: *A dialogue* and *A second dialogue between an antinomian and his friend*.[32] The year 1751 witnessed Wesley's publication, anonymously, of *Serious thoughts upon the perseverance of saints*.[33] The following year he released *Predestination calmly considered*, his most devastating assault to date.[34]

From 1741 to 1758 the Calvinists were on the defensive. Unable to ignore Wesley's paper barrage, they returned the fire. They made few attacks without first being provoked. To counter Charles's verse, especially "The

27 John Wesley, *Serious considerations concerning the doctrines of election and reprobation* (London: [W. Strahan], 1740).

28 John Wesley, *Serious considerations on absolute predestination* (Bristol: S. Farley, 1741).

29 Charles Wesley, *Hymns on God's everlasting love* (Bristol: S. Farley, 1741).

30 John Wesley, *A dialogue between a predestinarian and his friend*, in *BEWJW*, 13:229–38.

31 John Wesley, *The Scripture doctrine concerning predestination, election and reprobation* (London: W. Strahan, 1741).

32 John Wesley, "A dialogue between an Antinomian and his friend" in *Works* (Jackson), 10:266–76, and "A second dialogue between an Antinomian and his friend," *Works* (Jackson), 10:276–84.

33 John Wesley, "Serious thoughts on the perseverance of the Saints" in *BEWJW*, 13:239–57.

34 John Wesley, *Predestination Calmly Considered,* in *Works* (Jackson), 10:204–58.

horrible decree," Thomas Gurney (1705–1770), the famed eighteenth-century shorthand writer and Calvinist, composed a twenty-four-page poem entitled *The nature and fitness of things.*[35] Gurney's lines contain invective enough to match his opponent's. Throughout the poem Gurney affirmed the sovereignty of God, an attribute he believed Wesley had disfigured by controverting the doctrine of election. The Arminians, Gurney charged, had turned God into an indecisive, inconsistent, and imperfect deity. In branding Wesley's tenets Arminian, Gurney suggested that the Methodist leader should move to Rome, where he would be more at home theologically:

> What tongue thy horrid crime can tell?
> Put saints to sing the song of hell!
> Haste hence to Rome thy proper place;
> Why should we share in thy disgrace?
> We need no greater proof to see
> Thy blasphemies with theirs agree.[36]

The label "papist" became one of the favorite epithets flung at the Arminian wing of Methodism by the predestinarians. An early friend of the evangelical revival, Anne Dutton, a prolific hyper-Calvinist author, became one of Wesley's fiercest theological foes.[37] Part of her eighty-eight-page open letter to John Wesley was directed at Charles's anti-predestinarian poems.[38]

The reissuing of Charles's *Hymns on God's everlasting love* in a third edition in 1770 drew a heated response from an anonymous author who contended that it was "a wretched compilation" full of "horrid expressions" and "unheard of imprecations." A mischievous publication, its effect was to "blacken the character of those who strenuously defend the truths of God."[39]

Three major replies were issued to Wesley's dialogue on predestination. Two anonymous predestinarians responded in the same literary form in which

---

35 152B-Ba. [Thomas Gurney], *The nature and fitness of things* (London: no printer, 1742). The poem is also included in 551-Gr. Thomas Gurney, *Poems on various occasions* (Sudbury: W. Brackett, 1790).

36 Ibid., 16.

37 Anne Dutton was the widow (1743) of Benjamin Dutton, Baptist minister at Great Grandsen, Huntingdonshire.

38 146-Gr. [Anne Dutton], *A letter to the Rev. Mr. John Wesley in vindication of the doctrines of absolute unconditional election* (London: John Hart, 1742). See especially 31–32, 79–85.

39 467-Gr. *A faithful warning to the followers of the Rev. Mr. John Wesley* (London: printed for Keith, Buckland, Lewis and Mathews, 1774), 12, 17, 19.

they had been attacked—dialogue.[40] Both authors objected to Wesley's use of labels for those who espoused predestination. The anonymous author of *Some remarks on a dialogue* took exception to Wesley's labeling all those who believed predestination as "Calvinist," as if they agreed with Calvin on all points. Dowars was critical of Wesley for implying that predestinarians were antinomians, but his stated dislike of epithets did not prevent him from labeling Wesley a "papist."[41]

The author of *Some remarks on a dialogue* found much to criticize in Wesley's analysis of the predestinarian position. He chided Wesley for quoting predestinarian authors out of context and for selecting passages for their "shock" value merely to cast election in a "frightful appearance."[42] In Dowars's *Errors in part discovered*, Wesley's arguments against predestination were alleged to be so weak that even a woman untrained in theology could refute them.[43]

Much of Anne Dutton's letter to Wesley (mentioned earlier) was devoted to an attack on Wesley's *Dialogue on predestination*. She reaffirmed the doctrine of election, and insisted, against Wesley's arguments to the contrary, that it was scriptural. The main burden of her pamphlet was, however, that Wesley's doctrines destroyed the sovereignty of God.[44]

Wesley's two dialogues on antinomianism grew out of the question posed at the Bristol Conference in 1745: "What can we do to stop the progress of antinomianism?"[45] At the heart of the question was the fear that the Calvinist teaching on the "imputed" righteousness of Christ to humans in justification encouraged Christians to be passive toward the means of grace, and to believe "actual" righteousness was not demanded by the gospel. William Cudworth (1717–1763), minister of the Independent Chapel in Margaret Street, London,

---

40 129-Gr. *Some remarks on a dialogue . . . between a predestinarian and his friend* (London: no printer, 1741). Cf. 205C-Ki. W. D. [William Dowars], *Errors in part discovered* (Bristol: for the author, 1746), 4, 18.

41 129-Gr. *Some remarks on a dialogue . . .* , 5; 205C-Ki. [Dowars], *Errors in part discovered*, 4, 18.

42 129-Gr. *Some remarks on a dialogue . . .* , 4, 15.

43 205C-Ki. [Dowars], *Errors in part discovered*, 3.

44 146-Gr. [Dutton], *Letter to the Reverend Mr. John Wesley in vindication of the doctrines of absolute, unconditional election*, 15–20.

45 See John Bennet's Copy of the Minutes of Conference 1744, 1747, and 1748. Number 1 of *Publications of the Wesley Historical Society* (London: Charles Kelly, 1896). Bennet lists (p. 26) this as question 25. The answer is "1. Pray without ceasing that God would speak for Himself. 2. Write one or more dialogues."

and for a number of years an associate of Whitefield (responsible for the operation of the Tabernacle school) before forming his own connection, took Wesley to task in two dialogues.[46] Cudworth objected strenuously to the opprobrious designation "antinomian" for those who taught that Christ's righteousness was imputed to the Christian at justification. He believed that Wesley's abhorrence of antinomianism had warped his understanding of the Calvinist position. The imputation of Christ's righteousness to humans freed them from having to perform good works for salvation, but it did not free them from engaging in works: "We affirm constantly that they which have believed should be careful to maintain good works." Wesley, Cudworth believed, taught the unscriptural and popish doctrine of works righteousness.[47] Wesley's emphasis on works, said Cudworth, led to the establishment of a new legalism. The law's proper work was "to give the knowledge of sin . . . and be a ministry of condemnation, [not to be a] ministry of righteousness and life."[48]

Wesley's 1751 attack on the doctrine of the perseverance of the saints evoked a number of rejoinders. Thomas Gurney issued a revised edition of his *The nature and fitness of things* with an expanded preface (more than twice the original length) attacking Wesley's tract.[49] Robert Cruttenden (ca. 1690–1763), a London businessman, formerly a Dissenting minister who had lost his faith but had been converted to Calvinism under the preaching of John Cennick, devoted a section of his pamphlet in defense of George Whitefield to a slight attack on Wesley's rejection of the doctrine of perseverance.[50]

A major exchange took place between Wesley and John Gill (1697–1771), Baptist minister of Horseleydown, Southwark (later the chapel near London Bridge). An Old Testament scholar, Calvinist theologian, and ardent controversialist in the cause of ultra-Calvinism, Gill defended the doctrine

---

46 189-Gr. William Cudworth, *A dialogue between a preacher of inherent righteousness and a preacher of God's righteousness* (London: J. Hart, 1745). See Cudworth's second dialogue: 201-Gr. William Cudworth, *Truth defended and cleared from mistakes and misrepresentations* (London: J. Hart, 1746). When Wesley reprinted his dialogs in *A preservative against unsettled notions in religion* (Bristol: E. Farley, 1748), Cudworth responded in 272B-Ki. *A preservative in perilous times* (London: G. Keith, 1758).

47 189-Gr. Cudworth, *A dialogue between a preacher of inherent righteousness and a preacher of God's righteousness*, 7; 201-Gr. Cudworth, *Truth defended and cleared from mistakes*; 272B-Ki. Cudworth, *A preservative in perilous times*.

48 272B-Ki. Cudworth, *A preservative in perilous times*, 57.

49 152B-Ba. [Gurney], *The nature and fitness of things*.

50 246-Gr. [Robert Cruttenden], *The principles and preaching of the Methodists considered in a letter to the Reverend Mr. ***** (London: printed for James Buckland, 1752).

of perseverance in 1752 in *The doctrine of the saints['] final perseverance*, charging that Wesley had manipulated the Scriptures to fit his Arminian presuppositions. Gill summed up his charges thus:

> It [Wesley's doctrine] makes the love of God changeable; the covenant of grace failable; the redemption and satisfaction of Christ insufficient; and the work and graces of the Spirit loseable; and so must consequently fill the minds of the children of God with great doubts, fears, and distresses, if not despair; since their state and condition is so precarious: what comfort can a believer take in his present circumstances, if they are such as by a single act of sin, to which he is liable every moment, he may be removed from a state of grace into a state of condemnation; and, not withstanding all the favours bestowed on him, and grace given him, he may perish everlastingly?[51]

Wesley, unable to ignore Gill's attack (as he did with most Calvinists in this period), devoted a long section of his next anti-Calvinist pamphlet, *Predestination calmly considered* (1752), to an assault on his adversary's criticism.[52] The Baptist minister, the only opponent to venture into print against this new publication against predestination, refuted both Wesley's rejoinder to him and the new tract.[53] Gill denied vigorously that the doctrine of perseverance invited antinomianism. On the contrary, he suggested, it evoked holiness. Wesley had skirted the issues, he said, and had changed the subject from perseverance to predestination because he knew his arguments on the former had been defeated. Gill found Wesley's arguments against predestination unconvincing. Wesley did not debate sensibly about predestination, but "harangue[d] upon it; and that only a part of it, reprobation." What the Methodist leader wrote concerning reprobation was, in Gill's opinion, "mere noise."[54]

Wesley, realizing the futility of continuing the dispute at a theological level, replied to Gill in verse marked by biting sarcasm. Tongue in cheek,

---

51 233-Gr. John Gill, *The doctrine of the saints final perseverance* (London: printed and sold by G. Keith and J. Robinson, 1752), 54.

52 John Wesley, "Predestination calmly considered," *Works* (Jackson), 10:204–59.

53 234-Gr. John Gill, *The doctrine of predestination stated* (London: printed and sold by G. Keith, J. Robinson, Mr. Edwards, 1752).

54 Ibid., 4, 26.

Wesley entitled his poem: *An answer to all which the Revd. Dr. Gill has printed on the final perseverance of the saints.*[55] If Gill was unable to summon the poetic muse to his defense, Thomas Gurney was able. His twelve-page *Perseverance: A poem* matched Wesley's in acerbity and castigated him for not replying to Gill in a more befitting manner:

> Was ever such an empty answer seen?
> So weak, so wicked, foreign, false and mean?
> The author only beats the air in vain,
> And aims at something which he can't explain.
> In fine, the whole this mighty piece affords,
> Is spite, and pride and strange unmeaning words:
> Pleas'd with perverting sacred writ, to shew
> Salvation's not of grace, but what we do.[56]

Although the majority of anti-Wesley tracts from 1741 to 1758 were, as already noted, responses to the Methodist leader's own pamphlets, there were a few that were not provoked by his publications. Joseph Humphreys, one of Wesley's earliest lay helpers, who had left him to join Whitefield, published an open letter to members of the Methodist societies in London and several other cities, the pulpits of which were no longer open to him because of his Calvinist views. He was firmly persuaded that his former colleagues in Wesley's connection did not understand the doctrine of election in its true light since Wesley had represented it to them "in a most horrible colour." He raised questions, also, concerning Wesley's doctrine of perfection, charging that Wesley taught "sinless" perfection. Although he did not develop his criticism of this tenet fully, Humphreys raised a central issue for the Calvinists.[57]

Some of Anne Dutton's animus was also in fact directed against Wesley's doctrine of Christian perfection. It was the subject of her *Letters to the Reverend Mr. John Westley* in 1743—a series of four respectful, serious, and well-argued letters.[58] Wesley, she maintained, had set perfection too low.

---

55 John Wesley, *An answer to all which the Revd. Dr. Gill has printed on the final perseverance of the saints* (London: by the author, 1754).

56 253A-Ba. [Thomas Gurney], *Perseverance* (London: printed for G. Keith, J. Robinson, and M. Anderson, 1755), 5.

57 136A-Ba. Humphreys, *A letter to the members of the religious societies*, 8, 13–14, 16–17.

58 153-Gr. [Anne Dutton], *Letters to the Reverend Mr. John Westley against perfection* (London: J. Hart, 1743). Wesley's diary contains references to correspondence with Mrs.

Perfection was unattainable by humans in this life, and to be seen only on earth in the life of Christ. Whereas Wesley spoke of God's "imitable perfections," Anne Dutton avowed: "I see so much imperfection in my graces and duties, that I am glad to run by faith out of my imperfect self, into my perfect Jesus, and to see my beauty in his fairness, and my blackness, swallow'd up in his comeliness."[59]

The unpublished minutes of the 1744 Conference prompted John Green (d. 1774), an Anglican evangelical and master of a school in Great St. Andrew's Street, Seven Dials, and an early supporter of Wesley, to attack him in print.[60] The Conference had established the necessity of good works for final justification. Green believed that Wesley had turned his back on the doctrine of justification by faith alone and had established a doctrine that was "anti-scriptural, popish, and pharisaical." In opposition to Wesley, he contended that repentance was not the antecedent to saving faith, that faith alone was the condition of everlasting salvation, and that justification and sanctification were one and the same thing.[61]

In summary, between 1741 and 1758 the initiative in controversy rested with Wesley—his publications, and the rejoinders they evoked were the blows that drove in the wedge between Arminian and Calvinist. By 1758 the cleavage between the two had become a chasm separating two firmly entrenched positions.

Controversy over James Hervey's *Theron and Aspasio*

The publication of James Hervey's *Theron and Aspasio* in 1755 initiated a theological controversy that widened and deepened the chasm between

---

Dutton, October 25, 1739; August 22, 1740; December 23, 1740; February 28, 1741. On January 5, 1741, Wesley notes that he "read Mrs. Dutton's Letters." In all probability Mrs. Dutton's pamphlet contains her part of the correspondence during this period and was published in 1743 because of the growing antagonism between Wesley and the Calvinists.

59 Ibid., 50.

60 205B-Ba. John Green, *An appeal to the oracles of God*. An early supporter of Wesley, Green had assisted him in the oversight of the London Society. On October 4, 1746, John and Charles visited Green in a fruitless attempt to reconcile their differences. Cf. Wesley, October 4, 1746, in *BEWJW*, vol. 20, *Journal and Diaries III (1743–1754)*, 143–44. After his falling-out with Wesley, Green frequently preached for Lady Huntingdon at Norwood and supplied the pulpit at Whitefield's Tabernacle.

61 Ibid., 25–26, 31.

Calvinistic and Arminian Methodism. James Hervey (1714–58),[62] curate of Weston Favel, and one of Wesley's former Lincoln College pupils and member of the Oxford Holy Club, remained an admirer of the Methodist leader, although, having become a Calvinist, he did not see eye to eye with him in all theological issues. Their friendship was sadly interrupted when Wesley, in response to a request from Hervey for a critique of his manuscript of *Theron and Aspasio; or a series of dialogues*, and then a second request for a more thorough revision of his manuscript, made numerous alterations, wounding his former pupil with the severity of his critique.

Hervey published his work in February 1755.[63] Many months later, in October 1755, Wesley informed Hervey privately, in a long letter, of further criticisms arising out of the published version of *Theron and Aspasio*. He rebuked Hervey for teaching the "imputed righteousness" of Christ—an expression Wesley believed to be unscriptural. But Wesley's concern was not just theological; he feared that the phrase would encourage antinomianism: "I have abundant proof that the frequent use of this unnecessary phrase, instead of 'furthering . . . progress in vital holiness,' has encouraged [Christians] to work all uncleanness with greediness."[64] In 1758 Wesley published this letter, along with some of his other controversial writings, in *A preservative against unsettled notions*.[65]

Hervey had not replied to Wesley's 1756 letter but had sketched out a rejoinder in eleven letters. He died prematurely in 1758, making a deathbed wish that his reply never be printed. In 1764, however, a pirated edition appeared, and in 1765 William Hervey (James's brother) released a corrected version, which only served to exacerbate the existing hostility. Hervey's *Letters* were highly Calvinistic. Although he pulled no punches, he was not abusive. He rebuked Wesley for labeling his tenets antinomian: "I would incessantly inculcate, both the indispensable necessity, and the manifold utility of holy obedience. We are redeemed, that we may be zealous of good works—The

---

62 *ODNB*.

63 James Hervey, *Theron and Aspasio: or a series of dialogues and letters, upon the most important and interesting subjects*, 3 vols. (London: Rivington, 1755).

64 John Wesley, "Letter to James Hervey, October 15, 1756," *BEWJW*, 13:321–44. Wesley quotes from *Theron and Aspasio* and then replies seriatim.

65 John Wesley, *A Preservative against Unsettled Notions in Religion* (1756), in *Works* (Jackson), 14:254.

child obeys because he is beloved; because he is the heir."[66] Not content, however, to defend his own position, Hervey launched an attack on Wesley for teaching works righteousness and suggested that Wesley had entered a theological coalition with Rome.[67] Hervey went on to charge Wesley with changing his mind—a common Calvinist criticism of him. Indeed, much of what Wesley had condemned in *Theron and Aspasio*, he himself had taught in the early days of the revival.[68]

Wesley took offense at Hervey's *Letters* out of all proportion to their attack on him. In a long preface to *A treatise on justification extracted from Mr. John Goodwin* (1765), Wesley took his deceased friend to task.[69] Wesley hit hard. Some of his blows were unfair, unjustly accusing Hervey of stigmatizing him "as a knave, a dishonest man, one of no truth, justice or integrity."[70]

As Scotland, with its long association with Calvinism, found Hervey's theology congenial, it was not surprising that winds from the north fanned the flames of this controversy. Prefaced by a virulent attack of his own on Wesley, John Erskine (1719–1803), minister of Old Greyfriars Church, Edinburgh, published a Scottish edition of Hervey's *Eleven Letters*.[71] When James Kershaw, one of Wesley's itinerants, attacked Erskine's preface in *An earnest appeal to the public*, Erskine's response was to reprint and defend his preface.[72] He did not stop at this, however, but broadened his attack to include Wesley and Scottish Methodism. His aim was twofold—first, to reach members of Wesley's societies in Scotland and convince them that their leader was "by no means so orthodox as they . . . [had] hitherto imagined;" second, to warn those who adhered to the Westminster Confession not to put themselves

---

66 361-Gr. James Hervey, *Eleven letters from the late Rev. Mr. Hervey . . . to . . . John Wesley* (London: Charles Rivington, 1765), 64.

67 Ibid., 56, 77, 123.

68 Ibid., 213.

69 John Wesley, *Preface to A Treatise on Justification, extracted from Mr. John Goodwin,* in *Works* (Jackson), 10:316–46. Later in the year he reprinted this attack under the title *An answer to all that is material in letters just published under the name of the Reverend Mr. Hervey* (Bristol: William Pine, 1765).

70 Ibid.

71 363-Gr. [Erskine], *Mr. Wesley's principles detected.*

72 James Kershaw, *An earnest appeal to the public in an honest, amicable and affectionate reply to the preface of Aspasio Vindicated* (Edinburgh: Auld and Smelie, 1765). James Kershaw was one of Wesley's early itinerants. After a brief time as an independent minister, he returned to the itinerancy. In 1767 he ceased itinerating and settled at Gainsborough, Lincolnshire.

under the direction of a "teacher [Wesley] whose principles must oblige him to undermine," if possible, that statement of faith.[73] Wesley, unwilling to allow Erskine's attack to pass in silence, rushed off a short rejoinder, not in the hope that he would convince the Scot to change his mind, but in the belief that he owed it to his societies in Scotland to vindicate himself from such a vicious attack.[74] Matters did not rest there, Samuel Martin (1739–1829), minister at Monimail, Fife, Scotland, took up the cudgels against Wesley in answer to the attack on Erskine.[75] There could be no doubt that this bitter conflict prejudiced many in Scotland against Wesley and his preachers, hindering the progress of Arminian Methodism in the north.

England did not escape the bitterness of this controversy. An anonymous author who entitled his 1765 tract *Brief animadversions on some passages in the eleven letters*, although concentrating his attack on Hervey, was unsympathetic to Wesley as well. He ridiculed the unchristian bickering between the two men who had "so strenuously exerted themselves in the cause of Christianity and would be thought the pillars of the truth."[76] One zealous advocate of Hervey's *Letters* released *The Jesuit detected; or, The Church of Rome discover'd in the disguise of a Protestant*, alleging that Wesley and Rome taught identical doctrines of justification.[77]

The English Calvinistic critics reveled in Wesley's alleged theological inconsistency. Two authors, one in 1765, the other in 1766, set out to embarrass Wesley over his alleged inconsistent statements concerning imputed righteousness. In the anonymously published *John against Wesley; or, A dialogue on the imputation of Christ's righteousness,* readers eavesdrop on a schizophrenic Wesley talking to himself. As one part of him presents passages from *The Christian Library*, the other responds with contradictory statements from the *Preservative against unsettled notions, A treatise on justification, The principles of a Methodist,* and *Explanatory notes upon the New Testament.* The dialogue ends in utter disagreement, as Wesley remarks to John: "You and

---

73 363-Gr. [Erskine], *Mr. Wesley's principles detected,* 1, 24.

74 John Wesley, *Some Remarks on a Defence of the preface to the Edinburgh edition of Aspasio Vindicated, in Works* (Jackson), 10:346–57.

75 376-Gr. [Samuel Martin], *A few thoughts and matters of fact concerning Methodism* (Edinburgh, sold by William Gray, 1766). See especially 13–22.

76 363A-Ba. A sincere friend to the true religion of Jesus Christ, *Brief animadversions on some passages in the eleven letters to . . . John Wesley* (London: printed for John Payne, 1765).

77 410C-Fi. *The Jesuit detected* (London: printed for J. Johnson, M. Folingsby, J. Law and M. Smith, 1768).

I shall never agree upon these points, nor can all the wisdom of men make us agree."[78] Wesley's attempt in 1766 to clarify his position on imputed righteousness by preaching and publishing his sermon *The Lord our Righteousness* did not have the desired effect; it further heightened the controversy.[79] Another author, possibly William Parker, took passages from the sermon and placed them in parallel columns alongside extracts from Wesley's other writings on the subject, rebuking him for asserting contradictory tenets.[80] Walter Sellon, formerly a Methodist preacher and master at Kingswood, but later an ordained Anglican settled at Smithsby, rallied to Wesley's side during the conflict with two pamphlets, the first in 1766, the second in 1767.[81] The abusive tone of his criticism of the Hervey brothers and Cudworth did not help Wesley's cause. A severe, though not wholly unfair, critique of Sellon appeared in *A friendly reproof to a country clergyman* by "Calvinisticus." Sellon's zeal in defaming a dead colleague, Calvinisticus wrote, was "of the devil's kindling,"[82]

It would be futile to attempt to apportion the blame between Wesley and Hervey, or the Arminians and Calvinists, in this unfortunate dispute. But there can be no doubt that this squabble fanned the fires of enmity between the two camps—fires that would explode into a greater conflagration in the 1770s.

The Calvinistic Methodist Feud with the Church of England

Open warfare between the Calvinistic Methodists and the Church of England occurred from 1768 to 1770, but there had been a long history of tension and controversy between the two. With the Restoration, Calvinism within the Church of England suffered a heavy blow. Arminian tenets were substituted for Calvinistic ones. Indeed, by the onset of the evangelical revival, proponents of Calvinism within the Church of England, though not totally eclipsed, were rare. In the 1730s Robert Seagrave, one of the Calvinist remnant in the Church of

---

78 367-Gr. *John against Wesley* (London: for E. and C. Dilly, [1765]). The probable author was William Mason, an eighteenth-century poet, author, editor, publisher, and landscape designer. See *ODNB*.

79 John Wesley, Sermon 20, *The Lord our Righteousness*, in *BEWJW* 1:444–65.

80 375-Gr. [William Parker], *A letter to the Rev. Mr. John Wesley, concerning his inconsistency with himself* (London: H. Hart, 1766).

81 A Clergyman [Walter Sellon], *Some strictures on a few places of the late Reverend Mr. Hervey's letters* (London: no printer, 1766). Country Clergyman [Walter Sellon], *An answer to Aspasio Vindicated* (n.p.: no printer, 1767).

82 387A-Ki. Calvinisticus, *A friendly reproof to a country clergyman* (London: E. and C. Dilly, 1767), 19.

England, witnessed to the unpopularity of the Calvinistic interpretation of the Church's doctrinal standards.[83] It is not surprising, then, that when Whitefield began in 1739 to preach doctrines that leaned toward Calvinism, a hostile reaction from Anglican divines quickly ensued. Joseph Trapp complained that the young evangelist was teaching discredited doctrines.[84] Others charged that Whitefield and his fellow preachers were reviving "obsolete doctrines; . . . absurd doctrines, so derogatory to the divine attributes."[85]

Whitefield's Calvinism continued to be an issue all through the 1740s. Not only did Wesley assail Whitefield in the 1740s over the doctrine of predestination; Anglican writers also published repudiations of it. This and his other Calvinistic doctrines, they said, had no place in the eighteenth-century church.[86] During the 1750s and early 1760s, Calvinistic Methodist interpretations of the doctrine of justification sparked heated exchanges.[87]

The squabble between the Calvinistic Methodists and the Church of England came to a head in 1763 over the ejection of six Calvinistic Methodist students from St. Edmund's Hall, Oxford, on the grounds of enthusiasm and holding religious meetings in private houses. In the pamphlet feud that followed, the question soon shifted from the rightness or wrongness of the expulsion to a dispute over whether the Church of England's doctrines were Calvinist in foundation. Richard Hill had initiated the change in focus in his *Pietas oxoniensis*, almost half of which was devoted to a scathing attack on the Arminians of the Church of England and a defense of the Calvinist position. Hill asserted that justification by faith alone, the bondage of the human will, double predestination, and perseverance of the saints were all authentic Anglican tenets. They were the doctrines for which Cranmer and Ridley had been martyred.[88] Thomas Nowell, principal of St. Mary's Hall, Oxford, and one of the judges who examined the six students, was spokesman for the

---

83 See [Robert Seagrave], *A letter to the people of England occasion'd by the falling away of the clergy from the doctrines of the Reformation* (London: no printer, 1735). Seagrave (1693–1755?), a Cambridge-educated Anglican priest, hymnist, and pamphleteer, befriended and supported Wesley and Whitefield. *ODNB*.

84 010-Gr. Trapp, *The nature, folly, sin and danger of being righteous over-much*, 47–48.

85 007-Gr. E. B., *An expostulatory letter to the Reverend Mr. Whitefield, and . . . the Methodists of the Church of England* (London: printed for J. Noon, 1739).

86 126-Gr. *A comparison between the doctrines taught by the clergy . . . and . . . Whitefield.*

87 See chapter 3, "Doctrinal Deviation."

88 393-Gr. A Master of Arts of the University of Oxford [Sir Richard Hill], *Pietas oxoniensis* (London: for G. Keith, J. Millan, E. and C. Dilly, M. Folingsby, 1768), 29–66.

Anglicans. Half of his pamphlet reply to Hill was a refutation of the Calvin-istic interpretation of the Church of England's theological standards.[89] Other clergy rallied to Nowell's support. The bone of contention was the doctrine of predestination.[90]

The Predestination Controversy

The pamphlet warfare between the two wings of the revival in the decade of the 1770s had its origins in the controversy between Calvinistic Methodists and Anglicans over predestination.[91] Though he may have been sympathetic to the six young men from Oxford so unjustly treated, Wesley sided with Angli-can opponents of the Calvinist wing on the matter of doctrine. Convinced that Nowell's *Answer to pietas oxoniensis* said "quite enough to clear the Church of England from the charge of predestination,"[92] Wesley remained aloof from this controversy until 1769 when Augustus Toplady issued two trenchant attacks on Arminianism: the first, entitled *The Church of England vindicated from the charge of Arminianism*,[93] argued heatedly for the Calvinism of the Church of England and the *Articles of Religion*; the second, a translation of a Latin treatise by Zanchius, was entitled *The doctrine of absolute predestination stated*.[94] While Walter Sellon worked on a refutation of the first of Toplady's

---

89 394-Gr. Thomas Nowell, *An answer to a pamphlet entitled 'Pietas oxoniensis,'* 75–142.

90 396-Gr. A Member of the Church of England, *A letter to the author of a pamphlet intitled 'Pietas oxoniensis'* (London: for E. Johnson, 1768), 24–25; 412-Gr. [William Jones], *A letter to a young gentleman at Oxford* (London: for Robinson and Roberts, and M. Folingsby, 1769); 417A-Ki. John Allen, *The enthusiast's notion of election to eternal life disproved*; 426-Gr. Haddon Smith, *Methodistical deceit* (London: for H. Turpin, 1770); 411A-Ki. William Hawkins, *The pretences of enthusiasts considered* (Oxford: Clarendon, 1769), 9–12.

91 For the later phase of the Calvinist controversy, see chapter 12, "'Horrible Decrees': Methodism in the 1770s and the Calvinist Controversy," in Rack, *Reasonable Enthusiast*, 450–61 (see chap. 4, n. 2).

92 John Wesley, November 19, 1763, *BEWJW*, vol. 22, *Journal and Diaries V (1765–1775)*, 164.

93 416-Gr. A Presbyter of the Church of England [Augustus Montague Toplady], *The Church of England vindicated from the charge of Arminianism* (London: for Joseph Gurney, 1769).

94 417-Gr. The Author of the *Church of England vindicated from the charge of Arminianism* [Augustus Montague Toplady], *The doctrine of absolute predestination stated* (London: for Joseph Gurney and James Matthews, 1769). Jerome Zanchius (1516–1590) was an Italian Protestant clergyman, theologian, and educator. Among his publications are: *Confessions of the Christian Religion, Observation on the Divine Attributes,* and *The Doctrine of Absolute Predestination.*

assaults,[95] Wesley turned his attention to the second, publishing in 1770 an abridgment of it (under a shortened title) with the initials "A. T." affixed to a final paragraph of his own, summarizing in caricature the Calvinist doctrine: "One in twenty (suppose) of mankind are elected; nineteen in twenty are reprobated. The elect shall be saved, do what they will. The reprobate shall be damned, do what they will."[96] Furious, Toplady poured out the vials of his wrath in an open letter to Wesley, full of vicious personal attack and scandalous stories. Insult was heaped upon insult. Wesley was "a restless Arminian," a "lurking, sly assassin," endeavoring to palm off "pernicious doctrines . . . [on] credulous followers, with all the sophistry of a Jesuit, and the dictatorial authority of a pope." Toplady called for all-out war: "Commence the siege and welcome. Open your trenches and plan your batteries. Bring forth your arguments . . . If I cannot beat you back, I'll freely capitulate, and own myself conquered."[97] Wesley's publication of Toplady's extract of Zanchius with its caricature was unjustified, but so, too, was the irate young Calvinist's vitriolic response.

Wesley kept the fires aflame by adding more fuel with the printing of *The consequence proved* (1770).[98] Toplady's reply, *More work for Mr. John Wesley*, though more temperate, contained phrases of undue asperity. It seemed impossible for Toplady to write without slinging mud. Wesley ignored it, but Fletcher replied.[99] From 1770 to 1774 Toplady kept up a brisk assault on Arminian Methodism, with an occasional condemnatory remark about Wesley interspersed, through the publication of some of his sermons.[100] While the tone of these was less rancorous, Toplady's massive two-volume *Historic*

---

95 Walter Sellon, *The Church of England vindicated from the charge of absolute predestination* (London: E. Cabe, 1771).

96 John Wesley, "The Doctrine of Absolute Predestination" (1770) in *BEWJW*, 13:410–21, esp. 421.

97 424-Gr. Augustus Montague Toplady, *A letter to the Rev. Mr. John Wesley relative to his pretended abridgement of Zanchius* (London: for Joseph Gurney, 1770).

98 Wesley, "The Consequence Proved" (1771) in *BEWJW*, vol. 12, *Doctrinal and Controversial Treatises II*, 422–28.

99 447-Gr. Augustus Montague Toplady, *More work for Mr. John Wesley* (London: for James Matthews, 1772). Toplady claimed to have rid the work of offensive remarks, but see 5, 13. [John Fletcher], *An Answer to the Rev. Mr. Toplady's 'Vindication of the Decrees'* (London: no printer, 1776).

100 427-Gr. Augustus Montague Toplady, *A caveat against unsound doctrines; 472A-Fi.* Augustus Montague Toplady, *Good news from heaven* (London: for J. Matthews and G. Keith, 1775); 478-Gr. Augustus Montague Toplady, *Free-will and merit fairly examined* (London: for J. Matthews and G. Keith, 1775).

proof of the doctrinal Calvinism of the Church of England was tarnished by a renewal of rankling bitterness against Walter Sellon and Wesley.[101] None of Toplady's later assaults brought a reply from Wesley. The Methodist leader's 1771 tract, *The consequence proved,* was the last in which he engaged the young Calvinist hothead in debate, having dismissed him as "too dirty a writer" to meddle with.[102]

When in 1774 Wesley released his *Thoughts upon Necessity,* defending human freedom of will and refuting those who concluded that a person's sense of freedom was a delusion,[103] Toplady could not allow it to pass without comment. He issued a long rejoinder, the purpose of which, he stated, was to "invade and carry the arms of truth into the enemy's own territory."[104] Fletcher repulsed the invasion with a long counterstatement.[105] Much of Toplady's tract was just as abusive as his earlier works. Although this pamphlet was the last doctrinal tract he published against Wesley, he continued to hound him through the columns of the *Gospel Magazine,* the editorship of which he held from December 1775 to June 1776. In 1775 personal animosity against Wesley drove Toplady, under the pseudonym "Hanoverian," to blast him unmercifully for his *Calm Address to our American Colonies.*[106]

Controversy surrounded Wesley and Toplady even in the latter's final illness and death. Rumors abounded that Toplady had expressed a strong desire during his long and severe illness to see Wesley in order to recant his predestinarian principles. So strong were the rumors that Toplady, though deathly ill, found it necessary to issue a refutation from the pulpit on June 13, 1778, blaming "malicious and unprincipled persons" among Wesley's followers for spreading lies. Not even the pulpit denial quashed the rumors. Hearing from a friend that Wesley's preachers were circulating the false news that he had recanted from the pulpit, Toplady published his repudiation

---

101 464-Gr. Augustus Montague Toplady, *Historic proof of the doctrinal Calvinism of the Church of England* (London: for J. Keith, 1774), 2 volumes.

102 See John Wesley to George Merryweather, June 24, 1770, in *Letters* (Telford), 5:192.

103 John Wesley "Thoughts upon Necessity" (1774), in *BEWJW,* 13:526–46.

104 472-Gr. Augustus Montague Toplady, *The scheme of Christian and philosophical necessity asserted* (London: for Vallance and Simmons, 1775).

105 [John Fletcher], *A reply to the principal arguments by which the Calvinists . . . support the doctrine of absolute necessity* (London: R. Hawes, 1777).

106 See chapter 7, "Methodism and Politics."

under the title *The Reverend Mr. Toplady's dying avowal of his religious sentiments.*[107]

Toplady died of tuberculosis on August 11, 1778. An early appraisal of his life by Thomas Wilkins affirmed that he died a staunch Calvinist and remained an opponent of Wesley.[108] In spite of this, malicious rumors about Toplady persisted. Richard Hill inserted a letter to Wesley in the *General Advertiser,* October 3, 1779 (under the pseudonym "Veritas"), challenging Wesley to assert publicly that he had never made the malicious remark that Toplady had died in "black despair, blaspheming." When Wesley ignored the newspaper letter, Hill issued his challenge in the form of a pamphlet. If Wesley remained silent, people must assume, wrote Hill, that the Methodist leader was "the raiser and fabricator of this most nefarious report."[109]

Controversy over the 1770 Minutes of Conference

By 1770 Wesley and his branch of Methodism were increasingly concerned that the doctrine of election was dangerously antinomian and would result in greater sin:

> Blest all who seek to wrangle and to fight,
> Such mount from seas of blood to worlds of light;
> Go riot, drink, and every ill pursue,
> For joys eternal are prepar'd for you.
> Fear not to sin, till death shall close thy eyes,
> Since as you please, yours is the immortal prize.[110]

Fear of antinomianism led the 1770 Conference of Wesley's preachers to adopt anti-Calvinist statements, which read as follows:

> Take heed to your Doctrine.

---

107 513-Gr. Augustus Montague Toplady, *The Reverend Mr. Toplady's dying avowal* (London: for J. Mathews, J. Buckland, and T. Vallance, 1778), 3.

108 514A-Ki. T.W. [Thomas Wilkins], *An elegy on the death of the Rev. A. M. Toplady* (London: W. Oliver, 1778).

109 524A-Ki. Sir Richard Hill, *A letter to the Rev. John Wesley, wherein that gentleman is called upon to declare whether he be . . . the author of . . . calumnies on the late Rev. Augustus Toplady* (London: for J. Mathews, 1780), 5, 13.

110 608–Ki. *Methodism indeed; or, A satirical poem, in reply to on[e] composed by a Partialist, with a view to making the doctrine of universal salvation (by Jesus Christ) appear odious* (n.p.: no printer, no date), broadside.

We said in 1744, "We have leaned too much towards Calvinism." Wherein?

1. With regard to man's faithfulness, Our Lord himself taught us to use this expression, and we ought never to be ashamed of it. We ought steadily to assert, on his authority, that if a man is not "faithful in the unrighteous mammon," God will not give him the true riches.

2. With regard to working for life. This also our Lord has expressly commanded us. "Labour" ἐργάζεσθε, literally, "work for the meat that endureth to everlasting life." And, in fact, every believer, till he comes to glory, works for, as well as from life.

3. We have received it as a maxim, that "a man is to do nothing, in order to justification." Nothing can be more false. Whoever desires to find favour with God, should "cease from evil, and learn to do well." Whoever repents, should do "works meet for repentance." And if this is not in order to find favour, what does he do them for?

There followed a succinct eight-point review, which stressed the role of works, not as "meriting," but as a "condition" of justification. Wesley's position is best seen in points 4–6:

4. Is not this "salvation by works"? Not by the merit of works, but by works as a condition.

5. What have we been disputing about for these thirty years? I am afraid about words.

6. As to merit itself, of which we have been so dreadfully afraid: we are rewarded "according to our works," yes, "because of our works." How does this differ from for the sake of our works? And how differs this from secundum merita operum? As our works deserve? Can you split this hair? I doubt, I cannot.[111]

These propositions were loosely worded (especially the fourth and sixth statements in the "review") and open to grievous misunderstanding. A six-year controversy ensued between the two wings of Methodism. It was marked by increasing severity, bitterness, and hostility. If Calvinists were guilty of

---

111 "Annual Minutes of Some Late Conversations, 1770," in *BEWJW*, 10:392–94.

personal invective against their opponents, Wesley and Fletcher were not entirely blameless.

Lady Huntingdon, incensed by the doctrinal *Minutes* of 1770, branded them as "popery unmasked."[112] In January 1771 the countess decided to dismiss everyone at her college at Trevecca who supported Wesley's *Minutes*. The headmaster, Joseph Benson, (formerly a master at Wesley's Kingswood school) was dismissed, and Trevecca students who failed to disavow Arminian tenets were expelled. John Fletcher, college president, after failing to explain the *Minutes* to the countess's satisfaction, resigned his position in March 1771, insisting that if assent to dogmatic Calvinism was required, it was no longer the place for him. The purge of her ranks did not appease Lady Huntingdon's anger, and she set out to attack her Arminian opponents, and their commander-in-chief, John Wesley.

A circular letter was dispersed throughout England, Scotland, and Wales under the signature of Walter Shirley (1725–1786).[113] He was rector of Loughrea, Ireland, and one of the chaplains (and first cousin) of the Countess of Huntingdon. The letter called upon clergy and laity who disapproved of Wesley's *Minutes* to meet in Bristol to oppose the "dreadful heresy." The circular further proposed that those who gathered should invade Wesley's Conference as a body "and insist upon a formal recantation of the said *Minutes*, and in case of a refusal, that they sign and publish their protest against them."[114] A postscript to the document provided the names of individuals to whom the circular should be addressed and offered accommodations for those who wished to accept the invitation. Accompanying the circular were a copy of Wesley's *Minutes* and the proposed statement of protest.[115] Soon after, there appeared *A comment or paraphrase on the extract from the Minutes*

---

112 Thomas Jackson, *The Life of Charles Wesley* (New York: G. Lane and P. F. Sandford, 1844), 629. This phrase appears in a letter from Lady Huntingdon to Charles Wesley. Jackson prints the letter in full.

113 Walter Shirley, educated at New College, Oxford, was an Anglican priest, hymn writer, revivalist preacher, and controversialist. Initially friendly with John and Charles Wesley, he entered into heated debate with John over justification and antinomianism. *ODNB*.

114 434-Gr. Walter Shirley, *A circular letter* (n.p.: no printer, 1771). No copy of the circular appears to have survived. It was, however, reprinted in full in the *Gospel Magazine*, August 1771, 367–68, and in 436-Gr. Walter Shirley, *A narrative of the principal circumstances relative to the Rev. Mr. Wesley's late conference* (Bath: printed by W. Gye for T. Mills, 1771).

115 For the text of the letter, see Aaron Seymour, *The Life and Times of Selina, Countess of Huntingdon* (London: William E. Painter, 1839), 2:239–40.

of the Rev. Mr. Wesley.[116] Ostensibly, an Arminian explication of Wesley's *Minutes*, the pamphlet was in reality a bitterly sarcastic vindication of the Calvinist position. Wesley's *Minutes* was quoted in italics; the comments within brackets. A sample of its misrepresentation will suffice:

> 7. *As to merit itself, of which we have been so dreadfully afraid.*
> [We were brought into fear, where no danger was. Merit is a
> very harmless word. We may safely apply it to our works and
> plead it before God].[117]

A massive confrontation between the two forces seemed inevitable. Fletcher objected to the violence of Shirley's proposal, insisting that he had no right to intrude into Wesley's Conference, but the countess's chaplain refused to recall the circular. Before the Conference met, however, Lady Huntingdon's attitude softened, and she wrote to Wesley on August 2, 1771, apologizing for the circular's offensive tone. Following the countess's lead, Shirley also wrote, regretting his early aggressive attitude, and requesting that he and several of his friends be allowed to discuss their objections with the Conference.[118]

The Conference assembled in Bristol on August 6, 1771, and, on August 8, graciously received a Calvinist deputation consisting of Shirley, two of Lady Huntingdon's preachers (Mr. Glascot and Mr. Owen), three laymen (John Lloyd, James Ireland, and H. Winter), and two students of Trevecca College. After some discussion Shirley produced a "declaration" he had drawn up, requesting that "something at least analogous to it might be agreed to." Upon reading it Wesley made some "not very material" alterations, and he and fifty-three of his preachers attached their signatures. By their subscription they admitted that the wording of the 1770 *Minutes* had not been "sufficiently guarded" and declared that the *Minutes* were not to be understood as favoring justification by works.[119] Shirley, having agreed to issue a statement that he

---

116 435-Gr. *A comment or paraphrase on the extract from the Minutes of the Rev. Mr. Wesley*
     (London: printed for the author, 1771). This was reprinted in the June 1771 issue of the
     Gospel Magazine, 260–71.

117 Ibid.

118 These letters were published by Shirley (after the Conference had met) in 436-Gr. Walter
     Shirley, *A narrative of the principal circumstances relative to the Rev. Mr. Wesley's last
     Conference*, 8–12.

119 Ibid., 1–15. The text of the declaration and the names of those who signed are found on
     14–15.

had also made mistakes and had misunderstood the meaning of the *Minutes*, sent a certificate to Wesley to that effect a few days after the meeting.[120]

With irenic gestures from both sides, the controversy might have ceased had not Wesley insisted on the publication of John Fletcher's *Vindication of the Rev. Mr. Wesley's last Minutes occasioned by a circular printed letter*. Fletcher's manuscript, written after receipt of the circular letter, had been sent before the settlement of August 8 by Wesley to William Pine with instructions to print and publish. Despite Fletcher's pleas to suppress the work in its present form, Wesley, believing a public explication of his *Minutes* was necessary to combat the false impression widely dispersed in the circular, had resolved to release it as soon as it came off the press.[121]

Walter Shirley remained conciliatory. His *Narrative of the principal circumstance; relative to the Rev. Mr. Wesley's last Conference* was not an attack on others, but a defense of his role in the controversy. Unfortunately, he gave the mistaken impression that Fletcher had wanted the full suppression of his *Vindication*.[122] Fletcher rushed immediately to defend his first pamphlet, stating that he had no regrets about vindicating the *Minutes*, but was sorry he "did not write in a general manner, without taking notice of the circular letter."[123]

The peace had been shattered. Shirley retired from the battle, and Sir Richard Hill (1732–1808), second baronet of Hawkstone, Shropshire, replaced him as champion of the Calvinistic Methodist cause.[124] From 1771 to 1774 he lambasted Fletcher and Wesley with tracts tarnished on occasion by abusiveness. In 1771 he released two attacks on Wesley's doctrinal *Minutes*. In *An answer to some capital errors in Minutes of some late conversations between the Rev. Mr. Wesley and others*, extracts from the Minutes are compared with

---

120 Ibid., 17.

121 A lover of quietness and liberty of conscience [John Fletcher], *A vindication of the Rev. Mr. Wesley's last Minutes occasioned by a circular printed letter* (London: R. Hawes, 1775). Shirley printed a copy of the letter from Fletcher, dated August 15, expressing his wish that the publication would not reach the general public. Wesley's determination to go ahead with the release of Fletcher's *Vindication* is clearly stated in his letter of August 14, 1771, to Lady Huntingdon. See *Letters* (Telford), 5:274–75.

122 436-Gr. Walter Shirley, *A narrative of the principal circumstances relative to the Rev. Mr. Wesley's late conference,* 19.

123 The vindicator of the Rev. Mr. Wesley's Minutes [John Fletcher], *A second check to antinomianism* (London: W. Strahan, 1771).

124 Sir Richard Hill, educated at Magdalen College, Oxford, was a Tory member of Parliament, a prominent revivalist preacher, and a controversialist. *ODNB*.

quotations from Wesley's sermons, journals, *Earnest appeal*, and *Notes upon the New Testament*, to demonstrate Wesley's theological inconsistency.[125] The pamphlet closes with a satirical comment on the Declaration signed by Wesley and his preachers in Bristol in 1771:

> Whereas the religion and fate of three nations,
> Depend on th' importance of our conversations;
> Whereas some objections are thrown in our way,
> and words have been constru'd to mean what they say;
> Be it known from henceforth to each friend, and each brother
> Where'er we say one thing, we mean quite another.[126]

Wesley's equivocation on theological matters was one of the issues discussed in *A conversation between Richard Hill, Esq., the Rev. Mr. Madan, and Father Walsh*.[127] The central object of this tract, however, was to show that Wesley's doctrinal views were more Pelagian than those of Rome. "Popery," said the author, "is about the midway between Protestantism and Mr. J. Wesley."[128]

The Calvinist Arminian controversy in the 1770s revolved around the pamphlets of John Fletcher and Richard Hill. John Fletcher's *Vindication of Wesley's 1770 Minutes* was the first in a sprawling but well-organized series of essays he called *Checks to Antinomianism*.[129] Fletcher distinguished four degrees of justification: (1) that which is bestowed upon infants, without any action on their part; (2) that which the sinner receives by faith, and is given freely; (3) that which comes from bringing forth good works; and (4) final salvation which is bestowed at the last judgment, and is conditional upon faith and good works.[130] Fletcher, in rejecting the Calvinist notion that the sinner does nothing toward his or her initial justification, countered with the argument that belief in Christ and repentance, requirements the Calvinists accepted, were, in fact, actions performed before the individual is justified.

---

125 439-Gr. [Sir Richard Hill], *An answer to some capital errors* (London: for E. and C. Dilly, 1771).

126 Ibid., 11.

127 437-Gr. [Richard Hill], *A conversation between Richard Hill, Esq., the Rev. Mr. Madan, and Father Walsh* (London: sold by E. and C. Dilly, 1771).

128 Ibid., 14–15.

129 See John Fletcher, *The Works of the Reverend John Fletcher*, 2nd ed. (New York: John Wilson and Daniel Hitt, 1809).

130 Ibid., 2:45–48.

He pointed out that Scripture in many places stated that justification was conditional upon the performance, where possible, of "works meet for repentance." This did not mean that works merited or purchased justification. Like Wesley, Fletcher drew a clear distinction between "merit" and "condition." At the final justification on the last day, Fletcher asserted that humans are saved (or condemned) by the Judge according to their works. An individual is thus rewarded (or punished) for his or her works. This does not mean, however, that Christians merit their salvation by their works in the sense that it is earned—works have no power to save.[131]

Richard Hill, as champion of the Calvinistic theological position, became Fletcher's chief antagonist, counterattacking in a set of successive rejoinders to the *Checks*.[132] Though Hill was capable of debating theological issues coolly (his *Five letters* is a good example), much of his later writing in this controversy (particularly his *Review of all the doctrines taught by the Rev. Mr. John Wesley*) was marred by hyperbole and sarcasm.[133] Hill claimed that there was hardly a single paragraph in Wesley's controversial writings that was "exempt from cutting sneers and low sarcasm."[134]

Like Wesley, Fletcher believed that Calvinism led inevitably to antinomianism, and antinomianism led to hypocrisy and immorality. Hill castigated Fletcher roundly for "making Calvinism and antinomianism synonymous and convertible terms, thus injuring the reputations of numerous God-fearing Christians. Observation should have convinced Fletcher, said Hill, that antinomianism was not the inevitable result of holding Calvinist views.[135] Despite Hill's objection to Fletcher's name-calling, it did not prevent him from engaging in the same kind of practice. Wesley's doctrines, he declared, were a "mixture of Pelagianism, semi-Pelagianism, Arminianism, Popery, Mysticism,

---

131 Ibid., 2:45–48; 1:280–85, 287–96, 302–7.

132 438-Gr. A friend, the author of *Pietas Oxoniensis* [Hill], *Five letters to the Reverend Mr. F____r* (London: for E. and C. Dilly, 1771); 449-Gr. The Author of *P. O.* [Hill], *A review of all the doctrines taught by the Rev. Mr. John Wesley*; 450-Gr. The author of *Pietas Oxoniensis* [Hill], *Some remarks on a pamphlet entitled 'A third check to antinomianism'* (London: for Edward and Charles Dilly, 1772); 456-Gr. Hill, *The finishing stroke, containing some stricture on the Rev. Mr. John Fletcher's pamphlet* (London: Edward and Charles Dilly, 1773); 461-Gr. Hill, *Three letters . . . to the Rev. J. Fletcher.*

133 449-Gr. The author of *P. O.* [Hill], *A review of all the doctrines taught by the Rev. Mr. John Wesley.*

134 Ibid., 31.

135 456-Gr. [Hill], *The finishing stroke*, 30; 450-Gr. [Hill], *Some remarks on A third check to antinomianism*, 15.

and Quakerism."[136] Wesley and his preachers, Hill dismissed as "universalists, free-willers, perfectionists, and merit-mongers."[137]

Hill attacked the doctrinal views of Fletcher and Wesley on all fronts, but objected in particular that (1) Wesley's *Minutes* exalted humans, and did not take human depravity seriously enough; (2) by extolling one's power to do good works, the *Minutes* detracted from Christ's role in salvation; (3) humans play no part in their justification since believing is not a condition of justification; (4) the doctrine of second justification is unscriptural and popish—it inculcates legalism, and puts human merits in the place of divine grace; (5) good works are not "meriting" causes of an individual's justification but are witnesses to the effects of it.[138] Hill contended that once people are justified by faith, Christ's righteousness is imputed to them, and they remain in a state of "finished salvation."[139]

Hill's critique of Fletcher and Wesley did not stop at their doctrine of justification. He censured their teaching on Christian perfection, maintaining that the doctrine had arisen in the fifth century among the Pelagians, and had been fostered chiefly by Rome, until Wesley became its chief advocate. Hill offered little serious criticism of the doctrine. Rather, he mocked it and ridiculed those who espoused it.[140] In 1773 Hill showed reluctance to continue the controversy, entitling his rejoinder to the *Fourth check* by Fletcher, *The finishing stroke*, and commenting: "I believe that among real Christians more are the better for writing, and few if any are the better for reading controversial divinity. And with regard to people of the world, it is certain that altercations of this sort rather tend to set them against all religion."[141]

If these sentiments were genuine, they did not stop Hill from issuing, almost simultaneously, with his reply to Fletcher, *Logica wesleiensis*, an attack on Wesley's *Some remarks on Mr. Hill's Review.*[142] This new assault on the

---

136 449-Gr. The Author of *P. O.* [Hill], *A review of all the doctrines taught by the Rev. Mr. John Wesley*, 92. Cf. 20–21.

137 456-Gr. [Hill], *The finishing stroke*, 31.

138 438-Gr. A Friend, the Author of *Pietas Oxoniensis* [Hill], *Five letters to the Rev. M. F—r.*, 10–11, 19–20, 50, 222. 449-Gr. The Author of *P. O.* [Hill], *A review of all the doctrines taught by the Rev. Mr. John Wesley*, 4–5, 12.

139 Ibid., 5–6.

140 449-Gr. Author of *P.O.* [Hill] *A review of all the doctrines taught by the Rev. Mr. John Wesley*, 46–48, 104–5, 109–10.

141 456-Gr. [Hill], *The finishing stroke*, 39.

142 455-Gr. Richard Hill, *Logica wesleiensis* (London: E. and C. Dilley, 1773).

Methodist leader shows Hill at his angriest and most vindictive. He blamed Wesley for the bitterness existing between the two wings of Methodism and ridiculed Wesley's claim that his writings were irenic. Instead, Hill suggested, they had engendered discord:

> But hence, ye horrid spawn of hell,
> who hearken not to me;
> Blasphemers, devils, liars, fiends
> Who credit God's decree
> With love and meekness long I try'd
> To bend each stubborn mind;
> But hard as rocks and knotted oaks,
> Calvinian hearts I find.[143]

Hill's final shot at the Arminian camp took the form of a publication that contained, along with a bitter attack, three letters he had sent to Fletcher privately, making overtures for reconciliation. In this correspondence Hill, still insisting that his opponents' principles were erroneous, apologized for his intemperate remarks on occasion, and announced that he had requested his bookseller to stop the sale of his anti-Arminian publications. There matters would have rested had Hill's efforts at reconciliation not been betrayed by someone who, in misrepresenting his reasons for declining further controversy, spread a rumor that he had recanted his Calvinist tenets and begged Wesley's pardon for having written against his doctrines. Angered by what he thought a treacherous act, Hill not only published his correspondence with Fletcher, adding a preface full of invective and a postscript entitled *A creed for arminians and perfectionists* (signed J. F., J. W., and W. S.), cruelly caricaturing Wesley's theology in eleven articles, but he revoked his earlier instructions to halt sales of his antinomian tracts by ordering that sales be recommenced.[144]

Calvinists of lesser stature joined Hill in the assault on Fletcher and Wesley. Rowland Hill, Richard's younger brother, having stood aloof in the early stages of the controversy, entered it in 1772 in response to the publication of Fletcher's second and third *Checks*, believing that "to be neuter any longer . . . [would] be criminal."[145] But Rowland Hill added nothing new to the debate.

---

143 Ibid., 48.

144 461-Gr. [Sir Richard Hill], *Three letters . . . to the Rev. J. Fletcher*.

145 451-Gr. [Rowland Hill], *Friendly remarks occasioned by the spirit and doctrines contained in the Rev. Mr. Fletcher's 'Vindication,'* 4.

Fletcher's *Fourth Check* inspired a heavily satirical attack, issued under the pseudonym "Candid Calvinists," entitled *Much ado about nothing; Or, Arminian Methodism turned out rank popery at last.* As the title suggests, the pamphlet contended that Fletcher and Wesley had reintroduced the popish doctrine of salvation by works. The author announced that there would never be peace between the two wings of Methodism while the Arminians were plunging their "dagger into the very vitals of divine grace and truth."[146] In 1773 there appeared, anonymously, *Doctor Crisp's ghost; or, a Check upon checks,* directed at Fletcher, who had attacked the seventeenth-century Calvinist (an idol of their eighteenth-century counterparts) as an antinomian.[147] As late as 1780 there appeared a tract from an anonymous Calvinist author attacking Wesley's *Minutes* and Fletcher's *Checks* under the title *The friendly retrievers.*[148]

During 1774 and 1775 Fletcher released a massive attack on his opponents in five pamphlets totaling almost six hundred pages.[149] No Calvinist pamphlet came in reply. Attacks continued to come, however, from two periodicals, the *Spiritual Magazine* and the *Gospel Magazine,* whose editorial policy was to espouse and defend the Calvinist position. The columns of these magazines kept controversy alive by assaults on Arminian doctrine and by bitter personal attacks on Wesley and his followers. It was to neutralize the effect of the two Calvinist journals that Wesley launched his own partisan organ, which he called the *Arminian Magazine,* converting the label "Arminian" into a badge to be worn with pride just as he had done with the earlier epithet

---

146   458A-Ba. Candid Calvinists, *Much ado about nothing* (London: M. Lewis and J. Matthews, 1773), 15.

147   460-Gr. *Doctor Crisp's ghost* (London: no printer, 1773). Tobias Crisp (1600–1643) was an English Calvinist theologian whose antinomian tendencies drew him into controversy.

148   525E-Ba. *The friendly retrievers* (n.p.: no printer, 1773).

149   Author of *Checks to Arminians* [John Fletcher], *The fictitious and genuine creed* (London: R. Hawes 1775); [John Fletcher], *Logia genevenesis,* 2nd ed. (Bristol: W. Pine, 1774); [John Fletcher], *Logica genevensis continued,* 2nd ed. (Bristol: W. Pine, 1774); The author of the *Checks to Antinomianism* [John Fletcher], *The first part of an equal check to Pharisaism and Antinomianism,* 4th ed. (London: G. Storey, 1803); [John Fletcher], *Zelotes and Honestus reconciled* (London: R. Hawes, 1775).

"Methodist."[150] As Wesley tried to distinguish between writing on controverted topics and actual controversy, his magazine carried no personal attacks.[151]

Minor Skirmishes 1774–1791

Even after the pamphlet debate over the 1770 *Minutes* had ended, Wesley remained the target for rancorous attacks from Calvinist antagonists. The hostility that had been engendered took a long time to dissipate. In 1774 William Parker, an earlier opponent, gave some attention to Wesley in *Some account of the state of religion in London*. In contrast to the lavish praise he bestowed on Whitefield, Romaine, and Madan were unsympathetic statements concerning the Arminian wing. Parker urged that, since Wesley's doctrines obscured the gospel, respect for his "venerable grey hairs" ought not to prevent Calvinists from opposing his theological errors.[152] Also published in 1774 was a tract entitled *A faithful warning to the followers of the Rev. Mr. John Wesley*, renewing the attack on Charles's *Hymns on God's Everlasting Love* and taking John to task for his 1749 *Letter to a Roman Catholic*. The author concluded that Wesley's doctrine was identical to that of Rome.[153] A vulgar burlesque entitled *A necessary alarm and most earnest caveto against tabernacle-principles*, ridiculed Wesley's preaching tour in Cornwall in August and September 1775. The author was peeved that Wesley claimed to be the central figure of the revival.[154]

John Wesley's sermon at the ceremony for the laying of the foundation stone for his New Chapel in City Road, London, on April 21, 1777, reviewing the providential rise and progress of Methodism, occasioned a virulent rejoinder from the young Rowland Hill, entitled *Imposture detected, and the dead*

---

150 For Wesley's statement of purpose in establishing the *Arminian Magazine*, see John Wesley, Letter to Thomas Taylor, January 15, 1778, in *Letters* (Telford), 6:294–96, and the preface to the first issue in *Works* (Jackson), 14:278–81.

151 For a discussion of the material printed in the *Arminian Magazine*, see Thomas Walter Herbert, *John Wesley as Editor and Author* (Princeton: Princeton University Press, 1940), 34–45.

152 463A-Ba. [William Parker], *Some account of the state of religion in London* (London: for J. Matthews, G. Keith, and W. Harris, 1774), 18–19, 22, 24–34.

153 467-Gr. *A faithful warning to the followers of the Rev. Mr. John Wesley*, iv, 7, 12–19.

154 489-Gr. J. W., Master of (very extraordinary) Arts, *A necessary alarm and most earnest cavetto against tabernacle-principles* ([London]: sold by the bookseller of London and Bristol, 1776). No copy of this tract appears to have survived. Augustus Toplady, however, reviews it in the October 1776 issue of the *Gospel Magazine*, 475–78, commending it as a "delicate satire on Wesley," and reprinting several sections.

vindicated—a masterpiece of vituperation and scurrility.[155] Wesley, said Hill, despite his "pious ejaculations" of loyalty to the establishment, went about "raising dissenting congregations, and building dissenting meeting houses the kingdom over; patronizing a set of preachers, very many of whom . . . [are] licenced under the Act of Toleration," and was thus the real Dissenter. Wesley's appropriation of the term "Methodist" for himself and his followers, and his unwillingness to recognize the right of the other wing of the movement to use it, angered Hill, as did Wesley's inference that he himself had been the central figure of the revival. Hill designated Whitefield "the mighty beginner of this work," and accused Wesley of blackening his former colleague's name. Not content with such criticism, Hill stooped to character assassination by rehashing scurrilous rumors about Wesley's personal life.[156]

Wesley defended himself with *An answer to Mr. Rowland Hill*.[157] Among those who rushed to Wesley's support were Thomas Olivers, one of his preachers; Matthew Goodenough, a "mechanick" of Bishopsgate Street; an anonymous author who claimed to differ with Wesley on both theological and political issues; and one who signed his pamphlet "A Calvinist." All agreed—Hill's attack was scurrilous.[158] *Imposture detected* had been issued in June 1777. By September, Rowland Hill had an apology in the press, and by early October it had been released under the title *A full answer to the Rev. J. Wesley's Remarks*.[159] Although he admitted that the tone of his earlier work was "far too ludicrous and severe," and disclaimed responsibility for some of the more rancorous statements, explaining that he had not seen them till he read them in print, Hill refused to retract the essence of his former charges, reiterating them instead. His credibility had been destroyed, however, and he did not venture into print against Wesley again.[160]

The year 1780 witnessed a virulent attack from Wesley's old friend and former preacher, John MacGowan, now one of his Calvinist opponents.

---

155 496-Gr. Hill, *Imposture detected, and the dead vindicated.*

156 Ibid., 5, 6, 15.

157 John Wesley, "An Answer to Mr. Rowland Hill's Tract entitled 'Imposture detected,'" in *Works* (Jackson), 10:446–54.

158 *Remarks on some 'Gentle strictures'* (Bristol: W. Pine, 1777); Thomas Olivers, *A rod for a reviler* (London: J. Fry, 1777); A Calvinist, *An expostulatory letter to the Rev. Rowland Hill*; Matthew Goodenough, *The Slanderer chastised* (London: R. Hawes, [1777]); Matthew Goodenough, *The snake in the grass discovered* (London: by the author, [1777]).

159 497-Gr. Hill, *A full answer to the Rev. J. Wesley's remarks.*

160 Ibid., 3, 32–33.

Although part of his *Foundry budget opened* concerned Wesley's theology (attacking a number of his early anti-Calvinist publications), much of the pamphlet degenerated into personal inventive.[161] In 1780 Wesley was deep in controversy with Roman Catholics because of his support of the intolerant Protestant Association. Despite this, MacGowan continued to label Wesley "a papist" and insist that Methodism was a breeding ground for popery. Furthermore, MacGowan claimed that many of Wesley's followers in Manchester and Lancashire found Roman Catholic services of worship as congenial as Methodist society meetings.[162]

MacGowan's pamphlet was the last important one to come from the ranks of the Calvinist evangelicals. In 1784, however, John Muirhead launched an ill-informed assault on the Methodist leader, basing much of his criticism on the controversial tracts of Hervey, Toplady, and the Hill brothers.[163] In 1787 Robert Moody's *Observations on certain prophecies in the Book of Daniel and the Revelation of St. John* was published. This tract is worth mentioning here only because it was the most curious of all the Calvinist attacks on Wesley. It is shot through with millenarian references: the date of Christ's second coming was set for Eastertide 1791; Whitefield was believed to be the seventh angel heralding the jubilee of the Lord; John and Charles Wesley were the Antichrist tearing down true doctrine [Calvinism] to replace it with popery; and the Arminian–Calvinist controversy was the work of the Antichrist.[164]

Hume's comment, "It is a just remark that the more affinity there is between theological parties the greater is their animosity," aptly describes the relationship between the Arminian and Calvinist wings of the evangelical revival.[165] At the 1745 Conference Wesley's preachers agreed that the "truth" of the gospel lay "very near to both Calvinism and Antinomianism," indeed, "within a hair's breadth."[166] And yet it was this debate that separated Wesley's

---

161 525-Gr. MacGowan, *The foundry budget opened.*

162 Ibid., 17, 47.

163 531-Gr. John Muirhead, *A review of the principles of such Methodists as are under the direction of . . . John Wesley* (Kelso: printed by J. Palmer, 1784).

164 537-Gr. R. M. [Robert Moody], *Observations on certain prophecies in the Book of Daniel* (London: for the author, 1787).

165 See David Hume, *History of England by Hume and Smollett; with a Continuation by the Rev. T. S. Hughes, B.D.* (London: A. J. Valpy, 1834), 1:90; see also "animosity," Oxford English Dictionary, vol. 1, 336.

166 The 1745 Conference noted that the truth of the gospel [lay] very near both to Calvinism and Antinomianism, indeed "within a hair's breadth." It came "to the very edge" of Calvinism in "1. Ascribing all good to the free grace of God. 2. In denying all natural free

connection from most of the other evangelicals in the eighteenth century and made cooperation between them difficult, if not impossible. Although he claimed to have had no taste for controversy, Wesley kept up a barrage of anti-Calvinist tracts, and John Fletcher occupied his leisure for seven years with writing his *Checks to Antinomianism*. From the other side numerous Calvinists responded with unrelenting vigor. The anti-Arminian arsenal of men like Augustus Toplady and Richard Hill appeared to be almost inexhaustible.

Viewed in retrospect, it is hard to understand the reasons for the enormous amount of time and energy spent in argument and counterargument. Why were people who shared a common goal of reforming the Church and nation the bitterest of foes? The key to understanding this question lies in the deeply felt convictions of the contending parties that the future of the revival was at stake. Wesley, as he observed the spread of Calvinist views among his societies leading to antinomianism, feared the collapse of the revival into quietism and immorality. The Calvinists, on the other hand, convinced that Wesley's doctrines had begun to approximate those of Rome, feared that the Reformation truth of salvation by grace through faith, so central to the revival, was in danger of being obscured.

On the whole the controversy is unedifying. Little fresh light was shed upon the subjects discussed, but much heat was generated. Constructive debate was impossible, because the opponents began with different sets of presuppositions. While both professed strict adherence to Scripture as their ultimate authority, and they used identical texts, they arrived at widely divergent positions. Each believed the other misinterpreted the doctrine of justification. Each thought the other defamed the character of God.

The Calvinist–Arminian debate, so central to early Methodist theology because it addressed the pivotal mystery of God's dealing with humanity, has in twenty-first-century mainline religious discourse become a matter of peripheral concern.[167]

---

will, and all power antecedent to grace. And 3. In excluding all merit from man; even for what he has or does by the grace of God," and to the very edge of antinomianism in "1. Exalting the merits and love of Christ. 2. In rejoicing evermore." See questions 22–25, in "The Bristol Conference of August 1–3, 1745" in *BEWJW* 10:153.

167 Henry D. Rack, "The Great Debate: Calvinism, Arminianism, and Salvation, Book Notice," *ProcWHS* 44 (September 1983): 30–39.

Epilogue

From its inception the Methodist movement was embroiled in pamphlet controversy. The intensity of attack varied, but hostile publications flowed from British presses for more than half a century. Some hostility sprang from ignorance: misunderstanding of the movement's aims, and apprehension of its novel emphases and irregular methods. Some originated in deliberate efforts to misconstrue Methodism's purposes and practices. Rumors and lies concerning the evangelicals were printed under the garb of factual statements. There were clashes of personality and vested interests. Revenge for personal grievances motivated other attacks.

It would be easy to leave the impression that the Methodists were the injured party, innocent of incurring the wrath of their detractors, but this would ignore the facts. Whitefield's hastily published and poorly edited journals and egotistical biography provided many with their first (and, unfortunately, lasting) impressions of Methodism. From the outset rational English clergy were prejudiced against what they believed was a revival not of religion but of enthusiasm. Nor was Wesley entirely free from blame. Certainly, he was more cautious in print than his younger and more flamboyant colleague, George Whitefield, but some of the material in Wesley's early journals gave the impression of enthusiasm, especially accounts of the paroxysms accompanying Methodist conversion. Then, too, some of his early doctrinal statements (particularly on justification, assurance, and perfection) were not fully developed, and well-intentioned critics challenged him. Controversy became the anvil on which he forged a more mature theology.

Caricature was a favorite device of both anti-Methodist and Methodist. While opponents depicted Methodists as irrational, insane, censorious, immoral, heretical, and hypocritical, Whitefield and other Methodists were guilty of rash outbursts against the parochial clergy, caricaturing them as covetous, litigious, loose-living, unconverted drunkards. To attempt to apportion blame between the contending parties in the conflicts surrounding the revival would be futile. Printed controversy, however, could have been minimized had the Methodists acted and published with greater caution and their opponents exercised appropriate restraint in criticizing. The Calvinist–Arminian warfare is a vivid example. Wesley's protest that he had no taste for controversy did

315

not stop him from engaging in an unrelenting battle with the Calvinists. On the other hand, Christian charity did not prevent the Calvinists from issuing some of the most bitter of accusations against Wesley and his followers. Both sides resorted to oversimplification and caricature, and matched hostile epithet for hostile epithet. How different things might have been had not zeal impaired charity and good judgment!

Appendix

Peak Periods of Anti-Methodist Pamphlet Activity

Pamphlet attacks against Methodism were prolific and multifarious. Those published in the British Isles between 1738 and 1800 number 651. If those publications that merely contained unfavorable allusions to Methodism, were in newspapers or periodicals, or were published in America were also to be included, the number would be in the thousands. The vast majority of the printed attacks were brief. Three-quarters were shorter than fifty-five pages, a good number were below twelve pages, and some were broadsides.[1] Only a handful contained one hundred pages or more. Most publishers kept the price of items low in order to attract as large a reading public as possible. At least one (Henry Stebbing's *Earnest and affectionate address*) was distributed free of charge. Between 1738 and 1800 there was no year in which anti-Methodist polemic did not roll off the presses in England. In a few years only two or three were published: 1748, 1754, 1779, 1781, 1786, 1787, 1793, 1796, 1797, and 1798. Mostly, however, the annual output of pamphlets was anywhere between four and fourteen.

Five clusters of intense anti-Methodist pamphlet activity (measured by 15 or more new titles, reprints, or new editions in a single year) may be distinguished: 1739–45, 1758–63, 1766–69, 1771–77, and 1788–92.[2]

1739–1745

The first cluster, 1739–45, saw 188 pamphlets issued, 67 of which were published in 1739.[3] This cluster comprises the period of most consistent and concentrated anti-Methodist literary assault. This is hardly surprising, since it was the half decade when the emerging Methodist movement began to take shape in theology and organization. Whitefield was the prime target of the early pamphlet attacks. No fewer than 50 of them were specifically directed at him.

1758–1763

A second crest in the intensity of the pamphlet warfare was reached in the years 1758–63, (except 1762, when there were only 13 new pamphlets). The increase in

---

1 Broadsides: 109-Gr.; 138C-Fi.; 152A-Ba.; 205B-Fi.; 222A-Ba.; 285B-Fi.; 298A-Fi.; 431A-Fi.; 525B-Ki.; 525E-Ba.; 534A-Ba.; 541-Gr.; 565C-Fi.; 598-Gr.; 607-Ki.; 608-Ki., 609-Ki.

2 The statistics are derived from Clive Field, *A Revised Bibliography*, especially Appendix 5, and his *Supplemental Bibliography*.

3 Clive Field, *A Revised Bibliography*, Appendix 5. The statistics in Appendix 5 were amended to include the 42 new Anti-Methodist works discovered by Field.

anti-Methodist output was related to a number of events. In 1758, John Free (1711–91), a London priest, began an all-out attack on a number of aspects of the revival, blasting Methodism in a volley of seven pamphlets.[4] The year 1759 also witnessed pamphlets opposing evangelical Anglicans, who, although without connection with Wesley or Whitefield, were dubbed "Methodist" because of their emphasis on the doctrine of justification by faith alone. Evangelical Anglican clergymen Henry Venn, William Romaine, and Richard Elliott were the chief subjects of criticism. In 1760 and 1761 the increase (70 pamphlets) was occasioned by the theater production of Samuel Foote's *The minor*, and Israel Pottinger's comedy, *The Methodist*, renewing attacks primarily on Whitefield, both in dramatic and pamphlet form.

1766–1769

Two clusters of pamphlets may be discerned in this period: the first centers on pamphlets by several authors defending the late James Hervey from alleged assaults by John Wesley on Hervey's character and Calvinist theology;[5] the second was due in large measure to the furor aroused in 1768 by the expulsion from St. Edmund's Hall, Oxford, of a group of six of the Countess of Huntingdon's protégés. The paper war that ensued did not involve Wesley or his wing of Methodism.

1771–1777

This cluster was marked by the continued battle between the Arminian and Calvinist camps of Methodism over Wesley's 1770 Minutes of Conference. Augustus Toplady, Richard Hill, and Walter Shirley of the Calvinist camp were the most prolific pamphlet authors in this period.[6] From 1775 to 1778 it was Wesley's *A Calm Address to our American Colonies* that caused a rise in antagonistic pamphlet activity.[7]

1788–1792

The last peak of attacks came in John Wesley's final years, particularly 1791, the year of his death, as authors rushed to print biographies of the deceased leader.

---

4 273-Gr.; 274-Gr.; 275-Gr.; 276-Gr.; 277-Gr.; 278-Gr.; 286A-Ki.

5 See the following examples: 373-Gr.; 376-Gr.; 387A-Ki.; 416-Gr.; 421-Gr. See "Controversy over James Hervey's *Theron and Aspasio*," in chapter 9, "Calvinist 'Elect' and Arminian 'Saint' at War."

6 See chapter 9, "Calvinist 'Elect' and Arminian 'Saint' at War."

7 See chapter 7, "Methodism and Politics."

Anti-Methodist Pamphlets 1738–1800

A Short Title Bibliography

1738

002-Gr. SILVESTER, Tipping: *The scripture doctrine of regeneration stated* (London: for Charles Rivington, 1738).

003-Gr. BEDFORD, Arthur: *The doctrine of assurance* (London: Charles Ackers, 1738).

004-Gr. WARNE, Jonathan: *Arminianism the back-door to popery* (London: J. Noon and T. Cooper, 1738).

005-Gr. G., T. [T. Gib]: *Remarks on the Reverend Mr. Whitefield's journal* (London: for the author, [1738]).

1739

005A-Ba. TUCKER, Josiah: *Bristol, March 30, 1739* ([Bristol]: no printer, 1739).

006A-Ba. GENTLEMAN OF OXFORD, A [Ralph Jephson]: *Methodists dissected* (Oxford: by the author, [1739]).

007-Gr. B., E.: *An expostulatory letter to the Reverend Mr. Whitefield* (London: for J. Noon, 1739).

008-Gr. SKERRET, Ralph: *The nature and proper evidence of regeneration* (London: for C. Davis, 1739).

009-Gr. LAND, Tristram: *A letter to the Rev. Mr. Whitefield* (London: for J. Roberts, 1739).

009A-Ba. I have deregistered this item, "The Kennington song," in consultation with Field. It is not anti-Methodist but is a ballad in praise of George Whitefield.

010-Gr. TRAPP, Joseph: *The nature, folly, sin and danger of being righteous over-much* (London: for S. Austen, L. Gilliver and J. Clarke, 1739).

011-Gr. S-Y, T. [Richard Finch]: *A congratulatory letter to the Revd. Dr. Trapp* (London: for J. Roberts, 1739).

011A-Ki. HEWLETT, Ebenezer: *Mr. Whitefield's chatechise* (London: for sale by the author, 1739).

012-Gr. SCRUB, Timothy: *A letter to Robert Seagrave, M.A.* (London: for J. Roberts, 1739).

014-Gr. *Observations and remarks on Mr. Seagrave's conduct* (London: for S. Austen, 1739).

015-Gr. DEIST IN LONDON, A: *The true character of the Rev. Mr. Whitefield* (London: printed and sold by Mrs. Dodd, Mrs. Nutt, Mrs. Cook, Mrs. Bartlett, 1739).

017-Gr. STEBBING, Henry: *A caution against religious delusion* (London: for Fletcher Gyles, 1739).

018-Gr. WILDER, John: *The trial of the spirits* (Oxford: at the Theatre, for the author, 1739).

021-Gr. WHEATLY, Charles: *St. John's test of knowing Christ* (London: for J. Nourse, 1739).

022-Gr. GARNOR, William: *A dialogue between the Rev. Mr. Whitefield and Mr. Garnor* (London: for J. Crichley, 1739).

023-Gr. ANTIMETHODIST: *A letter to the Right Reverend the archbishops and bishops* (London: for J. Brett, 1739).

024-Gr. *Enthusiasm no novelty* (London: for T. Cooper, 1739).

025-Gr.   *The mock-preacher* (London: C. Corbett, 1739).

026-Gr.   *The Methodists: An humorous burlesque poem* (London: for John Brett, 1739).

027-Gr.   *The accomplished Methodist* (London: for J. Brett, 1739).

029-Gr.   [GIBSON, Edmund]: *The Bishop of London's pastoral letter* (London: S. Buckley, 1739).

030-Gr.   *Dr. Codex's pastoral letter versified* (London: for J. Brett, 1739).

031-Gr.   *An earnest appeal to the publick* (London: sold by J. Roberts, 1739).

032-Gr.   CURATE IN THE COUNTRY, A: *Observations on the Reverend Mr. Whitefield's answer* (London: for John Clarke, [1739]).

034-Gr.   BATE, James: *Methodism displayed; or, Remarks upon Mr. Whitefield's answer* (London: for J. Carter, [1739]).

035-Gr.   CURATE OF LONDON, A: *A short preservative against the doctrines reviv'd by Mr. Whitefield* (London: H. Whitridge, 1739).

036-Gr.   [TUCKER, Josiah]: *A compleat account of the conduct of . . . Mr. Whitefield* (London: sold by C. Corbett, 1739).

037-Gr.   *A plain address to the followers and favourers of the Methodists* (London: for H. Whitridge, [1739]).

039-Gr.   B., J. [John Brownsword]: *Remarks on the continuation of Mr. Whitefield's journal* (London: for T. Cooper, 1739).

040-Gr.   IMPARTIAL HAND, An [Josiah Tucker]: *The life and particular proceedings of the Rev. Mr. George Whitefield* (London: for J. Roberts, 1739).

041-Gr.   TRAPP, Joseph: *The nature, usefulness, and regulation of religious zeal* (London: for Lawton Gilliver, [1739]).

042-Gr.   BATE, James: *Quakero-Methodism* (London: John Carter, [1739]).

043-Gr.   BROWNSWORD, John: *The case of the rich young man in the gospel* (London: for George Strahan, 1739).

044-Gr.   VINEY, Richard: *A letter from an English brother of the Moravian persuasion* (London: for J. Roberts, 1739).

045-Gr.   *Enthusiasm explained* (London: for T. Gardner, 1739).

048-Gr.   MUGGLETONIAN, A: *The amorous humours and audacious adventures of one Whd.* (London: for the author, [1739]).

048A-Ba.   BERRIMAN, William: *A sermon preach'd to the religious societies* (London: for John Carter, 1739).

049-Gr.   CHURCH, Thomas: *An explanation and defense of the doctrine of the Church of England* (London: for J. Roberts, 1739).

050-Gr.   [ANNET, Peter]: *Judging for ourselves* (London: for the author, 1739).

050A-Ki.   *Enthusiasm display'd* ([London]: C. Corbett, 1739).

070-Gr.   H., T.: *The Methodists: A satirical poem* (London: sold by C. Corbett, 1739).

077-Gr.   *The conduct and doctrine of the Reverend Mr. Whitefield vindicated* (London: for A. Dodd, 1739).

089-Gr.   LAMB, William: *Remarks on the 'Plain account of the Methodists'* (London: for R. Minors, 1739).

092A-Fi.   COOKE, [Thomas]: *The mournful nuptials* (London: for T. Cooper, 1739).

092B-Fi.   *Remarks on several passages of Mr. Whitefield's sermons* (London: no printer, 1739).

1740

093-Gr.   [TRAPP, Joseph]: *The true spirit of the Methodists and their allies* (London: for Lawton Gilliver, 1740).

094-Gr.   BOWMAN, William: *The imposture of Methodism display'd* (London: for Joseph Lord in Wakefield, 1740).

095-Gr. WHISTON, Thomas: *The important doctrines of original sin* ([London]: for John Whiston, 1740).

098-Gr. [WELLER, Samuel]: *The trial of Mr. Whitefield's spirit* (London: T. Gardner, 1740).

100-Gr. *Free grace indeed! A letter to the Reverend Mr. John Wesley* (London: H. Kent, 1740).

101-Gr. CRISTIANUS: *A letter to the Reverend Mr. John Westly occasion'd by his sermon against predestination* (London: for D. Midwinter and A. Ward, 1740).

103-Gr. [WARNE, Jonathan]: *The Bishop of London's doctrine of justification* (London: for T. Cooper, 1740).

104-Gr. PRESBYTER OF THE CHURCH OF ENGLAND, A: *A modest and serious defence of the author of 'The whole duty of man'* (London: for J. Roberts, 1740).

104A-Ki. *The life of the Most Reverend Father in God, John Tillotson* (London: George Foster, 1740).

105-Gr. HEWLETT, Ebenezer: *A vindication of Arch-bishop Tillotson* (Bristol: by the author, 1740).

105A-Ki. SMYTH, Aquila: *A curious letter from a gentleman to Mr. Whitefield* (London: for the author, 1740).

106-Gr. *A collection of papers lately printed in the 'Daily Advertiser'* ([London]: no printer, [1740]).

107-Gr. WATERLAND, Daniel: *Regeneration stated and explained* (London: for W. Innys and R. Manby, 1740).

109-Gr. *The parallel reformers* (London: J. Lewis, 1740).

110-Gr. [GREY, Zachary]: *The Quaker and Methodist compared* (London: for J. Millan, 1740).

111-Gr. WARNE, Jonathan: *The Church of England turn'd dissenter at last* (London: T. Cooper and J. Oswald, 1740).

112-Gr. WARNE, Jonathan: *The spirit of the martyrs revived, Part 1* (London: T. Cooper, 1740).

115-Gr. *Methodists impostors* (London: for E. Curl, 1740).

1741

116-Gr. WHITEFIELD, George: *A letter to the Reverend Mr. John Wesley in answer to his sermon entituled 'Free-grace'* (London: W. Strahan, 1741).

117-Gr. FRIEND TO TRUE RELIGION, A [Joseph Nicoll]: *The sentiments of Archbishop Tillotson and Sharp on regeneration* (London: C. Corbett, [1741]).

118-Gr. TREVOR, J.: *A short history of the Donatists* (London: for T. Cooper, 1741).

119-Gr. *An extract of sundry passages taken out of Mr. Whitefield's . . . sermons* (London: reprinted and sold by J. Oswald, 1741).

123-Gr. TRAPP, Joseph: *A reply to Mr. Law's 'Earnest and serious answer'* (London: for L. Gilliver, 1741).

124-Gr. *Mr. Whitefield's doctrines considered and confuted* (Ipswich: W. C. for the author, 1741).

125-Gr. INGLEFIELD, Thomas: *An answer to a sermon preach'd at Rotherhith* (Sarum: for the author, 1741).

126-Gr. *A comparison between the doctrines taught by the clergy . . . and . . . Whitefield* (London: for A. Smith, 1741).

127-Gr. HART, Joseph: *The unreasonableness of religion* ([London]: for the author, 1741).

129-Gr. *Some remarks on a dialogue . . . between a predestinarian and his friend* (London: no printer, 1741).

130-Gr. BEDFORD, Arthur: *The doctrine of justification by faith stated* (London: for C. Rivington, 1741).

131-Gr.   FLEETWOOD, William: *The perfectionists examin'd* (London: for J. Roberts, 1741).

132-Gr.   [WELLER, Samuel]: *The remarks on the controversy between the author of 'The trial of Mr. Whitefield's spirit' and Mr. Benjamin Mills* (London: T. Cooper, 1741).

132A-Fi.   [WELLER, Samuel]: *An answer to the examination of 'The remarks on the controversy'* (London: T. Cooper, 1741).

133-Gr.   LAND, Tristram: *A second letter to the Rev. Mr. Whitefield* (London: for J. Roberts, [1741]).

134-Gr.   NELSON, Gilbert: *The use of human reason in religion* (London: for the author, 1741).

135-Gr.   A. (B) C.: *The controversy concerning free-will and predestination* (London: for R. Minors, 1741).

136A-Ba.   HUMPHREYS, Joseph: *A letter to the members of the religious societies* (Bristol: Benj. Hickey, 1741).

137-Gr.   *A letter from a gentleman in the country to his friend in Edinburgh* (Edinburgh: no printer, 1741).

137A-Ki.   RIDGWAY, Edward: *Truth defended; or, The awful sovereignty and righteousness of God* (London: John Wilson, 1741).

138A-Ba.   *Harlequin Methodist* ([London]: sold at the print and pamphlet shops, [1741]).

138B-Fi.   *Conference betwixt a conformist . . . and a nonconformist* (Edinburgh: W. Cheyne, 1741).

138C-Fi.   *Remarks on Mr. Whitefield* (Edinburgh: no printer, 1741).

1742

140-Gr.   M., A.: *The state of religion in New England* (Glasgow: Robert Foulis, 1742).

142-Gr.   GIB, Adam: *A warning against countenancing the ministrations of . . . Whitefield* (Edinburgh: for David Duncan, 1742).

143-Gr.   SECESSION CHURCH-Associate Presbytery: *Act of the Associate Presbytery anent a publick fast* (Edinburgh: no printer, 1742).

144-Gr.   *The declaration of the true Presbyterians* (Glasgow: no printer, 1742).

144A-Fi.   HEARTY FRIEND TO THE CHURCH OF SCOTLAND, A: *A letter to the Moderator of the Presbytery of Dumfermling* (Edinburgh: no printer, 1742).

145-Gr.   GENTLEMAN IN BOSTON, A [Charles Chauncy]: *A letter from a gentleman in Boston to Mr. George Wishart* (Edinburgh: no printer, 1742).

146-Gr.   [DUTTON, Anne]: *A letter to the Reverend Mr. John Wesley, in vindication of the doctrines of absolute, unconditional election* (London: John Hart, 1742).

148-Gr.   TRUE LOVER OF THE CHURCH AND COUNTRY, A: *Some observations upon the conduct of the famous Mr. W—field* (Edinburgh: no printer, 1742).

149-Gr.   BISSET, John: *A letter to a gentleman in Edinburgh* ([Aberdeen]: no printer, 1742).

149A-Ki.   FISHER, James: *A review of the preface to a 'Narrative of the extraordinary work at Kilsyth'* (Glasgow: for John Bryce, 1742).

150-Gr.   TUCKER, Josiah: *A brief history of the principles of Methodism* (Oxford: for James Fletcher, 1742).

152-Gr.   WARNE, Jonathan: *The downfall of Arminianism* (London: for T. Cooper and S. Mason, 1742).

152A-Ba.   WILLIAMS, Robert: *The life and conversation of that holy man Mr. John Wesley* (Bristol: no printer, 1742).

152B-Ba.   [GURNEY, Thomas]: *The nature and fitness of things* (London: no printer, 1742).

1743

153-Gr.   [DUTTON, Anne]: *Letters to the Reverend Mr. John Westley* (London: J. Hart, 1743).

154-Gr.   ESTE, Thomas: *Methodism display'd: A farce* (Newcastle upon Tyne: for the publisher, [1743]).

154A-Ba.   TWELLS, Leonard: *Twenty-four sermons preach'd at the parish church of St. Mary le Bow* (London: no printer, 1743).

155-Gr.   [POPE, Alexander]: *The dunciad* (London: for M. Cooper, 1743).

156-Gr.   IMPARTIAL HAND, An: *The progress of Methodism in Bristol* (Bristol: J. Watts, 1743).

156A-Ba.   DOCKWRAY, Thomas: *The operations of the Holy Spirit imperceptible* (Newcastle: John White, [1743]).

160A-Ba.   [SMITH, George]: *The notions of the Methodists fully disprov'd* (Newcastle: no printer, 1743).

160B-Ba.   [SMITH, George]: *The notions of the Methodists farther disprov'd* (Newcastle: J. White, 1743).

160C-Fi.   *The scoundrel scourged* (n.p.: no printer, 1743).

161-Gr.   [SHARP, Thomas]: *Remarks on a book intitled 'An earnest appeal to men of reason'* (Newcastle: no printer, 1743).

161B-Fi.   ERSKINE, Ralph: *Fraud and falsehood discover'd* (Edinburgh: printing-house in the Parliament-close, 1743).

161C-Fi.   *A brief and impartial account of . . . Whitefield and . . . Wesley* (Edinburgh: no printer, 1743).

1744

161D-Fi.   ANDREWS, John: *Of speaking as the oracles of God* (London: J. Tilly for E. Duncombe, 1744).

164-Gr.   [GIBSON, Edmund]: *Observations upon the conduct and behaviour of . . . Methodists* (London: E. Owen, 1744).

165-Gr.   CHURCH, Thomas: *A serious and expostulatory letter to the Rev. Mr. George Whitefield* (London: for M. Cooper, 1744).

166-Gr.   B., J./ GENTLEMAN OF PEMBROKE COLLEGE, OXON, A: *A letter to the Reverend Mr. Whitefield, occasion'd by his pretended answer to the first part of the 'Observations on the conduct and behaviour of the Methodists'* (London: for M. Cooper, [1744]).

167-Gr.   [SMALBROKE, Richard]: *A charge deliver'd to the . . . clergy in . . . the diocese of Lichfield . . . 1741* (London: for J. and P. Knapton, 1744).

168-Gr.   HEWLETT, Ebenezer: *The support of popery discover'd* (London: for M. Cooper, 1744).

169-Gr.   WHITEFIELD, George: *A brief account of . . . a late trial . . . at Gloucester* (London: for J. Robinson, 1744).

170-Gr.   [GIBSON, Edmund]: *The case of the Methodists briefly stated* (London: for Edward Owen, 1744).

172-Gr.   SECESSION CHURCH-Associate Presbytery: *Acts of the Associate Presbytery* (Edinburgh: T. W. and T. Ruddimans, 1744).

172A-Ki.   FRASER, James: *The lawfulness and duty of separation from corrupt ministers* (Edinburgh: for George Paton, 1744).

173-Gr.   *Some papers giving an account of . . . Methodism at Wednesbury* (London: for J. Roberts, 1744).

174-Gr.   EUSEBIUS [Caleb Fleming]: *A fine picture of enthusiasm* (London: for J. Noon, 1744).

174A-Ba.   HOWDELL, William: *Religion productive of joy and consistent with politeness* (York: Caesar Ward, 1744).

175-Gr.   HEARD, William: *The Methodists vindicated* (London: for the author, 1744).

176A-Ba.   [GIBSON, Edmund]: *Directions given to the clergy of the diocese of London* (London: Edward Owen, 1744).

1745

185-Gr.   CHURCH, Thomas: *Remarks on the Reverend Mr. John Wesley's last journal* (London: for M. Cooper, 1745).

186-Gr.   SINCERE PROTESTANT, A [Zachary Grey]: *A serious address to lay Methodists* (London: for William Russell, 1745).

187-Gr.   CENNICK, John: *An account of the late riot at Exeter* (London: J. Hart, 1745).

188-Gr.   IMPARTIAL HAND, An [George Coade]: *A brief account of the late persecution . . . of the Methodists* (Exon: no printer, 1745).

188A-Ki.   LAYMAN OF THE CHURCH OF ENGLAND, A: *Remarks on a late pamphlet intitled 'A brief account of the late persecution'* (Exon: A. and S. Brice, 1745).

188B-Fi.   BRICE, Andrew: *The play-house church* (Exon: no printer, 1745).

189-Gr.   CUDWORTH, William: *A dialogue between a preacher of inherent righteousness and a preacher of God's righteousness* (London: J. Hart, 1745).

190-Gr.   *The question whether it be right to turn Methodist considered* (London: for M. Cooper, 1745).

191-Gr.   MAUD, John: *An apology for the clergy in a letter to a gentleman of fortune* (Cambridge: R. Walker and T. James, 1745).

194-Gr.   IMPARTIAL HAND, An: *An essay containing evident proofs against the Methodists* (London: for the author, [1745]).

197-Gr.   LAYMAN, A [Sir John Thorold]: *Extracts of letters relating to Methodists and Moravians* (London: for B. Dod, 1745).

200-Gr.   B., A. [Henry Stebbing]: *An earnest and affectionate address to the people called Methodists* (London: J. Oliver for B. Dod, 1745).

200A-Fi.   SMITH, Luke: *A preservative against separation from the established Church* (London: for the author, 1745).

200B-Fi.   HILL, Mary: *An essay on schism* (Salisbury: Benjamin Collins, 1745).

200C-Fi.   PIMM, Katharine: *A true and faithful account of some of the transactions . . . of Doctor Westley* (Southwark: for T. Hinton, [1745]).

1746

201-Gr.   CUDWORTH, William: *Truth defended and cleared from mistakes* (London: J. Hart, 1746).

202-Gr.   [SMALBROKE, Richard]: *A charge delivered to the clergy of the diocese of Lichfield and Coventry . . . in the years 1744 and 1745* (London: for John and Paul Knapton, 1746).

204-Gr.   McCONNELL, James: *Mr. Cennicks laid open* (Dublin: J. Gowan, 1746).

205-Gr.   CHURCH, Thomas: *Some farther remarks on the Rev. Mr. John Wesley's last journal* (London: M. Cooper, 1746).

205A-Ba.   BIRT, William: *The doctrine of predestination defended* (London: for the author, 1746).

205B-Ba.   GREEN, John: *An appeal to the oracles of God* (London: J. Hart, 1746).

205C-Ki.   D., W. [William Dowars]: *Errors in part discovered* (Bristol: for the author, 1746).

205D-Fi.   [FIELDING, Henry]: *The female husband* (London: for M. Cooper, 1746).

205E-Fi.   TOMLINSON, Matthew: *The Protestant's birth-right* (London: for R. Dodsley, 1746).

1747

206-Gr. [GIBSON, Edmund]: *The charge of the Right Reverend Father in God, Edmund, Lord Bishop of London . . . 1746 and 1747* [London: no printer, 1747].

206A-Ki. B., T. [Thomas Burton]: *A friendly letter to John and Charles Wesley* (London: for the author, 1747).

206B-Ki. [DUTTON, Anne]: *A letter on perseverance*. This item has not been seen but is referred to in *Notes and Queries, Twelfth Series*, ii (July–December 1916), 338, *ProcWHS*, xi (1917–18), 47.

206C-Ki. DOWARS, William: *Calvinism supported by the Word of God* (London: for the author, 1747).

1748

207A-Ba. CURTIS, John: *A letter to the author of a pamphlet entitled 'A letter to a person lately join'd to the people called Quakers'* (Bristol: S. Farley, 1747–48).

208-Gr. WHITE, George: *A sermon against the Methodists* (Preston: for the author by James Stanley and John Moon, 1748).

208A-Ba. [FRY, John]: *Some remarks on a pamphlet intituled 'A letter to a person lately join'd with the . . . people called Quakers'* (Bristol: S. Farley, 1748).

1749

209-Gr. SLADDIN, John: *A brief description of the Methodists* (York: Caesar Ward, 1749).

210-Gr. FLETCHER, Nathaniel: *A Methodist dissected* (York: Caesar Ward, 1749).

212-Gr. CLERGYMAN OF THE CHURCH OF ENGLAND, A: *An answer to a late pamphlet entitled, 'A plain account of the . . . Methodists'* (London: for E. Withers, 1749).

213-Gr. [LAVINGTON, George]: *The enthusiasm of Methodists and papists compar'd* [Part 1] (London: for J. and P. Knapton, 1749).

213A-Ki. [LAVINGTON, George]: *The enthusiasm of Methodists and papists compar'd* [Part 2] (London: for J. and P. Knapton, 1749).

214A-Ki. HAWKINS, Joanna: *A letter to John Wesley* ([London]: no printer, 1749).

216A-Ba. PHILOSOPHICAL SOCIETY, The: *An account of the rise, progress and nature of Methodism in Corke* (Corke: no printer, 1749).

216B-Ki. *A plain and familiar dialogue between a steady and a wavering Christian* (London: for the author, 1749).

216C-Fi. LAYMAN OF THE CHURCH OF ENGLAND AND TRADESMAN OF THE CITY OF LONDON, A: *A letter to the Rev. Mr. George Whitefield* (London: for J. Fuller, [1749]).

1750

217-Gr. KIRKBY, John: *The impostor detected* (London: for M. Cooper, 1750).

217A-Ki. FLETCHER, Nathaniel: *A vindication of the 'Methodist dissected'* (Halifax: no printer, 1750).

218-Gr. FISHER, George *pseud.* [John Bailey]: *A letter to the Rev. Mr. Wesley* (Cork: no printer, 1750).

219-Gr. PHILALETHES [John Bailey]: *A second letter to the Rev. Mr. Wesley* (Cork: no printer, 1750). No copy has survived. For a partial reconstruction based on Wesley's reply see *BEWJW*, vol. 9: *The Methodist societies, history, nature and design and certain related open letters*, ed. Rupert Davies (Nashville: Abingdon, 1989), 565–56.

222-Gr. *A letter to the Reverend Mr. George Whitefield occasioned by his remarks upon a pamphlet entitled 'The enthusiasm of Methodists and papists compared'* (London: for M. Cooper, 1750).

222A-Ba. *Rules of the band societies* (n.p.: no printer, 1750).

222B-Ki. MASTER OF SHORT-HAND, A: *Christ the physician of the soul* [London: no printer, 1750].

222C-Fi. CRISPIN: *The cobler's letter to the Methodists* (Waterford: Jer. Calwell, [1750]).

222D-Fi. LAYMAN OF THE CHURCH OF ENGLAND, A: *Sion comforted* (London: for the author and sold by J. and R. Swann, 1750).

222E-Fi. *A letter from the deists to the chief rulers amongst the Methodists* (Dublin: printed and sold by the booksellers and hawkers, 1750).

1751

224-Gr. *A vindication of the Methodists and Moravians* (London: for the author, 1751).

225-Gr. [LAVINGTON, George]: *The enthusiasm of Methodists and papists compared,* [Part 3] (London: for J. and P. Knapton, 1751). For parts 1 and 2 see 213-Gr. and 213A-Ki.

226-Gr. *A second letter to the Reverend Mr. George Whitefield* (London: for M. Cooper, 1751).

226A-Ki. ROCHE, John: *Moravian heresy* (Dublin: for the author, 1751).

231-Gr. PHILADELPHUS [James Relly]: *Remarks on a pamphlet intitled 'A dialogue between a true Methodist and an erroneous Methodist'* (n.p.: for the author, 1751).

231A-Fi. OLDKNOW, Gregory: *Serious objections to the pernicious doctrines of the Moravians and Methodists* (n.p.: no printer, 1751).

231B-Fi. *A serious caution against enthusiasm and religious delusion* ([Norwich]: no printer, 1751).

232-Gr. [GIBSON, Edmund]: *A caution against enthusiasm* (London: E. Owen, 1751).

232A-Ba. BOOKER, Moore: *Two letters concerning the Methodists* (Dublin: for J. Kelburn, 1751).

1752

232B-Ba. COUNTRY GENTLEMAN, A [William Evans]: *A letter to the Rev. Mr. M—re B—k—r* (Dublin: for Peter Wilson, 1752).

232C-Ba. BOOKER, Moore: *A letter in answer to a late one . . . concerning the Methodists* (Dublin: printed and sold by the booksellers, 1752).

233-Gr. GILL, John: *The doctrine of the saints final perseverance* (London: G. Keith, J. Robinson, 1752).

234-Gr. GILL, John: *The doctrine of predestination stated* (London: G. Keith, J. Robinson, Mr. Edwards, 1752).

235-Gr. [EVANS, Theophilus]: *The history of modern enthusiasm* (London: W. Owen and W. Clarke, 1752).

235A-Ba. *A general view of the principles and spirit of the predestinarians* (Dublin: for G. Faulkner, J. Smith, W. Smith, A. Bradley, and P. Wilson, 1752).

236-Gr. *A plain account of justification* (Norwich: W. Chase, 1752).

237-Gr. HURD, Richard: *The mischiefs of enthusiasm and bigotry* (London: for J. Gleed in Norwich, 1752).

238-Gr. *The story of the Methodist-lady* (London: for John Doughty, [1752]).

239-Gr. [LAVINGTON, George]: *The Bishop of Exeter's answer to Mr. J. Wesley's late letter* (London: for John and Paul Knapton, 1752).

240-Gr. *Candid remarks on some particular passages in . . . Mr. Whitefield's . . . sermons* (Reading: C. Micklewright, 1752).

242-Gr. P., C. [Charles Perronet]: *A summary view of the doctrines of Methodism* (Bristol: Felix Farley, 1752).

243-Gr. *An address to the Protestant dissenters* (Norwich: no printer, 1752).

243A-Ba. *A true and particular narrative of the disturbances . . . in . . . Norwich* (London: no printer, 1752).

1753

245-Gr.   PARKHURST, John: *A serious and friendly address to the Reverend Mr. John Wesley* (London: for J. Withers, 1753).

246-Gr.   [CRUTTENDEN, Robert]: *The principles and preaching of the Methodists* (London: for James Buckland, 1753).

248-Gr.   WEBB, John: *An appeal unto the honest and sincere-hearted among the . . . Methodists* (London: for the author, [1753]).

248A-Ba.   LAY-MAN, A: *A few queries concerning the growth of Methodism* (Dublin: no printer, 1753).

248B-Ba.   BLAIR, Samuel: *The doctrine of predestination truly and fairly stated* (Belfast: Reprinted for Robert Johnston, 1753). Original printing in Philadelphia, 1742.

248C-Fi.   *The anti-chronicle* ([Norwich]: for the author, 1753).

248D-Fi.   *The enthusiast; or, Methodism display'd* (Portsmouth: W. Horton, 1753).

1754

248E-Fi.   [LAVINGTON, George]: *Methodists still the same* ([Norwich]: no printer, 1754).

249-Gr.   BOWDEN, Samuel: *Poems on various subjects* (Bath: T. Boddely for the author, 1754).

1755

249A-Fi.   GREEN, Thomas: *A dissertation on enthusiasm* (London: J. Oliver, 1755).

250-Gr.   HORNE, George: *Christ and the Holy Ghost the supporters of the spiritual life* (Oxford: at the Theatre for S. Parker, [1755]).

251-Gr.   PHILALETHES: *Christian piety freed from the many delusions of modern enthusiasts* (London: J. Oliver, 1755).

251A-Ba.   DARNEY, William: *A sermon published for the order and discipline in the Church* [London: no printer, 1755].

252-Gr.   [DOUGLAS, John]: *An apology for the clergy, with a view to expose the groundless assertions of a late commentator* (London: for S. Bladon, 1755).

253-Gr.   CROOKE, Henry: *The Spirit no respecter of persons in his gifts and graces* (London: W. Faden, 1755).

253A-Ba.   [GURNEY, Thomas]: *Perseverance* (London: for G. Keith, J. Robinson, and M. Anderson, 1755).

253B-Ki.   CHRISTOPHILUS: *A serious inquiry whether a late epistle from . . . Charles Wesley to . . . John Wesley be not an evident mark of their being . . . fallen into one of the . . . wiles of the devil* ([London]: for the author, 1755).

253C-Fi.   *A letter to the Rev. Mr. Thomas Jones* (London: for M. Collyer, 1755).

1756

254-Gr.   GRIFFITH, Thomas: *The use and extent of reason in matters of religion* (Oxford: at the Theatre for S. Parker, 1756).

256-Gr.   ONE OF THE CLERGY/CLERICUS [Caleb Fleming]: *A letter to the Revd. Mr. John Wesley, occasioned by his 'Address to the clergy'* (London: for M. Cooper, 1756).

257-Gr.   *Two Letters to Mr. George Whitefield* (London: J. Marshall and Mrs. Chastel, 1756).

258-Gr.   BULLER, James: *A reply to the Rev. Mr. Wesley's 'Address to the clergy'* (Bristol: S. Farley, 1756).

259-Gr.   *The great secret disclosed* (London: for the author, [1756]).

260-Gr.   *The folly and danger of enthusiasm* (London: for A. and C. Corbett, 1756).

260A-Ki.   [CUDWORTH, William]: *A friendly attempt to remove some fundamental mistakes* (London: for G. Keith, 1756).

262-Gr.   [MASON, William]: *Methodism displayed and enthusiasm detected* (London: for Henry Cooke, 1756).

262A-Fi.   BOOKER, Moore: *The true gratification of the sensual appetites* (Dublin: Henry Saunders, 1756).

1757

263-Gr.   JOHN-BAPTIST, THE ARCH-TEACHER *pseud.* [John Baptist Malassis de Sulamar]: *A short examen of Mr. John Wesley's system* (London: J. Marshall, [1757]).

265-Gr.   B., W., C., G., M., J., etc. [Richard Fawcett]: *An expostulatory letter to the Rev. Mr. Wesley* (London: for J. Wilkie, 1757).

266A-Ba.   PROBATOR: *A letter to the Revd. Mr. George Whitefield* (n.p.: no printer, 1757).

267-Gr.   CLERGYMAN, A [Henry Stebbing]: *The doctrine of justification by faith in Jesus Christ* (London: for L. Davis and C. Reymers, 1757).

267A-Fi.   [SANDEMAN, Robert]: *Letters on Theron and Aspasio* (Edinburgh: Sands, Donaldson, Murray, and Cochran, for the author, 1757), 2 vols.

267B-Fi.   JOHN-BAPTIST THE ARCH-TEACHER [MALASSIS DE SULAMAR, John Baptist]: *The fall of the old serpent called the Devil* (London: J. Marshall and P. Fitzgerald, 1757).

1758

268-Gr.   [MORTIMER, Thomas]: *Die and be damned* (London: for S. Hooper and A. Morley, 1758).

269-Gr.   GREEN, Thomas: *Justification* (London: for J. Oliver and T. Payne, 1758).

269A-Ba.   EDWARDS, John: *A vindication of the Protestant doctrine of justification* (London: M. Lewis, 1758).

271-Gr.   GRANGE, C.: *Considerations on some modern doctrines and teachers* (London: no printer, 1758).

271A-Ki.   GREEN, John: *Eight sermons preached in the parish church of St. Saviour's* (London: for J. Fuller and J. Scott, 1758).

272-Gr.   POTTER, [Robert]: *On the pretended inspiration of the Methodists* (Norwich: W. Chase, 1758).

272A-Ki.   POTTER, [Robert]: *An appendix to the sermon on the pretended inspiration of the Methodists* (Norwich: W. Chase, 1758).

272B-Ki.   CUDWORTH, William: *A preservative in perilous times* (London: no printer, sold by G. Keith, M. Lewis and T. Smith, [1758]).

272C-Fi.   D., J. [John Dove]: *Remarks on the Reverend Mr. John Wesley's 'Sufficient answer'* (London: for M. Lewis, 1758).

273-Gr.   FREE, John: *A display of the bad principles of the Methodists* (London: for the author, 1758).

274-Gr.   FREE, John: *Rules for the discovery of false prophets* (London: E. Owen, for the author, 1758).

275-Gr.   FREE, John: *Dr. Free's edition of the Rev. Mr. John Wesley's first penny-letter* (London: E. Owen for the author, 1758).

1759

276-Gr.   FREE, John: *Dr. Free's edition of the Rev. Mr. John Wesley's second letter* (London: for the author, 1759).

277-Gr.   FREE, John: *Dr. Free's remarks upon Mr. Jones's letter* (London: E. Owen, for the author, 1759).

278-Gr.   FREE, John: *The whole speech, which was delivered to the Reverend clergy . . . of London* (London: for the author, [1759]).

279A-Ba.   A, B, C, D, E, F, &c., &c., &c. [VENN, Henry]: *'An humble address of their (as yet uninfected) parishioners'* (London: no printer, [1759]).

280-Gr.   DODD, William: *Cautions against Methodism* (London: for L. Davis and C. Reymers, and W. Faden, [1759]).

281-Gr.   ACADEMICUS [John Riland]: *A letter to the Rev. Mr. Elliot* (Oxford: for S. Parker, [1759]).

282-Gr.   DOWNES, John: *Methodism examined and exposed* (London: for John Rivington, 1759).

284-Gr.   METHODIST, A: *A discourse concerning plays and players* (London: M. Cooper, 1759).

284A-Ba.   MONCRIEF, Alexander: *The countenancing of Mr. Whitefield's administrations* (Glasgow: J. Bryce and D. Paterson, [1759]).

285A-Ki   *An apology for the parishioners of St. Dunstan's in the West* (London: C. Sympson, [1759]).

285B-Fi.   UMFREVILLE, Charles: *Discourses upon the following important subjects* (London: for the author and sold by Benj. Dod, 1759).

285C-Fi.   JOHN-BAPTIST THE ARCH-TEACHER [MALASSIS DE SULAMAR, John Baptist]: *A letter of John-Baptist the arch-teacher to the Most Reverend Doctor Thomas Secker* (London: J. Marshal and T. Jones, 1759).

1760

286-Gr.   *Original letters between the Reverend Mr. John Wesley and Mr. Richard Tompson* (London: for L. Davis and C. Reymers, 1760).

286A-Ki.   FREE, John: *A controversy with the people called Methodists* (London: W. Sandby, J. Scott, and R. Stevens, 1760).

286B-Ki.   [DOWNES, Ann]: *The widow Downes's answer to the Rev. Mr. John Wesley's letter* (London: by the author, [1760]).

287-Gr.   CLARK, James: *Montanus redivivus* (Dublin: H. Saunders, 1760).

288-Gr.   [PIKE, Samuel]: *Free grace indeed! Set forth in a scriptural view* (London: for J. Buckland, T. Field, and E. Dilly, 1760).

288A-Ba.   [PIKE, Samuel]: *Simple truth vindicated* (London: for J. Buckland, T. Field, and E. Dilly, 1760).

288B-Fi.   [CUDWORTH, W.]: *A defence of 'Theron and Aspasio'* (London: for G. Keith, 1760).

289-Gr.   MARTIN, Samuel: *Two discourses* (London: for P. Vaillant, 1760).

290-Gr.   HALLIFAX, Samuel: *Saint Paul's doctrine of justification by faith* (Cambridge: J. Bentham, 1760).

291-Gr.   OULTON, John: *A vindication of the seventeenth article of the Church of England* (London: Aaron Ward, 1760).

292-Gr.   *The scriptural account of justifying faith* (London: no printer, 1760).

292A-Ba.   PHILANTHROPOS [John Dove]: *Rational religion distinguished from that which is enthusiastic* (London: J. Buckland, [1760]).

293-Gr.   [BERRIDGE, John]: *A fragment of the true religion* (London: for J. Williams, 1760).

294-Gr.   ACADEMICUS [John Green]: *The principles and practices of the Methodists considered* (London: for W. Bristow, 1760).

295-Gr.   GOLDNEY, Edward: *Scriptural remedies for healing the unhappy divisions in the Church* (London: for the author, 1760).

296-Gr.   LAW, William: *Of justification by faith and works* (London: for J. Richardson, 1760).

297-Gr.   JEPHSON, Alexander: *A friendly and compassionate address to all serious . . . Methodists* (London: C. Jephson, 1760).

298-Gr.   FOOTE, Samuel: *The minor* (London: printed and sold by J. Coote, G. Kearsly, T. Davis, and C. Etherington, 1760).

298A-Fi. FOOTE, Samuel: *Epilogue to 'The minor'* (Deptford-Bridge: Kent Printing Office, [1760]).

299-Gr. MINISTER OF THE CHURCH OF CHRIST, A [Martin Madan]: *Christian and critical remarks on . . . 'The minor'* (London: for Mr. Keith, Mrs. Lewis, Mr. Andrews, Mr. Rolls, Mr. Burd, and Mr. Taylor, 1760).

300-Gr. *A satirical dialogue between the celebrated Mr. F—te, and Dr. Squintum* (London: for H. Ranger, 1760).

300A-Ki. *Friendly advice for Dr. Squintum* [London: no printer, 1760].

301-Gr. SQUINTUM, George *pseud.: A letter of expostulation from the manager of the theatre in Tottenham-Court* (London: for R. Stevens, [1760]).

302-Gr. METHODIST PREACHER IN THE COUNTRY, A: *A genuine letter from a Methodist preacher in the country* (London: for S. Vandenbergh, 1760).

303-Gr. FOOTE, Samuel: *A letter . . . to the Reverend author of the 'Remarks . . . on "The minor"'* (London: for T. Davies, T. Becket, and J. Coote, 1760).

304-Gr. MINISTER OF THE CHURCH OF CHRIST, A [Martin Madan]: *An exhortatory address to the brethren in the faith of Christ* (London: for G. Keith, M. Lewis, and J. Burd, 1760).

305-Gr. [POTTINGER, Israel]: *The Methodist: A comedy* (London: for I. Pottinger, [1760]).

309-Gr. *A letter to Mr. F—te* (London: printed for T. Pote, 1760).

310-Gr. GENIUS, A [James Boswell]: *Observations good or bad . . . on Squire Foote's . . . 'The minor'* (Edinburgh: no printer, 1760).

310A-Fi. JOHN-BAPTIST THE ARCH-TEACHER [MALASSIS DE SULAMAR, John Baptist]: *Demonstrative reflections of John-Baptist the arch-teacher* (London: for J. Marshal, 1760).

311D-Gr. [CHALLENOR, Richard]: *A caveat against the Methodists* (London: for M. Cooper, 1760).

312B-Fi. *Miss Kitty F—h—r's miscellany* (London: H. Ranger, 1760).

312C-Fi. PEEBLES, Robert: *The inconsistency of the Methodist's scheme of religion* (Armagh: no printer, 1760).

1761

313-Gr. *An additional scene to the comedy of 'The minor'* (London: for J. Williams, 1761).

314-Gr. REED, Joseph: *The register-office* (London: for T. Davies, 1761).

315-Gr. ACADEMICUS [John Green]: *The principles and practices of the Methodists farther considered* (Cambridge: J. Bentham, for T. and J. Merrill, 1761).

316-Gr. *An address to the Right Honourable—* (London: for W. Sandby, 1761).

317-Gr. ALLEN, John: *No acceptance with God by faith only* (London: for Messrs. Whiston, White, and Withers, and Messrs. Parker and Prince in Oxford, [1761]).

318-Gr. [CUDWORTH, William]: *The polyglott* (London: for E. Dilly, G. Keith, and T. Smith, 1761).

319-Gr. HARMAN, John: *The crooked disciple's remarks upon the blind guide's method of preaching* (London: for the author, 1761).

320A-Ba. *Memoirs of the life of a modern saint* (London: for H. Ranger, 1761).

321-Gr. N., N.: *Presbyters and deacons not commissioned to preach* (London: for W. Nicholl, 1761).

323-Gr. FLAGELLAN, Christopher *pseud.: A funeral discourse occasioned by the much lamented death of Mr. Yorick* (London: for W. Nicoll, 1761).

324-Gr. SNIP, Nathaniel *pseud.: A journal of the travels of Nathaniel Snip* (London: for W. Bristow and M. Cooper, 1761).

325-Gr. ROCK, [Richard]: *A letter to the Reverend Mr. G—e Wh—d, A. B., late of Pembroke College, Oxford* (London: no printer, 1761).

326-Gr. *The spiritual minor* (London: for W. Morgan, [1761]).

326A-Ba. *Mr. Sanddeman refuted by an old woman* (London: J. Hart, 1761).

327-Gr. HANWAY, Jonas: *Letters written occasionally on the customs of foreign nations* (London: for John Rivington, R. and J. Dodsley, and C. Henderson, 1761).

328-Gr. RELLY, James: *Antichrist resisted* (London: for the author, 1761).

329-Gr. HITCHCOCK, Thomas: *The mutual connexion between faith, virtue, and knowledge* (Oxford: at the Theatre for James Fletcher, [1761]).

330-Gr. HORNE, George: *Works wrought through faith a condition of our justification* (Oxford: Clarendon Press, [1761]).

332A-Ba. [DODD, William]: *A conference between a mystic, an Hutchinsonian, a Calvinist, a Methodist, and a member of the Church of England, and others* (London: for L. Davis and C. Reymers, 1761).

1762

335-Gr. LANGHORNE, John: *Letters on religious retirement* (London: for H. Payne and W. Cropley, 1762).

336-Gr. P., W.: *An Answer to Mr. C— P—'s letter to Mr. P—E.* (London: no printer, 1762).

336A-Ba. [HILL, Sir Richard]: *A letter of advice from a father to his son* (London: for George Keith, 1762).

337-Gr. *A plain and easy road to the land of bliss* (London: for W. Nicoll, 1762).

338-Gr. PENN, James: *Various tracts* (London: Charles Say for the author, [1762]).

340-Gr. RILEY, William: *Parochial music corrected* (London: for the author, 1762).

341-Gr. RANDOLPH, Thomas: *The use of reason in matters of religion* (Oxford: at the Theatre, [1762]).

341A-Ki. [SECKER, Thomas]: *The charge designed to have been delivered by the archbishop of Canterbury to the clergy of his diocese* (London: no printer, 1762).

341B-Fi. HOUGH, John: *The pastor* (London: Mr. Williams, [1762]).

341C-Fi. HELME, John: *A specimen of preaching* (London: for J. Bird, 1762).

341D-Ki. FOOTE, Samuel: *The orators as it is now performing at the New Theatre in the Hay Market* (London: for J. Coote, G. Kearsley, and T. Davies, 1763).

1763

342-Gr. [WARBURTON, William]: *The doctrine of grace* (London: for A. Millar and J. and R. Tonson, 1763).

343-Gr. RUTHERFORTH, Thomas: *Four charges to the clergy of the Archdeaconry of Essex* (Cambridge: J. Bentham, 1763).

344-Gr. [MASON, William]: *A seasonable antidote against religious delusion* (London: M. Lewis and J. Johnson, 1763).

345-Gr. [MASON, William]: *The scripture-doctrine of imputed righteousness* (London: E. Dilly, 1763).

346-Gr. BACKHOUSE, William: *The history of the man of God* (Cambridge: J. Bentham, 1763).

347-Gr. ROBINSON, John: *The Methodists: an eclogue* (Norwich: John Crouse, 1763).

348-Gr. CHARNDLER, Samuel: *An answer to the Rev. Mr. John Wesley's letter to William, Lord Bishop of Gloucester* (London: for the author, 1763).

349-Gr. HARDY, Richard: *A letter from a clergyman to one of his parishioners who was inclined to turn Methodist* (London: for the author, [1763]).

351-Gr. *A word in season* (London: no printer, 1763).

352-Gr. WALDER, James: *The ax laid to the root* (London: for James Buckland and William Lepard, 1763).

353A-Ba   PROFESSOR OF CHRISTIANITY, A: *A scriptural account of the doctrine of perfection* (London: H. Fenwick, 1763).

1764

354-Gr.   ENEMY TO PIOUS FRAUD, An: *A sovereign remedy for the cure of hypocrisy and blind zeal* (London: for T. Becket and P. A. de Hondt, 1764).

355-Gr.   PHILAGATHUS CANTABRIGIENSIS: *The Methodist instructed* (London: for R. Withy and C. Marsh, 1764).

356-Gr.   BLACKSMITH, A. T. *pseud.* [John Witherspoon]: *Enthusiasm delineated* (Bristol: for the author, [1764]).

357-Gr.   [BARNES, John]: *Twenty charges against the Methodists answered* (Carmarthen: J. Ross, for the author, 1764).

358A-Ki.   WALDER, James: *A defence of the 'Preservative against Methodism'* (London: for the author, 1764).

359-Gr.   *The use of reason and reflection on religious subjects* (London: for J. Fletcher and Co., 1764).

360-Gr.   BLACKSMITH, A. T. *pseud.* [John Witherspoon]: *A defence of Christianity against the power of enthusiasm* (Bristol: for the author, [1764]).

360A-Fi.   HARMAN, John: *Remarks upon the life, character, and behaviour of the Rev. George Whitefield* (London: by the author, 1764).

1765

361-Gr.   HERVEY, James: *Eleven letters from the late Rev. Mr. Hervey . . . to John Wesley* (London: Charles Rivington for John Rivington, 1765).

363-Gr.   [ERSKINE, John]: *Mr. Wesley's principles detected* (Edinburgh: for William Gray, 1765).

363A-Ba.   SINCERE FRIEND TO THE TRUE RELIGION OF JESUS CHRIST, A: *Brief animadversions on some passages in the eleven letters . . . to John Wesley* (London: for John Payne, 1765).

364-Gr.   *Mumbo Chumbo* (London: for T. Becket and P. A. de Hondt, 1765).

366-Gr.   PRESBYTER OF THE CHURCH OF ENGLAND, A: *The doctrines of Methodism examined and confuted* (London: no printer, 1765).

367-Gr.   [MASON, William]: *John against Wesley* (London: for E. and C. Dilley, [1765]).

371-Gr.   COUNTRY CURATE, A: *The self-commissioned apostle an impostor* (Chippenham: for the author, 1765).

371A-Ba.   [BOWDEN, Samuel]: *The Methodists welcome to Pewsey* ([London]: no printer, 1765).

372A-Ba.   *Diotrephes and Stentor* (London: no printer, 1765).

372C-Fi.   [STEVENS, George Alexander]: *The celebrated lecture on heads* ([London]: for J. Pridden, [1765]).

1766

373-Gr.   FREEMAN, W.: *An essay to quench the fire of Calvin* (London: for J. Cooke, 1766).

375-Gr.   [PARKER, William]: *A letter to the Rev. Mr. John Wesley, concerning his inconsistency with himself* (London: H. Hart, 1766).

376-Gr.   [MARTIN, Samuel]: *A few thoughts and matters of fact concerning Methodism* (Edinburgh: sold by W. Gray, 1766).

378-Gr.   PARAGRAPH, Peter *pseud.* [James Makittrick Adair]: *The Methodist and mimick* (London: for C. Moran, 1766).

379-Gr.   AUTHOR OF *The powers of the pew* and *The curate* [Evan Lloyd]: *The Methodist: A poem* (London: for the author, 1766).

380-Gr.   ROTHERAM, John: *An essay on faith and its connection with good works* (London: for W. Sandby, 1766).

381-Gr.   FORMEY, Jean Henri: *An ecclesiastical history from the birth of Christ* (London: for R. Davis, J. Newbery, L. Davis, and C. Reymers, 1766).

384-Gr.   TOTTIE, John: *Two charges delivered to the clergy of the diocese of Worcester . . . 1763 and 1766* (Oxford: at the Theatre, 1766).

384A-Ba. K., W.: *A very humble, earnest, and affectionate address to the bishops and clergy* (London: no printer, 1766).

385-Gr.   INDEPENDENT, An [Samuel Newton]: *The causes and reasons of the present declension among the Congregational churches* (London: for J. Johnson and B. Davenport, 1766).

386-Gr.   [ANSTEY, Christopher]: *The new Bath guide* (London: no printer, 1766).

386A-Ki. IBBETSON, James: *A charge to the clergy of the archdeaconry of St. Albans* ([London]: for Benjamin White, [1766]).

1767

387-Gr.   [LANCASTER, Nathaniel]: *Methodism triumphant* (London: J. Wilkie, T. Payne. T. Becket, and W. Cook, 1767).

387A-Ki. CALVINISTICUS: *A friendly reproof to a country clergyman* (London: for E. and C. Dilly, 1767).

388-Gr.   *The troublers of Israel* (London: G. Keith, 1767).

389-Gr.   *A dialogue between the Rev. Mr. John Wesley and a member of the Church of England* (London: F. Blyth, G. Keith, J. Johnson, and W. Watts, 1767).

389A-Ba. MEMBER OF THE CHURCH OF ENGLAND, A [William Green]: *A dialog between the pulpit and the reading desk* (London: for W. Nicoll, 1767).

390-Gr.   [MAXFIELD, Thomas]: *A vindication of the Rev. Mr. Maxfield's conduct* (London: G. Keith, Mrs. Danson, H. Heard, 1767).

391-Gr.   MOORHOUSE, Thomas: *A sermon preach'd . . . at Otley-Cross* (Leeds: no printer, 1767).

392A-Ba. TAYLOR, John: *A reply to the Reverend Mr. John Wesley's 'Remarks. . . on original sin'* (London: M. Waugh, 1767).

1768

393-Gr.   MASTER OF ARTS IN THE UNIVERSITY OF OXFORD, A [Sir Richard Hill]: *Pietas Oxoniensis* (London: for G. Keith, J. Millan, E. and C. Dilly, M. Folingsby, 1768).

394-Gr.   NOWELL, Thomas: *An answer to a pamphlet, entitled 'Pietas Oxoniensis'* (Oxford: Clarendon Press, 1768).

395-Gr.   AUTHOR OF *Pietas Oxoniensis* [Sir Richard Hill]: *Goliath slain* (London: for G. Keith, E. and C. Dilly, M. Folinsby, 1768).

396-Gr.   MEMBER OF THE CHURCH OF ENGLAND, A: *A letter to the author of a pamphlet intitled, 'Pietas oxoniensis'* (London: for E. Johnson, 1768).

397-Gr.   WHITEFIELD, George: *A letter to the Reverend Dr. Durell* (London: for J. Millan, E. and C. Dilly and M. Folingsby, 1768).

398-Gr.   C., W.: *Remarks upon the Reverend Mr. Whitefield's letter to the vice-chancellor* (Oxford: at the Theatre for J. Fletcher, 1768).

399-Gr.   GENTLEMAN OF THE UNIVERSITY, A: *A vindication of the proceedings against the six members of E— Hall* (London: for M. Hingeston, S. Bladon, and D. Prince, 1768).

401-Gr.   SHAVER, The [John MacGowan]: *Priestcraft defended* (London: for G. Keith, J. Johnson, and J. Payne, 1768).

402-Gr.   SHAVER, The [John MacGowan]: *A further defence of priestcraft* (London: for G. Keith, J. Johnson, and J. Payne, 1768).

402A-Ba.   MARTIN, Samuel: *Religious divisions considered* (Glasgow: William Walker, 1768).

403-Gr.   ROE, Samuel: *Enthusiasm detected* (Cambridge: Fletcher and Hodson, 1768).

404-Gr.   RANDOLPH, Thomas: *The witness of the Spirit* (Oxford: at the Theatre, 1768).

405-Gr.   RANDOLPH, Thomas: *The doctrine of justification by faith explained* (Oxford: at the Theatre, 1768).

407-Gr.   [MURRAY, James]: *Sermons to asses* (London: for J. Johnson, T. Cadell, and W. Charnley, 1768).

408-Gr.   *Enthusiasm reprehended* (Edinburgh: for W. Gray, 1768).

410A-Ba.   GRAHAM, Dougal: *An alarm to the Methodest [sic.] preachers* (Edinburgh: for the author, 1768).

410B-Ki.   ROE, Samuel: *Another pertinent and curious letter humbly offered to the public* (Cambridge: Fletcher and Hodson for the author, 1768).

410C-Fi.   *The Jesuit detected* (London: for J. Johnson, M. Folingsby, J. Law, and M. Smith, 1768).

1769

411-Gr.   BRAITHWAITE, Booth: *Methodism a popish idol* (London: no printer, 1769).

411A-Ki.   HAWKINS, William: *The pretences of enthusiasts considered* (Oxford: Clarendon Press, 1769).

411B-Ki.   HAWKINS, William: *The pretences of enthusiasts, as grounded in the articles of the Church, considered* (Oxford: Clarendon Press, 1769).

411C-Ki.   MATRICULATED BARBER, A: *The shaver shaved* (London: for J. Fletcher and Co., 1769).

411D-Ki.   NO METHODIST: *Strictures on an answer to the 'Pietas oxoniensis'* (London: for S. Bladon, 1769).

412-Gr.   [JONES, William]: *A letter to a young gentleman at Oxford* (London: for Robinson and Roberts, and M. Folingsby, 1769).

413-Gr.   LAYMAN OF THE CHURCH OF ENGLAND, A: *A letter to the Rev. Mr. George Whitefield, containing some remarks on his letter to the Rev. Dr. Durell* (London: for John Fuller, 1769).

414-Gr.   AUTHOR OF *PIETAS OXONIENSIS, The* [Sir Richard Hill]: *A letter to the Reverend Dr. Nowell* (London: for G. Keith, E. and C. Dilly, M. Folinsby, and Mr. Fletcher, 1769).

414A-Ki.   ONE WHO IS NOT A MASTER OF ARTS: *The contrast* (London: M. Lewis, 1769).

416-Gr.   PRESBYTER OF THE CHURCH OF ENGLAND, A [Augustus Montague Toplady]: *The Church of England vindicated from the charge of Arminianism* (London: for Joseph Gurney, 1769).

417-Gr.   AUTHOR OF *The Church of England vindicated from the charge of Arminianism* [Augustus Montague Toplady]: *The doctrine of absolute predestination stated* (London: for Joseph Gurney and James Matthews, 1769).

417A-Ki.   ALLEN, John: *The enthusiast's notion of election to eternal life disproved* (Oxford: for S. Parker and D. Prince, 1769).

418A-Fi.   [HILL, Sir Richard]: *An evening conversation between four very good old ladies* (Bath: S. Hazard, [1769]).

419-Gr.   TRUSTY, John *pseud.* [Sir Richard Hill]: *A letter from farmer Trusty to his landlord* (London: J. and W. Oliver, 1769).

421-Gr.   HERVEY, James: *Many made righteous by the obedience of one* (London: for Joseph Gurney and James Matthews, 1769).

423-Gr.   PRUDENTIA CHRISTIANIA [Mrs. MacCarthy]: *A letter from a lady to the Bishop of London* (London: for J. Brown, [1769]).

423A-Ki. BALGUY, Thomas: *A sermon preached at Lambeth Chapel on the consecration of the . . . Bishop of Llandaff* (London: for L. Davis and C. Reymers, 1769).

423B-Fi. AUTHOR OF *THE ALTERATIONS OF THE PLAIN DEALER*, THE [Isaac Bickerstaffe]: *The hypocrite* (London: W. Griffin, 1769).

1770

424-Gr. TOPLADY, Augustus Montague: *A letter to the Rev. Mr. John Wesley relative to his pretended abridgment of Zanchius* (London: for Joseph Gurney, 1770).

426-Gr. SMITH, Haddon: *Methodistical deceit* (London: for H. Turpin, 1770).

427-Gr. TOPLADY, Augustus Montague: *A caveat against unsound doctrines* (London: for Joseph Gurney, 1770).

428-Gr. BOYCE, Gilbert: *A serious reply to the Rev. Mr. John Wesley* (Boston [Lincolnshire]: C. Preston, 1770).

429-Gr. ADAMS, William: *A test of true and false doctrines* (London: for B. White and T. Cadell, 1770).

430-Gr. PARISHIONER OF ST. CHAD'S, A/SALOPIENSIS [Job Orton]: *Diotrephes admonished* (London: for B. White and T. Cadell, 1770).

430A-Ki. LOVER OF GENUINE CHRISTIANITY, A: *Some considerations on original sin* (London: for the author, 1770).

431-Gr. PARISHIONER OF ST. CHAD'S, A/AUTHOR OF DIOTREPHES ADMONISHED [Job Orton]: *Diotrephes re-admonished* (London: for B. White and T. Cadell, 1770).

431A-Fi. *A discourse on the true nature of the Christian religion* (London: no printer, 1770).

1771

433A-Fi. [FLEURY, George Lewis]: *Two sermons against the Methodists* ([Waterford]: no printer, 1771).

434-Gr. SHIRLEY, Walter: *A circular letter* (n.p.: no printer, 1771).

435-Gr. *A comment or paraphrase on the extract from the minutes of the Rev. Mr. Wesley* (London: for the author, 1771).

436-Gr. SHIRLEY, Walter: *A narrative of the principal circumstances relative to the Rev. Mr. Wesley's late conference* (Bath: W. Gye, 1771).

437-Gr. [HILL, Sir Richard]: *A conversation between Richard Hill, Esq., the Rev. Mr. Madan, and Father Walsh* (London: sold by E. and C. Dilly, 1771).

438-Gr. FRIEND, A/AUTHOR OF *PIETAS OXONIENSIS*, The [Sir Richard Hill]: *Five letters to the Reverend Mr. F—r* (London: for E. and C. Dilly, 1771).

439 -Gr. [HILL, Sir Richard]: *An answer to some capital errors* (London: for E. and C. Dilly, 1771).

444-Gr. CATHOLICUS, Johannes [John Rutty]: *An essay towards a contrast between Quakerism and Methodism* (Bristol: William Pine, 1771).

445-Gr. FOOTE, Samuel: *Apology for 'The minor'* (Edinburgh: for J. Wood, 1771).

446-Gr. [TOWERS, Joseph]: *A letter to the Rev. Mr. John Wesley in answer to his late pamphlet 'Free thoughts on the present state of public affairs'* (London: for J. Towers, 1771).

446A-Ki. PENRICE, W.: *The causes of Methodism set forth* (London: no printer, 1771).

1772

446B-Ba. [MAUDUIT, Israel]: *The case of the Dissenting ministers* (London: J. Wilke, 1772).

447-Gr. TOPLADY, Augustus Montague: *More work for Mr. John Wesley* (London: for James Mathews, 1772).

447B-Ki. CHRISTIAN WHIG, A: *A letter to the members of the Honourable House of Commons* (London: for W. Bower and J. Nichols, 1772).

447C-Fi.   CHRISTIAN WHIG, A: *A second letter to the members of the Honourable House of Commons* (London: for W. Bower and J. Nichols, 1772).

448-Gr.   FRIEND TO RELIGION, A: *A letter to the Rev. Mr. Fletcher* (Bath: W. Gye, [1772]).

449-Gr.   AUTHOR OF *P. O.*, The [Sir Richard Hill]: *A review of all the doctrines taught by the Rev. Mr. John Wesley* (London: for E. and C. Dilly, 1772).

450-Gr.   AUTHOR OF *PIETAS OXONIENSIS*, The [Sir Richard Hill]: *Some remarks on a pamphlet entitled, 'A third check to antinomianism'* (London: for Edward and Charles Dilly, 1772).

451-Gr.   [HILL, Rowland]: *Friendly remarks occasioned by the spirit and doctrines contained in the Rev. Mr. Fletcher's 'Vindication'* (London: for E. and C. Dilly, 1772).

452-Gr.   MADAN, Martin: *A scriptural comment upon the thirty-nine articles of the Church of England* (London: for John and Francis Rivington, 1772).

453-Gr.   TUCKER, Josiah: *Six sermons on important subjects* (Bristol: S. Farley, 1772).

453A-Fi.   LAND, Henry: *The nature of the Christian covenant considered* (Redding: J. Carnan, [1772]).

1773

454-Gr.   [GRAVES, Richard]: *The spiritual quixote* (London: for J. Dodsley, 1773).

455-Gr.   HILL, Sir Richard: *Logica wesleiensis* (London: for E. and C. Dilly, J. Matthews and W. Harris, 1773).

456-Gr.   HILL, Sir Richard: *The finishing stroke, containing some strictures on the Rev. Mr. Fletcher's pamphlet* (London: for Edward and Charles Dilly, W. Harris, and J. Matthews, 1773).

457-Gr.   BERRIDGE, John: *The Christian world unmasked* (London: for E. and C. Dilly, 1773).

458A-Ba.   CANDID CALVINISTS: *Much ado about nothing* (London: M. Lewis and J. Matthews, 1773).

458B-Ba.   *Curse ye Meroz* (Halifax: for the editor, [1773]).

459-Gr.   TOPLADY, Augustus Montague: 'A word concerning the bathing-tub baptism,' *The Works of Augustus M. Toplady* (London: for William Baynes and Son, 1825), 6 vols., 2:385–60.

460-Gr.   *Doctor Crisp's ghost* (London: no printer, 1773).

1774

461-Gr.   HILL, Sir Richard: *Three letters . . . to the Rev. J. Fletcher* (Shrewsbury: T. Wood, [1774]).

463A-Ba.   [PARKER, William]: *Some account of the state of religion in London* (London: for J. Mathews, G. Keith and W. Harris, 1774).

464-Gr.   TOPLADY, Augustus Montague: *Historic proof of the doctrinal Calvinism of the Church of England* (London: for George Keith, 1774). 2 vols.

465-Gr.   [HILL, Sir Richard]: *A lash at enthusiasm* (Shrewsbury: J. Eddowes and T. Wood, [1774]).

466-Gr.   AUTHOR OF *PIETAS OXONIENSIS*, THE [Sir Richard Hill]: *A gross imposition upon the public detected* (Shrewsbury: J. Eddowes, [1774]).

467-Gr.   *A faithful warning to the followers of the Rev. Mr. John Wesley* (London: for Keith, Buckland, Lewis, and Mathews, 1774).

468-Gr.   *Methodism a farce* (London: no printer, 1774).

469-Gr.   SAINT FROM THE TABERNACLE, A: *A sermon upon the turf* (London: for the author, 1774).

470-Gr.   *A supplement to Mr. Wesley's pamphlet entitled 'Thoughts upon slavery'* (London: H. Reynell, 1774).

1775

472-Gr.   TOPLADY, Augustus Montague: *The scheme of Christian and philosophical necessity asserted* (London: for Vallance and Simmons, 1775).

472A-Fi.   TOPLADY, Augustus Montague: *Good news from heaven* (London: for J. Mathews and G. Keith, 1775).

472B-Fi.   TOPLADY, Augustus Montague: *Joy in heaven and the creed of devils* (London: for Vallance and Simmons, 1775).

473-Gr.   T., J. [John Towers]: *Elihu's reply* (London: for the author, 1775).

475-Gr.   AMERICUS: *A letter to Mr. John Wesley* (n.p.: no printer, 1775).

476-Gr.   *A letter to a friend on the subject of Methodism* (London: printed and sold by the booksellers in town and country, 1775).

478-Gr.   TOPLADY, Augustus Montague: *Free-will and merit fairly examined* (London: for J. Matthews and G. Keith, 1775).

479-Gr.   HANOVERIAN, A [Augustus Montague Toplady]: *An old fox tarr'd and feather'd* (London: for John French, Mary Lewis, and booksellers at the Royal Exchange, 1775).

480-Gr.   *A constitutional answer to the Rev. Mr. John Wesley's 'Calm address'* (London: for E. and C. Dilly, and J. Almon, 1775).

480A-Ki.   GENTLEMAN OF NORTHUMBERLAND, A [James Murray]: *A grave answer to Mr. Wesley's 'Calm address'* [Newcastle upon Tyne: no printer, 1775].

481-Gr.   S., T.: *A cool reply to a 'Calm address'* (London: for the author, 1775).

482-Gr.   AMERICANUS [Caleb Evans]: *A letter to the Rev. Mr. John Wesley occasioned by his 'Calm address'* (Bristol: William Pine, 1775).

483-Gr.   EVANS, Caleb: *A reply to the Rev. Mr. Fletcher's vindication of Mr. Wesley's 'Calm address'* (Bristol: W. Pine, [1775]).

483A-Ba.   JUNIOLUS: *Fallacy detected* ([London]: no printer, 1775).

483C-Ba.   Y., W.: *A serious answer to Mr. Wesley's 'Calm address'* (Bristol: no printer, 1775).

483D-Ki.   *Resistance no rebellion* ([London]: for N. Maud, 1775).

484-Gr.   D., W. [W. Denham]: *A second answer to Mr. John Wesley* (London: for Wallis and Stonehouse, 1775).

485-Gr.   LOVER OF TRUTH AND THE BRITISH CONSTITUTION, A [Titus Hibbert]: *A letter to the Rev. Mr. John Wesley, on his 'Calm address to the American colonies'* ([Manchester]: no printer, 1775).

485A-Ba.   [SUTCLIFF, Dr. of Settle]: *Political propositions* (Leeds: no printer, 1775).

485B-Fi.   SOPHRONIKOS, Mr. *pseud.: A check to enthusiasm* (London: J. and W. Oliver, 1775).

485C-Fi.   CIVIS: *A letter to the Reverend John Wesley* (London: no printer, 1775).

1776

486-Gr.   *Political empiricism* (London: for J. Johnson, 1776).

486A-Ki.   FRIEND TO THE PEOPLE AND THEIR LIBERTIES, A: *A full and impartial examination of the Rev. Mr. John Wesley's address* (St. H—n's [St. Helens]: the author, [1776]).

487-Gr.   MEMBER OF THE CHURCH OF ENGLAND, A: *Naked thoughts on some of the peculiarities of the field-preaching clergy* (London: for J. Pridden, [1776]).

488-Gr.   HAWES, William: *An examination of the Rev. Mr. John Wesley's 'Primitive physic'* (London: for the author, 1776).

488A-Ki.   DETESTER OF HYPOCRISY: *To that fanatical, political, physical, enthusiast* (London: no printer, 1776).

489-Gr.   *A necessary alarm and most earnest caveto against tabernacle-principles* ([London]: no printer, sold by the booksellers of London and Bristol, 1776).

490A-Ki.   DAVIES, Thomas: *Rational religion recommended* (Lewes: William Lee, 1776).

491-Ki.   GREENWOOD, John Cox: *Remarks on a wild oration, or funeral sermon, in memory of William Austin, late Methodist preacher at Bledlow . . .* (London: no printer, [1776]).

491B-Fi.   MEMBER OF THE REV. MR. WESLEY'S SOCIETY, A: *The Rev. John Fletcher's arguments . . . considered* (London: no printer, 1776).

492-Gr.   EVANS, Caleb: *Political sophistry detected* (Bristol: W. Pine, 1776).

492A-Ba.   GENTLEMAN OF NORTHUMBERLAND, A [James Murray]: *A compleat answer to Mr. Wesley's observations upon Dr. Price's essay* (Newcastle: T. Robson and Co., [1776]).

492B-Ki.   *The foxes and vines* ([London]: no printer, 1776).

492C-Ki.   IT DOES NOT SIGNIFY WHO: *The ruin of Methodism* ([London]: for the author, 1776).

492D-Fi.   MOORE, William: *The addresses for blood and devastation* (London: T. W. Shaw for the author, [1776]).

1777

493-Gr.   BULL, Patrick: *A wolf in sheep's cloathing; or, An old Jesuit unmasked* (London: reprinted by Mary Trickett, [1777]).

495-Gr.   HERRING, Thomas: *Letters from the late Most Reverend Dr. Thomas Herring* (London: for J. Johnson, 1777).

496-Gr.   HILL, Rowland: *Imposture detected, and the dead vindicated* (London: for T. Vallance, 1777).

497-Gr.   HILL, Rowland: *A full answer to the Rev. J. Wesley's remarks upon a late pamphlet* (Bristol: sold by T. Mills, [1777]).

500-Gr.   [SMYTH, Edward]: *An account of the trial of Edward Smyth* (Dublin: William Kidd, 1777).

502-Gr.   THOMAS, John: *Two letters to the Rev. Thomas Coke* (London: sold by G. Robinson, 1777).

504-Gr.   LOFFT, Capel: *Observations on Mr. Wesley's second 'Calm address'* (London: for E. and C. Dilly, 1777).

504A-Ba.   J., W. [W. Jordan]: *W. J. against J. W.* ([London]: for the author, 1777).

1778

505-Gr.   Murray, James: *The finishing stroke to Mr. Wesley's 'Calm address'* (Newcastle upon Tyne: T. Robson and Comp., 1778).

505A-Ki.   AUTHOR OF *Royal Perseverance,* The: *Tyranny the worst taxation* (London: for J. Bew, 1778).

506-Gr.   HELTON, John: *Reasons for quitting the Methodist society* (London: J. Fry and Co., 1778).

507-Gr.   PRESBYTERIAN, A [Thomas Bennett]: *Terms of communion agreed upon by the Scots Methodists* (Edinburgh: no printer, 1778).

507A-Ba.   POULSON, James: *James Poulson further detected* (n.p.: no printer, 1778).

510-Gr.   *A calm inquiry into rational and fanatical dissention* (London: no printer, 1778).

511A-Ba.   *The doctrines of free grace and imputed righteousness asserted* (Leeds: printed and sold by the booksellers in town and country, [1778]).

512-Gr.   MAXFIELD, Thomas: *A short account of God's dealings with Mrs. Elizabeth Maxfield* (London: J. W. Pasham, 1778).

513-Gr.   [TOPLADY, Augustus Montague]: *The Reverend Mr. Toplady's dying avowal* (London: for J. Mathews, J. Buckland, and T. Vallance, 1778).

513A-Ba. *A memoir of some principal circumstances in the life and death of . . . Augustus Montague Toplady* (London: for J. Mathews, 1778).

514A-Ki. W., T. [Thomas Wilkins]: *An elegy on the death of the Rev. A. M. Toplady* (London: W. Oliver, 1778).

515-Gr. HILL, Richard, of Cambridge *pseud.: The gospel-shop* ([London]: Fielding and Walker, Richardson and Urquhart, Southern, Bab, Leacroft, [1778]).

516-Gr. [COMBE, William]: *The saints* (London: for J. Bew, 1778).

517-Gr. [COMBE, William]: *Perfection: a poetical epistle* (London: for J. Bew, 1778).

518-Gr. AUTHOR OF *THE SAINTS* [William Combe]: *The temple of imposture* (London: for J. Bew, 1778).

519-Gr. AUTHOR OF *THE SAINTS* [William Combe]: *The love-feast* (London: for J. Bew, 1778).

520-Gr. AUTHOR OF *THE SAINTS* [William Combe]: *Sketches for tabernacle-frames* (London: for J. Bew, 1778).

520A-Ki FOOTE, Samuel: *The Devil upon two sticks, a Comedy in three acts* (London: for T. Sherlock and T. Cadell, [1778]).

1779

521-Gr. [COMBE, William]: *Fanatical conversion* (London: for J. Bew, 1779).

522-Gr. *Methodism and popery dissected and compared* (London: for Fielding and Walker, 1779).

523-Gr. [COMBE, William]: *Voltaire's ghost* (London: for J. Bew, 1779).

1780

524-Gr. CALVINISTICUS: *Calvinism defended and Arminianism refuted* (Leeds: Binns, 1780).

524A-Ki. HILL, Sir Richard: *A letter to the Rev. John Wesley wherein that gentleman is called upon to declare whether he be . . . the author of . . . calumnies . . . on the late Rev. Augustus Toplady* (London: for J. Mathews, 1780).

525-Gr. MacGOWAN, John: *The foundry budget opened* (London: for G. Keith, J. Johnson, and James MacGowan, 1780).

525A-Ba. OLD FASHION FARMER, The [John Whittingham]: *To the Public* (Coventry: no printer, 1780).

525B-Ki. WHITTINGHAM, John: *To the public* (Coventry: no printer, [1780]).

525C-Ki. O'LEARY, Arthur: *Mr. O'Leary's remarks on the Rev. Mr. Wesley's letters* (Dublin: no printer, 1780).

525D-Ki. CONSISTENT WHIG: *Considerations on the late disturbances* (London: for J. Almon, 1780).

525E-Ba. *The friendly retrievers* (n.p.: for the author, 1780).

525F-Ki. [COMBE, William]: *A sketch of the times* (London: for J. Bew, 1780).

525I- Fi. PHILALETHES: *Popery exposed and John Wesley vindicated* (London: no printer, 1780).

1781

526-Gr. AUTHOR OF *Remarks on Dr. Hallifax's Preface to the Sermons of the Late Dr. Ogden* [John Mainwaring]: *An essay on the character of Methodism* (Cambridge: J. Archdeacon, 1781).

526A-Ki. *The nature of faith* (Northampton: T. Dicey, [1781]).

527-Gr. O'LEARY, Arthur: *Miscellaneous tracts* (Dublin: Tho. McDonnel, 1781).

1782

527A-Fi.   McKEAG, Patrick: *The eternal decree* (Dublin: Boucher, 1782).

527B-Fi.   SHERATON, Thomas: *A scriptural illustration of the doctrine of regeneration* (Stockton: R. Christopher, 1782).

527C-Fi.   *The adventures of an actor* (London: for the author, [1782]).

528-Gr.   C., T. [Thomas Coleman]: *A letter to a friend on Methodism* (Canterbury: no printer, 1782).

528A-Ba.   COBLER OF CRIPPLEGATE WARD, LONDON, A.: *Truth exploded* (Bath: no printer, 1782).

1783

528B-Ba   *A word to the Rev. Mr. John Wesley* (n.p.: no printer, 1783).

528C-Ki.   *A discourse setting forth the dangerous consequences of enthusiasm* (n.p.: no printer, 1783).

528D-Ki.   MOORHOUSE, Thomas: *A view of practical Methodism* ([London]: sold by all booksellers in town and country, [1783]).

528E-Fi.   [BARRINGTON, Shute]: *A charge delivered to the clergy of the diocese of Sarum* (Oxford: no printer, 1783).

528F-Fi.   HUNTINGTON, William: *The skeletons* (London: J. Rozea, [1783]).

1784

529-Gr.   LAY-MEMBER OF THE CHURCH OF ENGLAND, A: *A letter to the Honourable and Right Reverend Shute, Lord Bishop of Sarum* (Bath: S. Hazard, 1784).

530-Gr.   SANDILANDS, Richard: *Faith and works* (London: for the author, [1784]).

531-Gr.   MUIRHEAD, John: *A review of the principles of such Methodists as are under the direction of . . . John Wesley* (Kelso: J. Palmer, 1784).

531A-Ba.   [HAMPSON, John]: *An appeal to the Reverend John and Charles Wesley* (n.p.: no printer, 1784).

1785

532-Gr.   MOORE, William: *An appeal to the inhabitants of the town of Saltash* (Plymouth: R. Trewman and B. Haydon, [1785]).

532A-Ba.   LAYMAN OF THE METHODIST SOCIETY, A: *Free thoughts concerning a separation of the people called Methodist* (London: no printer, 1785).

532B-Ba.   LADY, A [Mary O'Brien]: *The pious incendiaries* (London: for the author, 1785).

533-Gr.   METHODIST OF THE CHURCH OF ENGLAND, A [Charles Wesley]: *Strictures on the substance of a sermon preached at Baltimore* (London: sold by G. Herdsfield and the booksellers of town and country, 1785).

534A-Ba.   *A receipt how to make a true Methodist* [London: no printer, 1785].

1786

535-Gr.   [OSWALD, John]: *Ranae comicae evangelizantes* (London: E. Macklew, 1786).

535A-Ki.   MOORHOUSE, Michael: *An appeal to all honest men* (n.p.: no printer, 1786).

536A-Ki.   CROFT, George: *Eight sermons preached before the University of Oxford* (Oxford: Clarendon Press, 1786).

1787

537-Gr.   M., R. [Robert Moody]: *Observations on certain prophecies in the book of Daniel* ([London]: for the author, 1787).

538A-Fi. MANNERS, Nicholas: *A full confutation of the Rev. Mr. John Fletcher's appeal* (London: R. Hindmarsh, 1787).

538A*-Ki. HORSLEY, Samuel: *The analogy between the light of inspiration and the light of learning as qualifications for the ministry* (Gloucester: R. Raikes, [1787]).

1788

539-Gr. KINGSFORD, William: *A vindication of the Baptists* (Canterbury: J. Grove, 1788).

540A-Ba. MANNERS, Nicholas: *Remarks on the writings of the Rev. J. W.* (Hull: George Prince, 1788).

540B-Ba. MANNERS, Nicholas: *Preachers described, and the people advised* [Hull: no printer, 1788].

541-Gr. *The secret disclosed* (Lichfield: no printer, 1788).

542A-Ba. ATTENTIVE, Thomas *pseud.*: *A friendly address to the preachers and principal members of the M—d—ts* (n.p.: no printer, 1788).

542B-Ba. [ATLAY, John]: *A reply to what the Rev. Dr. Coke is pleased to call the state of the Dewsbury house* (n.p.: no printer, 1788).

542C-Ki. NORMAN, Samuel: *Authentic anecdotes of George Lukins* (Bristol: G. Routh, [1788]).

542C*-Fi. NORMAN, Samuel: *The great apostle unmask'd* (Bristol: for S. Johnson, 1788).

542D-Fi. [HILL, Sir Richard]: *An important case argued* (London: sold by Buckland, Mathews, Wilkinson, and Scollick, 1788).

1789

542E-Fi. GRIFFITH, Amyas: *Miscellaneous tracts* (Dublin: W. Corbet, 1789).

543-Gr. *Methodism unmasked* (London: G. Riebau, [1789]).

543A-Ki KINGSFORD, William: *Three letters to the Rev. Mr. Wesley* (Canterbury: J. Grove, for the author, 1789).

544-Gr. MANNERS, Nicholas: *A full confutation of the Rev. John Fletcher's appeal* (Hull: T. Briggs, 1789).

545-Gr. MOORHOUSE, Michael: *The defence of Mr. Michael Moorhouse* (Leicester: Ann Ireland, 1789).

548-Gr. AUTHOR OF *The critique on the conduct of the Rev. John Crosse, Vicar of Bradford and the Rev. William Atkinson, Fellow of Jesus College, Cambridge,* The [Edward Baldwyn]: *Remarks on two of the most singular characters of the age,* second edition (London: for the author, 1790). First edition seems to have been published in 1789.

549-Gr. AUTHOR OF *The critique on the conduct of the Rev. John Crosse, Vicar of Bradford and the Rev. William Atkinson, Fellow of Jesus College, Cambridge,* The [Edward Baldwyn]: *Further remarks on two of the most singular characters of the age* (London: T. Knott and J. Debrett, 1789).

549A-Ba. PRICE, Richard: *A discourse on the love of our country* (London: George Stafford, 1789).

549B-Fi. *A serious conversation . . . between a gentleman brought up to the law and a Methodist* (n.p.: no printer, 1789).

1790

550-Gr. TRIM [Edward Baldwyn]: *A congratulatory letter to the Rev. William Atkinson* (London: G. Kearsley, 1790).

550A-Ba. [ATLAY, John]: *Letters that passed between the Rev. John Wesley and Mr. John Atlay* (London: J. Matthews, W. and J. Stratford, J. Murgatroyd, [1790]).

551-Gr. GURNEY, Thomas: *Poems on various occasions* (Sudbury: W. Brackett, 1790).

551A-Ba.   *A letter addressed to the M—t p—s . . . October 16, 1790* ([London]: no printer, 1790).

551B-Fi.   *An original Methodist sermon* (West Smithfield: R. Eastin, [1790]).

1791

552-Gr.   *A congratulatory address to the Rev. John Crosse* (London: for the author, 1791).

552A-Ba.   *An epitaph on the late Rev. Mr. John Wesley* [London: no printer, 1791].

553-Gr.   HUNTINGTON, William: *The funeral of Arminianism* (London: for G. Terry, J. Davidson, J. Baker, and Mr. James, 1791).

553A-Ba.   KING, Thomas: *A check to uncharitableness* (London: for the author, 1791).

554-Gr.   PRIESTLEY, Joseph: *Original letters by the Rev. John Wesley and his friends* (Birmingham: Thomas Pearson, 1791).

555-Gr.   *A review of the policy, doctrines, and morals of the Methodists* (London: for J. Johnson, 1791).

556-Ki.   [Horne], George: *A charge intended to have been delivered to the clergy of Norwich* (Norwich: Yarrington and Bacon, 1791).

557-Gr.   DAVIS, Mark: *Thoughts on dancing* (London: C. Paramore, 1791).

558-Gr.   COLET, John Annesley: *An impartial review of the life and writings . . . of . . . John Wesley* (London: for the author, 1791).

559-Gr.   BALDWYN, Edward: *Remarks on the oath, declarations, and conduct of Johnson Atkinson Busfield* (London: G. Kearsley, 1791).

560-Gr.   LACKINGTON, James: *Memoirs of the first forty-five years of the life of James Lackington* (London: for the author, [1791]).

560A-Ba.   HOBROW, William: *The doctrines of the Methodists*, third edition (Liverpool: E. Johnson, 1792). First published 1791.

560B-Ba.   HAMPSON, John: *Memoirs of the Late Rev. John Wesley*, 3 vols. (Sunderland: for the author by James Graham, 1791).

561-Ki.   [HORSLEY], Samuel: *The charge of Samuel, Lord Bishop of St. David's, to the clergy of his diocese, delivered at his primary visitation in the year, 1790* (Gloucester: R. Raikes, 1791).

1792

562-Gr.   EDWARDS, William Embury: *A letter from the . . . minister of Westbury-upon-Trym* (Bristol: J. Rudhall, 1792).

563-Gr.   *Transactions of the London Methodist parsons* (London: for C. Stalker, J. Parsons, and A. Cleugh, 1792).

564A-Ba.   *To the members of the Methodist societies* ([Liverpool]: H. Hodgson, 1792).

564B-Ba.   MEMBER OF THE ESTABLISHED CHURCH, A: *Remarks on a sermon of the late Rev. John Wesley* (Dublin: James Moore, 1792).

565-Gr.   TATHAM, Edward: *A sermon suitable to the times* (London: sold by J. F. and C. Rivington, 1792).

565A-Fi.   *A blister for Methodism* (London: no printer, 1792).

565B-Fi.   PHILLIPS, Catherine: *Reasons why the people called Quakers cannot so fully unite with the Methodists* (London: James Phillips, 1792).

565C-Fi.   BENTLEY, Thomas: *A few queries to the Methodists in general and especially to teachers* (London: no printer, 1792).

1793

566-Gr.   METHODIST LAYMAN, A: *Remarks concerning the present government of the Methodist societies* (London: no printer, 1793).

566A-Fi. RUSSEL, William: *A few hints for the consideration of the Methodists* (Worcester: J. Tymbs, 1793).

566A*-Fi. [RUSSEL, William]: *A short address to the public* (n.p.: no printer, 1793).

1794

566B-Fi. RUSSEL, William: *A calm reply to the fallacious arguments . . . in Mr. Joseph Benson's 'Farther defence'* (Wolverhampton: J. Smart, 1794).

567-Gr. CLAPHAM, Samuel: *How far Methodism conduces to the interests of Christianity* (Leeds: J. Binns, [1794]).

567A-Ba. ONESIMUS [Garnet Terry]: *An affectionate address to the members of the Methodist society* (Leeds: Thomas Hannam, A. Newsom and T. Wright, 1794).

568-Gr. *The fair Methodist*, 2 vols. (London: for J. Bell, 1794).

568A-Ba. GREAT BRITAIN–Court of Chancery: *Attested copies of three several depositions* (London: no printer, 1794).

569-Gr. WOOLLEY, William: *A cure for canting* (London: no printer, sold by Jordan and Ridgeway, 1794).

570-Gr. MEMBER OF THE ESTABLISHED CHURCH, A [Alexander Knox]: *Considerations on a separation of the Methodists from the Established Church* (Bristol: Bulgin and Rosser, 1794).

571-Gr. AUTHOR OF *Considerations on a separation of the Methodists from the Established Church* [Alexander Knox]: *Candid animadversions on Mr. Henry Moore's reply* [to 570-Gr.] (Bristol: Bulgin and Rosser, 1794).

1795

572-Gr. *The triumph of religious liberty over the spirit of persecution* (London: no printer, 1795).

573-Gr. CLERGYMAN, A [James Franks]: *Memoirs of pretended prophets* (London: for J. Johnson, 1795).

574-Gr. CROFT, George: *Thoughts concerning the Methodists and the established clergy* (London: for F. and C. Rivington, 1795).

575A-Fi. *Remarks on several passages in the works of the late Rev. John Wesley* (Bristol: R. Edwards, 1795).

575B-Fi. BELCHER, William: *Belcher's cream of knowledge* (London: these and the author's other works may be had of the booksellers and at his house, [1795]).

575C-Fi. *The wolf in sheep's cloathing: A fragment* (London: no printer, 1795).

575D-Fi. *Lucifer's lectures; or, the infernal tribune* (London: for the president of the Stygian Council, [1795]).

1796

576-Gr. HALL, Robert: *A friendly address to the Methodists* (Nottingham: C. Sutton, 1796).

577-Gr. [HOWELL, William]: *Free grace, the experience and triumph of every true Christian* (Leeds: for the author, 1796).

1797

577A-Fi. HURLOTHRUMBO [Samuel Johnson of Gawsworth]: *A curious letter from a mountebank doctor to a Methodist preacher* ([Edinburgh]: for the book-sellers, 1797).

1798

578-Gr. AUTHOR OF *Free grace*, The [William Howell]: *The trial of Arminian Methodism* (Leeds: no printer, 1798).

578A-Ba.   MAYER, Joseph: *Candid animadversions on the Rev. Thomas Whitaker's four letters* (Stockport: J. Clarke, 1798).

580-Gr.   CANNON, Thomas: *The Calvinist and Lutheran's family library* (London: for the benefit of the gospel, [1798]).

581-Gr.   HOPKINSON, Samuel: *A sermon preached at the visitation held in Grantham* (Stamford: R. Newcomb, 1798).

1799

582-Gr.   GREAVES, Alexander Benjamin: *A letter addressed to ministers of state* (Sheffield: J. Crome, for the author, 1799).

584-Gr.   POLWHELE, Richard: *A letter to the Rev. Robert Hawker* (London: anti-Jacobin Press, 1799).

585-Gr.   CLERGYMAN OF THE CHURCH OF ENGLAND, A: *A treatise on inspiration* (York: William Blanchard, 1799).

585A-Fi.   WOLLASTON, Francis: *A country parson's address to his flock* (London: for G. Wilkie, 1799).

585B-Fi.   BARRY, Edward: *The friendly call of truth and reason* (Reading: for the author, 1799).

585C-Fi.   [FRANCIS, D.]: *Queries addressed to a Methodist* ([Shrewsbury]: T. Wood, 1799).

1800

586-Gr.   HILL, Sir Richard: *Daubenism confuted* (London: J. Smeeton, 1800).

587-Gr.   HASTINGS, Theophilus Henry: *Nine sermons upon the 16th. chap. of the Revelation to St. John* (Loughborough: Adams, 1800).

588-Gr.   TOPLADY, Augustus Montague: *The liturgy of the Church of England explained* (London: J. Barker, 1800).

589-Gr.   [TOMLINE, Sir George Pretyman]: *A charge delivered to the clergy of the diocese of Lincoln* (London: for Cadell and Davies, Rivingtons, White, Hatchard, Lunn, Deighton, 1800).

590-Gr.   WHITAKER, Thomas Dunham: *An history of the original parish of Whalley* (Blackburn: Hemingway and Crook, 1800–01).

591-Gr.   *Report from the clergy of a district in the Diocese of Lincoln* (London: Bye and Law, 1800).

591A-Ba.   POLWHELE, Richard: *Anecdotes of Methodism* (London: T. Crowder, 1800).

591B-Fi.   FRANCIS, D.: *Remarks upon the Rev. J. Gill's answer* (Shrewsbury: T. Wood, 1800).

591C-Fi.   POLWHELE, Richard: *A third letter, on the itinerancy and non-conformity of the vicar of Charles, Plymouth* (London: for Cadell and Davies, and Chapple, 1800).

Undated

597-Gr.   *Some queries humbly offered to those who profess sinless perfection* (n.p.: no printer, no date).

598-Gr.   *A wolf in sheep's clothing: The words of a gentleman of wit* (n.p.: no printer, n.d.), broadside.

607-Ki.   *Preaching for bacon* (n.p.: no printer, n.d.), broadside. This item, previously numbered by Frank Baker as 009B-Ba and dated by him as 1739, was accepted by Clive Field for his revised anti-Methodist Bibliography. No eighteenth-century editions have yet been located. Three nineteenth-century issues are located in the Bodleian Library, Oxford.

608-Ki.   *Methodism indeed; or, A satirical poem, in reply to one composed by a Partialist, with a view to making the doctrine of universal salvation (by Jesus Christ) appear odious* (n.p.: no printer, n.d.), broadside.

609-Ki.   *The Methodist turned poet* (n.p: no printer, n.d.), broadside.

Index

CPSIA information can be obtained
at www.ICGtesting.com
Printed in the USA
BVHW082253260123
657282BV00017B/105